DETROIT:
Who Built Her?

Who Broke Her?
by
Douglas Jamiel

Copyright © 2022 Douglas Jamiel.

All rights reserved. No part of this publication may be reproduced, distributed, or transmitted in any form or by any means, including photocopying, recording, or other electronic or mechanical methods, without the prior written permission of the publisher, except in the case of brief quotations embodied in critical reviews and certain other noncommercial uses permitted by copyright law. For permission requests, write to the publisher, addressed "Attention: Permissions Coordinator," at the address below;

jamiel2995@comcast.net

Library of Congress Control Number: 1-11608412951

Front cover image by Douglas Jamiel.
Book design by Douglas Jamiel.

First printing edition 2022.

Introduction

*H*istorian *– an unsuccessful novelist.*

This characterization of the historian's craft by H.L. Mencken is certainly thought provoking. It suggests that, out of a failure to enjoy the same success with fiction as, say, Daniel Defoe's "Robinson Crusoe," Edmond Gibbon settled instead on writing an epic history of the Roman Empire. Or, perhaps, out of envy over the success of Fitzgerald's "Gatsby," G.M. Trevelyan penned a definitive history of England to assuage his frustration. Though it is likely that Mencken's intent was entirely comedic, the comparison nevertheless invites a more in-depth investigation.

Both the novelist and the historian confront the same societal forces, yet, each shapes them to markedly different ends. Whereas, for the novelist, the facts and events of the real world are subsumed in a fictive narrative creatively constructed, the historian is confined to the very real and ready-made narrative of actual events. Hence, the novelist invents; the historian sorts. Sorts what? The societal forces and personalities he/she believes have influenced and shaped the course of history. Nature abhors a vacuum; so does history. No place's history – whether Detroit, Denmark, or Dubai – develops whole-cloth from purely local forces. This is especially true of Detroit whose past, for the first two-hundred years, was almost entirely derivative, the course of its development, year by year, decade by decade, inextricably tied to events and countries across the Atlantic. In particular, France and England.

The Detroit, Michigan even remotely like the one we know today did not begin to take shape until the early 1800s. However, in order to understand the history of the Great Lakes region at any point in its history, context is everything. Before the mid-1800s, what is now Michigan was little more than an ocean of trees punctuated by crude outposts, a place where French trappers sparred with British soldiers for control of the peltry trade, and French Jesuits worked to capture the souls and loyalty of Native Americans for the Catholic Church. It begs the questions: who were the Jesuits? Who were the *coureur de bois*? And who were the British soldiers, many of whom were orphans ,plucked from the streets of English cities to be reared in public foundling homes where they would, ultimately, be trained to become the cannon fodder for British imperialism and wars of conquest. Hundreds of years before Ford and his automobile, names like Pontiac and Cadillac referred to real people, and the fate of the region depended on men with names like Amherst and Picoté de Belestre. Even as the faint outlines of the State of Michigan began to emerge, it was fed by external forces, i.e. immigration by property-less and impoverished workers fleeing the growing exploitation of the industrial east and heeding the jingoistic call of "manifest destiny" that would come to mean, in reality, genocide for Native Americans.

One has to admire the sheer dedication and tenacity of a Gibbon or a Trevelyan who, long before the magical digital portal of the internet, were relegated to the lowest tech resources: libraries, private collections and the painfully slow cycle of printed newspapers and journals. While the pros and cons of the digital milieu are certainly debatable, there is an unmistakable advantage for the modern historian who, with the stroke of a key, can access some historical document in some archive on the other side of the planet. Considering this powerful resource, it is easy for today's historian to accumulate and sort facts quickly and accurately, thus creating the all-important historical element – context. Like a satellite that can image the entire globe one second, then focus on a single building the next, it is easy for the historian to exploit this flexibility, alternately zooming in and out in order capture the forces – macro and micro – that feed the history of any place, especially Detroit. This is precisely what I have attempted to do in this, the first volume of "Detroit: Who Bulit Her? Who Broke Her?" which covers the period of Detroit and Michigan's history from very beginning, when Etienne Brulé's canoe slid onto the shores of Upper Michigan, to pre-industrial Detroit where stove production and ship-building and maintenance were the industrial core of the city long before the automobile.

In 1976, amidst the hoopla of the U.S. bicentennial, my family moved to Colorado. With me came twenty-five years of memories built in 1950s and '60s Detroit. During that time, Detroit's reputation as an industrial behemoth and the "arsenal of democracy" still legitimately defined it. But its image as "automaker to the world" was already waning as more and more cars with German, Japanese, Swedish names darted around on its streets. Ugly names like "rice-grinder" betrayed the resentment of a populace whose industrial dominance was slipping away. As American management and human resource theorists struggled to understand and, perhaps, incorporate the German and Japanese management models in U.S. factories, their efforts did little to upend an entrenched U.S. system that had little patience for industrial processes based on cooperation, worker involvement, and something other than the unaccountable enrichment of absent shareholders with no interest in the company other than to extract its wealth. American industrial giants could not – would not – adjust to the global economic reality, nor entertain an increased role for workers in the production process, preferring instead the easy exploitation of Third-World labor.

But even more than its dedication to anachronistic management methods and outdated car designs, something deeper, more corrosive and destructive had eaten away at Detroit since the first blacks settled in the city in the ante-bellum days. Like so many other northern cities whose governing documents professed the language of equality, Detroit had, since before the Civil War, confined its black population to certain areas – in Detroit, it was Black Bottom. Even the Emancipation Proclamation and the franchise was not potent enough for Detroit's blacks to overcome the subtle power of red-lining, segregation, and a white populace that, over decades, had fled the city for the safe haven of the white dominated suburban periphery. There, in the time while Nash Ramblers, Falcons, Fairlanes, and Comets enjoyed their heyday, the language of segregation was inculcated around the dinner table, couched in veiled references to the neighbor whose house was for sale and who, it was rumored, was "thinking of selling to coloreds." This portended the self-fulfilling scenario of plummeting real estate values that had nothing to do with blacks, and everything to do with massive flight from the neighborhood for no reason other than racial animus. For a boy navigating the natural insecurities of his age, the consciousness to challenge these notions, absent deliberate intervention from parents who themselves were prisoner to the same ignorant misconceptions, was simply not there yet.

And the city fathers (yes, I mean fathers since they were mostly men back then) made it easy to ignore, to conveniently bypass the reality of a separate, wholly black enclave. Certainly, the national freeway system enabled this, whisking white commuters quickly from the suburbs to the city center. Even the bus system did its part. For example, my daily trip to Cass Tech High School downtown mimicked this diversion. In the early hours, I would dutifully walk with my french horn to the bus stop where I would catch the Hayes Express. "Express" is, here, the significant word. Once the doors closed at the last stop at the end of Hayes Street, the bus would make its way, without ever stopping, down a great length of Gratiot Ave, past the Vernors factory, the Strohs brewery and, more importantly, past the black neighborhoods. Considering my age and my as yet unchallenged social consciousness, I considered this more convenient than devious. It would take a momentous and violent event to shake my world and open my eyes to the city's original sin of segregation and injustice. It would take a riot.

In the early hours of July 23, 1967, police raided an after-hours drinking club on 12th Street in a black neighborhood where a party was being held for returning (black) veterans. Police arrested 82 individuals. (It is difficult to escape the irony that these were black veterans who probably had been drafted and forced to serve in Vietnam, a conflict concocted by a very white government and studiously avoided in any way possible by young white men.) Locals – already angry and disaffected by the city's segregation and constant police harassment – witnessed this mass arrest and took to the streets in a rage, looting and burning the businesses they viewed as exploiting their situation and their neighborhood with high prices for limited goods, and only low-paying service jobs for employment. Sirens and occasional gunshots could be heard in the distance. For five days, a big portion of the city burned. Eventually, federal troops were called to the city to restore order. The park up the street where I played touch football with my buddies was filled with uniformed soldiers, bivouacked, armed and ready to impose order on the recalcitrant black population which, to my amazement, was burning and looting its own neighborhoods. "Why would they do this?" I asked myself. As we listened to the constant sirens and watched the burning buildings on TV, I could no longer ignore the ugly reality of my city and its history, a history filled with other black riots in 1833, 1863, and 1943. This was the city I left and didn't give much thought. For a very long time, Detroit was, for me, simply a nice place to be "from."

After thirty-six years, in 2012, I returned to Detroit to visit my sister who was ill. As we drove east to her home in St. Clair Shores, even the uninterrupted access of the freeway could not conceal the wasteland that peeked out above, stretching for miles along the highway. Its blighted state was betrayed by mile after mile of collapsed roofs and hulks of buildings, abandoned and left to waste. They told the story: the Detroit I knew was gone, brought to ruin by decades of segregation, white flight, predatory real estate practices, and corporate decisions to forsake the city that gave it life. Places where I walked without concern as a young man I dared not go: the walk through Chandler Park up to the library.; the walk down to the bookstore on

Harper, across from the movie theater. They were now as forbidding and unwelcome as a war zone. How did this happen? How did this once great city become a decrepit skeleton of its former self? Who did this? It is precisely those questions that gave rise to this, the first volume of my series called, "Detroit: Who Built Her? Who Broke Her?" Though this effort, I hope to elucidate a way forward for Detroit by shining a light on its long past.

D.J.

Table of Contents

Chapter 1. The French and Before

Étienne Brûlé, the beaver, and the land of Michigan .... 1.
Indian tribes of early Michigan .... 2.
European religious strife .... 3.
Jean Bodin and the growth of monarchy .... 4.
New France, the coeurer de bois, and Cardinal Richelieu .... 5.
Jesuits: their history and influence .... 6.
French culture, guns, and alcohol .... 11.

Chapter 2. Rule Britannia

French, English, Dutch and the struggle for control .... 15.
Mayflower Compact, colonies and their charters .... 16.
John Calvin and the Puritan Zion .... 17.
Thomas Hobbes and the Leviathan .... 20.
Cadillac and Detroit. France confronts England .... 23.
Britain, France and black slavery .... 24.
Cadillac and the outpost at Detroit .... 27.
French and Indian war and Pickawillany .... 28.
General Braddock's defeat at Monongahela Valley .... 29.

Chapter 3. Adam Smith's Bookends

Picoté de Belestre, Robert Rogers and British rule at Detroit .... 32.
Adam Smith's "Theory of Moral Sentiments" .... 35.
General Jefferey Amherst, British trappers, and Native Americans .... 39.
Sir William Johnson ("Warraghiyagey") and the Indians .... 40.
Chief Pontiac, Neolin, and the Indian rebellion .... 42.
Smith's "Wealth of Nations" .... 46.
Smith and the economic realities at Detroit and the colonies .... 51.
War and piracy as a source of early U.S. fortunes .... 53.

Chapter 4. Liquor, Lies, and Laissez-Faire

Britain and its proxy Iroquois army resist U.S. settlement .... 54.
General Anthony Wayne and the Battle of Fallen Timbers .... 55.
Bacon and Shay's rebellions, the Constitution, and the new republic .... 57.
Treaty of Paris: re-drawing Great Lakes' borders .... 58.
New Gnadenhutten and the nascent Michigan real estate market .... 60.
Ancrum, Askin and the Moravian settlement .... 61.

The Northwest Ordinance ..... 62.
John Jacob Astor and the great fur trading companies ..... 64.
Lewis Cass and the Michigan survey expedition ..... 71.
Lewis Cass and confiscatory treaties ..... 74.
Lewis Cass and corrupt surveys ..... 76.
Andrew Jackson, Indian Removal Act, and Indian expulsions ..... 77.
Andrew Jackson, ethnic cleansing and the Trail of Tears ..... 79.

Chapter 5. Wood, Water, and Fire: After the Beaver

Evolution of Wayne County ..... 81.
Michigan judge cabal and the "Woodward Code" ..... 82.
John Gentle and the judge cabal ..... 83.
Detroit fire ..... 84.
William Hull and the surrender of Detroit ..... 86.
"Council of the Territory," Lewis Cass, and the marketing of Michigan ..... 87.
Logging in Michigan: antiquity and early 1800s ..... 88.
Harvey Miller and the first steam-powered sawmill ..... 92.
Steamships, immigrants, and the Illinois-Michigan Canal ..... 94.
Erie-Kalamazoo Railroad ..... 95.
Henry Bessemer and the Bessemer steel process ..... 96.

Chapter 6. The Not So Calm Before the Storm

Alexis de Tocqueville: wealth and land in America ..... 98.
Hamilton and Bank of United States (BUS) ..... 99.
Jackson, Calhoun, anti-bank sentiment, and Tariff of Abominations ..... 101.
Loose money, speculation, and the "Specie Circular" ..... 102.
Rampant speculation and the Panic of 1937 ..... 104.
Early Detroit business ..... 107.
Detroit population growth: 1850 to 1870 ..... 108.
Black segregation and discrimination in ant-bellum Detroit ..... 109.
The Black Codes and the Blackburn riots ..... 110.

Chapter 7. A Melting Pot, Boiling

Immigrants, industrialization, and the devolution of labor ..... 114.
German immigration to Michigan ..... 116.
Canut and Swing riots ..... 117.
European labor rebellions – 1848 ..... 119.
Professors' Parliament and the "48ers" ..... 120.
Ante bellum political parties in Detroit and Michigan ..... 122.
John Calhoun and the economics of slavery ..... 124.

    Dred Scott and Bleeding Kansas..126.
    Fugitive Slave Act and Kansas-Nebraska Act ....127.
    Birth of Republican Party ....128.
    Anti-Black sentiment in Detroit, John Brown and Harper's Ferry ....129.

Chapter 8. A Rich Man's War, A Poor Man's Fight

    Confederate victory at Fort Sumter..132.
    Recruitment at Detroit..133.
    Southern politicians secede..135.
    Friederich List and U.S. protectionism ....137.
    Henry Charles Carey and early U.S. industry ....139.
    Francis Wayland ....139.
    Salmon Chase and Civil War fundraising...141.
    Jay Cooke and Civil War bonds..142.
    Key battles, cost, and the Thirty-Seventh Congress ....144.
    Congress creates Internal Revenue Service ....145.
    Revenue Act, Railroad Act, and the Morrill Land Grant College Act passed.....................146.
    Anti-recruitment mob at Campus Martius ....147.
    Emancipation Proclamation and effect ....149.
    Northern labor unrest ....141.
    Enrollment Act and reaction ....150.
    Draft riots ....152.
    Henry Barnes and the Black Regiment ....155.

Chapter 9. In God We Make Trusts

    Lee's surrender at Appomattox..156.
    Mechanization and labor...157.
    Richard Trevelick and the WTA in Detroit ....160.
    Early business development in Detroit ....161.
    Work, management and ownership in early Detroit ....161.
    Work and social stratification in Detroit, 1880...163.
    James McMillan ....165.
    Jay Cooke and the failed Great Lakes railway..167.
    Movement to a national railway system ....168.
    Pacific Railway Act and Crédit Mobilier..169.
    The Michigan salt monopoly, John D. Rockefeller, South Improvement Co.,
    Failure of Jay Cooke's bank, and the Panic of 1873...170.
    National strikes and their suppression, 1877 ....172.
    Working black ostracism from Detroit unions..173.

Chapter 1
The French and Before

He who goes about to reform the world must begin with himself, or he loses his labor.
Ignatius Loyola[1]

Before the French, there was the beaver. Before the forests blanketing the land of Michigan echoed with the Gallic tones of the *coureur de bois*, – those "rovers of the woods" — there were the Indians and their simple dance with the unspoiled rivers and woodlands. When, in 1620, Etienne Brulé's boat slid onto the soft sand of Sault Saint Marie, how could he know that that small slice in the Michigan shore would be just the first of many wounds? How could he know – in his blameless quest to satisfy the need for hats and coats in Paris, London, and Vienna – that stowing away in the boats of those to come would be the hatreds, vices, and disease that had, for centuries, roiled the European continent across the water? Eventually, the natives would offer their hand to the French, and their help. That simple

"Étienne Brûlé at the mouth of the Humber" **(F.S. Challener. Art collection of the government of Ontario. 619849)**

gesture presaged first their dependence, and then their undoing. For the time being, though, Michigan was an ocean of trees, rich with fur-bearing animals of every sort and, – more importantly for Richelieu and Louis XIII– the potential to become yet another jewel in the growing collection of French colonies.

To eyes not merely covetous of its lustrous coat, the beaver is a model of industry, close social ties, and family stability: all virtues esteemed by their human counterparts who are the only species better at engineering. Beavers mate for life, their fidelity ending only, in many unfortunate instances, when one of their partner's legs has a close and deadly encounter with a steel trap, thus ending its days on a shelf in a milliner's shop or a haberdashery. For safety's sake, the beaver prefers a private aquatic entrance to its lodge: a dome-like structure of branches and mud in the middle of a

Beaver with baby. **(Picryl. Public domain.)**

biodiversity and act like a natural sponge, helping to keep erosion in check, raise the water table, and filter water.[2] Thus, without the advantage of human reflection or cerebral gymnastics, nature provides in the beaver an instinct-driven example of self-interest that also redounds to the benefit of many – an outcome humans, in their own unique greed and self-interest, have yet to master.

Before the Jesuits with their strange clothing and even stranger ideas, there were the Indians and their intimate relationship with the forests, the lakes, and the rivers. The Indians were farmers, mostly, producing corn, beans, peas, squash, and pumpkins. Their primitive tools and techniques limited the size of their plots and, therefore, their impact on the pristine environment.[3] As a culture, the Indians were peripatetic, never staying in one place too long and exploiting the indigenous flora and fauna only in amounts necessary for survival. In the winter months they hunted beaver, muskrat, raccoon, deer, elk, bison and black bear for meat and hides. The warmer months were devoted to agriculture, with sugar being a staple of the Indians' diet.[4] Those tribes living along the shoreline of the lakes relied on fishing as well, especially around what is now Sault St. Marie. Though the forested interior of early Michigan was dense and impassable, the rivers that snaked their way through it became highways for the natives who developed an elaborate, watery network for traversing the region.

Imagining Michigan, as it often is, in the image of a mitten (one over the left hand), it is easy to describe the distribution of Indian tribes at the time of the first white man's arrival.[5] Michigan's upper peninsula (in French, the *Pays d'en Haut*) touches the top of the glove like a finger. It was there that Brulé and later Jean Nicolet in 1634 – coming down from Canada, the first foothold of "New France" – made the first inroads into the region, encountering the native Ojibwe and Menominee who were primarily hunters and fisherman because of the cold climate. The Potawatomi occupied most of the land mass of lower Michigan at this time, encompassing an area that would, using our imaginary mitten, include all the fingers and – moving from the index finger leftward to the pinky – down most of the palm to the wrist. The Sauk and the Fox controlled the area around the thumb (which would come to include Detroit), with the Miami and the Kickapoo just below them at the base of the hand at the wrist. Though all had separate cultures and traditions and sometimes warred over territory, they all were reluctant to share their traditional methods and techniques with the newcomers, a healthy apprehension fate would prove warranted.

Indian tribes of early Michigan

As for the *coureur de bois* – the French trappers – beyond the historical record, one can only speculate about the men, their state of mind, and their motivation. Would, for instance, the simple desire to make a living have been enough to cause them to confront the dangers and uncertainties of this wooded expanse across the ocean, with its frequently hostile inhabitants and inhospitable environment? Indeed, it would when viewed in an historical context, because tucked away in the psyche of many of these men might have been

Chapter 1   *The French and Before*

enough to cause them to confront the dangers and uncertainties of this wooded expanse across the ocean, with its frequently hostile inhabitants and inhospitable environment? Indeed, it would when viewed in an historical context, because tucked away in the psyche of many of these men might have been memories of the savagery French Protestants and Catholics had visited upon each other in their home country between 1562 and 1589. At the height of that period, known as the French Wars of Religion, ten thousand French Protestants (called "Huguenots") were massacred by Catholics on St. Bartholomew's Day in 1572.[5] Who wouldn't choose the sounds of the forests – the wind in the trees, rustling rivers, and squawking birds – over the carnage of zealous armies set one upon the other in the name of God?

Such chaos was, it should be noted, not confined to France. The sectarian violence reverberated throughout Western Europe and the Netherlands, later to find its own unique political expression in Calvinist Cromwell's England. In 1589, after 27 years of mutual slaughter, cooler heads prevailed for a time; at least in France. Despite his Catholic roots, philosopher Jean Bodin saw the wisdom of compromise over carnage and imagined a force powerful enough to bring the warring factions to heel: an all powerful monarch. (A notion predating Hobbes' own theories of a unitary monarchy by seventy-five years.) Even at the height of the violence, there existed deep in the consciousness of the French people, no matter what their convictions, a nebulous idea of a French nation that vibrated beneath the conflict like a barely discernible figured bass. But it

Perhaps many French trappers – or, *coureur de bois*, as they were called – came to the New World not just for furs, but to escape the carnage and brutality of Europe's religious wars. **(Painting of St. Bartholomew's Day Massacre by Huguenot artist, Francois Bubois. Wikimedia Commons.)**

Chapter 1 *The French and Before*

Jean Bodin **(Wikimedia Commons)**

was an idea too weak and too cerebral to overcome the all-consuming emotional vortex of religious warfare. What was needed was a tangible symbol of the nation's power embodied in a single person, one who could inspire fear not just because he (gender intended) was above the law, but also because he was divinely invested with the power to dictate or liquidate it at his whim. No one could question or contradict him. His rule would be, in other words, absolute; so potent, in fact, that he – the living expression of French sovereignty – could suck the energy from the warring factions by the sheer gravitas of his being and bend their destructive inclinations to the more positive and broader will of the state.

However, as Bodin went to great lengths to point out, the mechanics of government were something different than the sovereign state, and while the privilege and purview of the monarch as its expression was eternal and irreproachable, the actual act of governance was unrestrained by such philosophical niceties and could be executed by anyone with the loyalty and will to do so, no matter what their religious persuasion. Anything goes, as Machiavelli had so pointedly described, when it came to managing and preserving the well-being – i.e., "governing" – the state, even, if necessary, dispatching its detractors. It was the early French Renaissance version of Realpolitik, and it made a clear distinction between the agents of governance, and the unquestioned authority of the monarch from which their authority derived. "Whatever power and authority the sovereign prince confers upon others, his own person remains excepted" writes Bodin.[6] While England was cobbling together a rudimentary system of parliamentary checks on the monarch's power, French governance suffered no such bifurcation (a fact that would ultimately prove to be its undoing).

Though the first glimmers of French absolutism appeared in the reign of Henry IV in 1601, it came to full flower under Louis XIII, his nine-year old son, who rose to the throne upon the assassination of his father at the hands of a Catholic fanatic in 1610. Though one so young was perfectly qualified to assume the symbolic duties of monarchy, the details of governance, on the other hand, fell to a cleric by the name of Richelieu, whose brilliance and ruthlessness would become legend. Through Richelieu's iron-fisted cultivation of the French monarchy, it assumed its unyielding nature, a characteristic that would ultimately meet its end with Louis XVI's head in a basket in 1793. What is significant for this inquiry is the fact that at the time of the first French incursions into the Americas, every aspect of French power – from religion to the economy – was under the control of the French crown, which, for

Chapter 1

The French and Before

much of that period, actually meant Armand Jean du Plessis, otherwise known as Cardinal Richelieu.

At the time of Louis XIII, therefore, the power of the French monarchy did not stop at the water's edge, and the mere width of the Atlantic Ocean was not great enough to diminish the sovereign's reach into the tiny French enclaves which, at this time, were regarded as "New France." The *coureur de bois*, for their part, were economic vassals of the French crown, and could never really act legally as independent agents of business, even in the North American wilderness. They were, in fact, the bottom of an economic hierarchy at whose apex sat wealthy French outfitters who, in concert with the crown and even the church, subsidized the provisions and necessary equipment for the trappers' sojourns in the wilderness. The French fur trade was a monopoly with its epicenter in Montreal.[7] Control of the trade could reside in a corporation, a single investor or group of investors, and even the commander of a settlement as part of his compensation. All operated at the behest of the monarchy, and strict laws were enacted regulating price and distribution.[8] But passing laws and enforcing them from such a great distance were two very different matters.

As newcomers, the early French trappers were at the mercy of the natives who were not eager to surrender their knowledge of the wilderness or their skills acquired over generations. What the French did have to offer were metal tools, artifacts, and textiles produced in French factories and workshops, and, tragically, liquor. All of these items went a long way toward chipping away at the Indians' resistance, and the natives gradually came to share much of their culture with the woodsmen. In the process, an enduring symbiotic relationship developed between the French and the Indians, one that transcended the merely economic. The *coureur de bois* not only adopted much of the lifestyle of the Indians, many took Indian women as wives and lived among the natives. As Juen and Nasseney have suggested,[9] the fur trade "… was the glue that bound the French to their native allies." But the trade might never have occurred had the French not first collaborated in the Indian ritual of gift giving. For the natives, western concepts of trade and private property were alien notions. Exchange was more about gifts. Those who gave gifts were held in high esteem, and those who received them were obligated to the giver.[10] One could not trade with an enemy. Because the monopoly, which generated from the home country, guaranteed prices no matter what the supply of fur, it was often woefully inefficient from an economic standpoint. Nevertheless, the French embrace of the native culture ensured the Indians' allegiance and would win them as allies in the struggle against future British encroachments on the trade, proving their alliance with the Indians to be, perhaps, an asset more valuable than the fur trade itself.

As a group, the *coureur de bois* were free-spirited, adventurous, and many did assimilate with the native population. Still others were less than sterling in character and (as Ida Johnson recounts in a 1919 passage indicative of the enduring racism of her own era) not above the merely mercenary: "…the *couerer de bois*…struck boldly into the wilderness, trading with and cheating the savage [sic] to their hearts content, in spite of trading companies and French decrees."[11] These were the unlicensed traders who, under leaders like Daniel Greyselon Du Luht (the eponymous founder of present day Duluth) "…erected rude forts or palisades at various points which they occupied as long as it suited their purpose, and then abandoned them for their next corner."[12]

As the trappers began to cut their own paths across the wilderness with less and less help from the Indians, there sprung up certain way stations at places like Sault St. Marie, Michilimackinac, St. Joseph, and a little outpost called Detroit where the men could meet to barter, drink, and find respite from the rigors of the forests and lakes. Though these men led a free-wheeling lifestyle, they were captive to circumstances to which they were born. Whether in a canoe, inside a stockade, or stalking some furry creature, mere survival trumped self-realization in a world with no social mobility. In both old France and New, the most an individual could do was to assume his place in the cosmic hierarchy, one overseen by an all-powerful God and the absolute monarch just below him.

In truth, French imperialist designs in New France were never more than half-hearted for much of the 17th century. French ministers from Sully under Henry IV to Colbert under Louis the XIV deemed it, frankly, unworthy of effort and resources. Attention should be focused, each argued, on truly scarce resources like sugar, spices, and tea, available only in southern climes. This is not to say there were not advocates for expansion in the Americas back in France; their ambitions, however, were stymied by men closer to the seat of power, men whose fingers were actually on the national purse. As a result, funding did not issue from state coffers alone, but had to come from some combination of three sources: the crown, the commercial sector, and the church, all of whom heard constantly from importunate speculators and adventurers, regaling these monied authorities with tales of possible riches from the forests, lakes, and rivers of New France.[13] If history shows one thing about this period, it is this: If Old France had been tethered to the New by the mere economic thread of the fur trade, it would have certainly snapped much sooner. A more enduring vanguard of French influence in these times was religious, and came in the form of the religious order called The Society of Jesus, or, as they are otherwise known, the Jesuits.

So important is the Jesuits' role in New France at this time that, in order to truly understand the affairs of the day, an understanding of their order, its philosophy, and its governance is helpful. Depending on who is telling the story, the Jesuits were either selfless apostles in the service of God, or manipulative, power-hungry scoundrels who twisted religious doctrine to satisfy secular ambitions. Probably a little of both is true depending on which side of the Atlantic is under scrutiny, and which level of the order's hierarchy is being considered. Though all their professed loyalties were to the Almighty, many of their actions would seem to indicate a more earthly fealty to the reigning pope and the "General" of the society instead. (That this powerful, shadowy character was referred to at the time as the "Black Pope" is an indication of the contemporary distrust held for the order). The fact that the Jesuits were as comfortable in the chambers of power as they were running a university or ministering to the sick and diseased speaks to their unique history and organizational flexibility, making them the ideal – if not, perhaps, the only – religious order equal to the task of claiming the North American wilderness and its inhabitants for France.

Stone Relief of Jesuit Seal on of the Church of the Gesu, Rome. **(Wikimedia Commons)**

The Jesuits who followed in the footsteps of the trappers and endured the hardships of the wild frontier across the ocean were generally from the hard-working, humble, and sincere lower ranks of the Jesuit

Chapter 1 *The French and Before*

organization. Their mission was not to capture beaver's fur, but rather the souls of the natives for Christendom. Unlike the *coureur de bois*, they tended to stay in one place, working with individual tribes to learn their language and customs, sincerely hoping their message might penetrate the thick wall of Indian custom and win them for Christ – in most cases an unlikely outcome. Back in Europe, however, their order had developed a more checkered reputation and had, from the beginning, been viewed with suspicion, not only by secular authorities who distrusted their gradual encroachment on local governments wherever they established themselves, but also by rival orders like the Dominicans and Franciscans who resented them for their preferential treatment by the papacy, their doctrinal liberalism, and their closely cultivated relationships with the powerful and aristocratic.[14]

What, then, might account for the Jesuits' stalwart courage and discipline, so firm that they would risk death willingly, not only in the wilds of the Americas, but in such far-flung corners of the world as China, Japan, and India? How did the order secure such unquestioned obedience from its clerical legions? As with many successful organizations, old and new, the key was indoctrination. When it came to the novitiate, nothing was left either to chance or to the individual belief system of the aspiring member. Each was to be scrubbed clean spiritually and doctrinally, reduced to a tabula rasa upon which the order could write its own designs; and it did. The gateway to the Society of Jesus was both narrow and arduous, consisting of an exhausting, month-long regimen of self-examination and atonement formulated by its founder, Ignatius Loyola, called the "Spiritual Exercises." The Exercises grew out of Loyola's own religious ecstasies, the details of which are recounted in a 1913 book on the order by Joseph McCabe, himself a former member:

St. Ignatius Wearing Leg Splints by Antoine DeFavray **(Wikimedia Commons)**

"After a few months he found a cavern outside the town, at the foot of the hills, and entered upon the period of endless prayer and wild austerity in which he wrote his book, the Spiritual Exercises. He scourged himself until the blood came, three times a day: he ate so little, and lived so intense a life that he was sometimes found unconscious on the floor of the cave, and had to be removed and nursed; his deep black eyes seemed to gleam from the face of a corpse. Thus he lived for six months, and wrote his famous book."[15]

Though the Exercises still play a role in Jesuit training today, this brief description of the process by Catholic apologist Francis Parkman shows the deep impress and the dark, lingering aspects of the master's own experience on them:

"The novice, in solitude and darkness, day after day and night after night, ponders its images of perdition and despair. He is taught to hear, in imagination, the howling of the damned, to see their convulsive agonies, to feel the flames that burn without consuming, to smell the corruption of the tomb and the fumes of the infernal pit. He

Chapter 1   *The French and Before*

must picture to himself an array of adverse armies, one commanded by Satan on the plains of Babylon, one encamped under Christ about the walls of Jerusalem; and the perturbed mind humbled by long contemplation of its own vileness, ordered to enroll itself under one or the other banner. Then, the choice made, it is led to a region of serenity and peace, and soothed with images of divine benignity and grace."(16)

This is martial imagery, and reveries and self-mortification were hardly unique to Loyola and his times. He no doubt knew, from a Catholic history rich with such histrionics, that a visually dramatic contempt for the physical self was merely one of the necessary components of a holy man's bona fides; another being the outward demeanor and look of an abject beggar. The latter was a persona Ignatius and his followers mastered early on. Like Francis of Assisi, who was also from a wealthy family, he forsook his worldly possessions and wandered about in rags in a town where his family was still held in high esteem. By this behavior he brought ridicule upon himself, and the moniker "Father Sackcloth" from cajoling children and annoyed townspeople. But unlike St. Francis, there was an element of disingenuousness and a studied theatricality to his behavior, for his ministrations were very often performed for public consumption, some of whom he probably hoped might regard his efforts as worthy of acclaim, endorsement, and indicative of a properly sanctimonious contempt for the self.

Contained in this somewhat false and calculated mendicancy was, in fact, the seed of the all-important (and useful) persona of the Jesuit as a self-less champion of the downtrodden and the ill, willing to throw himself headlong into a population of the sick and diseased without regard for his own well-being. Though any attempts to help the sick and the poor would certainly be laudable for people of any persuasion, one gets the feeling it was for the Jesuits a little something more; that is, a dramatic and effective way to insinuate themselves among an unsuspecting and vulnerable population in order to cultivate a physical dependence on their attention and care.(17) More importantly, this is a plan of action that could work just as well in the wilds of America as in a little town in Spain. After all, from simple aid could come a hospital, then a school, then a local government inhabited (and influenced) by the alumni of Jesuit schools and colleges. In this way was Jesuit influence– and by extension, papal power– disseminated; a potent antidote to a world poisoned with heretical Protestant notions and the threat of Muhammadism (Islam) pressing at the borders of the Catholic realm.

The spirit of the Exercises was, then, not preparation for a life of chanting in the cloistered vaults of a monastery or passing one's days in ascetic isolation. Its stark images of banners and armies squared off on the eternal plain of Good and Evil

Unus non sufficit orbis - One world is not enough - from the 1640 centenary Jesuit publication *Imago primi saceuli Societatis Iesu.*" **(Wikimedia Commons.)**

Chapter 1

The French and Before

suggest the Jesuits were not simply missionaries, but warriors in the cause of a Catholic church in the throes of an existential crisis. The induction period spent with the Spiritual Exercises could even be regarded as a sort of doctrinal boot camp. Catholic dogma had long since been constructed by thinkers like Augustine and Aquinas and the faith did not need, in those troubled times, another philosophical brick added to that edifice. What it needed was a soldier to defend it, and, as fate or coincidence is often wont to do, provided him in the person of Ignatius Loyola.

Like the order he created, Ignatius Loyola is a complex amalgam of saint and soldier. In order to understand him, one must walk a tightrope between history and hagiography. Like St. Paul on the road to Tarsus, the heavens opened to him through a physical trauma. While defending the Spanish town of Pampelona against a French siege in 1521, the legend goes, Loyola's leg was badly broken by a cannon ball. During the long weeks of convalescence, he passed the time reading a book on the lives of the saints. One can imagine him – his leg permanently damaged – reflecting on the trials, tribulations, and glory of the esteemed personages about whom he read, all the while realizing that his own life of soldierly exploits and courtly ambitions were now irreparably broken. He had cut, after all, a dashing figure in the court where a wealthy aunt had placed him, and had experienced "…the flash of swords, the smile of princes, the softness of silk and of women's eyes, and all the hard deeds and rich rewards of the knight's career."[18] No Quixote or windmills here; he had truly experienced the smell of smoke and death in battle. Now that was gone. But someone like Ignatius was not easily disabused of the chivalric ideal after which he'd striven until that day. What else could he do, then, but transpose that code of chivalry onto the wider realm of God's universe? What else for a crippled man, unlikely now to put a sparkle in a lady's eye, but to dedicate himself to the eternally sexless icon of the Virgin Mary?

Loyola was no scholar and the limited education he had was hard-won. But despite his simple Basque background, Loyola proved to be a consummate politician, controlling very closely at first the first few members of his nascent order who were, in fact, scholars themselves. He cultivated relationships with the powerful, and positioned himself and his coterie of followers who immersed themselves among the sick when necessary, engaged in intellectual discourse with prospective converts and ideological enemies, and assumed whatever role they needed to enhance the influence of the order which, in their minds, was no different than furthering the cause of the faith. By the time Pope Paul III officially recognized the Society of Jesus in 1540, their reputation had preceded them, and many others of the faith set little store in the pope's decision. However, it was a wise move for the Vicar of Christ, for Loyola had made it clear to the pontiff that though he and his followers would certainly promote the faith, they would, above all, be the right hand of the papacy itself:

> "The rules of the new order were designed to develop a flexible, disciplined, and efficient body of ecclesiastical shock troops for the papacy. The Jesuit wore no distinctive habit; he dressed as his job might require, as priest, teacher, missionary, or secret agent…He was carefully selected and trained for the most dangerous and difficult tasks the Church might require, from serving as confessor to a king, to venturing into Protestant countries where he might be executed as a traitor…The Jesuits were spectacularly successful. They strengthened the pope's control over the Church itself; they ran the best schools in Europe; and during the late sixteenth century they won back most of

Chapter 1

The French and Before

Bohemia, Poland, Hungary, and southern Germany from Protestantism."[19]

The humble clerics who ministered to the Indians in New France were, then, the most benign wing of a complex, multi-faceted Jesuit order. Though France's ambitions in the Great Lakes region were dashed early on, that French influence in Canada and southern states like Louisiana endures to this day can be credited to religious, rather than economic forces; in particular, the Jesuits.

In the twenty-five years, or so, after Brulé's boat came ashore in the Great Lakes region in 1620, the waves of European culture, religion, and technology that lapped at the simple culture of the natives were gentle and predominantly French. Extending the metaphor, one could characterize them as a low tide of influence owing to France's half-hearted investment, the willingness of the French on the ground there to assimilate, and the moral brake on predation exerted by Jesuit evangelism. Ultimately, of course, the Indians would be ravaged by a typhoon of disease, genocide, and exploitation once the British and the Americans had their day. That, however, is a tale for later. For now, it is important to look at bit closer at the actual interaction of French and Indian cultures, for the realities of that engagement are quite different than much of the literature has led us to believe.

Fortunately, the racially tinged narrative that dominated the study of Indian history – one characterizing the Indians as hapless primitives bowing irresistibly to the paternalism and superiority of the white culture – has been supplanted since the fifties by genuine, objective scholarship.[20] Archeological and anthropological finds at sites like Fort St. Joseph, on the St. Joseph River (which flows through southwestern Michigan, dips briefly into Indiana, and empties into Lake Michigan), reveal a mix of traditional and European items, indicating that the native tribes were resourceful, discriminating, and not always quick to accept wholesale the white man's metal tools, cookware, and firearms. However, once the Indians acquired a taste (and even a dependence) on certain of these items, they became linked to the inexorable chain of supply and maintenance that stretched back to Europe. Parts and powder for guns, cloth and jewelry, and metal pots pulled them closer to the land across the water, and served to alter, each in its own way, some aspect of Indian society and habits.

"Father Marquette and the Indians."
(Painting by William Alfred Lamprecht, 1869. Wikimedia Commons)

Where domestic items were concerned, the Indians were certainly insightful enough to appreciate the durability and efficiency of metal cookware like brass kettles, metal knives, and axes as opposed to traditional clay vessels or tools of stone. Though they utilized metal versions in some instances, they did not necessarily prefer metal in all cases. Archaeological finds at sites like Rock Island – along the western shore of Lake Michigan – indicate a predominance of bone over metal fishing tools.[21] Nor did the natives hesitate to re-purpose metal items for different uses. According to Juen and Nasseney: "Natives recycled worn out kettles into new goods such as arrow points, scrapers,

Chapter 1

The French and Before

and awls, and ornaments such as tubular beads, pendants, and tinkling cones."[22] Textiles followed a similar pattern, the obvious advantages of woven textiles being obvious, especially to Indian women who, by utilizing them, were freed from the onerous process of manufacturing their own apparel from indigenous resources. Like the metal, however, this came with a price: an ongoing relationship with the white merchants who dealt with the home country for these items, one requiring payment for the transaction in the prevalent currency of the area: beaver pelts. This development is significant in the life of the Indian in that the beaver became transformed from a creature of subsistence, to a fungible commodity exchanged for some foreign article.

The commoditization of the beaver (and other fur-bearing animals) meant, as with any marketable item, an increased pressure for greater supply over and above subsistence. In short, production trumped subsistence, and the creature needed to be killed more quickly and in much greater numbers to satisfy demand. Firearms facilitated this, their introduction posing a profound and dramatic change in the life and worldview of the Indian. Thus, with the advent of beaver pelt as currency, the Indians had their first, often brutal, lesson in the rudiments of European market economies. Indirectly, though, it strengthened the alliance with the French because the guns needed maintenance, and that meant closer ties with French gunsmiths. Just as with domestic items, however, the natives did not completely abandon

French Inroads in "New France"

Antoine Lamothe de Cadillac

"Fur Traders in Canada, Trading with the Indians." 1877. **(From "A map from the inhabited part of Canada..." 1777 by William Faden)**

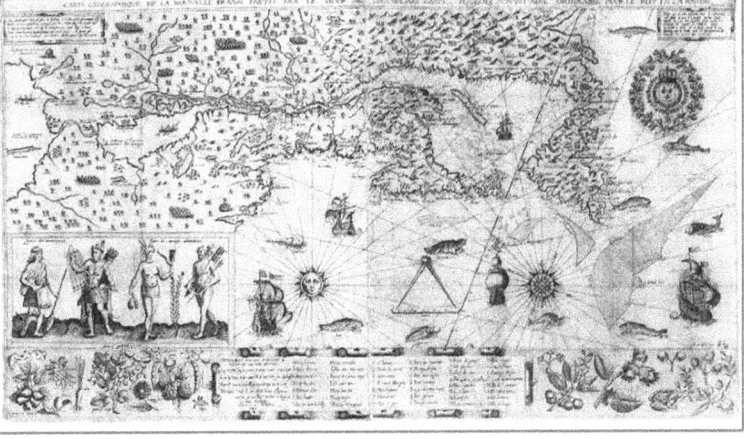

Map of New France drawn by Champlain in 1632. **(© Samuel de Champlain/Library and Archives of Canada/NMC-51970)**

Chapter 1   *The French and Before*

their traditional weapons, in great part because these early firearms were notoriously inefficient and undependable, often posing a greater danger to the user than those on the receiving end.[23] Sadly, the gun also took on its darker aspects as a weapon, used, ironically, against anyone threatening one's niche in the fur trade. As we shall see, once the French fur trade – and, by proxy, their Indian allies – were threatened by British and Dutch interests, the gun and violence it wrought dictated other alliances with more deadly consequences.

Perhaps the most fateful and tragic European import for the Indians was alcohol. Like other characterizations of the Native American, the image of the drunken Indian is also a pervasive and carelessly wrought stereotype in much of the historical record. What is absent – and, in all fairness to the early French soldiers and trappers, not always malicious in intent – was the white man's role in facilitating and molding the natives' negative relationship with alcohol. Even an authority like Ida Johnson shows her own dereliction in this passage: "The Indian imbibed a taste and love for the white man's brandy, so strong that he would gladly exchange the costliest furs for a drink."[24] Though it is true that alcohol grew to be a tragic part of many fur trading transactions with the Indians, the author makes no attempt to contextualize the behavior, to investigate the white man's culpability in shaping it, or the predisposition of the Indian to seek in intoxication a false religious significance.

Before the arrival of the Europeans, the Native American population had very limited experience with alcohol. Though some tribes traditionally produced rather tame types of fermented brews that were used primarily in religious ceremonies, drink was not produced in anywhere near the strength or volume consumed by the Europeans. Alcohol in copious amounts, on the other hand, was a way of life among the soldiers, licensed traders, and *coureur de bois* who no doubt resorted to it in order to cope with the twin scourges of boredom and danger posed by life in the intractable wilderness. Initially, simply being present at any of the white man's liquor-soaked festivities would have been a powerful inducement for the Indian to participate, literally and figuratively, in the spirit of the occasion. As the competition for furs of all kinds increased, and as the natives' lack of resistance to alcohol became apparent to the foreign traders, the Europeans began to employ liquor as a deliberate tool to steer the transactions to their own advantage.[26] Eventually the violence and debauchery wrought by the ocean of liquor among the natives and the foreigners was a profound source of frustration for the Jesuits who, as the official moral compass of both populations, found it nearly impossible to steer any of them onto a pure and godly path. Parkman recalls the despair of Father Etienne Carheil at the depraved state of affairs among the inhabitants at the outpost at Michlimackinac:

> 'Our missions," he says, "are reduced to such extremity that we can no longer maintain them against the infinity of disorder, brutality, violence, injustice, impiety', impurity, insolence, scorn, and insult, which the deplorable and infamous traffic in brandy has spread universally among the Indians of these parts.... In the despair in which we are plunged, nothing remains for us but to abandon them to the brandy sellers as a domain of drunkenness

and Indian society had no normative structure to deal with the type of violent, irrational behavior modeled by the intoxicated Europeans. The psychotropic substances, peyote, and tobaccos of various sorts had indeed been a part of Indian culture, but were employed as a positive part of religious ceremonies where the underlying intent was to unite them spiritually with tribal

Chapter 1 *The French and Before*

members, not inebriation for its own sake. This, the Indians learned from the white men with whom they dealt.[26]

The plaints of the good Father and his fellow clerics did not fall on deaf ears. In 1679, Louis the XIV issued a decree mandating progressively increasing fines for traders trafficking liquor to the Indians. This was followed in 1694 by a complete ban on the trade of liquor in the Michigan territories. But even the long arm of Louis did not extend far enough to stop the practice. The recalcitrance was thorough all the way up the chain of command, for, as Johnson reminds us, the "…governor and commandants winked at its importation and sale, while the blame was heaped on the shoulders of the *coureur de bois*."[27]

Intellectuals across the water – philosophers like Hobbes who never experienced an environment any wilder than a drawing room – seized, purely for the purpose of argument, on the image of the native North Americans as indicative of a savage "state of nature" characterized by lawlessness and chaos.[28] However, those Jesuits, traders, and voyageurs who actually lived among the Indian found a culture quite different than the unredeemed, lawless, and forsaken people of Hobbes' imagination. After all "…there were towns," says Parkman, "where savages lived in thousands with a harmony which civilization might envy."[29] The Indian, Parkman continues, was governed by a universal code of courtesy and generosity, one which – in a natural inclination to please the Jesuits or anyone else – often compelled them to act as though they had succumbed to the clerics' proselytizing when, in fact, they neither understood what they seemed to agree to, nor had any intention of assuming the behavior of a genuine convert. It was this incipient good nature that the Europeans, with their guns, liquor, and irresistible trinkets, dismantled: a fragile, social firewall that protected the Native American from the excesses and negative behavior of the white men.

In their quest to convert the natives to Christianity, the Jesuits confronted a formidable philosophical barrier in the panthesim at the very core of Indian religion. Spiritually, the two cultures were, in fact, on opposite trajectories. For the Christian Scholastics – whose teachings posited a material world entirely subordinate to an-all powerful God and a hierarchy of being clearly defined in the Garden – all creation existed for the pleasure of humans, who, created in God's image, held exclusive license to its exploitation. Even Descartes and his method (himself a graduate of the Jesuit school at La Flèche in 1615) deduced a physical world that was illusory and inferior to a thought world that was the realm of God and humans alone:

> "But because I had already recognised very clearly in myself that the nature of intelligence is distinct from that of the body, and observing that all composition gives evidence of dependency, and that dependency is manifestly an imperfection, I came to the conclusion that it could not be a perfection in God to be composed of these two natures, and that consequently He was not so composed."[30]

For the Indian, there was no such troubling dichotomy. "A mysterious and inexplicable power resides in inanimate things…" Parkman explains. "They, too, can listen to the voice of man, and influence his life for evil or for good. Lakes, rivers and waterfalls are sometimes the dwelling-place of spirits; but more frequently they are themselves living beings, to be propitiated by prayers and offerings."[31] In fact, humans

Chapter 1

The French and Before

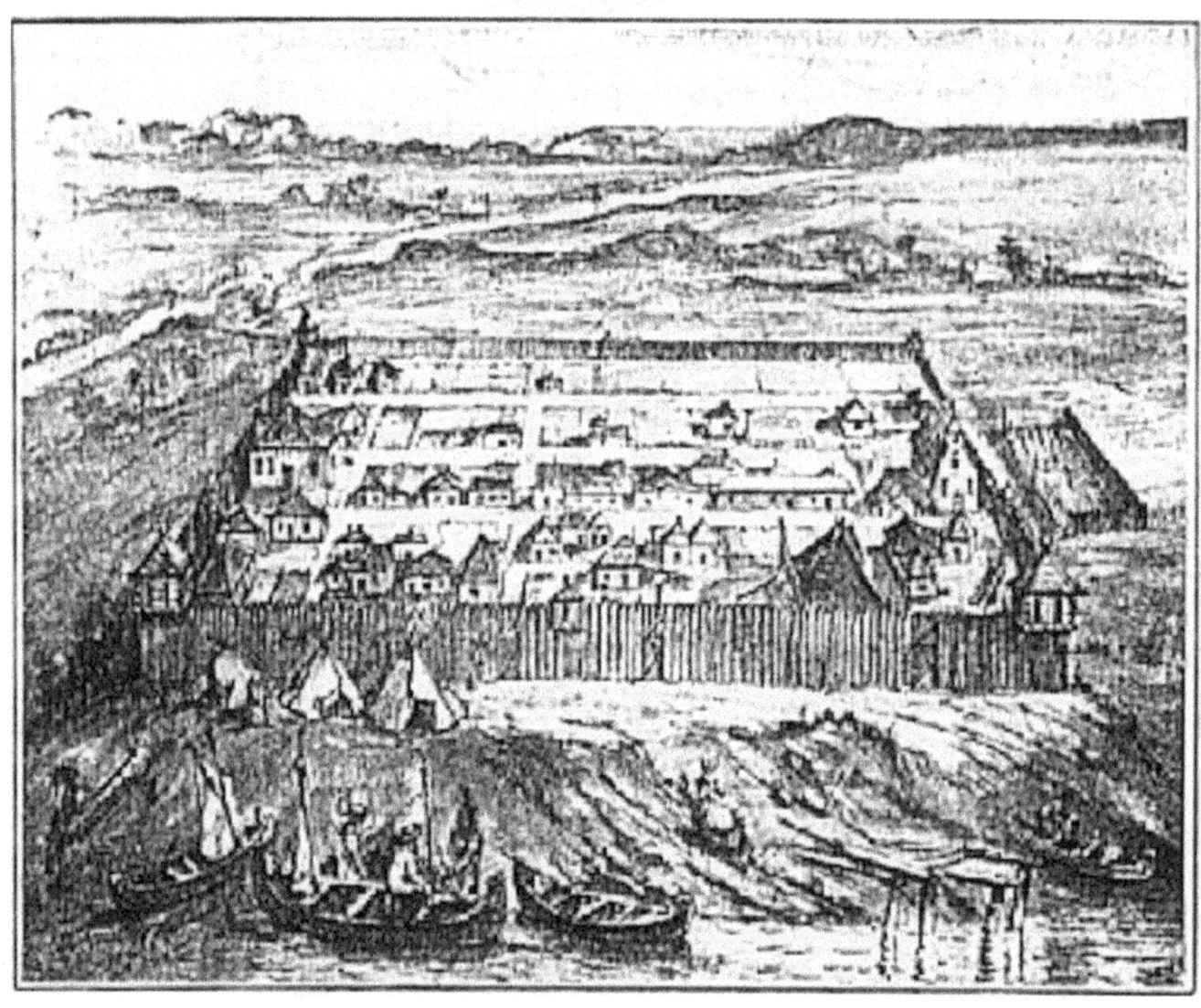

Fort Ponchartrain – renamed "Detroit" (the French word for "strait,") in 1701. **(Archives nationales d'outre-mer. France. Wikemedia Commons)**

were, for the Indians, descendants of archetypal animals that exist in some larger form somewhere. In their role as human progenitors, animals were, consequently, treated with respect and reverence. Prayers and propitiation were offered to the spirit of the animal before killing it in appreciation of its sacrifice, and to acknowledge its natural connection with the hunter. For the Europeans – who saw the forest as merely a killing field filled with marketable commodities – overcoming the Indians' intimate association with the physical world (to the point where they could recruit the natives to this cold, utilitarian enterprise) was a difficult task, one the Europeans accomplished with vigor and persistence. This process had begun even before the incursion of the Dutch and the British who would, as we shall see, take the subjugation and cultural indifference to an even higher level, thus transforming and objectifying a relatively peaceful and subsistence oriented Indian culture into an instrument for their own transplanted wars of domination, and a reliable market for European goods, guns, and alcohol.

Chapter 1   *The French and Before*

Chapter 2
Rule Britannia

While the French were taking their first tentative steps among the lands and natives of New France in the two decades after 1620, English and Dutch colonies had been struggling to gain a foothold on the Atlantic coast since the beginning of the century. These colonies and their inhabitants were separated from the French not only by wooded expanses and huge bodies of water, but also by an even greater cultural and philosophical chasm that mirrored the socio/political landscapes of the nations they had left. The hard-won beliefs, fears, and convictions they forged in their mother countries crossed with them and crashed into the reality of an American continent whose wilderness and indigenous

Oliver Cromwell, Lord Protector of England, 1670. (**National Army Museum, U.K. Artist unknown.**)

peoples seemed, at first, impervious to their ambitions and worldviews.

As to the situation in France, were there any questions regarding either the future of Protestantism in that country or the limits of Louis XIII's absolute power, they were laid to rest by Richelieu whose ubiquitous reach into every corner of French society (with aid from the Jesuits) effectively neutralized the gains the Protestant Huguenots had won through the fragile peace brokered twenty years earlier in 1585 by Henry IV called the "Edict of Nantes." Neither minister nor monarch could countenance pockets of Protestant

Richelieu presents painter Nicolas Poussin to Louis XIII. 1817 painting by Jean-Joseph Anisaux. (**Museé des Beaux-Arts, Bordeaux.**)

influence with the potential to politically threaten or limit the king's sovereignty, something already underway across the channel in England. There, Charles I (of Catholic sympathies with a Spanish, Catholic wife) attempted to rule without parliament: a body jealous of its increasing role as arbiter of taxation and, more importantly, as a foil for unrestrained monarchical power.

Like many conflicts of the time, political strife in England was merely a subtext for the much broader and older Protestant/Catholic schism, the sort of divide which – as the bloody religious conflicts of the previous century throughout Europe had shown – could not be bridged peacefully through existing institutions. Therefore, king and commoner squared off in the fens and fields of England in yet another internecine bloodletting to decide whether Charles I would be forced to come to parliament and beg money for his wars, and to ensure that papists would not have the royal ear. The savage and destructive civil war that pitted Calvinist against Catholic between 1642 and 1646 supplanted the fear of a potential despot with the reality of a religious republic headed by a de facto (although never self-professed) dictator: Oliver Cromwell. Cromwell oversaw a commonwealth of Calvinist bigots whose diktats were enforced with the power of the anti-royal military. Ironically, as Trevelyan has suggested, the failure of the victorious Republicans to broker a sensible and fair peace with the royal-leaning nobles merely exchanged an intolerant Catholic regime for a militant Protestant one, and laid the groundwork for a return of the monarchy in the Restoration to come once anarchy ensued.[1]

Preoccupied, then, with the collective slaughter of the civil war, England posed little threat to France's hegemony over what was then the American frontier in the wilds of Canada and what was to become Michigan. More importantly, the tsunami of violence that engulfed

Creating the Mayflower Compact – a painting by Jean Leon Gerome Ferris, 1899. **(Library of Congress.)**

the island nation produced hardly a ripple in its coastal colonies on the other side of the ocean. This left these infant communities in great part un-tethered from control by the government in London and free to experiment within the bounds of their respective charters. Some colonies had no charter, others created their own, a notable and iconic example being the Mayflower Compact.[2] Crafted to accommodate the fact that a storm had blown them north to Cape Cod –

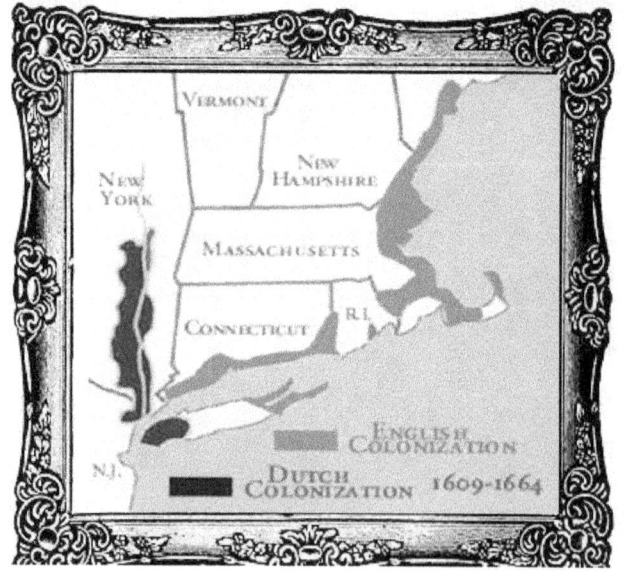

Keen to exploit the fur trade, Dutch trappers established outposts along the Hudson River, well before the English settled on the Eastern Seaboard. **(Map: National Park Service)**

Chapter 2 *Rule Britannia*

600 miles off course – instead of their intended destination in the already established (and royally chartered) colony at Jamestown, Virginia, the Puritan passengers cobbled together their own makeshift charter, at once pledging themselves to development while still swearing a tenuous allegiance to the mother country. Though the colonies did not, however, have formal political rights at this point, their more liberal atmosphere – with elected representative assemblies and generally egalitarian civic institutions – empowered the inhabitants, thereby enhancing personal initiative, local political involvement, and economic development, a fact that served as an impetus for English expansion (and, ultimately, dominance) in America even as French and Dutch colonies were languishing.[3] That the British rather than their French and Dutch rivals would ultimately prosper and proliferate outward from the Atlantic coast to the interior of Michigan and beyond is directly attributable both to the nature and intent of its colonies, the religious and political sensibilities of those who crossed over, and the commitment of the British government to an agenda of empire.

Dutch East India fleet returning with goods from their far-flung market empire. The East India logo – "VOC", or "Vereenige Oost-Indische Compagnie" – in Dutch is superimposed on a black and white version of the painting. **(Painting (1701) by Ludof Bakhulzen . Louvre.)**

Though the Dutch presence in North America was relatively brief and limited geographically in scope, its footprint was consequential enough to merit brief examination. Their involvement in the Hudson Bay area began with the establishment of a few trading posts by the Dutch East India Company beginning in 1606. Then, in 1621, the Dutch West India Company was formed in order to promote more serious colonization. The fact that the latter's stock was open for purchase by anyone was not only testament to its apolitical, non-sectarian nature,[4] it also belied a lack of interest in immigrating on behalf of people in the Netherlands who felt, perhaps, the incentive to leave to be too little, and the potential hardship too great.[5] Furthermore, unlike the French whose presence was also anchored by a religious component in the form of the Jesuits and their mission to evangelize, the Dutch were neither persecuted in their home country, nor possessed of the wanderlust of the *couerier de bois*, nor were they keen to propagate a particular faith. The Dutch wanted simply to reap from this possession what they hoped from all their others: profit. Though they never really expanded beyond the Hudson River Valley and their influence had ended by 1664, Dutch entrepreneurs established a series of trading posts, towns, and forts up and down the Hudson River.[6] Arguably, the most profound and lasting legacy of the Dutch was their relationship with the Indians, one characterized by shameless exploitation and regard for them only in so far as the natives could help facilitate the fur trade, a practice, tragically, continued by the British.

English colonies, on the other hand, were both economic and religious. The colonies at Massachusetts Bay and Jamestown, Virginia serve as perfect examples of each type. At the core of the archaic and effusive language of the Massachusetts Bay Charter of 1629 is the notion of a Puritan Utopia, one that envisioned a model polity[7] governed by Christian principles while

Chapter 2

Rule Britannia

still protecting individual liberties (liberties closely constrained, that is, within their "puritanical" worldview) through clearly defined legal and judicial bodies and elected representatives. It was to be a civic vehicle driven exclusively by religious men. In the language of the document:

> the "Ende of the Plantacion, [should be] soe as their good Life and orderlie Convesacon, maie wynn and incite the Natives of Country, to the Knowledg and Obedience of the onlie true God and Saulor of Mankinde, and the Christian Fayth…"[8]

There were, however, no wild eyed and pious prelates anxious to create the Puritan Zion at Jamestown. Its charter had been issued by James I in 1606, and the eponymous colony had been formed for the pursuit of one prize: gold. But as winter approached and the specter of starvation and malaria loomed, the inhabitants realized that their futile pursuit of the elusive ore had distracted them from learning the more useful skills of farming and husbandry. Facing this crisis, their leader, John Smith, forced the colony into a hard turn toward survival, proclaiming that everyone would "work or starve," and mandating too that everyone would spend at least four hours a day farming. The colony's fortunes changed when they realized that their real gold could be mined from tobacco, a crop perfectly suitable to the Virginia climate.[9]

More than charters or the efforts of zealots in pursuit of a religious utopia, the engine of English development in North America (and anywhere else, for that matter) would not have left the station had its initial head of steam not been stoked by Calvinist philosophy. For anyone other than a stern-faced prelate or a divinity student, Calvinist theology probably offers little of interest. It is hard to imagine that anyone with a modicum of self-esteem or pride would be drawn to Calvin's world, a universe where a petulant and vindictive deity toys with his followers by designating an elect group to share in his divine bounty, all the while not revealing just who these lucky chosen might be. The faithful are, then, left to fret and worry whether they are in God's good graces and, more importantly, whether they will share the common and inescapable fate of eternal damnation that is the certain end of the non-elect.

Before Luther, Calvin, and the Reformation, Church dogma mandated help for the poor and preached the moral obligation of the aristocracy to see to the needs of their earthly subordinates. Charity was a major casualty of Calvinism, twisting the dynamic of helping someone less fortunate into a crippling and enabling gesture fostering laziness. Suddenly, the individual was given wider latitude, with religion now blessing

John Calvin – Reconciled Christian theology with early capitalist commercialism. Pen and ink by George Osterwald (1803 – 1884).

Chapter 2 *Rule Britannia*

personal industry and, to a degree, aggrandizement British economist R. H. Tawney characterized it thusly:

> "The law of nature had been invoked by medieval writers as a moral restraint upon economic self-interest. By the seventeenth century, a significant revolution had taken place. "Nature" had come to connote, not divine ordinance, but human appetites, and natural rights were invoked by the individualism of the age as a reason why self-interest should be given free play."[10]

Whether English or Dutch, a culture whose moral compass is forever fixed on the true north of commercial advantage and a libertine marketplace will do nearly anything to advance its economic agenda, up to and including upsetting the balance of power among a native population by giving one tribe firearms to use against another, by luring young men from the home country into indentured servitude, or even the wholesale enslavement of a different race as a cost-effective labor strategy. The hedonistic calculus was ascendant, and proof that it worked was everywhere.

Having sanctified the marketplace and bade the faithful to find proof of God's favor in their coffers rather than the cathedral, Calvin broke the links in God's Chain of Being and loosed the human appetite, held back only by the tenuous link of personal restraint and the strength of human character. Ever the good Calvinist, Cromwell implemented the prelate's teaching with a vengeance, abetting every commercial and imperial venture with all the resources – both economic and military – the commonwealth could bring to bear. For after all, wasn't the commonwealth, as Hobbes would claim, merely a powerful amalgam of the nation's collective wills and selves? Sincere in his goal to establish a Puritan Zion – that ideal republic shorn of royalist and papist influence – his greatest mistake was imagining that his fellow citizens shared his sincerity, lofty sentiments, and unimpeachable intent. Nearly a

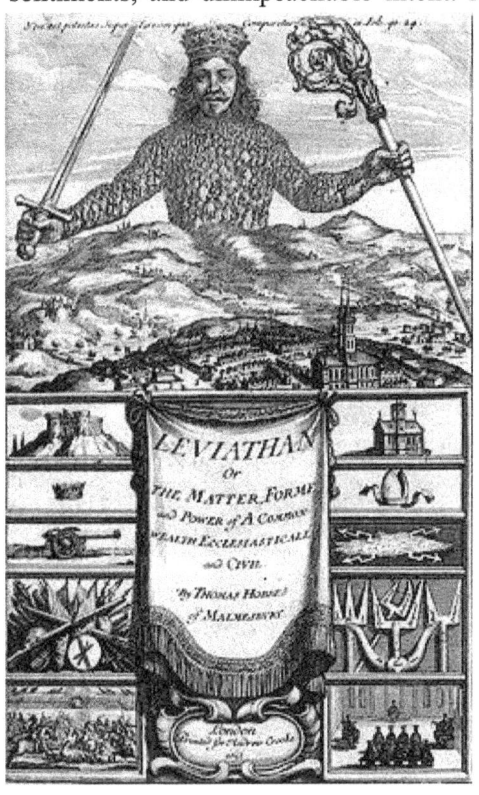

Frontispiece for Hobbes "Leviathan," Engraving by Abraham Bosse (1651).

quarter million had been sacrificed in the civil war (many more to disease and starvation) to make this New Zion a reality. At the end of his life, as Schama suggests, Cromwell must have been profoundly disappointed to look out on the realm and see not the army of virtuous men at the helm of a model Christian republic, but rather "… a lot of England undisturbed – the England that most of the bigwigs who now ran it…had grown up with, were partial to and, for all the sound and fury of 1649, had never dreamed of doing away with it in the name of some imagined new Jerusalem."[11] Though prosperity was, for Cromwell, all well and good, something was missing: that divine spark that was to illuminate God's presence in the enterprise of empire.

Sadly, no roiling issues, religious or political, were resolved by the carnage or the tenure of the

Chapter 2 *Rule Britannia*

Commonwealth. Back in England, it was still essentially unsettled as to whose interests had primacy in the culture, or whose religion received God's nod. Nevertheless, some things did seem indisputable. First of all, by 1700 it was clear that England's colonies along America's Atlantic coast had survived their sometimes- brutal initiation to the continent in the face of hostile natives, and, at times, an even more hostile climate, obtaining a solid foothold from which to take their first footsteps into the interior for the glory of *Pax Britannia*. The senseless death and brutality of the conflict also seemed to make clear that the natural state of humankind was neither generous nor compassionate, but, instead, violent, covetous, impulsive, and anti-social. What could be done, then, to contain a society potentially filled with self-interested reprobates? England was in a crisis of governance, caught in a hard choice between the dull, draconian morality of the Calvinist republic and the fear of an unchecked, unaccountable, and whimsical absolute monarchy. Certainly, there must be a middle way, one free of religious zealotry or royal privilege and narcissism, one recognizing and validating the citizenry as the core of the nation, yet, more importantly, one inspiring loyalty and obedience. Thomas Hobbes had a solution.

That hope of national unity, endlessly frustrated by stubborn sectarian strife and disputes over sovereignty, could perhaps be obtained after all by looking at the situation differently. Imagine the nation, Hobbes challenged, not as a plaything for a narcissistic monarch, nor an ill-governed conglomerate of well-meaning republicans, but as an institution deliberately conceived for the specific purpose of effecting peace and security, not in spite of the citizenry, but in league with it and in its interests. Humans, Hobbes asserts, craft machines for all kinds of jobs, their parts cooperating to perform tasks, free of human foibles and prejudices. Why not, then, craft a state in the same way, uniting all of a nation's people into one "Artificial Man"?:

> "Art goes yet further, imitating that Rational and most excellent worke of Nautre, Man. For by Art is created that great LEVIATHAN called a COMMON-WEALTH, or STATE…which is but an Artificiall Man…"[12]

> **"Charity was a major casualty of Calvinism, twisting the dynamic of helping someone less fortunate into a crippling and enabling gesture fostering laziness. Suddenly, the individual was given wider latitude, with religion now blessing personal industry and, to a degree, aggrandizement."**

What, then, would drive this Leviathan? What would be reasonable and powerful enough to compel the body politic to check their natural right to do anything they wish in a government-less state of "Warre" at the door of the commonwealth? Part of the answer was in the mechanism at the heart of England's bustling economy and its old, venerable, and trusted legal system: the contract. But for Hobbes, an everyday contract – that legal instrument ensuring that tea and spices moved successfully from India and cotton from the southern American colonies – was just a pale imitation of a much older, more consequential contract, one presented to Moses on Mt. Sinai and embedded as the bedrock of all morality in the Abrahamic religions,[13] no matter what the sect. What was required was a covenant :

> "For where no Covenant hath preceded, there hath no Right been transferred, and every man has a right to every thing; and consequently, no action can be Unjust. But when a Covenant is made, then to break it is

Unjust: And the definition of INJUSTICE, is no other than The Not Performance Of Covenant."[14]

Hobbes, who "...read and wrote at four, learned Greek and Latin at six, and went to Oxford at fifteen,"[15] knew a thing or two not just about covenants; he also had personal experience with reprobates as well. The son of a vicar who abandoned the family after a drunken brawl, he had a well-to-do uncle who took him under his wing and shepherded him into a more rarified social class. This stroke of luck combined with his keen intellect made him a doyenne of the aristocracy.

Penned a full five years after Cromwell's rise to power in 1651, Hobbes' "Leviathan" was written, ironically, in France – the very belly of absolute monarchy, where he'd fled the violence of the civil war. In it, Hobbes says that two things must happen before a society can achieve a modicum of peace and stability. First of all, it must accept that without an overarching power to "keep them in awe,"[16] – to compel them to behave a certain way – people not only do whatever they want, but, frankly, have every right to do so. Next, once people accept this uncomfortable fact about themselves, a further realization must be made that this state of affairs is destructive and to no one's benefit, and that in order to avoid it, individuals must agree to surrender the unlimited rights they had in a state of "Warre," and subject themselves to the restraining power of civil law; that is, enter into a covenant. "The Desires, and other Passions of man," Hobbes continues, "are in themselves no Sin. No more are the Actions, that proceed from those Passions, till they know a Law that forbids them"[17]

"Hobbes filed, one might say, the jagged edges of monarchy and republicanism, fitting them together in a new political paradigm, one, in great part, absent the volatility that had previously characterized British politics."

And who exactly will preside over this Leviathan, issue its laws, and see to the well-being of its citizenry? Unlike Louis and Charles, both of whose crown was bestowed simply a matter of sanguinity, sovereignty could be invested in Hobbes' commonwealth in either a person, an assembly, or a privileged faction, regardless of lineage or alleged social entitlement:

"...there can be but Three kinds of Commonwealth. ...When the Representative is One man, then is the Common-wealth a MONARCHY: when an Assembly of All that will come together, then it is a DEMOCRACY, or Popular Common-wealth: when an Aseembly of Part onely, then it is called an ARISTOCRACY."[18]

True to his inherent cynicism, in deciding which form to embrace, Hobbes says a society must not only consider the nature of each form when it is functioning positively, but also what it could look like when it devolves and becomes ineffective. In decline, Hobbes suggests, a monarchy (of one person), becomes a tyranny. A democracy, on the other hand (run by a democratic assembly) would most likely devolve into anarchy. And, finally, an aristocracy (rule by a privileged class) has the potential of becoming an oligarchy. Which should be chosen? Hobbes suggests it depends on "...the difference of Convenience, or Aptitude to produce the Peace, and Security of the people; for which end they were instituted."[19]

This was a new element of expediency in social policy not seen before. And what was his choice? Because Hobbes felt the country's ills were in great part due to a too diffuse and conflicted power structure, that power or sovereignty focused in one person would be the most ideal.

Assemblies and parliaments, he felt, were too apt to lapse into self-interest than to truly tend to the needs of all the people, something more easily accomplished by one person – a monarch. After all, "a Monarch cannot disagree with himselfe, out of envy or interest; but an Assembly may; and that to such a height, as may produce a Civill Warre."[20] The dark specter of another civil way haunted and inspired much of Hobbes' work.

Hobbes filed, one might say, the jagged edges of monarchy and republicanism, fitting them together in a new political paradigm, one, in great part, absent the volatility that had previously characterized British politics. Given this realignment, everyone – commoner and aristocrat – could get down to the business of empire, now that the essence of British imperial power was now defined and codified. The British government could now lend its resources to its colonies along the American coast, offering them the security of trade, and the bulwark of defense should it be needed; and it would be. Trevelyan defines the functions of the colonies at this point in a memorable passage from his "History of England":

> "The overseas possessions were valued as fulfilling a twofold purpose. First as supplying an appropriate outlet for the energetic, the dissident, the oppressed, the debtors, the criminals and the failures of old England – a sphere where the energies of men who were too good or too bad not to be troublesome at home, might be turned loose to the general advantage."[21]

In addition to their role as a repository for England's troublesome and disaffected elements, the colonies were a lucrative marketplace for the mother country, supplying raw materials and, in turn, finished goods for the colonies' inhabitants. More consequential for the future of the empire, each colony had its own unique ethnic and religious character, lending it a diversity unlike England's stable, homogeneous population, one whose variety ranged from the "self-dependent Puritanism" of New England to the ugly racism of the southern plantation owners.[22] Once the colonies were settled in their respective cultural patterns, more adventurous and mercenary elements – those not rooted to the quotidian demands of agricultural life – began to look westward and southward to the areas along the St. Lawrence and around the Great Lakes. That was the frontier, and, as Trevelyan explains, "…the frontier in American history does not mean, as in Europe, a fixed boundary paraded by sentries, but is the term used for that part of the wilderness into which the white man has most recently penetrated."[23] But there was a further complication: the French had already been there for decades and, as has already been shown, had established deep-rooted relationships with the predominantly Algonquin Indians who dominated the region from southern Michigan up to what would come to be the Canadian border.

Like the original forays of the French into the Americas, the impetus for British encroachment westward and southward into French territory was due in great part to the furry little engineer – or perhaps, more correctly, the lack of it – with the coveted coat. British interests had, for some time, been siphoning furs from the interior from points at Albany and Hudson Bay.[24] The Dutch and English, in league with their Iroquois allies armed with guns, had depleted the beaver stock around the Hudson Bay, Hudson River area. Those colonists not disposed to hard agricultural toil in the settled communities along the coast sought to continue exploiting the easier rewards of the beaver trade. These ambitions were, however, destined to collide with the French who were only too aware of British designs.

Chapter 2 *Rule Britannia*

For reasons already described, the French presence had eroded toward the end of the seventeenth century, leaving Sault Ste. Marie completely abandoned and Michilimackinac rendered almost insignificant. What was needed to check the English advance and reinvigorate the French presence were outposts in strategic positions along the main waterways like the St. Lawrence and the Great Lakes. Having been commandant at Michilimacknac, Antoine le Mothe de Cadillac was familiar with the region and seized on Detroit as one possible spot to inhibit the English advance because of its location on the Detroit River, the strait connecting Lake St. Clair with Lake Erie. After petitioning the French government, Cadillac was granted permission to found the post in 1701, and to affirm the sincerity of the commitment, a hundred French and Canadian soldiers were sent with him.[25]

Violence in the region had been festering for more than sixty years prior to Cadillac's re-establishment of the post at Detroit. These hostilities were directly related to the depletion of the beaver in the part of the country where English and Dutch presence had been prevalent. Until mid-century, this had been Iroquois territory, an area representing just a small portion of the total Native American population that was dominated region-wide by the Algonquin tribes, most of who were in the French camp. The decimation of the beaver in this area posed a significant hardship for the Iroquois for whom the beaver pelts were the principle currency to buy firearms and European goods upon which they had grown dependent.

French Canadian hero Adam Dollard des Ormaux repelling England's proxy Iroquois army in the battle of Long Sault, 1660. **(Artist unknown.)**

Their way of life was now so profoundly altered by the influence of the English and Dutch that a return to their previous independent existence, one in harmony with the earth, was impossible. The links to Europe were now unbreakable. This redounded to the benefit of the Europeans who had no difficulty or qualms about recruiting the Iroquois as proxies in their fight against the French. What resulted was a very violent period in North American history known as the "Beaver Wars."[26] Even before the presence of the white man, there had always been a back and forth over territory between the Indians. But these hostilities – which ensued intermittently between 1642 and 1698 – were particularly savage, pitting the Algonquin and Iroquois tribes against each other for control of the now all-important trade in beaver peltries.

With the help of European firearms, the Iroquois greatly expanded their range northward into Canada (at one point even blockading Montreal), altering radically the balance of power among the Indian nations, and tilting it in the direction of their English allies who before long would also gain control of Newfoundland and Nova Scotia from the French as part of the Treaties of Utrecht 1713, the pacts that ended the Wars of Spanish Succession.[28] Clearly, the stars were aligning for the British geographically, and the Dutch succumbed as well to the English juggernaut, undone by something approximating international law of the time. Since Elizabeth, there had been an agreement among Christian (Catholics excluded) nations not to pursue colonies in a place that had already been settled by another Protestant Christian nation. Though the Dutch

Chapter 2   *Rule Britannia*

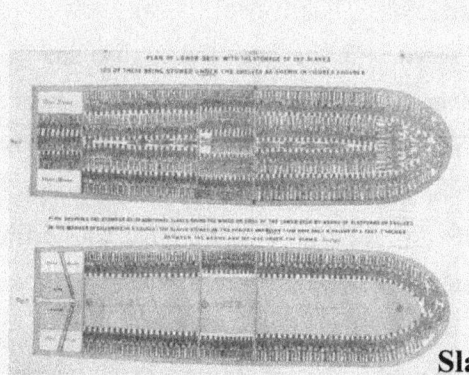
Diagram of slave ship maximizing human cargo. (Plymouth chapter of the Society for Effecting the Abolition of the Slave Trade.)

Slave auction, Charleston, South Carolina

The irony that an empire so noisily advertised as an empire of free Britons should depend on the most brutal coercion of enslaved Africans is not just an academic paradox. It was the condition of the empire's success, it is original sin: a stain that no amount of righteous self-congratulation at its eventual abolition can altogether wash away.(31) **Simon Schama**

had already been settled by another Protestant Christian nation. Though the Dutch traced their North American holdings back to 1623, the English had had a settlement at Jamestown in 1606 and another at Plymouth since 1620. In addition, James I had declared the whole American coast between the 38th and 45th parallel for England.[29] England's most devastating weapon against the Dutch, however, was the Navigation Act.[30] Passed under Cromwell's commonwealth in 1651, it forbade the import or export of any goods into the Atlantic coast by anything other than English vessels. Already relegated to a small area around present-day New York and finding it nearly impossible to attract committed immigrants to its colonies, the Dutch had no choice but to engage the English in a naval war for their colonies' survival, one which they lost. Consequently, New Amsterdam became New York and the British gained another significant chunk of the North American coastline: another platform from which to launch its assault on the entrenched French to the west.

By 1664, the Dutch imperial star was waning and Spanish influence, once a behemoth, had finally been critically weakened. Whatever traumas England had suffered over religious or political issues, her ships were the finest and the fastest, plying the oceans to far-flung colonies stretching from India, to the Bahamas, to North America. She had, without question, the strongest economy in the world, and what else was there to do but make it stronger and bigger? After all, Hobbes had smoothed out some of the rough edges, the sovereign regarded now not as a menace, but, in fact, the very symbol of Britain's power. Calvin, on the other hand, had made it okay to make a little money without that old, nagging, and very Catholic specter of usury. For England, then, the secret to dealing with all the weighty issues of the past was to drown them in its prodigious ocean of commerce and somehow forget about them. Once that was done, John Q. Brit could sit and relax with a cup of tea from India, stay warm with a shawl that had started its life with cotton from a plantation in the American south, and enjoy a glowing pipe full of tobacco grown at Jamestown, Virginia.

But the glorious, glimmering sheen of empire was just a patina. England's robust economy masked a dark sickness at its core: a Faustian-like compact with the morally indifferent devil of enterprise, one that swallowed all other impulses. As for the French, their moral compass in New France, at least, was still pointed at traditional Catholic values of charity, humility, and concern for the poor. Such shadows did not darken England's path to empire. Ironically, like the Spanish papists who they reviled, the English could not have cared less about the spiritual state or the souls of the "savages" who they manipulated and exploited as needed, and even murdered wholesale when it served the agenda of *Pax Britannia*. Those not wedded to "England Incorporated;" those not safe and secure under its umbrella as full-fledged members of imperial Britain, were quite simply *persona non grata* and, without the privileges of full membership in the empire, one might very well be made to serve it instead. After all, if you weren't part of the covenant, as Hobbes declared, then you were in a state of "Warre" where you would be (justifiably, it seems) at the mercy of those stronger and more organized. Without question, Britain at the beginning of the eighteenth century was both.

For over a hundred years, great orators had thundered in Parliament, in leaflets, and on street corners about liberty. They railed against papal and royal oppression and taxation without parliamentary oversight. But when it came to liberty, the dark-skinned people who toiled in the heat cutting England's sugar cane and tobacco leaves need not apply. Even the wretched refugees with appropriate skin color – those desperate souls who sought relief from the squalor of London, Edinburgh, and Galway only to be tricked into endless, involuntary servitude on plantations in the Bahamas and at Jamestown – came to understand the downside of contracts. But neither the treatment of the Indian nor the indentured servant could approach the misery and inhumanity visited on the Africans who provided the slave labor on plantations throughout the Caribbean and the American south.

"The irony that an empire so noisily advertised as an empire of free Britons should depend on the most brutal coercion of enslaved Africans is not just an academic paradox. It was the condition of the empire's success, its original sin: a stain that no amount of righteous self-congratulation at its eventual abolition can altogether wash away."[31] No matter what country, commerce reigned. For both France and Britain there had been significant investment in coastal plantations, places in the "low malarial coast regions" where the climate was conducive to labor-intensive crops like cotton, tobacco, rice, and sugar, but woefully inhospitable to light-skinned European laborers.[32]

Land was cheap and labor was scarce in the narrow swathe that was colonized America at this time. The cost of legitimate wage labor would, therefore, have been prohibitive. Black slave labor was the perfect solution to problems posed by climate and economics, and the dependence of the home countries on these commodities was too important to be compromised by such rarified concepts as human freedom and dignity. Besides, one had only to look to scripture and/or the civil code for some tortured assurance that such inhumanity was not only religiously and legally justified, but deserved as well. Slave traders and plantation owners invoked the ancient Greek view that African natives were worthy of servitude by virtue of a

"Cruelties of slavery." **(The New York Public Library Digital Collections.)**

lack of intelligence, or the Roman notion that vanquished peoples were the property of the victors, destined to serve their masters in any way required. British slave owners escaped their own opprobrium by taking refuge in civil law, gleaned, ironically, by Anglican clerics who washed their hands of the whole issue. Since in the eyes of English law black slaves were regarded as property, their status was, or so the prelates decided, a matter for the courts and legislature, not the vicars of Christ.[33] Thus the ancient Manichean metaphor equating darkness with evil had again found its way into human experience, investing skin color with its simplistic and destructive dualism. And for all of France's historic crowing about *liberté and egalité*, at the end of the day it led the pack in the black African slave trade well into the nineteenth century, making almost three times more slaver voyages than Britain, and transporting two-and-a-half times more slaves than Britain to plantations in America and their own plantations in the West Indies.[34] The French port of Nantes lives to this day with its infamous reputation as the once busiest French clearinghouse for the slave trade.[35]

In New France, Indians fared better than their dark-skinned brethren toiling under the lash on the coastal plantation s. Certainly, their historic cooperation with the French in the peltry trade earned them an elevated status more like partners (albeit, partners often swindled and manipulated). And it probably didn't hurt that the Native American was viewed as a darker shade of normal, virtuous, and intelligent white rather than black or brown. As a proud, resistant, and indigenous population used to subsistence living, Indians could not be yoked easily to routine repetitive tasks that supported alien European institutions like property and ownership, so they made poor laborers. Black Africans, however, were "...tractable, capable of hard work, hardy, and easily and cheaply maintained."[36]

When France, under Cadillac's auspices, decided to make a new, more serious effort at an outpost at Detroit in 1701, they had no need for black slave labor. The Indians, on the other hand, were not only tolerated, they were embraced and invited to the newly

"When France, under Cadillac's auspices, decided to make a new, more serious effort at an outpost at Detroit in 1701, they had no need for black slave labor. The Indians, on the other hand, were not only tolerated, they were embraced and invited to the newly established outpost."
Painting by Émile Louis Vernier (1887).
"Conference between the French and Indian Leaders..." Public Domain.)

Chapter 2   *Rule Britannia*

established outpost. Cadillac issued the call, and the Indians – mostly Huron, Ottowa, and Pattawatomi – flocked to the settlement. On July 23rd, the day of Detroit's founding, there were one-hundred people at the site. Within six months the population had swelled to around six thousand, mostly Indians, who not only hoped to partner with the French in the fur trade, but also to join forces to repel their fierce and common enemy, the Iroquois.[37]

The re-constitution of the outpost at Detroit is a watershed moment in the history of the area. It bears scrutiny because it reflects diminishing French influence in New France and their attempts to reverse this decline. In Cadillac's mind, French goals at Detroit were threefold: to establish a firmer French presence in the region by encouraging actual settlement, to secure their place in the regional fur trade, and to have a secure post from which to repel British encroachment. Despite Cadillac's good intentions, however, the French government could not disabuse itself of its counterproductive economic policies, practices grounded in monopoly, restriction, and mercantilist principles. Instead of entrusting control of the trade to Cadillac, the government in France implemented restrictions that worked against him. In response to the glut of beaver pelts that flooded the market at this time, peltry traffic was restricted exclusively to the fort. Officers, soldiers, and settlers were strictly forbidden from participating in the market for furs.[38] Adding insult to injury, just one year later in 1702 control of the post was turned over to the monarchy's appointed business agent, The Company of the Colony. Headed by a group of lawyers and accountants ill-suited to the task of running a far-flung outpost like Detroit, the men of the Company were "skilled only in drawing up deeds; and the others, merchants who knew little beyond selling to advantage…"[39] In addition, alcohol was banned at post, a situation in great part orchestrated by the Jesuits – a group with whom Cadillac had issues and generally mistrusted. While morally laudable, the move served to hamper the trade with Indians who, given their weakness for it, were apt to deal with anyone more likely to indulge their taste for the spirits. This situation lasted until September, 1705 when, after many complaints to Count Ponchartrain, full control of the fort was once again handed over to Cadillac.

The fort was structurally more like a *villein*, with Cadillac serving as the Marquis de Detroit, a title for which he had petitioned. As seigneur, control and the day-to-day operation of the outpost fell on him. Real estate inside the palisades was parceled out in small, twenty by twenty-five-foot plats. In purchasing these plats, the buyer would promise to cultivate it and pay Lord Cadillac an annual stipend – a

DESTRUCTION OF FORT PICKAWILLANY.

By 1752, The French could no longer tolerate the British/Miami Indian presence at Pickawillany, in present day Ohio. The French attacked the outpost, killing two Miamis and two British traders, causing Britain to swear vengeance. **(C.W. Williamson, In:** *History of Western Ohio and Auglaize County*. **Linn & Sons, 1905)**

Chapter 2   *Rule Britannia*

pool of money meant to cover the costs of maintenance, soldiers' upkeep, and a small income for Cadillac and his family.[40] Neither taxes nor real estate values in the modern sense existed. Outside the fort was an ocean of trees – a wilderness where land could be had simply for the claiming. But it was dangerous. The value of a plat inside the fort was, then, not reckoned in an economic sense, but was more a reflection of what Cadillac felt was a fair price for the protection the fort provided. Inside the palisades, civilians owned their own homes. Cadillac owned the soldiers' homes, but they were allotted small gardens of about half an acre. Lord Cadillac owned the mill as well, which contributed that much more to the upkeep of the outpost.[40] As for the alcohol problem, Cadillac's response was ingenious. While he restored the right to imbibe on the post, all the alcohol was locked in a store house and was doled out in amounts in measured sensible amounts.[41]

After just seven years as head of Detroit, Cadillac – against his will – was transferred to Louisiana in 1710. He was followed by a long line of mostly unremarkable leaders who, each in his own way, attempted to regulate commerce (meaning the peltry trade) in order to continue Cadillac's success in making Detroit both a regional hub for the fur trade, and a bulwark against British power. By 1742, however, the British had become a menacing presence, inciting the Indians to warfare and wooing the *couerier de bois* (whose patriotism often took a back seat to personal gain) with a greater price for their pelts. Detroit was right in the midst of the increasing warfare between the Ottowas and the Hurons stoked by the British, making the fur trade a more and more dangerous undertaking. Faced with increasingly hostile Indians, the French government was forced to make protection a priority to the exclusion of commerce.[42] In order to deal with the situation, the leader of Detroit at this time, Sieur de Céloron, implemented certain measures like forbidding trade in English goods and enjoining the British from trapping for beaver, something obviously difficult if not impossible to enforce.[43] But events were on an unstoppable trajectory to a wider conflict, one involving not just the Indians, but the French and British as well.

The start of the French and Indian War – the North American theater of a world-wide conflict called the Seven Years War – has been historically set at 1754. This conflict in North America pitted French colonists and their Indian allies against Britain and tribes of the Iroquois Confederacy for control of trade in the region. Often considered the first "world war," the Seven Years War included hostilities that extended to a struggle for control of Western Europe, India, and the Mediterranean as well. An argument could be made that the conflict in New France had already begun years earlier with the French attack on the settlement at Pickawillany (near the present-day town of Piqua, on the western edge of Ohio). Pickawillany was settled by Miami Indians who, tired of paying exorbitant prices for French goods, transferred their allegiance to the British.[44] By 1751, according to Wraxall,[45] Pickawillany had not only become one of the biggest Indian towns in the region, it had evolved into a center of British trade with up to fifty British trappers doing business there, something the French could not countenance. This impacted the trade at Detroit enormously. In an attempt to regain the Indians' loyalty and business, Céloron (then leader at Detroit) paid a visit to the settlement in 1750 and unsuccessfully attempted to win back the loyalty and the business of the Indians. After failing in this endeavor, the French attacked the fort in 1752, killing two Miamis and capturing two British traders.

By 1754, the fall of Pickawillany to the French accomplished, to a degree, what Céloron's visit had not. While the Delawares and the Shawnees had been eager partners to the British when it came to the peltry trade,

Chapter 2 *Rule Britannia*

their fear and contempt for those who sought to settle on their land (a problem they did not have with the French) trumped their more mercenary inclination to cooperate with the English. The French exploited this propaganda effectively, convincing the Indians that the goal of the English and American colonial settlers was to confiscate their hunting grounds. Not only had this already occurred in the Juniata Valley,[46] that the British saw settlement as an effective tool for expansion is given credence by the fact they offered 500,000 acres of land to any American colonists willing to establish a fort in the disputed area between the Niagara River and the head of the Ohio River.[47] In the same year, the British mounted a failed attempt – led by an upstart lieutenant colonel by the name of George Washington – to expel the French.

Britain, of course, could not countenance such a setback and devised a grand plan to avenge Washington's defeat. General Edward Braddock, a steely-eyed leader and disciplinarian with impeccable credentials, would mount a massive offensive to subdue the Ohio country and finally send the French packing. At the head of two regiments, he would administer Britain's wrath in a plan that included attacking and capturing the French forts at Louisbourg and Niagara, while Braddock himself would shepherd his own force in an attack on Fort Duquesne (the place where Washington had been rebuffed). Though dark clouds were ahead for relations between England and its American colonists, for now, Braddock's force was regarded as a blessing by the colonists who showed their gratitude by outfitting them with a repast which ultimately would ensure their disastrous undoing.

"Cruelties of slavery." The New York Public Library Digital Collections. As Schama recounts, each officer was supplied "…with the equivalent of the imperial pantry: 6 pounds of rice, raisins, chocolate, coffee and sugar; a pound each of green and Bhea black tea; half a pound of pepper; a whole Gloucester cheese; 20 pounds of best butter; two hams; 2 gallons of Jamaica run and two dozen bottles of Madeira."[48] Though an army does indeed run on its stomach, a more practical view of this necessity is the manner in which its supplies are transported. In Braddock's case, its gastronomic treasures required 150 wagons and 500 pack horses. While such a caravan might enjoy unfettered mobility across the open spaces and well-worn routes in many parts of Europe, the dense foliage along the Monangahela River yielded passage only after painstakingly slow efforts to widen the road by cutting a passage. Braddock's Mingo Indian guides had warned him about the logistical folly of dragging the resplendent train behind them. But why would the general, a seasoned champion of the white man's empire, entertain the counsel of mere savages? As the Mingo chief, Scarouady remarked, "…he treated them barely better than dogs." But, as Schama notes, "The dogs could bite." And they did:

> "The 'contemptible savages' fighting for the French did not form up in the open like sporting Jacobites to take on Braddock's light infantry, but raked them with fire from invisible positions deep inside the forest…As his boxed in infantry attempted to return fire into the piny nowhere he remained imperturbable in the saddle, riding the line, encouraging the soldiers even as they fell in hundreds: a deliberately perfect target for the inevitable musket ball in the chest. Down went the redcoats like lead soldiers in text-book platoon formation, their fellows taking their place in the firing line, staying put as they dropped. By the time a modicum of self-preservation took over, and men actually began running for their lives, two-thirds of

Chapter 2   *Rule Britannia*

Braddock's force was dead or critically wounded."[49]

This bloody defeat occurred on July 9th, 1755. By the end of 1757, the hue and cry in Britain over the fiasco set in motion redoubled efforts to revitalize the war effort with new enthusiasm and resources. Leading this campaign was Secretary for Southern Affairs, William Pitt who assumed the task with the vigor of one divinely mandated. Through his prodigious powers of persuasion (and support from a British populace unwilling to suffer the ignominy of a French victory) Pitt raised 5.5 million pounds and marshaled 50,000 troops for the war. The French could match neither the money, nor the manpower. The British military received a shakeup as well, its leadership infused with new blood catapulted from the ranks to generalship: ambitious young men in their thirties, hungry for fame and glory; men like James Wolfe, the hero of the Battle of Abraham.[49] Pitt's efforts bore fruit. One by one the French citadels fell: Louisbourg, Frontenac, Fort Duquesne, Niagara, Ticonderoga, Crown Point, and Quebec. Finally, surrounded by three British armies with no viable options, the governor of Montreal – Vaudreuil de Cavagnal – surrendered this, the last bastion of French Power in North America to General Jeffrey Amherst on September 8th, 1760.

A little more than a month later, on October 25th, 1760, George III ascended to the throne upon the death of his father. Unlike his Hanoverian father and grandfather (George I spoke only German), the young king was English by birth and, unlike his predecessors, was not only unwilling to cede the reins of power to anyone like Pitt, he had come to question the wisdom and the cost of Pitt's war and was anxious for peace. The French government, on the other hand, was broke, bloodied on land and sea, and eager for peace. It finally came in August, 1763 with the Treaty of Paris. Though many, like Pitt, wanted the French to be vanquished and walk away from North America with nothing, the French were forced to cede Canada and lands east of the Mississippi (they kept New Orleans), as well as west Louisiana. Along with retaining valuable fishing rights off the coast of Newfoundland, French Canadians were allowed to continue practicing Catholicism within the strictures of British law enjoining them from political participation.

Though the French colors were struck after 1763 at outposts throughout New France, and the Union Jack replaced the *fleur-de-lis*, many French Canadians still lived at outposts like Detroit and did their best to adjust to a new life under British overseers after the Treaty of Paris. Ironically, the consequences of the peace were less impactful on those French who remained than the American colonists whose relationship, up until the British victory, had been one of dependence, relying, as they had, on the British military for protection from the now vanquished French and their Indian allies. The conflict had been devastatingly expensive for both sides; especially the French. The French threat now absent, the colonists began to cultivate a separate identity and see themselves as different from the mother country, a prospect the British government was far from ready to entertain. After all, the mother country had just expended much blood and treasure to ensure a steady stream of raw materials and a dependable market for English goods in the colonies. Great sums were spent for the colonists' protection, so it was only fair they should give tangible expression to their gratitude by willingly replenishing the exhausted British coffers with money in taxes and fees. The American colonists, needless to say, did not agree, and therein the course of future events was written.

Chapter 2 *Rule Britannia*

Chapter 3

Adam Smith's Bookends

What improves the circumstances of the greater part can never be regarded as an inconveniency to the whole. No society can surely be flourishing and happy, of which the far greater part of the members are poor and miserable.
    Adam Smith – *The Wealth of Nations*[1]

On September, 8th, 1760, the British Army under General Jeffrey Amherst surrounded Montreal, forcing its governor, the Marquis de Vaudreuil-Cavagnial, to surrender the city. News of the city's capitulation traveled very slowly. Certainly, it had not yet reached Detroit (about 550 miles away), and as far as Detroit's French commandant, Picoté de Belestre, knew, hostilities had not yet ended. Nor could he have known that on his way to take over his command – Detroit and its Fort Ponchartrain – was the storied commander, Robert Rogers who had been tasked by Amherst to collect two companies of his Rangers[1] from Fort Pitt, then proceed to subdue the remainder of the French forts along the Great Lakes. As Rogers made his way along the shoreline, he encountered some Ottawa Indians who he told of the latest developments and British control.[2] The Ottawas, in turn, ran ahead and informed Belestre of the approaching force and of Montreal's surrender which effectively ended French power in North America. The two men, it seems, exchanged communiqués before they met. This much is implied in Rogers' memoirs of the event:

"Sir,

I acknowledge the receipt of your two letters, both of which were delivered to me yesterday. Mr. Brheme has not yet returned. The inclosed letter from the Maquis de Vaudreuil will inform you of the surrender of all Canada to the King of Great Britain, and of the great indulgence granted to the inhabitants; as also of the terms granted to the troops of his Most Christian Majesty. Captain Campbell, whom I have sent forward with this letter, will shew you the capitulation. I desire you will not detain him, as I am determined, agreeable to my instructions from General Amherst, speedily to relieve your post. I shall stop the troops I have with me at the hither end of the town till 4 o'clock, by which time I expect your answer; your inhabitants under arms will not surprise me, as yet I have seen no other in that position, but savages waiting for my orders. I can assure you, Sir, the inhabitants of Detroit shall not be molested, they and you complying with the capitulation, but be protected in the quiet and peaceable possession of their estates; neither shall they be pillaged by my Indians, nor by your's that have joined me.

I am, &c.
R. Rogers."
To Capt. Beletsre,
commanding at Detroit.[3]

The encounter was momentous. Such a display of civility between these two fierce warriors would have been unimaginable just a few months earlier when they might very well have met on the battlefield instead. Rogers was already the stuff of legend. Belestre – himself a captain in the French army – had been part of the force in the Monongehela Valley that was Braddock's undoing. Certainly, there would be more violence of one sort or another. For now, however, the warring giants had ceased. The French had left the field, leaving the Brits to sort out the spoils of victory in North America. And with the peace came a respite for the land, so long merely an arena for marauding, marching armies whose men of arms in the heat of war robbed it of its bounty with no thought of replenishing it. Now, with the long, violent issue of ownership settled for the time being, the French outposts could shake off their identities as forts – as mere places to hide – and become communities; settled places where the fructifying impulse could finally be indulged. When Rogers raised the colors over Detroit, it was obvious that the town, despite the conflict, had already begun this process. Later, Rogers' successor, Captain Donald Campbell, would remark that Fort Ponchartrain "…was the finest we'd ever seen."[4]

Though a then depressed fur trade was Detroit's economic mainstay, farms extended for some distance beyond the village. All of them were very narrow, yet long, extending to a depth of from 40 to 80 arpents. (One arpent equaled 197.75 feet, meaning the farms extended from one-and-a-half to three miles.) Each farm fronted a common road that ran next to the river. Often, however, the road would be impassable, whereupon farmers resorted to canoes to travel about via the water. The houses were very close together for easy and quick communication in the event of an emergency or an imminent attack.[5] The farmers grew very little, leading to an unfortunate and only partially correct historical conclusion that the French inhabitants were somehow apathetic or even lazy when it came to cultivation. Even though the soil was potentially very productive, there was little incentive to grow more than needed. Since the population was so small and each family had a farm, there would have been no market for the surplus produce.[6] The village itself, according to Campbell's description:

> "…occupied a space of about two acres of land, was surrounded by a high fence or palisade made of young trees…The houses within the enclosure were huddled together – the streets were very narrow – ten or twelve feet, with the exception of St Anne street – which was about twenty feet wide."[7]

The majority of the farmers were French Canadian. Most accepted the British takeover without resistance. Compliance, nevertheless, was ensured, as one of the

Chapter 3   *Adam Smith's Bookends*

tasks assigned to Rogers' successor – Captain Donald Campbell – by General Amherst was to confiscate the weapons of any Frenchman deemed a threat to British authority.[8] This would have been a crucial blow to the French settlers who, in season, also doubled as hunters and trappers, selling their furs to the traders at the post for extra income. The English, however, were not denied their firearms. Naturally, then, they came to monopolize the fur trade, alienating the French and leaving many of them to simply rely on their farms or to join ranks with Indians who were also becoming increasingly disaffected by another Amherst directive that decreased their ammunition. This, of course, impacted the Indians' ability to hunt as well and, coupled with a contempt for them born of an ugly paternalism and racism on the part of the British, helped sow the seeds of rebellion.[9] As if this weren't enough, Campbell implemented a system of taxation far more burdensome than the French had demanded. Annual taxes for each settler were a full 184 pounds, payable in skins or farm products. This differed from the French who had assessed proportionately according to one's land holdings. And whereas the French sent all taxes back to France, British taxes went directly to the support of the garrison. Settlers were also required to provide two cords of wood per acre.[10]

Though Detroit had come a long way toward becoming an established community at the time of Montreal's capitulation, it was, however, still a frontier village, its fortune and destiny now shaped by English

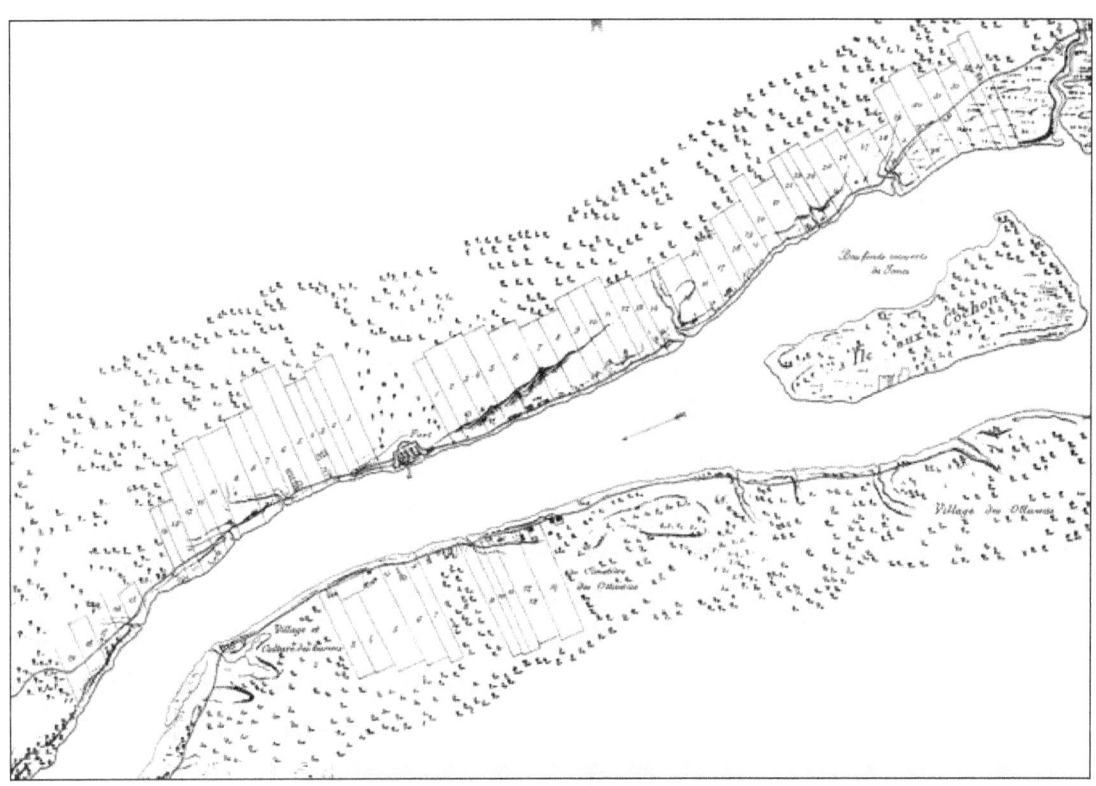

Though this map of early Detroit is from slightly later – 1796 – (long after the British presence at Detroit), over time, French farms had developed a pattern perpendicular to the river as a thoroughfare linking all the properties when roads were muddy and impassable. (**Map from "Detroit796 DETROITography"**)

Chapter 3 *Adam Smith's Bookends*

culture and government. Britain had won the day with its military power, so it was logical for the English to govern the colonies like a garrison. But the unyielding letter of British law was ill-suited to a still wild land whose indigenous peoples and free-spirited colonists did not defer to the glory of the British imperium. Given their new hegemony – and absent French power – the British should have been able to press their agenda with impunity. But even in victory the English fist remained clenched; quite unlike the French who had entered the Americas with open hands and hearts over a century before.

The driving force of British power was trade, and at the center of this commercial milieu was the newly empowered individual whose self-interest was now indulged within a broad arena of far-flung markets protected by British military might, especially by sea. While Neo-liberalism would indeed liberate this individual, it redounded to the benefit of only a small portion of English society. The bulk of British citizenry – the majority of the population not privileged by virtue of sanguinity or money – were consigned to either abject toil as tenants on the Lord's manor in the countryside, or laboring under oppressive conditions in myriad small craft shops where production was often overseen by despotic masters, unaccountable in their demands either by official policy or individual conscience. The center of British life was still the village, and the large landowners were the unquestioned masters in the countryside. Despite their dominance of the government in London, Whig politicians left rural England to the discretion of the aristocrats, both Whig and Tory.[11] For their part, (for now, at least) the average citizen did not question this order and accepted their exclusion from power stoically and peacefully.

England's burgeoning economy offered proof of the practical effectiveness of self-interest, but in its nascent state it either did not nor could not define the ethical boundaries between self-interest and selfishness. Nor would the truly ugly consequences of failing to define those parameters not manifest, as Trevelyan indicates, until already existing abuses of the workforce became obvious once production was gathered under one roof in a factory system many decades later.[12] Adam Smith's theoretical conception of a perfect balance of market forces still seemed possible in England and America's pre-industrial, pre-monopolistic economy still dominated and constrained by small craft production and the influence of the master/apprentice guild system. It would be for Smith to codify these notions in his "Wealth of Nations" seventeen years later. But in 1760, the work that would earn him initial acclaim was a treatise on moral philosophy called "The Theory of Moral Sentiments," a work he'd published a year earlier in 1759. This is logical, since moral philosophy was one of the principal disciplines in universities of the 18th century. It would, in fact, be Smith himself who would later lay the groundwork for the study of political economy with his "Wealth of Nations."

The two works and their relationship, putative or otherwise, has been the stuff of scholarship for over two centuries. What is clear is that more than his mentors – Francis Hutcheson[13] and David Hume [14] – Smith

> "But the unyielding letter of British law was ill-suited to a still wild land whose indigenous peoples and free-spirited colonists did not defer to the glory of the British imperium…even in victory the English fist remained clenched; quite unlike the French who had entered the Americas with open hands and hearts over a century before".

Chapter 3   *Adam Smith's Bookends*

anchored his moral theory in individual judgment rather than its utility to society: the perfect philosophical predisposition for Smith's later economic model that would conflate the material well-being of the individual with that of society. By the time Smith penned his capitalist theory in "Wealth of Nations" in 1776, the empire had already been humming along upon these as yet un-iterated principles for some time. Smith, so to speak, merely cataloged the elements of a dynamic economic system that was already coming to fruition on its own.

Whether Detroit, Devonshire, or Delhi, Smith's moral and economic writings chart both the economic and moral trajectory of Pax Britannia at this point in time as well as its full-throated embrace of commercialism and self-interest. As such, the "Moral Sentiments" and "Wealth of Nations" are like philosophical and historical bookends. They stand at opposite ends of Britain's experience in North America in the eighteenth century, bracketing a seventeen-year period between its nadir of dominance and its defeat at the hands of the colonists, their French allies, and its own native son, George Washington. Imbued with the spirit of Smithian economic and moral philosophy, a merchant or entrepreneur navigating the uncharted waters of business, seizing economic opportunities as they arise, would not want to be anchored to a pre-existing system of normative values (especially a church-inspired injunction against usury) that ineluctably dictated "right" and "wrong." Though the British government still adhered to mercantilist policies that viewed colonies as generators of raw materials and dedicated markets for the home country's finished goods, trade was becoming increasingly laissez-faire in character. This was decidedly more efficient than the cumbersome system of controlled monopolies that had hampered French trade in New France. For the moment, however, Smith's moral writings deserve close scrutiny because they serve as an intellectual foundation from which to judge the disparity between his ideal, self-driven ethical system – principles that essentially served the interest of the monied, educated, and aristocratic class – and the reality of daily life in Britain and its colonies where draconian rule, exploitation, and injustice for the natives and colonists was often the order of the day.

"England's burgeoning economy offered proof of the practical effectiveness of self-interest, but in its nascent state it either did not or could not define the ethical boundaries between self-interest and selfishness."

Like Hutcheson and Hume, Smith grants that moral character and virtuous behavior neither occur in a vacuum, nor exist as general principles prior to experience. Normative structures are forged out of a sort of ethical alchemy in the crucible of human experience and social relations: from being and living in the world among other humans with whom we interact, observe, and, most importantly, judge. Smith agrees with his teacher, Hutcheson, and his friend Hume that moral judgments serve a useful purpose to society, but he goes further and asserts that beyond their utility, every moral judgment also has a certain propriety in its own right; that is, it is morally appropriate or inappropriate to a given situation. This assessment, furthermore, cannot occur solely upon private introspection. Someone raised alone on a desert island[15] would have no concept of ethical judgment or morality since, as Smith states, the propriety of an action is gauged through observation; by observing the behavior of others in certain scenarios and "…conceiving what we ourselves should feel in the like situation."[16] If we would act the same in that situation, then, says Smith, we are in sympathy with that action and we "...either approve or disapprove of the conduct of another man according as we feel that, when we bring his case home to ourselves, we either can or cannot "sympathize" with the sentiments and motives that directed it."[17] With regards to the utility of moral judgments, Smith famously asserted:

> "...it seems impossible that the approbation of virtue should be a sentiment of the same kind with that by which we approve of a convenient and well-conceived building; or that we should have no other reason for praising a man than that which we commend a chest of drawers."[18]

Known as the "Muir Portrait," after the family who owned it, this is the only known image of Adam Smith. However, whether the man pictured is indeed the famous economist is in question. **(The painting hangs in the Scottish National Gallery.)**

For Smith, society is like a touchstone one uses – moving from one interaction, one agent to another – to scrutinize others' actions and decide if one would, or not, act similarly in the same circumstances. In the course of our ethical life we all assume, from one moment to the next, either the role of observer, or observed. When we are not absorbed in our own moral dramas, we are spectators. The depth of scrutiny and sympathy we bring to this interaction is gauged by 1) how closely the observed agent's feelings resonate with us; and 2) how successful we are in not projecting our own values on a situation. Both are preconditions for a truly "impartial" observation, according to Smith. Though a perfect state of impartiality is impossible (we can never remove ourselves completely from a situation), we are closest to this goal – in other words, we truly "sympathize" with the observed agent(s) – when our own values are not imposed on the situation.[19] Stripped of as many prejudices as possible, Smith conceives in the impartial spectator a sort of abstract human capable of judging a moral scenario as nearly as possible on its own merits. This abstract human finds "...the intersection of the values of the parties concerned, and then judges whether the action under consideration is in line with the shared values."[20] This exclusion of the self from the process holds even more true for moral self-reflection, a situation in which we endeavor to see ourselves as someone else would. This "man within the breast,"[21] as Smith calls him, is synonymous with "conscience" and is divinely inspired.

By rejecting utility as the core of normative value, Smith shifts the ethical center of gravity from the good of society to the judgment and well-being of the individual, an approach that is more problematic and less applicable to behavior than simple usefulness.

Chapter 3

Adam Smith's Bookends

Quite simply, morality is, for Smith, not a noun, but a verb: a process out of which moral judgments emerge inductively through social interaction. But if moral life is so dynamic and personal, how, then, do common values emerge from the galaxy of individual judgments from moment to moment? Are not moral codes redundant if not shared? Though Smith grounds his theory in the primacy of the individual, he is led full circle back to some form of shared value system, even if it has been built from the ground up. And contrary to those objectivists (i.e., Ayn Rand and her ilk) who would claim him as the architect of pure libertarianism, Smith did not advocate a solipsistic rejection of society or collective values. He certainly did not regard selfishness as a virtue, but rather as a vice. On the contrary: the ethical self exists and evolves within a social framework. Not only does the average human, Smith asserts, crave the approval of other humans,[22] this desire for approbation (or, the shame of disapprobation with the attendant threat of ostracism) is enough to make a person change their behavior and/or re-orient around another moral perspective, because, as Smith claims: "…we are mortified to reflect that we have justly merited the blame of those we live with…."[23] Hardly the view of someone advocating a purely narcissistic outlook.

For Smith there are no pre-existing moral absolutes. Yet, there is still a need for moral order in society. While his theory goes to great lengths to indulge the freedom and discretion of the individual – and though he sets great store in the value of benevolence – benevolence is, frankly, not necessary to society;

> **"Smith shifts the ethical center of gravity from the good of society to the judgment and well-being of the individual, an approach that is more problematic and less applicable to behavior than simple usefulness. Quite simply, morality is, for Smith, not a noun, but a verb: a process out of which moral judgments emerge inductively through social interaction."**

justice, however, is. "Society may subsist," he asserts "though not in a comfortable state, without beneficence; but the prevalence of injustice must utterly destroy it."[24] Whereas the individual is indulged in much of Smith's moralizing, the principles of justice are, conversely, "…accurate in the highest degree, and admit of no exceptions or modifications…"[25] In other words, justice is a compulsory, collective virtue to which everyone must submit for the good order and well-being of society: echoes of Hobbes. Justice is realized in the codified laws that ensure what needs to happen in a society, in fact, happen as well as guaranteeing redress when harm is done to one's self or neighbor.

History shows, however, that some neighbors were more important than others in Smith's England. Justice was limited in scope, its definition encompassing a narrow and quite selective concern for the rights of property rather than human rights in general, an enlightenment notion only just incubating in the minds of intellectuals across the channel in Louis XV's France. Of all the more egregious examples of injustice at work in the empire he could have chosen, Smith seizes on the mundane issue of "breach of contract" as a paramount instance of injustice: "What I ought to perform, how much I ought to perform," he asserts, "when and where I ought to perform it, the whole nature and circumstances of the action prescribed, are all of them fixt and determined."[26] Apparently, that the scions of England's economic empire should be appeased and settled in their contracts is of more consequence than the moral lacunae filled with the misery of those in the work houses and debtors' prisons, or the even more grievous injustice of millions of black slaves ferried on British ships from Africa to English sugar plantations in Barbados and beyond.

Whereas for Smith the theater of morality is played out in the material world among humans with all their foibles, the final critic and arbiter of morality is the Deity from whom all justice flows, and who ultimately avenges all injustice in the after-life. In contrast to Greek morality that stresses the logic of virtuous action as reason enough to subscribe, our duty to act virtuously is in the end, says Smith, divinely mandated. It is as though Smith, after great effort developing an empirically nuanced theory of morality and how it is conceived out of human behavior, retreats into the cathedral and surrenders his system to traditional medieval and heavenly compulsion. Unlike his friend Hume who at least flirted with agnosticism (thus earning for himself a reputation as "the Scottish infidel"[27] among the clergy), Smith's fidelity to Christianity was never in question. In fact, moral life and existence was, for him, grounded in the love and glory of God whose existence and authority is never to be doubted: again, echoes of Hobbes.

Smith's impartial spectator – this, "man within the breast" –reveals the disinterested truth of moral behavior when he is successful. He is himself a "demigod," performing at these times "…suitably to his divine extraction…,"[28] according to Smith. In this way, God provides humanity with a moral compass Smith calls "General Rules," aimed ever at the true north of the moral life as He intended it. Yet these General Rules are only loosely derived and do not carry the same weight as the "exact" laws of justice. They are, Smith explains, "…ultimately founded upon experience of what, in particular instances, our moral faculties, our natural sense of merit and propriety, approve, or disapprove of."[28] Naturally, in their moral musings, humans ultimately arrive at similar conclusions about the morality of a situation so frequently that they become habituated as moral givens. These General Rules, though loosely configured and derivative, provide a sort of shortcut, a "remedy" as Sidgwick has characterized them,[29] for those instances when the "man within the breast" is "…perverted from truth by the internal influence of passion and self-regard." [30] Thus, Smith creates an ethical system with its head in heaven and its hands in the material world of commerce, one ideally suited not just to English merchants and their hunger for world markets, but infant commerce in the colonies as well.

Its national energies underwritten by a self-interested philosophical outlook embodied in Smith's "Moral Sentiments" and "Wealth of Nations," England's conquest of Canada expanded its empire prodigiously, giving it control of the North American fur trade. But like a modern corporate takeover, much of the structure of the business, painstakingly built by the French over decades, remained intact. Thus, when British traders finally ventured into what before had been exclusively French territory, they found a ready-made system consisting of trading posts and a skilled force of French traders and

> "…our duty to act virtuously is in the end, says Smith, divinely mandated. It is as though Smith, after great effort developing an empirically nuanced theory of morality and how it is conceived out of human behavior, retreats into the cathedral and surrenders his system to traditional medieval and heavenly compulsion."

Chapter 3 *Adam Smith's Bookends*

trappers who, easier-going and more stoic than their English counterparts, generally accepted the new reality of British control and attempted to adapt.[31] It was, however, disastrous for the French economy. The river of French goods that had for so long flowed to the Indians from Paris to New France now generated from London, and the furs from the region were re-routed to the English market. Detroit, along with the post at Michilimackinac, was and remained a major entrepot for the exchange of peltries even after the British flag was raised over the village. Though the resources were basically the same, the rules were not. The British abolished the tightly controlled system of leased posts and lifted many of the restrictions on the fur trade, throwing it open to virtually anyone willing to subscribe to the now much looser regulations.[32] A flood of new English trappers filled the breach, many of who, absent the respect and restraint exercised by the French trappers and the limits on their activity formerly dictated by government control, were boundlessly mercenary and bigoted in their treatment of the Indian, so much so that they have earned a place in history as "the scum of the earth."[33] One might say that, due to these liberalized trade practices, not only was Smith's impartial spectator noticeably absent from the region, there was little moral reflection to be found at all when it came to business, especially the fur trade and the treatment of the native population.

For a while after assuming power, the English continued the French practice of currying favor with the Indians by supplying them with clothing, blankets, knives, and similar articles.[34] This, frankly, had always been the cost of doing business with the Indians whose access to the interior made them the primary source of peltries. France's success with the Indians was due, in great part, to both their acceptance of this reality and their willingness to assimilate with them as well.[35] But, for the English, it soon became evident that the cost of doing business with the natives was not just prohibitive, but unconscionable and not worth it. No one felt this more strongly than General Jeffery Amherst who, as Governor General of British North America, made a fateful decision to end the practice, one he viewed as merely purchasing good behavior.[36]

Racist and iron-fisted in his command, 1st Baron Jeffery Amherst was the very face of British power in North America. **(Portrait by Joshua Reynolds 1765. National Portrait Gallery. Wikimedia Commons.)**

For Amherst, the Indians were "an execrable race," unredeemable and undeserving of preferential treatment. In his eyes, their only duty was to kowtow willingly to the new reality of British power, or be compelled to do so by methods up to and including terror.[37] It would be naïve to suppose that a patrician like Amherst would be driven in his views toward the

Indians by anything other than the same racist sentiments that also allowed slavery to be compartmentalized in Britain's national psyche. The practical wisdom of continuing to reward the Native Americans for cooperation was certainly not powerful enough to override the emotional tendency, abroad throughout the empire, that might was not just right, but white; and English for good measure. It is logical Amherst would view his charge as newly conquered domain. As such, he felt he was entitled to control it as he would any investment. America was now British "property" in the Lockean sense; that is, a possession they had not only made their own by applying their labor, but blood and treasure as well. They had, therefore, not just the right, but a duty to govern it in their own best interest, even if that meant taking the "savages" to task for their professed right to the land, or the faint rumblings of self-determination and independence from the "provincials," as Amherst called the colonists.

Fortunately for Amherst, his point person on the front lines with the Indians was someone more compassionate and practical, an Irish-born immigrant who had actually lived and fought among them. Sir William Johnson, dubbed "Warraghiyagey" – "one who does much"– by the natives had indeed done very much. As head of a force of Mohawks, other Iroquois, and colonial militia, he had helped the British wrest control of Lake George from the French in 1755, and capture Fort Niagara in 1759. For these and other efforts he was awarded the title of Baronet by a grateful British government. Recognizing his obvious value, the government had already appointed him Superintendent of Indian Affairs for the northern colonies in 1756. In this capacity, he managed to sustain Britain's sometimes wobbly alliance with the Iroquois Confederacy through his intimate knowledge and respect for Indian culture and his command of the Mohawk language. Such gestures are epitomized by a meeting with natives Williams had in Detroit 1761:

> "Sir William's was a great name, and his coming among the western Indians was like the entry of a king on his possessions…His fleets of ten or a dozen boats, loaded with gifts and provisions, were often separated, and his cargo became damaged before he reached Detroit. There he received a great welcome, and for some days spent a lively time between holding audiences of the Indians and settling matters with them, leading balls, which lasted until seven in the morning, and in general making a deep impression personally and by his official authority."[38]

More than his diplomatic or linguistic skills, Johnson's success with the natives was simply a matter of human decency. He cut through the hypocrisy and racism so indicative of Amherst and his administration, considering the Indians' behavior less as a product of some innate flaw in character and more as the response of an otherwise proud and principled race to wretched exploitation by their British overseers:

> "On their hunts, as upon all other occasions, they are strong observers of meum and teum [sic], and this from principle, holding theft in contempt, so that they are rarely guilty of it, though tempted by articles of much value. Neither do the strong attempt to seize or oppress the weak; and I must do them the justice to say that unless heated by liquors or inflamed by revenge, their ideas of right and wrong, and their practices in consequence of them, would, if more known, do them much honor."[39]

Chapter 3   *Adam Smith's Bookends*

In considering England's dealings with the Native Americans, it is necessary to recall the alliances that had been cemented between the various tribal groups and the foreigners, both French and British (and Dutch), since the earliest European incursions. Until the end of the French and Indian Wars in 1763, clear and firm alliances had evolved between the Algonquin tribes and

Known and beloved by the natives as "Warraghiyagey," or, "he who does much, "Sir William Johnson indeed "did much" to soften the tyrannical hand of British rule. **("Sir William Johnson talking to a Mohawk chief." From "History of the City of New York: its origin, rise and progress" by Martha J. Lamb 1896)**

the French. The British, on the other hand, inherited the strong relationship with the Iroquois originally cultivated under now moribund Dutch influence. As has been noted, the roots of the French/Algonquin relationship were deep, personal, and so closely entwined that the British could never really hope to transplant them into the soil of their own imperial designs once they assumed control. Their failure to do so was a factor instrumental in quickly brewing Algonquin discontent and the subsequent uprising under Pontiac.

The British relationship with the Iroquois Confederacy[40] was much less personal, as one would expect given the English propensity for feelings of cultural and racial superiority. Yet, for their own part the Iroquois were equally restrained for different, more practical reasons. As Wraxall has indicated,[41] the Iroquois were very aware of their role as intermediaries between the generally inaccessible tribes in the interior, and the markets, like Albany, in the east. To this end, they were quite opportunistic, pursuing a measured attitude toward both the French and the English, leaning whichever way proved more advantageous once the two powers became embroiled in a struggle. Certainly, they were faster allies with the British, not just because they shared the more business-like outlook of the British, but also because they bore an historic grudge against the French going all the way back to Champlain who, upon first arriving on North American shores, killed an Iroquois chief. Cold or warm, vengeance was a dish the Iroquois were bent on serving over and over again.

From the beginning, Amherst and his administration made the egregious error – one Warraghiyagey never made – of mistaking Indian ritual for rapacity. That Amherst so totally misunderstood the Indian's concept of gift giving cannot be stressed enough. Far from motivated by greed, gifts were, for the Native American, an act of restitution and good faith to be offered to the Indian for the sacrifice made by all their fallen warriors who gave their lives for the foreigners. This sentiment was expressed unequivocally in 1761 in the presence of a British trader by the name of Alexander Henry who, while at Michilimackinac, heard the legendary Chippewa Chief Minnevana offer these words of approbation to their new British overlords:

> "…the spirits of the slain are to be satisfied in either of two ways; the first is by spilling of the

bold of the nation by which they fell; the other by covering the bodies of the dead [sic], and thus allaying the resentment of their relations. This is done by making presents."[42]

Minnevana's next statement was filled with ominous implications for the British:

"…your king has never sent us any presents, nor entered into any treaty with us, wherefore he and we are still at war; and until he does these things we must consider that we have no other father, nor friend among the white men than the King of France."[43]

Amherst's malice toward the Indians was particularly focused on the group of tribes traditionally residing in the northern Great Lakes area known collectively by the autonym Anishnaabeg. From the Chippewa/Ojibwe word meaning "The People," the Anishnaabeg refers to a mix of tribes consisting of the Chippewa, Ojibwe, Ottawa, Potowatomi, Fox, Cree, and Menominee, all members of the Algonquin linguistic group. The mounting discontent of the tribes needed only a leader around whom they could coalesce. This emerged in the person of Pontiac, a powerful and charismatic leader who – along with an influential prophet from the Delaware tribe by the name of Neolin – began to stoke the fires of resistance. While Pontiac's contribution is common knowledge, Neolin's role as the spiritual animus for the revolt is less known. Neolin saw the plight of the Indian as divine retribution for assimilating with the Europeans and adopting their tools and ways. The only path to redemption, and an eventual heaven devoid of Europeans, was to purge their land of the foreigners by force.[44] The revolt, however, began not with a full-scale assault, but with a now well-chronicled and failed act of subterfuge on the part of the Indians at Detroit in May, 7, 1763.

Pontiac's foiled plot to peacefully gain access to the interior of Detroit and mount an attack is now the stuff of legend, the event immortalized in a painting by American painter, Frederic Remington. Having been forewarned of the plot, the then commander of the post, Major Henry Gladwin, played along with the ruse, allowing Pontiac and a group of three hundred Indians with concealed weapons to enter the fort. The plan was simple: the Indians would enter the fort, whereupon Pontiac would merely turn an extended belt, thus signaling the attack. But to the chief's surprise he was greeted by a complement of fully armed soldiers. No signal was given, and the attack did not come off as planned. In his journal, Amherst himself recounts the event as conveyed to him by Gladwin:

"The 7th he came [Pontiac], but luckily the night before, Major Gladwin was informed it was with an intention to surprise him, and took such precautions that when they entered the fort, tho' they were about 300 and armed with Knives, Tomohawks, and many with guns cut short hid under their blankets, they were so surprised at seeing his disposition for receiving that they would scarcely sit down to Council, as they saw their designs were discovered."[45]

The Commander at Michilimackinac, Major George Etherington, was not so lucky in foiling a similar plot just a month later. On a pleasant Sunday, June 4th, 1763, two groups of Chippewa and Sauk men – about a hundred each – squared off outside the walls of the outpost at Michilimackinac for what appeared to be an innocent game of Baug-ah-ud-o-way (or, "baggataway," an antique version of modern

Chapter 3

Adam Smith's Bookends

lacrosse).(46) Staged, purportedly, in honor of George III's birthday, the Indians invited the Major and his troops to gather outside the fort's walls to observe the game. Gates open and weapons inside, the garrison settled outside the walls to watch the game, ostensibly honoring their king. Like Gladwin, Etherington had not only been warned by French traders at the post that the Indians were planning something, he had also ignored an increase in the sale of tomahawks to the Indians in the preceding days. He also failed to notice the Indian women lining the walls, dressed in bulky clothing despite the heat of the summer's day. The Major's indifference proved fatal. At the signal, the Indians retrieved weapons concealed under the women's clothing and stormed the fort. After a few hours, half of the one-hundred-man garrison was killed and Etherington was taken prisoner.(47)

The fire behind Pontiac's rebellion was not only fed by a deep-seated hatred for the British, there was also an element of false hope that their traditional benefactor, the King of France (known to the Indians as "Orontio"), would come to their aid. This was, however, impossible given France's signature on the Treaty of Paris ending the Seven Years War and their involvement in the region. Pontiac and his forces struck swiftly over a broad area, capturing nine forts including Michilimackinac and Fort St. Joseph, driving every white man out of the Ohio Valley. However, the Trojan horse gambit that had worked so well for Chief Minnevana up at Michilimackinac failed at Detroit, thanks to the warning given to Major Gladwin and his

"Chief Pontiac's Siege of Detroit": famous painting by Frederic Remmington recalling the Anishnaabeg chief's 1763 attack on the Biritish ouposet at Detroit after his attempt to gain access through subterfuge was foiled by post commander, Major Henry Gladwin. **(Public Domain)**

Chapter 3 *Adam Smith's Bookends*

decisive response. Foiled in their subterfuge, Pontiac and his forces settled in for a long siege against Detroit, hoping to starve the British inhabitants into submission.⁽⁴⁸⁾ The British, however, remained minimally supplied and did not capitulate. As Fall ensued, enthusiasm within the Indian ranks waned and many returned to their hunting grounds to prepare for winter. Although not formally conceding, Pontiac withdrew, delivering word to Sir William Johnson that if Warraghiyagey wanted to talk peace, the now chastened chief could be found in Miami country. On December 7th, 1765, Johnson and representatives of the Ottawas, Ojibways, Potawatomis, Miamis, Sacs and Wyandottes passed the pipe of peace at Oswego, finally acknowledging King George as their new father.⁽⁴⁹⁾

For his part, Pontiac never gave up hope of liberating the region of the British overlords. In 1769, he was living at the busy village of Cahokia in the Illinois country where a British trading post had replaced the former French store. The Illinois still harbored the same hatred of the British and Pontiac hoped to rekindle the rebellion. But fate had something else in store for the once great chief. A young warrior by the name of Pini attached himself to Pontiac, attending to him so obsequiously that the chief's bodyguards began to accept his presence. This was a mistake, as Pini was actually the nephew of an Illinois chief Pontiac had stabbed in an earlier dispute and was simply biding his time until the proper moment to exact retribution. One day, as Pontiac was leaving the trading post, Pini buried a tomahawk in the back of Pontiac's head, then stabbed him for good measure to ensure the chief's demise.⁽⁵⁰⁾

Pontiac's insurrection certainly represented an existential threat to British power in the Americas, but it was merely peripheral. Places like Detroit and

Posing for many years as a trusted confidant, an Indian named Pini bided his time and gained Pontiac's trust until the time when he could exact vengeance for Pontiac's murder of a fellow tribesman years earlier. (**"U.S. History Images." Found in Lossing (1), Benson J.** *Our Country***. New York: Johnson and Bailey, 1895.**

Mackinac were and remained frontier outposts, centers where the peltry trade continued to dominate as it had all along. Though the rugged interior was yielding somewhat to white trappers and traders, it was still a world inhabited and controlled by the Indian, and the British were savvy enough to understand, despite their feelings of racial and cultural superiority, that the Indians still had an important role to play in their agenda on the American frontier. Retribution was, then, less important than maintaining a working relationship with the tribes and showing them that such a relationship was, though lacking the emotional and

Chapter 3 *Adam Smith's Bookends*

social depth they'd enjoyed with the French, to their mutual benefit.

Ironically, the real threat to England was brewing among its own colonies along the eastern seaboard. With the rebellion quashed and the French threat neutralized, England – who had borne the brunt of the economic and human sacrifice in winning the French and Indian Wars – quite naturally expected her colonies to be brimming with gratitude that she, the mother country, had saved them from the French and Indian menace. Certainly, the provincials would enthusiastically shoulder the burden of the Crown's war debts amassed on their behalf. And it was indeed an enormous sum, incurred, after all, in keeping the colonists' scalps intact and ensuring that the lingua franca of North America would be English and not French. But now, absent the threat and the sounds of conflict that had dominated the region for so long, cries of independence issued from lecterns in Boston and Philadelphia instead, a message quite dissonant and unexpected to a British government that stubbornly refused to see its colonies as anything other than eternally captive consumers of British goods, and a dedicated source of raw materials for England's factories and looms.

The arrogance and myopia of Hanoverian England under George III, coupled with the indifference of the colonists to the needs of imperial Britain now that peace was secured, merely widened the growing chasm between a nascent American culture paying homage to equality (in word if not in deed), and an English society quite satisfied and bifurcated into a monied, propertied elite, and a majority of the British population serving their interests. Trevelyan captures the disparity between the two cultures brilliantly, offering a decidedly English view of a moment much revered and iconic in U.S. history:

> "English society was based on great differences of wealth, while in America property was still divided with comparative equality, and every likely lad hoped someday to be as well-off as the leading man in the township. In England political opinion was mainly that of squires, while in America it was derived from farmers, water-side mobs, and frontiersmen of the sforest." [51]

Each side of the Atlantic had its own unique form of hypocrisy. In the colonies, the hue and cry for liberty and self-determination rang hollow among the slavery in southern plantations, in the north where the franchise was limited to citizens of property and completely denied to women, and on the frontier where every means necessary, from subterfuge to violence, was used to dispossess the Native Americans of the land they had occupied for millennia.

In England, the very same year that John Hancock and his brethren put their signatures on America's Declaration of Independence – 1776 – Adam Smith published another work, thus bracketing the British experience in the Americas with a second intellectual bookend. This work would earn him everlasting acclaim. Intended to codify the principles of a burgeoning capitalism already at work in world trade,

> "…a careful reading of Smith's "The Wealth of Nations" betrays the disparity between the disinterested and ineluctable economic forces Smith imagines are humming underneath everyday commerce, and the greed, privilege, and exploitation that were the actual engines of both British and budding American commerce."

Chapter 3

Adam Smith's Bookends

a careful reading of Smith's "The Wealth of Nations" betrays the disparity between the disinterested and ineluctable economic forces Smith imagines are humming underneath everyday commerce, and the greed, privilege, and exploitation that were the actual engines of both British and budding American commerce.

The "shot heard around the world" a year earlier on the green at Lexington in April, 1775 had echoed faintly in faraway Detroit as well, compelling British authorities to increase the size of the garrison there. Although the British had their hands full with the growing rebellion hundreds of miles to the east, affairs at Detroit centered, as they always had, on two goals: 1) maintaining the working relationship with the Indians around the fur trade; and 2) retaining their allegiance while placating their fear of westward expansion by American colonists. In 1763, George III had aided the latter with a proclamation forbidding expansion past a line drawn along the Appalachian Mountains. Though this indeed went far in securing the loyalties of the Indian tribes on the frontier, the colonists perceived it as yet another onerous gesture of English tyranny. Furthermore, whatever the official English policy toward gift giving, its importance became immediately apparent to Detroit's new commandant, Colonel Arent Schuyler de Peyster, who by 1780 was apologetically passing on a record of the ever increasing costs of "…clothing, cheap blankets with bright colors, fancy knives, scarlet cloth, ruffled shirts, laced hats and other similar articles"[52] to his superior, General Frederick Haldimand. Faced with the colonial rebellion on the coast, imminent threats from American forces, an alliance with the Indian tribes on the frontier became a priority, despite the cost.

Though Detroit had no direct involvement in the American Revolution, it served as a rallying point for Indian war parties who, confronted with thirteen colonies filled with white settlers covetous of Indian land, switched their allegiance to the British. Because the conflict was occurring so far from the outpost, Britain retained firm control of Detroit, and with the exception of the fur trade, remained quite divorced from diverse and robust commerce on the eastern seaboard. Yet commerce – that is, true commerce as Smith defined it – saluted no flag and, in its unimpeded form as he imagined it, reached across borders and the globe. For Smith, the laws of economics were as immutable and dependable as Newton's gravity or the universal principles of motion. Confident and determined, he and other intellectuals began to reexamine and even reject the time-honored theological explanations of the origin and nature of the physical world. Science, ever objective and dispassionate by nature, ultimately gave theism a reprieve of sorts, opting to re-define rather than outright reject its relationship with the Deity. As Newton and his successors began to observe, understand, and formulate the very predictable laws governing the physical world, it was empowering, and they began to appreciate it for the intricate structure and inter-dependence it displayed. So impressive was it that they themselves saw the hand of God in it. But this was not Jehovah, stern and unforgiving; this was "God the Clockmaker." This was a new, "natural" theology," one where the almighty was more like a partner, much like themselves; just greater in power. One could come to it not just by faith, but also through the eyes as evidence of its divinely inspired intricacy was observable everywhere. One had only to look and understand.

Chapter 3

Adam Smith's Bookends

Smith was certainly no monastic, and though his belief in the natural theology of the time rescues him from the suffocating strictures and stained-glass attitude of revealed religion, elements of his Christian faith still run like a common thread through the weave of his philosophical tapestry. Notwithstanding his trust in the "impartial spectator" to make correct choices in the moral universe, or his belief that individual consumers unwittingly contribute to the well-being of the economic order by simply satisfying their own desires, it soon becomes obvious that Smith's faith in the ability of the individual to effect these positive outcomes is not boundless. Choice is, in the end, neither infallible nor a panacea. Sometimes compulsion is necessary to effect collective outcomes, even though Smith only grudgingly cedes any role to government as a deliberate element of his economic thought. (As the "Sentiments" asserted, a system of justice based on laws was, for instance, vital and non-negotiable.) Within both the moral and the economic world, choice has its limits, and the well-being of the body politic – as well as the individual soul – must sometimes be entrusted to something other than individual discretion. Smith distrusted government interference in most forms, preferring instead to recruit a sense of personal guilt and the power of the Deity for this all-important intervention. In this, he was forced to rely on the notoriously unreliable individual conscience as a substitute for public policy.

It is one thing to be reverent of self-interest, and another to have a myopic, self-serving view of it. Smith's consumer "…intends only his own gain," and in this is led by an "invisible hand to promote an end which was no part of his intention."[53] But beware of unintended intentions. The hand that shuffled the goods and services in the economy of Smith's day was indeed self-interested, but for the wretched poor in the work houses and debtors' prisons and the country folk driven from their meager plots by enclosure[54] to an uncertain fate in cities like London or Manchester, the hand was neither invisible nor, it seemed, divinely directed. It was, rather, the very real hand of the lord, cloistered and secure, drinking claret in the security of his manor. It was the manufacturer, exploiting the tiny fingers of children twelve to fourteen hours a day to line his pockets. Just as some of the moral agents inhabiting Smith's ethical realm never quite find their own way to the straight and "impartial" moral path, many in the world of commerce come to their fortunes precisely by thwarting those supposedly unimpeachable laws of economics rather than being guided by them.

Individual discretion is, then, the cornerstone of Smith's economic and moral edifice. But there are cracks in this foundation; glitches in Smith's otherwise ideal world of commerce which – were it not for the pesky predilection of humans not just to "truck, barter, and exchange"[55] – but to swindle, cheat, and exploit as well – would make for a perfect harmony of supply and demand and an always efficient use of capital to constructive ends. To his credit, Smith does give a nod to some of capitalism's pitfalls here and there in "Wealth of Nations." But references to such downsides as monopoly[56] or wage and price fixing and collusion

> **The hand that shuffled the goods and services in the economy of Smith's day was indeed self-interest, but for the wretched poor in the work houses and debtors prisons and the country folk driven from their meager plots by enclosure [4] to an uncertain fate in cities like London or Manchester, the hand was neither invisible nor, it seemed, divinely directed.**

are mere asides in the work, indicating that such conditions were an embarrassing reality in the economy of Smith's day. No doubt, Smith would have attributed their very existence to the protections and obstruction thrown up by still reigning British mercantilists and guilds. However, evidence that such conditions only worsened as Smith's capitalism took root and supplanted the economy of the empire can be found in any of Charles Dickens' writings or the paintings of William Hogarth.

Pervading both works is a tension between the power of the individual to choose, and the problem of choosing rightly, both for one's self and for the good of society. This conflict, however, only reveals itself to the careful reader, one not invested in Smith's notion that the natural laws of economics are the hidden hand of commerce, guiding individual choices in such a way that there is no conflict between self-interest and the interests of society. These are, in Smith's imagination, naturally conflated, and their intimate relationship depends on an acceptance of certain articles of faith with regards to production, division of labor, and a naïve belief in the equitable movement of goods and services based on supply and demand.

At the very outset of "Wealth," Smith makes an optimistic assumption about the salutary and universal effects of the division of labor, one not born out, as we shall see, in the reality of the day:

> "It is the great multiplication of the production of all the different arts, in consequence of the division of labour, which occasions, in a well-governed society, that universal opulence which extends to the lowest ranks of the people."(57)

An accounting of beggars in London produced by Matthew Martin in 1796 places their numbers in the city at 15,288, "…the vast majority of whom were women, frequently with children in tow."(58) This figure indicates that as Smith's political economy took root in British society, not only did much of the wealth not, as he supposed, percolate down to the "lowest ranks of the people," (a delusion persisting to this day as "Supply Side" theory) the presence of so many hopeless and destitute a full thirty years after the publication of "Wealth" proves that it was not so much mercantilism that was the cause of this misery as the increased acceptance of Smith's own laissez-faire ideas. Smith's invisible hand was, in fact, quite arthritic, distributing the social product so inefficiently that many of those not driven to overt begging in the street were consigned to one of the eighty-six workhouses in London and Middlesex, an institution conceived to address a social problem too great to be ignored, and whose very existence was barely tolerated by a society still gripped by a cruel species of Calvinism that equated poverty with mere laziness and divine disfavor.

The workhouses were inhabited by about two percent of the population of London and its environs, a third of whom were children under the age of fourteen

"Individual discretion is, then, the cornerstone of Smith's economic and moral edifice. But there are cracks in this foundation; glitches in Smith's otherwise ideal world of commerce which – were it not for the pesky predilection of humans not just to "truck, barter, and exchange" but to swindle, cheat, and exploit as well – would make for a perfect harmony of supply and demand and an always efficient use of capital to constructive ends."

years.(60) Intended to instill in the poor the individual industry and ambition the lack of which, or so the well-to-do claimed, was the cause of their penury, children and adults alike were subjected to a daily regimen of barely remunerated work and a wealth of religious proselytizing. Other options for the poor included parish charity schools that allowed entry only with a proper certificate issued by local authorities,(59) one attesting to the good character, trustworthiness, and personal industry of the applicant.

Whereas the legion of abandoned and/or orphaned infants were consigned to Thomas Coram's new Foundling Hospital,(59) boys who qualified were shepherded into the Marine Society, a naval academy conceived by social activist and philanthropist Jonas Hanover.(60) While the Society's avowed purpose was the rehabilitation of poor young boys, its ultimate effect was to provide a steady flow of cannon fodder for the British military and a reliable source of sailors for the empire's commercial fleet. And finally, those too sick or unable to work were simply thrown on the mercy of parish charities, each of which placed its own rigorous preconditions on its beneficence.

History sometimes makes strange bedfellows, and this is certainly the case with Smith's ideas of value. "Labour therefore," he writes, "is the real measure of the exchangeable value of all commodities."(61) On this, both he and Marx agree.(62) But in Smith's universe, even though he concedes that the only true value of a commodity is the labor expended to produce it, labor value is itself for him a totally abstract, inexpressible concept and therefore of little use in the real economy. Because, Smith asserts, true labor value can exist only in a world where a solitary person supplies all his own needs, labor in the real, collective economy must be pegged, like a commodity, to a tangible medium of exchange; that is, the money wage or some other form of remuneration. After all, says Smith, "…it is but a very small part of a man's wants which the produce of his own labour can supply."(63)

"And therein lies one of the fatal assumptions of Smith's capitalism: that the system will always endow the worker with a surplus from the sale of his/her own labor – an amount sufficient to purchase the goods and services required for survival."

How, then, does the worker obtain what he needs? He brings to the market "…that surplus part of the of the produce of his own labour, which is over and above his own consumption, for such parts of the produce of other men's labour as he may have occasion for."(64) And therein lies one of the fatal assumptions of Smith's capitalism: that the system will always endow the worker with a surplus from the sale of his/her own labor – an amount sufficient to purchase the goods and services required for survival. Yet, as the laborers in the work houses, the children at the looms, and even the fast-food workers of today will attest, this would be true only if capitalists were not, by nature, predisposed to extract as much labor as they can for as little wages as possible. That the rewards of production redound to the benefit of the worker to the same degree as the capitalist is, in Marx's words, "…a fundamentally perverted analysis," one that assumes, wrongfully, that the capital of society "…is laid out exclusively in the payment of wages."(65) In the end, Smith's unseen hand is not only very visible, but very stingy as well.

Chapter 3 *Adam Smith's Bookends*

Smith's selective vision with regard to the poor and the destitute, his lack of sympathy for their condition,[66] and his unawareness of the true systemic causes of it is equally misguided when he turns his analytical gaze to the economy of Britain's North American colonies. As far as Detroit is concerned, for the time being we must remain zoomed out on larger national forces to whose fate the village was still tied at this time. It is important to appreciate that though the rudiments of a stable, enduring community had developed in Detroit by the time of the revolution, it was still a frontier outpost without a unique identity, one still under tight British control, and one only peripherally affected by the ensuing insurrection on the eastern seaboard.

Though it had been founded around the same time as the now rebellious colonies, a history in time was, frankly, the only thing Detroit shared with its eastern counterparts. The forbidding geography of the region,

The Birth of U.S. Class and Inequality...

By 1700, the available landmasss of the American colonies was limited. Most of the safe property had long since been settled and claimed, actually creating a situation of scarcity quite unlike the cheap "waste lands" Smith imagined. However, quite ironically, because land could be had only at a premium within the secure confines of the colonies, Smith's laws of supply and demnad did create conditions whereby land was scarce, and the lack of land existing in an economy still dominated by agriculture created an army of poor and dispossessed people surviving at the margins of colonial society. Many teetered on the brink of starvation and destitution. In desperation, they were, as historian Howard Zinn has indicated, often driven to violent protest and rioting, a fact obscured by the mythology of an American revolution whose own elites successfully deflected that energy of popular protest from themselves to the wider existential threat of British hegemony. Fed by a steady flow of English, Scotish-Irish, German immigrants and black slaves, the population of the colonies swelled from 250,000 in 1700 to 1,600,000 by 1760.[65] The results of this increase would have been positive had wages, as Smith's theories supposed, been distributed in a reasonably equitable manner and capital in both agriculture and/or the nascent industrial secotro been applied efficiently. The opposite, in fact, happened. By 1770, Zinn observes, "...the top 1 percent of property owners owned 44 percent of the wealth."[67] The situation was worse in places like Boston where, Zinn recounts, "...the top 1percent of property owners owned 44 percent of the wealth, while the lowert 30 percent of the tax paying population had no taxable property at all.[68] In a time when only those who owned property could vote, this not only meant the property-less were denied the franchise, it also meant the political life of the community was in the hands of a few propertied elites.

Chapter 3 *Adam Smith's Bookends*

"Surrender of Cornwallis at Yorktown." From: Library of Congress Engravings: 1860 to 1880.

the resistance of its Native American inhabitants and its early association with the regressive economic policies of the French for the first hundred years or so of its existence kept Detroit quite apart from the fray. Deep-seated resentment of taxation, representation, violations of privacy, property, and the forced impressment of young men to the service of the crown could only have festered in a close and slowly souring association with the mother country like the one that existed in the east, one that ultimately grew unconscionable to communities that had hewn their own identities and needs out of the environment an ocean away from England.

Though Smith traveled widely and was acquainted with such intellectual notables as Hume, Turgot, and the physiocrat Quesnay (Smith considered dedicating "Wealth of Nations" to Quesnay, he never crossed the water to America. After reading Smith's section on colonies in "Wealth" (IV.7), one comes away with the feeling that he is torn in his assessment between his head and his heart. He rails against the undeserved mercantilist strangle hold British merchants have over the commerce of all the colonies, robbing them of their wealth, he claims, that would otherwise come with unfettered world trade. Because, he claims, British merchants played no positive part in their founding, they had no exclusive rights to the social product of the American colonies, entities not founded on "…wisdom and policy, but the disorder and injustice of the European governments which peopled and cultivated America."[69] In a moment of intellectual candor, he reminds the reader that the Puritans in New England and the English Catholics in Maryland were driven from the mother country by discrimination and oppression. On the other hand, while allegiance to his laissez-faire principles bade him embrace the colonies' right to free trade, a sense of patriotism compelled him to reject the American rebellion as so much ingratitude and disloyalty toward a mother country that had expended much blood and treasure in their defense.

Whether it was the product of anecdotal accounts, or simply a deduction based on his own economic principles, Smith made two questionable assumptions about land and wages in the American colonies, both of which assumed these two were more abundant than they actually were. "Waste lands of the greatest natural fertility are to be had for a trifle,"[70] he claims. To be useful, this land had to be cleared, and because of the lack of labor available to do so, workers in America had to be enticed with high wages – higher than in England. Indeed, a whole continent awaited the ax and the plow. Though the logic was sound, there was one problem: these lands were already inhabited by Native Americans; peoples whose claim was both historically legitimate, and jealously guarded. For those coveting the forests and pastures beyond outposts like Detroit and Pittsburgh, the prospect of higher wages was trumped by the possibility of extinction at the hands of hostile tribes. The southern colonies solved the labor problem with black slavery. In the north, white indentured servants toiled for years in their own unique sort of captivity.

The available landmass of the American colonies was, then, limited. Most of the safe property had long since been settled and claimed, actually creating a situation of scarcity quite unlike the cheap "waste lands" Smith imagined. However, and quite ironically, because land could be had only at a premium within the secure confines of the colonies, Smith's laws of supply and demand did create conditions whereby an economy still dominated by agriculture created an army of poor and dispossessed people surviving at the margins of colonial society. Many teetered on the brink of starvation and destitution. In desperation, they were, as historian Howard Zinn has indicated, often driven to violent protest and rioting, a fact obscured by the mythology of an American revolution whose own elites successfully deflected that energy of popular protest from themselves to the wider existential threat of British hegemony.

Fed by a steady flow of English, Scotch-Irish, German immigrants and black slaves, the population of the colonies swelled from 250,000 in 1700 to 1,600,000 by 1760 (see panel, page 50). The results of this increase would have been positive had wages, as Smith's theories supposed, been distributed in a reasonably equitable manner and capital in both agriculture and/or the nascent industrial sector been applied efficiently. The opposite, in fact, happened. By 1770, Zinn observes, "…the top 1 percent of property owners owned 44 percent of the wealth." The situation was worse in places like Boston where, as Zinn further recounts, "…the top 10 percent of Boston's taxpayers held about 66 percent of Boston's taxable wealth, while the lowest 30 percent of the taxpaying population had no taxable property at all."[71] In a time when only those who owned property could vote, this not only meant the property-less were denied the franchise, it also meant the political life of the community was in the hands of a few propertied elites.

The mythology of wealth in the United States would have us believe that the country's original fortune holders rose from humble beginnings through hard work and fortitude. While this might well have been true for some, a closer more honest look indicates that much early American wealth originated from less noble, unsavory sources.

The mythology of wealth in the United States would have us believe that the country's original fortune holders rose from humble beginnings through hard work and fortitude. While this might well have been true for some, a closer more honest look indicates that much early American wealth originated from less noble, unsavory sources. War, of course, has always and everywhere been a time-honored font of riches for those well situated to equip and feed the belligerents. This was true in the colonies as well where, after England's long struggle to oust the French from North America between 1754 and 1763, the bill for the French and Indian War roughly doubled its national debt.

On the plus side of this ledger were the merchants, both British and American, who supplied the grist – the provisions and credit – for this murderous mill of war. Despite the shadow these masters of war cast, history nevertheless affords them a measure of respectability for their dark service. Yet, for those daring enough to cast a more aggressive net and catch the wind with a trim sail, illegitimate booty from piracy offered riches reaped from the high seas. "Merchants in the American colonies of the 1690s," notes economic historian Kevin Phillips,[72] "often funded covert expeditions to plunder gold, silks, and ivory in the faraway waters off India, Arabia, and Madagascar." By the time of the American revolution, Phillips claims, "…it is reasonable to suggest that many of the thirteen colonies' richest merchant families owed 30 or 40 percent of their wealth to the fruits of war, privateering, and earlier piracy." Much as Smith imagined the colonies to be a petri dish for neo-liberal economics – bemoaning what he perceived as rule by the rabble – at the time of the colonies' rebellion, wealth distribution in the colonies resembled more the disparities of the mother country. The provincial gilded class was, in the end, fattened less by pulling up their bootstraps than by bombs, bayonets, and booty liberated from the holds of foreign merchants' ships.

On October 17th, 1781 the gates of besieged, British-occupied Yorktown swung open and a lone drummer followed by a British officer with a white flag slowly made their way to the American and French lines with a note requesting terms of surrender. The next day, notes passed back and forth between English General Cornwallis and Washington laying the groundwork for the surrender of the fort and the British forces inside. Through a combination of brilliant strategy, luck, and help from Louis the XVI's French army and navy, the revolutionary forces had delivered the British government a humiliating defeat. Its empire unraveling in India, Gibraltar, the West Indies and Ireland, the British parliament passed a measure resolving not to continue the conflict in North America (not directly, at any rate). By September, 1782 the deal was inked and the British presence in the American colonies officially ended.[73] But the Treaty of Paris was, apparently, a mere formality on the western frontier. Nearly a year later, on July 4th, 1783, an American contingent headed by Major Ephraim Douglass visited Detroit and was received cordially by British commander, Colonel DePeyster. DePeyster had not received orders to stand down, and when Major Douglass asked to meet with the Indians on July 6th to inform them of the change of government the British commander politely refused, then asked the Americans to leave.[74] The British retained control of Detroit for another fourteen years, administering the village as though it were simply an extension of the Canadian bureaucracy, appointing its own judges and applying British/Canadian law despite the treaty officially ending Britain's influence.[75] Only another war on the European continent would be a powerful enough catalyst to finally and in fact end British rule in and around the Great Lakes. Faced with the specter of a resuscitated French imperialism under Napoleon, the increasingly disaffected and dispossessed Native Americans were left to face, in part as British proxies, the encroaching waves of white settlers, hungry for Indian land.

Artist's rendering from a photo in an 1890 work titled "How the Other Half Lives" by Jacob A. Riis. The New York slum depicted is "Gotham Court." (Alamy stock photo no. D89B52.)

Chapter 3

Adam Smith's Bookends

Chapter 4
Liquor, Lies, and Laissez-Faire
Making Early Michigan

We believe, if the Indians do not emigrate, and fly the causes which are fixed in themselves, and which have proved so destructive in the past, they must perish.

Lewis Cass *Removal of the Indians*, 1830.

General Anthony Wayne. Engraving by Alonzo Chappel. (From: *National Portrait Gallery of Eminent Americans. Vol 1.* **Johnson and Fry, 1862**)

From the end of the conflict with its rebellious colonies, England had sat idly by, a neutral observer, as the revolutionary forces of France began their steamroller conquest of Europe. Inaction ceased to be an option in 1793 when Louis XVI and his wife, Marie Antoinette, were guillotined and the massive (and conscripted) revolutionary French army began advancing on the Dutch Republic. With its European trade routes threatened and its traditional monarchy in the sights of France's First Citizen, Napoleon Bonaparte, Britain was forced to turn its attention to the crisis at home. Despite its waning influence on the American frontier in what is present day Michigan, Ohio, Indiana, and Pennsylvania, it maintained a stubborn, rear-guard action by continuing to equip its Indian allies, urging the natives to resist the tsunami of white settlers gathering strength to the east (a not unrealistic admonition, as history would show). Native American resistance indeed proved formidable at first, repelling successive militia armies sent by the infant government to quell the rebellion. After ambushing and routing a Continental force led by Brigadier General Josiah Harmer in 1790, the natives – mostly Miamis – served up the same fate to a later expedition led by Major General Arthur St. Clair in 1791.

Leaders of the new republic were in a quandary. What could they do to turn the tide? How could they deal with opposing natives who, rather than confronting Continental forces in neat rows as the British had, used the same guerilla tactics instead, firing from the forest, then melting back into the safety of the woods? Ironically, it was the same strategy used so successfully by colonial forces and their then Indian allies against British General Braddock on the Monongahela four decades earlier. And with the tactic came an element of terror, one compelling enough to make some of the poorly trained volunteer militiamen break ranks and run away. It was, in short, a crisis of organization and discipline for an army consisting in great part of volunteers whose only qualification was the fact that they owned a gun. What it lacked, the young Congress decided, was professionalism, training, and a new identity. On March 5th, 1792, Congress approved the reorganization of the army as the Legion of the United States.[1] Based on a model conceived by the German general Baron Friedrich Wilhelm von Steuben – who had helped train the Continental Army – it divided the new military into four sub-legions, each with 1,280 men. The sub-legions were, in turn, to be commanded by a brigadier general overseeing two battalions of infantry, one battalion of riflemen, one company of artillery, and one company of dragoons. This restructuring, legislators hoped, would make the force more effective and tactically nimble. All that was needed was someone to lead it, and President Washington and Secretary of War Henry Knox chose Major General Anthony Wayne, recalling him back into service from civilian life where he was the owner of a rice plantation in Georgia.

General Anthony Wayne's newly trained "American Legion" defeats a proxy Indian army, the Miamis, at the Battle of Fallen Timbers on August 20, 1794. **(From a steel engraving in the "National Portrait Gallery of Eminent Americans") by Alonzo Chappel, 1862.**

Preparing for two years at an isolated outpost Wayne named "Legionville" on the Ohio River twenty miles from Pittsburgh, he molded his recruits into a credible fighting force according to principles laid down by von Steuben in his Blue Book drill manual.[2]

After talks with the Indians failed to make the serially swindled and distrustful natives capitulate, Wayne had just the excuse he needed to put his new army to the test. In August, 1794 Wayne and his troops reached their destination: a British/Indian stronghold the British had refused to surrender called Fort Miamis. Before they could reach the fort, however, Wayne's forces were ambushed in an area near present day Toledo known as Fallen Timbers, a place littered with trees felled years earlier by a tornado. The training proved decisive and, after a battle lasting less than an hour, the Indians were routed and forced to retreat back to the fort where their British allies refused to open the gates lest they – clearly in violation of the 1783 Treaty of Paris ending the Revolutionary War – be drawn into an embarrassing, unwanted conflict. Wayne's victory was momentous not just because it represented the last tangible act of British resistance, it was yet another defeat for an Indian

Chapter 4   *Liquor, Lies, and Laissez Faire*

Protesting a lack of protection from Indian attacks, Nathaniel Bacon leads a rebellion against Jamestown authorities in 1676. (From: *Harper's Encyclopedia of United States History: from 358 A.D. to 1905.* John Lessing, Ed.; Vol. 5 of 10.)

A seminal event inspiring, in part, the move to a new federal constitution the next year, Shay's rebellion – 1786 – was a violent reaction to intolerable economic conditions, wealth stratification, and burdensome taxation.(From: *People's History of the World, Edward Sylvester Ellis, Vol. 6, 1902.*)

population ever wary of its tenuous hold on territory it had dominated for centuries. Worse for the Indians, the treaty Wayne negotiated a year later in 1795 – called "The Treaty of Greenville" – seized another sizeable chunk of their traditional lands, throwing open the door to unmolested settlement in the Ohio Territory.[3]

Wayne's victory over England's proxy army at Fallen Timbers created a vacuum of sorts. With the old grip of European power loosened and the back of native resistance broken in the region, the Ohio territory was now opened for business. Settlers could claim what for so long had been the ancestral home of the Indians, dispossessed now by yet another lopsided treaty bargained under duress. For over a century, France and Britain had lorded over North America, casting their long shadows of empire over a burgeoning population not yet certain of its own cultural identity. Now those foreign giants were gone (in this part of the continent, at least), and into the breach once filled with their imperial arrogance and swagger flowed a river of settlers whose only agenda was the simple prospect of survival afforded by a patch of earth blessed with sun and rain and a secure environment free of attacks from its previous inhabitants.

Though the settlers were merely trying to survive, their turbulent encounters with the Native Americans were certainly nothing new. It was, in fact, an ugly dance that had been choreographed a hundred years earlier as poor white immigrants were pushed westward from already crowded coastal cities where working conditions were often intolerable and exploitive. They served, wittingly or not, as a useful human buffer zone between angry native tribes and a small eastern elite with a monopoly on property. The tension of constantly facing down attacks by Indians and the lack of an organized, government-sponsored entity to protect the

Chapter 4   *Liquor, Lies, and Laissez Faire*

settlers from them often reached the boiling point. Add to this problem of security an onerous system of taxation and an unforgiving, Calvinist contempt for debtors – no matter what the reason for their destitution – and all the elements were there for social upheaval.

Though long past at the time of the Revolution, the memory of Nathaniel Bacon and his 1676 rebellion against the masters of Jamestown still haunted the propertied elite at the time of the revolution.[4] Though Bacon had actually been a person of some distinction and was himself a property holder, his real frustration was with the threat from Indians attacks. After fruitlessly petitioning Virginia's Governor Berkeley for protection, Bacon organized a militia of his own and made the mistake of attacking a friendly Indian tribe, thereby setting up a chain of violent, mutual retribution. Bacon's revolt was eventually suppressed and the leaders were hung. Bacon himself escaped the hangman's noose by dying prematurely of dysentery, thus robbing authorities of a more formal exercise before the bar of justice. Nevertheless, thereafter his memory instilled a sobering and lasting fear of another rebellion and another Bacon-like agitator at the head of a disaffected army of poor whites, abused servants, and slaves. The propertied elite was ever wary, and preoccupied with some way to forestall future insurrections. Eventually, as Howard Zinn recounts, they happened upon the answer:

> "Those upper classes, to rule, needed to make concessions to the middle class, without damage to their own wealth or power, at the expense of slaves, Indians, and poor whites. This bought loyalty. And to bind that loyalty with something more powerful even than material advantage, the ruling group found, in the 1760s and 1770s, a wonderfully useful device. That device was the language of liberty and equality, which could unite just enough whites to fight a Revolution against England, without ending either slavery or inequality"[5]

Thus, was laid the philosophical cornerstone for the new constitution that would come in 1787, a document born, in part, by the failure of the Articles of Confederation to ensure the privilege of the wealthy, the lack of a central authority strong enough to guard against the chaos of yet another revolt, and an inability to settle the debt incurred by the Revolution. In 1786, only a year before the historic meeting in Philadelphia, yet another rebellion of the poor and disaffected erupted, this time under the leadership of Daniel Shays. Shay's Rebellion[6] sent a shudder through the colonial ruling class, convincing wealthy intellectuals like Madison, Hamilton, and Adams (Jefferson was in France at the time) that a stronger central government – one capable of maintaining order and fiscal solvency – was in order.

While colonial settlers were pushing against the periphery of the infant nation, Detroit – still a frontier outpost (albeit quite settled) – remained stubbornly under British control. Seven years before the decisive Battle of Fallen Timbers, while the Founders were hammering out the details of their constitutional meeting in Philadelphia, both the village by the Great Lakes and the territory of Michigan were gradually assuming the shape and character they would ultimately be.

Using a generous policy of gift giving coupled with assurances that the Crown's agenda was, unlike the colonial settlers, concerned with commerce and not confiscation, the English secured a shaky but enduring period of peace and collaboration with the natives. With the existential threat of their physical expulsion from the frontier off the table for the time being, successive British commanders (ten, to be exact, between the Treaty of Paris in 1783 and the British exit from Detroit

Chapter 4

Liquor, Lies, and Laissez Faire

in 1796) devoted their energies to the business of personal enrichment. An unintended consequence of this Smithian pursuit of self-interest was to define a rudimentary local real estate market, one that went a long way toward supplanting the patchwork of conflicting claims existing under foreign auspices.

With the Michigan and Ohio territories pacified and the vast (still Indian-inhabited) wilderness to the west beckoning, the vexing question arose: "who owns what," after all? England's persistent possession of frontier outposts like Detroit and the pile of treaties chronicling the elusive dance of sovereign ownership over the decades rendered the whole issue of borders and claims to the land and waterways quite nebulous. If nothing else, the history of the area showed how economies, from local to international, often develop a unique power and character. Commercial highways and waterways long trammeled and cemented in time create enduring borders of their own, borders drawn by the stubborn hand of commerce not easily undone with the simple stroke of a pen. Such areas, emptied of foreign ambitions and re-filled with a galaxy of powerless farmers or merchants more concerned with profit than sovereignty, was like a tempting tabula rasa to those with great ambitions and even greater resources:

Map from Library of Congress, "Treaty of Paris."

capitalists and politicians who, as we shall see, were anxious to draw those borders themselves in their own interest.

In 1783, when representatives of the new American republic and the English government sat down at the table in Paris to settle their differences, the diplomats drew a line they imagined would thereafter be the sovereign border between British Canada and the new nation. That line – beginning at the Appalachians and stretching westward along the northern shores of Lakes Superior and Huron – then moved south, following a portion of the Mississippi River in the west until it reached the northern border of Florida (then under Spanish control). From there it moved eastward to the Appalachians again, thereby enclosing a gigantic area bounded on the north by the Great Lakes, on the east by the entire length of the coastal states, and, on the west, by a great length of the Mississippi River. Its southern border followed the northern edge of Spanish Florida.[7] Bereft, finally, of European influence, other forces were poised to move in and reshape the region.

Nowhere, perhaps, was the disparity between the political and practical ramifications of the 1783 Treaty of Paris border more apparent than around the Great Lakes. For those merchants, no matter what their country of allegiance – who for over a century had

Chapter 4

Liquor, Lies, and Laissez Faire

shuffled goods around the network of rivers and lakes – these waterways had come to be nothing less than an established, transnational highway for the exchange of goods. Merchants in Detroit, for example, relied on credit and supplies emanating in Montreal, which was now across the border. Conversely, the new border effectively blocked Detroit merchants' access to lucrative foreign markets brokered in Montreal. Merchants in London who dealt with fur trading concerns in Quebec warned that the new boundary "…cuts off all the Trading Posts and almost all the Indian Nations; the Trade with whom was the grand object of the commercial Intercourse between Great Britain and the Province of Quebec."[8] The boundary was simply ignored for some time until, as Hatter suggests, "…local entrepreneurs at Detroit helped convert the political economy of the Great Lakes from a transnational network of patronage to a divided system of sovereign markets."[9] What might make this possible, or so they hoped, was a regulated real estate market that would eventually be underwritten by the new government, one that would replace the local system of exchange based on quasi-legal titles of questionable legality. It would, they further imagined, offer a more secure path to economic opportunity, one that would ultimately reshape the transnational environment to one of rival domestic markets.[10]

However, until 1796 Detroit was still (and quite illegally) under English control. The Proclamation of 1763 had precluded any white settlement west of the Appalachians and was still the official policy of the English government. Writing to his Lieutenant Governor, Jehu Hay, the Governor of Quebec, Frederick Haldimand, made it clear:

"I have to acquaint you that the claims of individuals, without distinction, upon Indian Lands at Detroit, or any other part of the Province, are invalid [sic], and the mode of acquiring lands by which is called Deeds of Gift, is to be entirely discountenanced."[11]

The Governor's concerns were based on the ever-growing and illegal use of land titles consummated under purely local authority, contracts drawn up without the imprimatur of the sovereign British government. Whatever authority existed in far-flung outposts like Detroit resided in the commandant who had the final say on most every matter. Therefore, an enterprising commandant could, in true Smithian fashion, exploit circumstances to his own advantage. This is exactly what the then commandant of Detroit, William Ancrum, did. Collaborating with Detroit businessman John Askin, Ancrum and his partner helped carve out the first Michigan real estate market. This nascent market is embodied historically in two important transactions: their purchase of the Moravian settlement twenty miles north of Detroit, and a speculative deal involving land around Cuyahoga River (near present day Cleveland).

In an environment like Detroit – one virtually devoid of sovereign authority at the time – there were few government agencies to make transactions official. One was, as Hatter suggests, the notary public:

"The office of the notary public was one of the few agencies of civil government accessible to Detroiters prior to 1796. Consequently, the notary's register became the repository of record for a wide range of private agreements between individuals, ranging from marriages to indentures."[12]

The notary's seal and the ledgers in which they were recorded "…created a demonstrable lineage of descent for land transactions, which was an important marker of legitimacy in English common law."[13]

Chapter 4 *Liquor, Lies, and Laissez Faire*

Among these records are documents chronicling the sale, in 1786, of the Moravian Settlement to Ancrum and Askin.

Located a little over twenty miles northwest of Detroit (near present day Mount Clemens), the

thereby questioned the Moravian's loyalty and subsequently expelled them from their home by the Muskingum in 1781.

In October of that year, the commandant of Detroit, Major de Peyster, sent for the leaders to answer the

Partnering with businessman John Askin, Detroit post commander William Ancrum purchased the Moravian settlement of New Gnadenhutten, beginning a nascent real estate industry, thereby contributing greatly to the region's identity and autonomy.

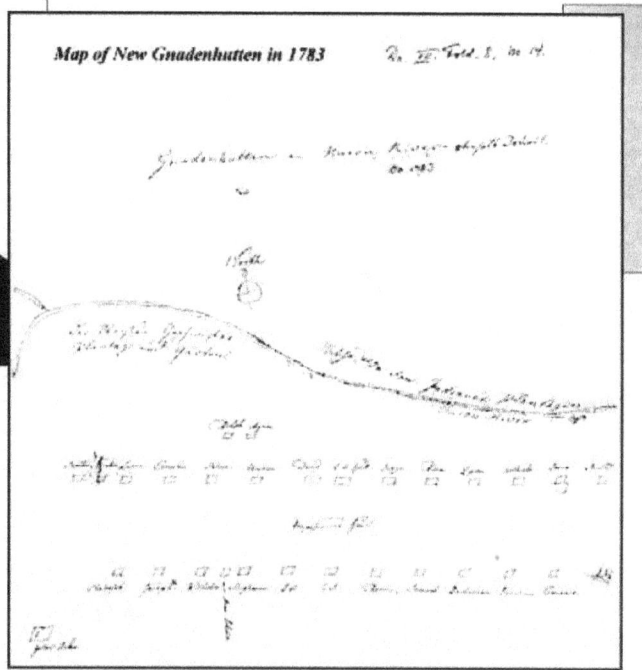

Re-established from its original site in Gnadenhutten, Ohio, residents of New Gnadenhutten did much to develop the area, including the first road.

In league with Detroit commandant William Ancrum, businessman John Askin began buying up land in the region, including the Moravian settlement at New Gnadenhutten.

settlement – which came to be known as New Gnadenhutten – had been established in 1782 by David Zeisberger and his assistant, John Heckewelder. Both were ministers and missionaries in the German Moravian Church. The pair headed a group of Christianized Delaware Indians forced to move from their original home by the Muskingum River in Ohio by British authorities who suspected them of collaboration with the Americans. Throughout the revolutionary conflict, the group professed neutrality; a standpoint viewed suspiciously by the warring parties who did not see neutrality as an acceptable option. The English

charges of treason leveled against them. Upon interrogation, the leaders must have apprised themselves well, for they eventually won over de Peyster who not only sent for the rest of the group and bade them settle on the nearby Huron River, the commandant also supplied them with enough provisions for six months.[14] Industrious residents of New Gnadenhutten not only created an enviable, thriving community consisting, as Heckewelder described in a letter to Askin dated February 26th, 1786, of "…some 24 log Houses, besides Stables, and other small Buildings,"[15] they had also begun work on what

Chapter 4

Liquor, Lies, and Laissez Faire

would be the first major road through the wooded landscape stretching twenty-one miles from their settlement to the gates of Detroit.

On April 28th, 1786 – after much back and forth over the deal and a survey of the prospective land – Askin and Ancrum purchased the Moravian settlement and its improvements for the sum of 200 dollars. The Moravian sale is a transformative moment in the region less because of the actual transaction than the impetus behind it. That Ancrum and Askin were interested in the property for its agricultural potential points to a shift in the economic paradigm of the region from furs to husbandry, a transition implying the type of cultivation that comes with settled communities rather than methodically depleting a region of its native fauna for profit. And while this indeed might be the case in the broader sense, the pair's own incentive for buying the property was decidedly more mercenary and self-interested.

That Askin's aim was ultimately to go into the provisioning business becomes obvious when in 1793 – just seven years after acquiring the property – he pulled enough strings with connections in Montreal to land a lucrative contract to provide supplies to England's largest fur trading company remaining on the continent, the Northwest Company. Another reason the Moravian deal is a watershed moment in the history of Michigan is that it points to a change in cultural forces from external foreign governments influencing from abroad to a local animus based on self-interest – an atmosphere arguably more conducive to long-term stability and growth. In addition, the very mechanics of buying and selling necessitated an accurate definition of boundaries, and this need could only be realized through the arduous mechanical process of surveying, a practice totally rooted in the white man's concept of ownership and property. Activities like surveying were alien to the Native Americans. How could they know that the clinking surveyor's chain dragged across the landscape and the bang of measurement poles being pounded in the ground was nothing less than noises heralding their own dispossession? It was, quite simply, the menacingly audible, step-by-step sound of present and future confiscation.

"Activities like surveying were alien to the Native Americans. How could they know that the clinking surveyor's' chain dragged across the landscape and the bang of measurement poles being pounded in the ground was nothing less than noises heralding their own dispossession? It was, quite simply, the menacingly audible, step-by-step sound of present and future confiscation."

During the decades under foreign influence, the desire of the landless masses on the eastern seaboard to migrate and exploit the wilderness to the west boiled like a teakettle, its lid held down firmly by a British government more interested in trade than settlement. England's desire to suppress this urge required the cooperation and a modicum of good will from the Indians. The English realized that neither could be cultivated while stealing Indian land. While such a practical outlook was possible for a power whose primary interests lay across the ocean, the attachment of those new generations who called the colonies home was much more emotional. They were, frankly, covetous of land otherwise available except for its inconvenient habitation by people they dismissed as unworthy and ignorant "savages."

As British influence was eroded then forcibly extirpated, the rebellious colonies were now free to turn their hungry gaze to the west where large swathes of unsettled territory awaited possible admission to the union. To their credit, members of the Second Continental Congress realized these territories should

Chapter 4   *Liquor, Lies, and Laissez Faire*

only be admitted in an orderly fashion and only after satisfying a list of legislative and judicial preconditions. This agreement, passed in July, 1787, came to be known historically as the Northwest Ordinance, thereby setting aside a huge piece of frontier known as the Northwest Territory.[16]

The Northwest Ordinance gave legal expression and a measure of governmental legitimacy to an appetite for land already at work in the young nation's collective consciousness. From a practical standpoint, the frontier loomed like a gigantic safety valve, just waiting to relieve the social pressure of congestion, unemployment, and civil strife. But in the eyes of some societal elites, this acquisitive impulse was also sanctified philosophically. Jefferson himself bore a physiocratic reverence for the soil, regarding the simple act of farming as a redemptive, character-building experience. For him, a life tilling the soil in sync with the rhythms of nature was not merely the most productive and valuable form of labor to a society (a physiocratic article of faith), in his opinion the act of husbandry by its vervy nature produced citizens of sterling character, at once unselfish, unaffected, and wise. The simple communion of the farmer with the plow would bring, or so Jefferson believed, deliverance from the "... panders of vice and the instruments by which the liberties of a country are generally overturned."[17] If the twin contagions of vice and violence were the products of crowded, cramped cities with their struggle for resources and opportunities, then the anodyne was land and open spaces.

The property-less and disadvantaged had only to set their sights on the wilderness to the west where they would find sustenance and fulfillment, a fruitful place they could bequeath to successive generations carved from the seemingly inexhaustible soil. Certainly no one at this time thought of the sprawling, unexplored continent as a finite resource, and even one as intelligent and wise as Jefferson succumbed to the notion that there would always be enough land for everyone. It would last, Jefferson imagined, "...to the hundredth and thousand generation."[18] His task, then, in no matter what capacity he served was to ensure an unending supply of *terra firma* to the citizenry, a mission he would fulfill beyond his dreams, once he became president, with the Louisiana Purchase.

Realizing territory should be admitted and organized in an orderly fashion, the infant government enacted the Northwest Ordinance which also stipulated the terms of property ownership in perpetuity with the power to sell or give it away. **(Free Software Foundation. Public Domain.)**

The victory over England had come at great cost to the new government. With triumph, however, came the spoils, one of which was the eternal problem of rewarding those who had sacrificed on the battlefield to make it so. With limited financial resources and absent, as yet, a strong federal mechanism to replenish them, it was both necessary and logical to award those who served with the treasure it imagined it now had (in theory, at least) in abundance: land. Never mind that

Chapter 4   *Liquor, Lies, and Laissez Faire*

this ocean of land beyond the frontier was as yet unexplored and filled with hostile people not anxious to surrender it, promises for a patch of it could be made to veterans and substituted for a handful of gold or silver. In fact, the unsettled nature of the frontier only enhanced the enterprise and the appeal, portraying the opportunity to anxious and desperate pioneers as an adventure – a trek at the end of which would come the security and physiocratic bliss of a fruitful piece of land. All the government had to do was make this promise tangible, and they did so by issuing scrip that promised precisely that. It was beautiful in its simplicity. It was a destiny that seemed almost manifest.

In the more stable atmosphere that ensued with England's exit, land, thereafter, attained a new significance as a speculative commodity. Notwithstanding the abstract, Jeffersonian security it still represented to the otherwise property-less farmer, for the banker and speculator, land became fungible – a tradable asset they hoped would bear fruit in the capital markets as well. And it wasn't just individuals who attempted to capitalize on land in the new, post-revolutionary environment. Except for a 120-mile strip of land called the Western Reserve that ran along the shore of Lake Erie from the Pennsylvania border to what is now Sandusky, Connecticut, for example, gave up its claim to most of its western lands after the revolution. However, needing money to fund a school system, the State of Connecticut sold this remaining "Western Reserve" in 1796, relinquishing control to a group of fifty investors who called themselves the "Connecticut Land Company" for 40 cents an acre.[19] A surveying party was formed to survey the Western Reserve. Led by General Moses Cleaveland, its leader is remembered as the inspiration for that eponymous city (minus the letter "a").

The sale of the Moravian Settlement by Ancrum and Askin and the purchase of the state-owned Western Reserve by a syndicate of investors signaled a shift from a national to an individual animus in terms of expansion in the Michigan region and beyond. This is not to say that the new national government was not interested in extending its borders; it merely substituted what before had been the overt imperialism of foreign powers with the subtler and more efficient prospect of home-grown individual acquisition and aggrandizement. In this way the new government ingeniously recruited ordinary people for its own national agenda.

Armed with newly minted notions conflating freedom and democracy with capitalism, humble farmers and entrepreneurs would fulfill the government's mandate by simply following their own ambitions for wealth and land. It had only, as Adam Smith urged, to step aside and turn the citizenry loose in order to realize their mutually beneficial goals in this new, free, post-mercantilist environment. The new laissez faire outlook was indeed an engine of economic progress. By definition it did not, however, set ethical limits. Lacking this distinction, it was likewise indifferent to the shadowy boundary between mere success and cupidity. It ignored that place where an honest desire for economic security devolves into a mindless quest for more and more wealth for its own sake by whatever means possible.

It is instructive at this point to recall the state of the fur trade at the time of Britain's exit, militarily, from North America. Their departure created a power vacuum the infant government was not quite able to fill. With the regions along the eastern seaboard stripped of their fur bearing animals by a century of predation, fur traders of every stripe, both corporate and individual, trained their sights on the vast, unexplored frontier west of the Great Lakes and northward to the Canadian border in the Pacific Northwest. Historian Ida Johnson eloquently captures the post-revolutionary atmosphere of the fur trade and the major players involved in it:

Chapter 4

Liquor, Lies, and Laissez Faire

"It was a period of systematic wholesale exploitation of the furred creatures of her forests by factory, fur-trading company, and independent trader, without thought of reservation or preservation; a period when the dollar took the place of the beaver pelt, salaries the place of the credit system, and the Yankee the place of the Briton; a period when her splendid forest and Indian hunting grounds were transformed into pastures and farms, and her trading rendezvous became the sites of villages and thriving cities; when the trapper and hunter and savage gave way to the man with the axe and the hoe, the lumberman, the merchant, and the farmer."[20]

Out of weakness, in part, and out of sympathy to an extent, the new government effectively conceded much of the economic activity on the frontier to two groups. The first were the powerful fur trading companies. The most prominent was the Northwest Company, a consortium of Canadian fur traders bent on capturing and maintaining a lock on all the furs in those areas of North America as yet unclaimed and unsettled by the new nation. In opposition to this powerful foreign interest was the equally forbidding American Fur Trading Company, an entity conceived, funded, and controlled by immigrant turned mogul, John Jacob Astor.

Through a combination of sheer economic prowess and careful manipulation of federal and local authorities, Astor positioned himself to inherit the huge block of trade held by the English once, or so he hoped, they were finally evicted from the continent. The other dominant players in the fur trade were the rogue, independent traders – unscrupulous and unaligned – who (like many of their predecessors, the *coeurier de bois*) swore no sovereign allegiance and were not accountable to any corporate entity or master. These independent traders, says Johnson, "…cared little for law, justice, and a square deal, so long as the main purpose of their undertaking prospered."[21] Despite their contempt for the Native Americans with whom they dealt, independent traders also realized that they needed the Indians to supply them with pelts. To facilitate these exchanges and to ensure the most profitable (and exploitive) outcomes, Indians were filled with "liberal quantities of liquor" before any business was transacted, thereby easily relieving "the savages" (through the fog of inebriation) of valuable furs, pelts often purchased for the price of a few worthless trinkets or, sadly, yet more liquor.

There was, in addition to the organized companies and rogue traders, a third player in the regional fur trade. Well aware of the near sociopathic indifference of the independent traders and corporate elements to the plight of the Indian, U.S. officials developed their own trading network to deal specifically with the Indians. They

John Jacob Astor. **(Painting by John Wesley Jarvis, 1825. National Portrait Gallery.)**

Chapter 4

Liquor, Lies, and Laissez Faire

appreciated, as did their English predecessors, the vital role the natives still played in the frontier economy. Not only did officials continue the very practical policy of subsidizing and funneling supplies to the Indians, they also professed a more magnanimous (and, frankly, half-hearted as we shall see) agenda by sheltering them, as best they could, from the greed and predation of independent and corporate traders. In 1796, Congress approved $50,000 in funds to purchase merchandise to be distributed to Indian tribes. The following year it "…granted the President the privilege of forming such establishments throughout the country for the purpose of carrying on trade with the various tribes."[22] Dubbed the "Factory System," those working for the new entity swore an oath not to use the system for private gain. In addition, they were forbidden to introduce alcohol of any kind into their transactions with the natives. The Indian population under jurisdiction of the government was divided into departments, each with its own head. The bureau was headed by the Superintendent of Indian Affairs. Department heads issued licenses to traders who were bonded and swore an oath to obey all rules and regulations. They were, unlike their profligate civilian counterparts, government employees.[23] Though well intentioned, the factory system exerted only tepid control over its private counterparts, injecting – or at least attempting to – an element of conscience and order into what was otherwise economic anarchy. Ultimately, as we shall see, it too succumbed to the same corruption that dominated the commercial fur trading sector.

The private sector, however, reigned supreme over the fur trade. Of the many personalities who shaped the history of Detroit, the Great Lakes, and the frontier all the way to the Pacific Northwest, John Jacob Astor's image looms large. Contrary to his reputation as the very model of honest self-industry and ambition, history shows the darker side of his business practices to be more consequential. To understand them and to paint a complete picture of Astor, one must separate history from hagiography, laying bare the distinction between mere wealth and how it is wielded.

For Astor, his riches became a cudgel – a weapon he used to bring competitors to heel, to buy influence, and to increase his fortune to the furthest limits for its own sake. Like all myths, Astor's legacy as the paragon of the self-made-man bears at least a grain of truth, drawn – much as the mundane feats of ancient heroes were inflated by poets and storytellers – from his humble beginnings as an immigrant who traversed the wilderness for furs, beating the skins with his own hands. But only a miniscule part of his fortune was gleaned from his personal efforts. Once his fortune swelled into the behemoth it became, his riches were great enough to buy the loyalty of an army of subordinates powerful and extensive enough to manipulate not just people, but the affairs of state as well. At that point, like many fortunes, his wealth took on a life of its own, regenerating effortlessly for Astor as though touched by Midas himself.

One must give Astor his due: he indeed came from humble beginnings. Accounts of his early life, however, differ. As Gustavus Myers recounts, eighteen-year-old

"But only a miniscule part of his fortune was gleaned from his personal efforts. Once his fortune swelled into the behemoth it became, his riches were great enough to buy the loyalty of an army of subordinates powerful and extensive enough to manipulate not just people, but the affairs of state as well. At that point, like many fortunes, his wealth took on a life of its own, regenerating effortlessly for Astor as though touched by Midas himself."

Chapter 4

Liquor, Lies, and Laissez Faire

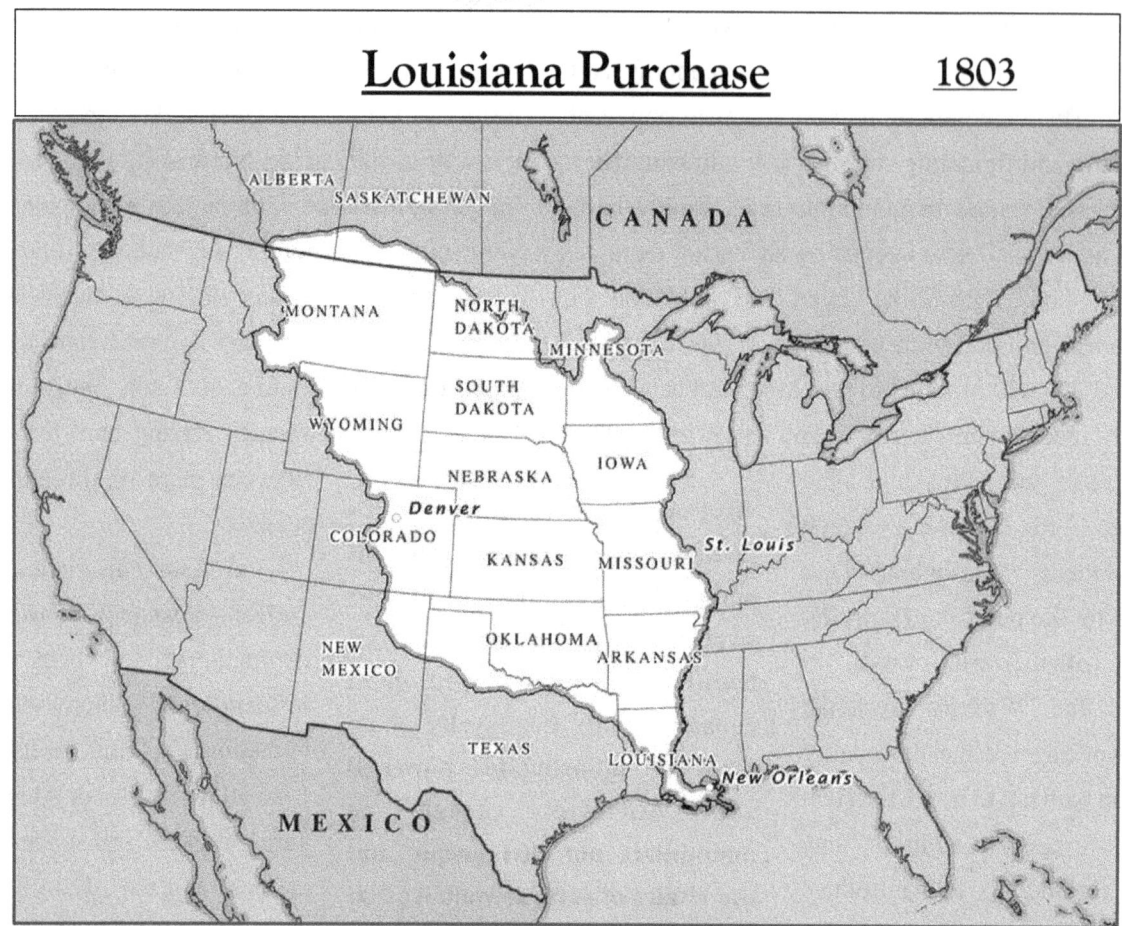

In part driven by then President Jefferson's physiocratic belief in the spiritual power of working the land and a desire to control the Mississippi River, the Louisiana Purchase opened up the vast mid-section of the continent, offering a potential haven for the impoverished and exploited masses cramped in the cities on the eastern seaboard. Never mind that this huge area was already inhabited by millions of Native Americans.

Astor made his way in 1781 from his birthplace in Waldorf, Germany to England where he stayed for two years helping his brother, George Peter Astor, sell musical instruments.[24] After two years, Astor left London and immigrated to New York. Here the story varies. One version has him apprenticed to one George Dietrich for whom he peddled cakes. Another has him taking a job beating furs for a New York merchant named Robert Browne; perhaps a more likely career path for the future czar of the North American fur trade. Here, according to Myers,[25] he had his first encounters with furs and the traders who brought them in. The eager young Astor absorbed all the lessons they were willing to share about furs and how best to acquire them.

Clearly, the root of Astor's fortune was furs. But one must realize that this part of his wealth played a mostly seminal role in his true money-making enterprises: business holdings that grew to span oceans through shipping and encompass huge swathes of urban and agrarian real estate at home. Much as one might like to attribute such aggregation to the mythical rubric of "hard work," in reality it represented the power of monopoly itself, a business model Astor cultivated

Chapter 4   *Liquor, Lies, and Laissez Faire*

assiduously and ruthlessly and one made no less venal by describing it as "vertical integration."

However one chooses to rhetorically scrub the practice, monopoly still involves the absolute control of production and distribution from source to sale. And again, to be fair, it is important to remember that in his time Astor's success and methods were generally a cause for celebration rather than reproach, his business practices different only in scale to businessmen of humbler means who, in the *laissez faire* spirit of the times, would have exploited the situation to the same extent had the opportunity presented itself. Thus, as Youngman suggests, the inevitable issue of Astor's greed and "wickedness" is perhaps better addressed within the larger context of a society that lionized such cupidity, offering the very fruits of monopoly and exploitation as proof of its legitimacy.[26]

While the ultimate object of our attention at this point is Astor's influence on the still important fur trading centers of Detroit, Michilimackinac, and Michigan in general, their importance can only be appreciated within the larger context of developments on the North American continent at the time, events which, since the early settlement of the continent, have resonated to conflicts, policy, and personalities at work in Europe. We therefore must remain at a distance from Michigan and focus on Europe where Napoleon Bonaparte was casting a long shadow at this time; so long, in fact, that it reached North America.

After 1801, Napoleon was desperately in need of cash to support his continuing aggression against other European powers; notably, England. He had always been eager to re-establish French power in North America and had secretly purchased the Louisiana Province from Spain a short time earlier. The U.S. government, under the newly elected Jefferson administration, was also interested in acquiring a foothold in this region, one that would give the U.S. access to the sea via New Orleans and lands lying along the Mississippi river to its mouth. For this, it offered the French two million dollars and was willing to up the ante to ten million.[27] Jefferson sent an additional envoy, James Monroe, to help clench the deal. Much to the envoys' surprise, however, the cash-strapped French offered a much grander proposition: the whole of the Louisiana Territory for fifteen million dollars. Despite his apprehension over spending such an immense sum for as yet unexplored wilderness, Jefferson closed the deal in April, 1803, thereby increasing the landmass of the new nation by 820,000 square miles.

"By virtue of its immense, unchallenged economic power operating with impunity in such a wild, unsettled environment, Astor's empire was (when it was not purchasing the government's complicity) effectively beyond the reach of any legal authority."

Whatever his moral shortcomings, Astor – forever an astute businessman – was keen to the economic potential of the pristine territory. Lewis and Clark's detailed accounts of their expedition down the Columbia River Basin from May 1804 to September 1806 told of an immense region rich with flora and fauna, all the way along its length until it emptied into the Pacific. It fired Astor's imagination: it was, he was sure, nestled among wilderness abundant with furs and filled with gullible native tribes as yet unseduced by his baubles and booze. But, at the time he gave corporate expression to this vision by founding his American Fur Company in 1808, his goal to exploit the resources of the Pacific Northwest was thwarted by the existence of the Northwest Fur Company. It too was eager to capitalize on the northwestern wilderness for Canadian and English interests and enjoyed the advantage of posts already established along the Fraser River, a tributary feeding the Columbia from the

Chapter 4 *Liquor, Lies, and Laissez Faire*

north.[28] His efforts, therefore, were relegated to the (albeit, still massive) region bounded by the Rocky Mountains to the west, the Mississippi River to the east, and the Great Lakes to the North, an area where the Northwest Company also menaced Astor's ambitions. Despite this impediment, Astor nevertheless forged ahead and established a post at the mouth of the Columbia in 1811, naming it, of course, Astoria.

Astoria was vital to Astor's plans, not just as a clearing house for goods moving down the Columbia from the interior, but as an international entrepot for his already prodigious trade with Europe and, particularly, China. Throughout his life, Astor had an uncanny ability to profit from others' misfortune. The commercial advantage he gleaned from the conflict in Europe between 1789 and 1815 is just one example. Because of the Napoleonic conflict, markets in France and Germany were off limits to English merchants. Astor, on the other hand, conducted regular business in London, Gothenburg, Hamburg and Havre.[29] In addition, unlike British and Canadian merchants who were barred from the Chinese trade (they were required instead to funnel all business through the East India Company) Astor could trade virtually without restrictions and he exploited this advantage with a vengeance.[30] From his trading posts along the Columbia and Missouri rivers, Astor generated and moved goods along a vast network, one that stretched from the interior of North America to the Pacific coast, Alaska, Europe, and China. The cycle generated immense profits despite the menacing presence of his Canadian and English detractors:

> "But most of the furs would be taken to the Columbia River and transported to a post or fort at or near its mouth. Vessels would carry goods and supplies to the Columbia; thence they would be taken to the interior. These vessels would also furnish supplies to the Russians in Alaska and would trade with the Indians on the Northwest Pacific Coast. These vessels would then return to the Columbia to obtain supplies of furs procured there and transported from the interior. These vessels would then sail to China, sell their cargoes of furs, purchase Chinese teas and merchandise and return to New York. Thus, three profits would result from each trip."[31]

War, however, proved to be a fickle benefactor for Astor. While his coffers grew enormously from exploiting the situation created by the Napoleonic conflict, his blindness to the clouds of war forming closer to home cost him the temporary loss of Astoria to British/Canadian interests in 1812. After 1808, Astor had expended much energy and money lobbying the government for their support (and protection) in exploiting the new wilderness and gaining control of trade on the Pacific coast. The best way to do this, he believed, was to legitimize his efforts under the umbrella of a government charter. For help in this endeavor, he petitioned such influential political figures as DeWitt Clinton, Thomas Jefferson, and Albert Gallatin without success.[32] In 1810, he funded two expeditions; one by land followed the route of Lewis and Clark and sought to demonstrate the feasibility of trade via the Missouri; the other, by sea, followed the well-established route around Cape Horn, "…sailed north and then west to the Hawaiian Islands for resupply, and finally to the Columbia River." According to the plan, the two parties would meet and establish the outpost at Astoria.[33]

In 1811, his coveted coastal trading post was finally established at immense cost, especially to the overland expedition which suffered great hardships at the hands of both the environment and hostile natives on the way. But Astor's control of the new post was

Chapter 4   *Liquor, Lies, and Laissez Faire*

Thomas Hart Benton

Astor's great wealth bought great influence, both in the nation's capitol and in the newly developing territory of Michigan. In Washington, Senator Thomas Hart Benton (MO.) - a fervid expansionist - gave legislative expression to Astor's agenda. In Michigan, Governor Lewis Cass - an unrepentant racist – set about clearing the land, not just of trees, but of the indigenous Indian population as well.

Lewis Cass

short-lived. A year after hostilities with England broke out in 1812, the British moved quickly, capturing Astoria and running the Union Jack up the flagpole on December 12, 1813. Unlike their American counterparts, their desire to support Canadian and English fur interests in the region was unequivocal, ordering Captain James Milligan of HMS Phoebe to "…render every assistance in your power to the British traders from Canada, and to destroy and, if possible, totally annihilate any settlements which the Americans may have formed…"[34] However, in one of the great ironies that often occur from war (and more evidence, perhaps, of Astor's luck) the British victory proved pyrrhic. The town was returned to American control by the Treaty of Ghent in December of 1814, the agreement that ended the conflict and further eroded English influence.

Astor indeed profited at times from good luck, but the bulk of his wealth was amassed by very purposeful business practices that bordered more on sociopathy than economy, exchanges which – far from the balanced Smithian model of mutual self-interest – celebrated and pursued self-aggrandizement at the expense of others. While the newly acquired territory was, technically, under the control of the U.S. government, its sovereignty was in name only. By virtue of its immense, unchallenged economic power operating with impunity in such a wild, unsettled environment, Astor's empire was (when it was not purchasing the government's complicity) effectively beyond the reach of any legal authority. "That it employed both force and fraud," Myers reminds us "and entirely ignored all laws enacted by Congress, is as clear as daylight from the Government reports of that period."[35]

The Bureau of Indian Affairs was a particular object of disrespect and a case in point. Astor and his agents treated that bureau's injunctions on the sale and use of alcohol with Indians contemptuously and indifferently. Penning a frustrated letter to then Secretary of War James Barbour from his post as Commander at Detroit in August, 1825, Colonel Snelling bemoaned the presence of alcohol in the face of government bans:

Chapter 4   *Liquor, Lies, and Laissez Faire*

"He who has the most whiskey carries off the most furs," wrote Snelling, and that the variables of that equation usually figured to Astor's advantage is evidenced by the fact that, as Snelling recounts, "…during that year there had been delivered by contract to an agent of Astor's North American Fur Company, at Mackinac…3,300 gallons of whisky and 2,500 gallons of high wines."[36]

Alcohol's use as a grease for crooked transactions played a foundational role in Astor's money-making machine. That was only the beginning of the process, one that did not involve the exchange of money for the furs in question, but rather cheap goods: "… especially woolens, made by underpaid adult and child labor in England and America…For these goods the Indians were charged one-half again or more what each article cost after paying all expenses of transportation."[37] The predation didn't stop there. "…for every dollar in cheap merchandise that the Astor company exchanged for furs, the company received $1.25 or $1.50 in fur values, undoubtedly by the trader's low trick of short weighing."[38] And to imagine that Astor's rapacity was visited only on Native Americans would be mistaken. His own employees bore the weight of his cupidity as well. In this pre-industrial time, before the confinement and misery of the factories and workhouses finally drove workers to organize, the simple urge to survive provided Astor with a pool of employees willing to promote his agenda on the frontier. So desperate – or, perhaps, in some cases so reprobate – were Astor's agents that swindling, blackmail, and even murder was merely a part of a day's work. Certainly, one imagines, the pay must have been quite good to purchase such Faustian loyalty. This was, as Myer reminds us, not the case:

"For all this what was their pay? It was the trifling sum of $130 for the ten or eleven months. But this was not paid in money. The poor wretches who gave up their labor, and often their health and lives, for Astor were themselves robbed…Payment was nearly always made in merchandise, which was sold at exorbitant prices. Everything that they needed they had to buy at Astor's stores; by the time they had bought a year's supplies they not only had nothing coming to them, but they were often actually in debt to Astor."[39]

If furs provided the foundation for Astor's fortune, real estate built the palace above it, and one wonders, as Youngman has: "…could any appreciable proportion of the $18,000,000 worth of real estate owned by him at the time of his death be held to represent a return due to his personal efficiency?"[40] Lest one imagine that such princely acquisition came by any other method than through harvesting the misery of others need only consider the fact that his holdings increased the most during the War of 1812 and the Panic of 1837, both times when the market was heavy with the low-hanging fruit of mortgage foreclosures and bankruptcies.[41] Clearly, Astor deserves less his reputation as the archetype of self-industry than as a puppet master, working the strings of his vast network from the security and safety of his New York headquarters.

As history so often shows, great wealth buys great influence. Not only was Astor an example of this eternal relationship, in his time he was, arguably, the very definition of it. Astor was never held to account for any legal or moral transgressions, a feat that would hardly have been possible for anyone of more average means, and an accomplishment that presupposes the protection of powerful allies in consequential positions. One was his own lawyer, Thomas Hart Benton who, conveniently, was also one of the leaders in Congress.

Chapter 4   *Liquor, Lies, and Laissez Faire*

Benton – a vocal proponent of westward expansion – introduced legislation not just helpful to Astor, but actually written by the mogul himself. But there were many corners in Astor's empire and the one of most concern to this narrative includes Michigan, Detroit, and the whole Great Lakes region. Astor's point man in this region was Lewis Cass, another figure who, like Anthony Wayne and Andrew Jackson, rose out of military conflict (in his case, the War of 1812) to become a political mover and shaker. In addition to his prodigious influence in his many roles as governor of Michigan, Secretary of War, Ambassador to France, and presidential candidate, historical evidence offers hints of a sub-rosa collaboration with Astor as well.

Cass's personality and character can be gleaned from his attitude toward two groups: Native Americans and the British. Whether his condescending paternalism toward the Indians exceeded his utter contempt for the British is debatable. Nevertheless, the fact remains that Cass's long career was shaped in response to these two factions. After a privileged upbringing that included an education at New Hampshire's exclusive Philips Exeter Academy, his aristocratic pedigree was further padded with law school and admission to the bar at the tender age of twenty. Cass thereupon joined the Ohio militia with the rank of colonel. At the outset of the 1812 war, fate placed him under the command of General William Hull (then, also, Governor of Michigan) whose retreat from Canada and subsequent surrender of Detroit to the British in August of 1812 darkened an otherwise distinguished military career with accusations of cowardice and capitulation.[42] As a member of Hull's contingent, Cass carried the burden of this shame by association, and the experience only sharpened his enmity toward the British who he continued to battle after the war in different ways. His military experience proved more positive as he rose through the ranks of General William Henry Harrison's army, earning ultimately the title of brigadier-general. As a one of the commanders in Harrison's defeat of the British and their Indian ally, Tecumseh, at the Battle of the Thames in October, 1813, Cass no doubt came away with a sense of personal empowerment and national destiny. These feelings shaped his actions in every public position he held thereafter, especially, as we shall see, during his eighteen-year tenure as Governor of the Michigan territory.[43]

At age thirty-one, in 1813, Cass was appointed governor of the Michigan Territory. It was a place unlike the state we know today. Cass's Michigan seemed an inhospitable wilderness, a conclusion supported by a report two years later in 1815 by Surveyor General Edward Tiffin who deemed the region generally unfit for cultivation and settlement. The government had ordered the survey with the idea of doling out parcels to veterans as a reward for service in the war. Tiffin, however, demurred after his work, characterizing the proposed "bounty lands" in his report as "…a poor barren, sandy land, on which scarcely any vegetation grows, except very small scrubby oaks."[44] As the new governor, Cass faced not only persistently encroaching British traders and, as he regarded them, recalcitrant Indians, his new domain had serious image problems as well. The first order of business, then, was to recast the state in a more positive image, something that would offer a second more positive look at the area Tiffin dismissed in his report to President Monroe as

> "…when it came to the Indian tribes whose presence compromised his plans for the settlement of Michigan, Cass had the power to effect change on the ground quickly and more effectively by systematically dispossessing his native nemesis through the use of treaties."

Chapter 4

Liquor, Lies, and Laissez Faire

filled with "swamps and lakes." Convinced Tiffin's conclusions about the state were unduly dismissive, Cass began with a public yet friendly rejection of his findings, pointing out the strategic value of the Great Lakes in moving goods around the region, and drawing on his military experience to emphasize the need for roads through Michigan to aid in national defense. In addition, he lobbied authorities in the federal government to fund another expedition to explore the Michigan region.[45]

Cass's timing was good. James Monroe had been elected two years earlier and his fervent desire to enhance the U.S.'s international reputation was matched by his ambition to expand the country westward. Monroe's new Secretary of War, John C. Calhoun (himself a crusader for states' rights, a slaveholder who ardently defended the slave economy, and a proponent of the concept of nullification)[46] shared these sentiments. He felt such an expedition would serve his own goal of enhancing the country's defenses and defense infrastructure. In January, 1820, Calhoun granted permission for the exploration, stipulating only that the budget for the undertaking not exceed a thousand dollars, the amount normally granted to Cass in his capacity as Superintendent of Indian affairs for the Michigan Territory.[47] Given the expedition's importance to him, Cass was not wont to trust anyone other than himself to head it. His personal involvement inspired the expedition's secretary, James Doty, to characterize Cass's participation in the "…general dangers and fatigues of the operations of that arduous campaign" as "a pledge of that decision of character, foresight, and personal courage, so necessary in the safe conduct of the voyage before us."[48]

On May 20th, 1820, Cass and forty-two men pushed off from the docks at Detroit in four large canoes. Among the expedition's avowed purposes, three were manifest: 1) to recast the Michigan Territory as a place more favorable to cultivation and settlement than previously thought; 2) to search for the source of the Mississippi River; and 3) to assess the existing relationships of the various Indian tribes with British traders and any attendant threat of British influence via their native allies. As to the first goal, Doty's chronicle of the journey, written in the effusive prose of the day, describes the picturesque and settled shoreline, peppering his narrative with geological observations no doubt supplied by another member of the party, Henry Schoolcraft, a trained mineralogist and geologist. "The banks of the river present a compact settlement along the American shore," writes Doty. "…Everything bears the appearance of having been long settled and well improved. The soil is a deep, black alluvion, of the richest quality…"[49]

The expedition did not, however, succeed in finding the source of the Mississippi, although it did add a wealth of information as to its characteristics and tributaries. Finally, in fulfilling the third purported aim of the mission – to assess the existing, post-war relationship between British traders and the Indian tribes – Doty's narrative takes on a darker aspect, echoing the then popular view of the Indian character as morally bereft and intellectually inferior. Bemoaning the French missionaries' failure to firmly Christianize the natives, he muses:

> "The savage mind," "habituated to sloth, is not easily roused into a taste of moral activity, and is not at once capable of embracing and understanding the sublime truths and doctrines of the evangelical law."[50]

These two themes –a potentially fecund Michigan, and culturally forsaken savages – occur like a leitmotif throughout Doty's journal of the 124-day mission which returned to Detroit on September 20th, 1820.

Chapter 4 *Liquor, Lies, and Laissez Faire*

In terms of improving Michigan's image, Schoolcraft's 1821 account of the journey (a tome with the stuffy title, "A Narrative Journal of Travels Through the Northwestern Regions...to the Sources of the Mississippi Rivers,") proved an immediate hit, selling out completely in Albany where it was published. It even enjoyed an audience in parts of Europe. Eastern newspapers like the New York Spectator began publishing articles depicting Michigan as both a place ideal for emigrants anxious to put down roots in rich soil, and the promise of lake-born commerce that would, it was argued, be quicker and cheaper than the laborious movement of goods over land and through the canal system. In addition, the expedition revealed continued and extensive collaboration between British traders and natives, a troubling fact for Secretary of Defense Calhoun who found the evidence compelling enough to press for more outposts throughout the Great Lakes region and roads to connect them; something Cass himself was keen to see happen. Though much of the historic record around and just after Cass's journey is salutary and positive, a close examination of his published writings as a supposed "authority" on Indian culture and affairs reveals a man whose racism is cloaked in a false mantel of paternalism and feigned concern for the native peoples in his charge.

In his struggle to rid the region of the last vestige of British influence, Cass wielded the powerful tool of legislation, aided in this endeavor by none other than John Jacob Astor who, in April, 1816, convinced Congress to pass a law forbidding foreigners to trade with Indians within the U.S. territories without permission, something that proved difficult to enforce.[52][53] On the other hand, when it came to the Indian tribes whose presence compromised his plans for the settlement of Michigan, Cass had the power to effect change on the ground quickly and more effectively by systematically dispossessing his native nemesis through the use of treaties. As the historical record shows, these agreements incrementally evicted the tribes from Michigan, forcibly pushing them west, vacating the land and thereby making it available for expansion. While the treaties themselves are a fact of history, the circumstances surrounding many of them are not as obvious, and speak to a contradiction between Cass's purportedly pristine image and the hypocrisy displayed in his actual dealings with the tribes. In his role as chief Indian affairs agent for the Michigan territories, Cass's official writings outwardly inveigh against the dangers of alcohol to the Indian population, condemning, in word at least, the use of alcohol as a tool to dull their senses and facilitate what can only charitably be regarded as "commerce" with them. His own journals, however, and those of his subordinates, betray the sad truth: many of the treaties were consummated at the end of a drunken stupor, intentionally induced by Cass and his agents.

> **"Peters recounts that in 1819, Cass – upon encountering resistance from Saginaw Chippewas to a treaty he was presenting – apparently decided that the impediment was not the terms of the treaty, but rather the sobriety of his native interlocutors.**

Evidence of the moral chasm between Cass's public condemnation of alcohol and his private use of it as a tool in his dealings with the Indians is not hard to find upon close examination of the historical record. Peters recounts that in 1819, Cass – upon encountering resistance from Saginaw Chippewas to a treaty he was presenting – apparently decided that the impediment was not the terms of the treaty, but rather the sobriety of his native interlocutors. In a letter to Secretary of War Calhoun, Cass admitted that in the face of the Indians' resistance to his terms, he was compelled to use a different strategy, writing that "some considerations

Chapter 4

Liquor, Lies, and Laissez Faire

more obvious in its effects & more congenial to their habits was necessary to insure a successful termination to their negotiations."[54] While it is possible that Indians or someone else introduced liquor into the proceedings, evidence of Cass's complicity is betrayed in his supply order of 31, August, 1819. Included among Cass's list for the usual complement of foodstuffs and practical necessities, directed to the storekeeper of the Detroit Military District, is a request for "Whiskey" – 20 barrels, in fact, which, by Cass's own reckoning "[= 662 gallons.];"[55] an amount far exceeding the needs of himself and his entourage.

From his own time to the present, Cass has been celebrated as an authority on Indians and their way of life. Yet, in addition to the de facto evidence of his contempt for Native Americans enshrined in the list of confiscatory treaties he helped broker over a period of twenty-three years at various levels of government, two documents – one penned three years into his governorship in 1816, the other, twenty years later in 1836 in his capacity as Secretary of War under Andrew Jackson – indicate an attitude, formed early on, filled with racist generalizations of Indian temperament and a blanket condemnation of the Indians' failure to embrace

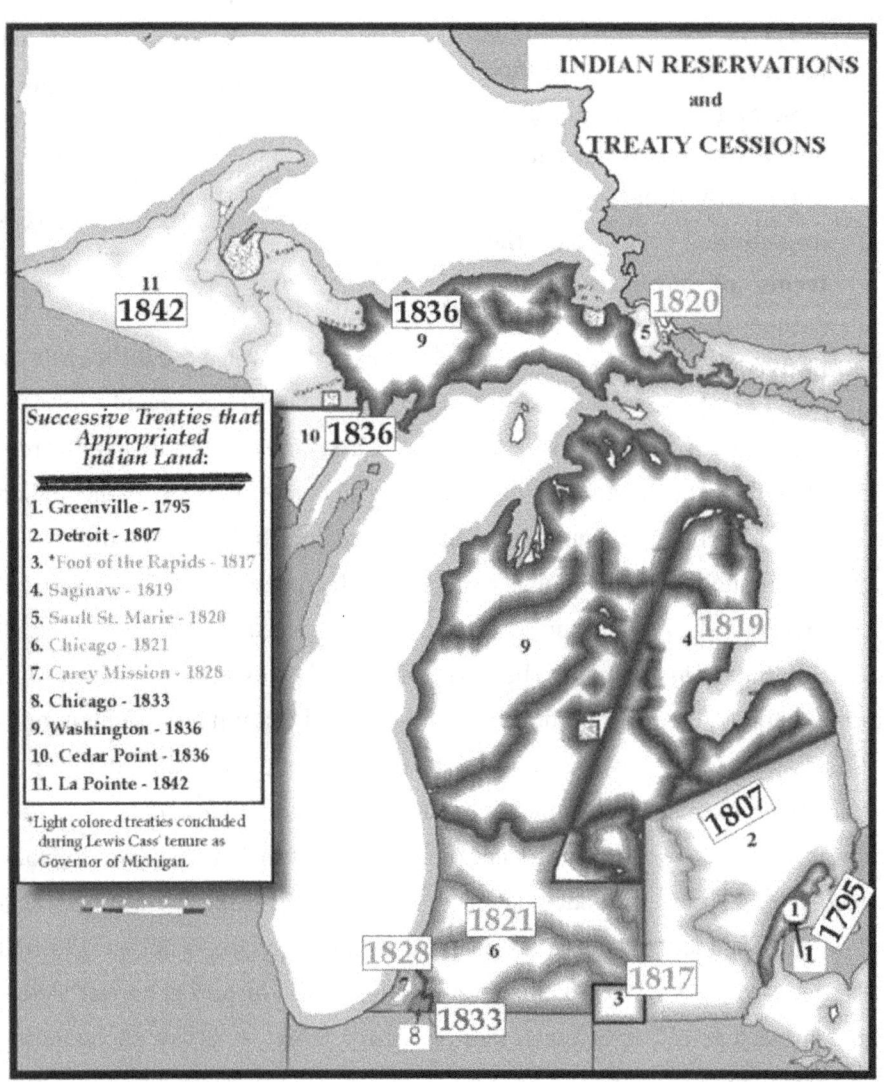

Of the eleven treaties concluded with Michigan's Indian tribes between 1795 and 1842, six were created during Lewis Cass's tenure as governor. Cass, who never disabused himself of the notion that Indians were naturally lazy and ignorant, felt that those Indians who could not be Christianized should be forcibly removed or done away with.

Chapter 4 *Liquor, Lies, and Laissez Faire*

the white man's reverence for property and husbandry. In an early reflection on the subject dated November 29, 1816 and sent to Calhoun, the young governor gave first formal expression to his conclusions that Indians were impulsive, irredeemably lazy, incapable of conceptual thinking and, because they could not be led like sheep into the white Christian fold, were therefore worthy of eviction and even extermination if the country's manifest destiny to subdue the continent demanded it.

If the two documents – one penned in 1816, the other in 1830 – illustrate anything, it is that Cass's attitude toward the native population never evolved over that entire fourteen-year period, carrying the same festering prejudices he had harbored as a novice into the twilight of his political career. In fact, in laying the two documents side by side, their sentiment is so similar that one might justifiably believe they were conceived days rather than decades apart.

For example, in the first, titled "Concerning a System for the Regulation of Indian Affairs," Cass sets the pervasive and enduring tone for all his Indian policies to come. Uppermost in this document is the professed (and, as he was to conclude early on, futile) need to redeem the savages; to, as Cass puts it "…reclaim them, as far as practicable, from the savage situation in which they are placed."[56] In the later document, an article published in a January, 1830 edition of the North American Review with the more direct and honest title, "Removal of the Indians," Cass once again recalls the failure of previous attempts by Catholic missionaries to subdue the Indian spirit, bemoaning "…insurmountable obstacles in the habits or temperament of the Indians, which has heretofore prevented and yet prevents , the success of these labors."[57] In each document, the struggle between lazy native and industrious white culture is filtered through Cass's own unyielding, philosophical prism: a bigoted, Calvinist Christian orthodoxy that equates progress with agriculture, and regards the Indian's preference for the freedom of a hunter-gatherer lifestyle as indicative of a flawed character and a fallen moral state. Totally possessed, therefore, of the white Christian notion that land is worthless unless it broken with a plow or a source of land rents, the next step in the chain of logic is to dismiss those who do not embrace the moral superiority of agriculture and business, insisting, therefore, that they (Native Americans) thereby forfeit their claim to the land. In a nineteenth century "If such people will usurp more territory than they can subdue and cultivate, they have no right to complain, if a nation of cultivators put in a claim for part."[58]

But, as history shows, settlers and politicians were not interested in just "part" or with sharing in any sense of word. Most politicians, including luminaries like John Calhoun and Andrew Jackson, were equally invested in this mindset that used Christian dogma to rationalize what amounted to ethnic cleansing. The principle tool for effecting this self-righteous confiscation was the treaty, a legal mechanism embodying European concepts of property that incrementally ate up Indian land in neat parcels codified by surveys, all the while pushing the Indian tribes further and further west. For his part, Cass's contribution to this effort – that is, systematically evicting Native Americans from the Michigan territory – was legion, and is expressed visually and effectively in the graphic above. As it illustrates, six of eleven major treaties that carved up the Michigan Territory between 1795 and 1842 were consummated during Cass's tenure as governor, a testament to his dogged determination to rid the region of what he regarded as its unworthy native occupants.

Surveys and the process of surveying itself was instrumental in appropriating Indian land. More specifically, it was a corruption of traditional surveying that helped confine and marginalize the Indian

Chapter 4 *Liquor, Lies, and Laissez Faire*

population on land deemed inhospitable to white settlers. The process was, for the most part, the same, using all the tools – such as a Vernier compass to calculate angles and a Gunter's chain to measure degrees – to carve the territory into a grid. But, as always, the devil was in the details, and although the tools and the procedures were the same, the grid was purposefully and artfully constructed to effect an ugly outcome: eviction and segregation of the native population. As Pearce recounts, surveyors accomplished this in a number of ways:

> "Their field notes were kept separately from their regular township and range field books. Section lines were not to be run through the reservations, nor were interior corners to be marked. The result was a township grid punctured by large "holes" ranging from a few acres to tens of thousands of acres in size."(59)

Whereas surveying under regular circumstances would have been conducted in a more disinterested manner and overseen by the surveyor general, the mission to empty Michigan land and render it marketable and conducive for settlement was apparently, for Cass, too important to be left entirely to such low-level functionaries. "Deputy surveyors," therefore, "received their instructions for how to proceed not from the surveyor general, but from the governor of Michigan Territory."(60) This was, of course, Lewis Cass. One example of the governor's tendentious instructions can be gleaned from a letter to James McCloskey, one of the surveyors. In this letter, Cass counsels McCloskey to be mindful, when drawing boundaries, of the course of the Raisin River. "I am informed," Cass writes, "that there are falls upon the River near the Wyandot improvements which will hereafter furnish valuable sites for mills. If you will run the lines, if possible, in such a manner as to exclude these falls from the Indian reservations."(61)

Between 1795 and 1856, a total of forty treaties created numerous reservations in this fashion, effectively emptying the Upper Great Lakes of its native peoples and evicting the resident Neshnabe and Wyandot tribes in the Lower Peninsula. With each territorial sacrifice, the natives who surrendered the territory held the false hope that the agreement finally afforded them security, peace, and an end to the conflict with the encroaching white settlers. They were, as Pearce suggests, mistaken:

> "For Native Peoples, the reservation boundaries signified where dispossession began and ended – the space through which the Public Land Survey would not run and thus where the Euro-American settlement could not penetrate. For the United States, the reservation boundaries signified temporary placeholders for a group of people perceived to be incompatible with white civilization and the settlement of the Old Northwest."(62)

The Indians' experience in Michigan was just part of a national campaign – couched in a mantel of feigned concern for the Indians' welfare and fully supported by the U.S. government – to rid the existing frontier west of the eastern seaboard of its indigenous people. In the south, cotton proved to be a difficult and insatiable crop, requiring ever more land. No wonder, then, that southern planters like Calhoun were at the forefront of westward expansion and, in turn, the anti-Indian agenda. President Jackson led the effort, using treaties

"Most politicians, including luminaries like John Calhoun and Andrew Jackson, were equally invested in this mindset that used Christian dogma to rationalize what amounted to ethnic cleansing."

Chapter 4 *Liquor, Lies, and Laissez Faire*

as a tool for appropriation just as Cass had done to the Northwest. Jackson's efforts were much wider and focused on the tribes in the south. Between 1814 and 1824, in whatever post he held, Jackson brokered treaties with the southern Indians, enabling whites to take over "…three fourths of Alabama and Florida, one-third of Tennessee, one-fifth of Georgia and Mississippi, and parts of Kentucky and North Carolina."[63] One example is the Battle of Horseshoe Bend in 1814 when he, along with a group of Cherokee allies whose allegiance he'd solicited with false promises of friendship, did battle with a larger, hostile Cherokee force. After swimming a river and successfully routing their Cherokee brethren, Jackson – then newly appointed treaty commissioner rewarded his Cherokee allies by brokering a treaty that effectively appropriated all Creek land, never distinguishing between friend or foe.[64]

Not every tribe resisted. Accepting the inevitability of white dominance, 17,000 Cherokees in Georgia, surrounded by 900,000 whites, gradually began to take on elements of white culture, learning trades like blacksmithing and carpentry and becoming owners of property. To facilitate this transition, their chief, Sequoyah, even developed a written form of their native language. This effort extended to government as well with the Cherokees creating a Legislative Council in imitation of the white government and even publishing

---

The National Park Service officially recounts the Indians' experience on the Trail of Tears:

> Families were separated-the elderly and ill forced out at gunpoint - people given only moments to collect cherished possessions. White looters followed, ransacking homesteads as Cherokees were led away.
>
> Three groups left in the summer, traveling from present-day Chattanooga by rail, boat, and wagon, primarily on the Water Route. But river levels were too low for navigation; one group, traveling overland in Arkansas, suffered three to five deaths each day due to illness and drought. Fifteen thousand captives still awaited removal. Crowding, poor sanitation, and drought made them miserable. Many died. The Cherokees asked to postpone removal until the fall, and to voluntarily remove themselves. The delay was granted, provided they remain in internment camps until travel resumed.
>
> By November, 12 groups of 1,000 each were trudging 800 miles overland to the west. The last party, including Chief Ross, went by water. Now, heavy autumn rains and hundreds of wagons on the muddy route made roads impassable; little grazing and game could be found to supplement meager rations.
>
> Two-thirds of the ill-equipped Cherokees were trapped between the ice-bound Ohio and Mississippi Rivers during January. As one survivor recalled, " Long time we travel on way to new land. People feel bad when they leave Old Nation. Womens cry and make sad wails. Children cry and many men cry...but they say nothing and just put heads down and keep on go towards West. Many days pass and people die very much."

Chapter 4   *Liquor, Lies, and Laissez Faire*

their own newspaper.[64] But southern plantation and mill owners were too hungry for land and refused to take "yes" for an answer from the Indians. In fact, Jackson, now president, turned the Indians' sincere gestures of adaptation against them, misrepresenting their efforts as a threatening attempt to establish a separate government. In 1829, Jackson introduced an Indian removal bill.[65] This false specter of a threatening, independent Indian state within the U.S. became a pretext for eviction, framed by Jackson as an ultimatum to accept the power of the state government where they reside, or move west of the Mississippi. The bulk of support for the bill came from the south; there was little support in the north where, in some corners, the Indians' right to stay was even championed. The southern interests prevailed in a close vote, giving an early glimpse of sectional rivalries that would devolve decades later into a bloody, protracted civil war.

Coincidentally, and probably not accidentally, the Indian Removal Act was approved in 1830, the same year gold was discovered on Cherokee land. Even before the tribe's eviction, Georgia held lotteries to give away land and gold rights to territory still occupied by the Cherokee. Midas' power proved too compelling. The bill was targeted at Cherokees and four other tribes in Georgia (the Chickasaws, Choctaws, Creeks, and Seminoles). Exploiting the advantage of their cultural adaptation, the Cherokees wisely opted for legal rather than futile, violent resistance and brought suit against the bill. The case made its way all the way to the Supreme Court where it won a judgment in its favor.

It was, however, a pyrrhic victory. After hearing of the court's decision, President Jackson remained unimpressed. In an overt gesture of contempt for the concept of judicial review, Jackson quipped "[Chief Justice] John Marshall has made his decision; let him enforce it now if he can."[66] Sensing, perhaps, the futility of resistance, a small minority of Cherokees resigned themselves to moving, but only if compensated. This cohort represented just a fraction of the other 15,000 Cherokees who rejected removal. This did not stop the government from negotiating only with the willing minority, presenting them with a deal in December, 1835 called the Treaty of New Echota, a place in Georgia of the same name. Only 300 to 500 came to the signing, and only twenty actually put their names to the agreement which ceded all Cherokee lands east of the Mississippi for five million dollars and the promise of a secure homeland west of the Mississippi. The signatories were neither officials of the Cherokee nation, nor authorized to represent the majority. Nevertheless, advocates for Indian removal were undaunted by questions of the treaty's legitimacy and, by May, 1836, had shepherded the treaty through Congress where it was ratified by just one vote.[67] The natives' fate was sealed. Despite their legal success at the highest levels of justice, they would be forced upon the same miserable and deadly trek already begun five years earlier by the Choctaws in Georgia who, not having the legal option the Cherokees would employ later in 1836, were forced from their homes. Zinn describes the conditions the Indians experienced on what became known as the "Trail of Tears."

The Choctaws began their long trek in wagons, on horseback, and on foot. Though they were to be accompanied by the army, the job was turned over to private contractors who, Zinn recounts, "...charged the government as much as possible, gave [s.i.c.] and the Indians as little as possible."[68] The winter of the first migration was one of the coldest recorded and many died of pneumonia; in summer, an outbreak of cholera pruned their ranks, killing hundreds. The seven thousand Choctaws remaining in Georgia refused to go, preferring to live under white domination than perish on the Trail. The Cherokees thought they would be able to remain as well and stayed put. They were mistaken.

Chapter 4

Liquor, Lies, and Laissez Faire

Once President Jackson had thumbed his nose at the court's decision over the legality of the Treaty of New Echota with impunity, it was open season on the Cherokee Nation in Georgia. In May, 1838 Federal and state militias began rounding up Cherokee families and confining them to a stockade. This was only the first step. In at least a meager gesture of remorse and remembrance in hindsight

Some drank stagnant water and succumbed to disease. One survivor told how his father got sick and died; then, his mother; then, one by one, his five brothers and sisters. "One each day. Then all are gone."

By March 1839, all survivors had arrived in the west. No one knows how many died throughout the ordeal, but the trip was especially hard on infants, children, and the elderly. Missionary doctor Elizur Butler, who accompanied the Cherokees, estimated that over 4,000 died-nearly a fifth of the Cherokee population."[69]

Citing figures from Michael Paul Rogin's definitive 1991 study of Jackson's presidency and psychology titled Fathers and Children, Zinn tallies up the effective and brutal result of the ethnic cleansing that resulted from Jackson's Indian removal policy:

> "In 1790, there were 3,900,000 Americans, and most of the lived within 50 miles of the Atlantic Ocean. By 1830, there were 13 million Americans, and by 1840, 4,500,000 had crossed the Appalachian Mountains into the Mississippi Valley – that huge expanse of land crisscrossed by rivers flowing into the Mississippi from east and west. In 1820, 120,000 Indians lived east of the Mississippi. By 1844, fewer than 30,000 were left. Most of them were forced to migrate westward."[70]

Settlers, speculators, and any other segment of the dominant white culture were now free to move in and realize their "manifest destiny." Given the government's systematic removal agenda championed by Jackson, it is clear that Cass's contribution to this effort in Michigan was just a small part of this undertaking. More importantly, his efforts were not merely a matter of sympathy, but federal policy. The Indian "problem" was solved.

The ethnic cleansing of the Cherokee nation by the U.S. Army, 1838. **(Painting by Robert Lindneux, 1942. Public Domain.)**

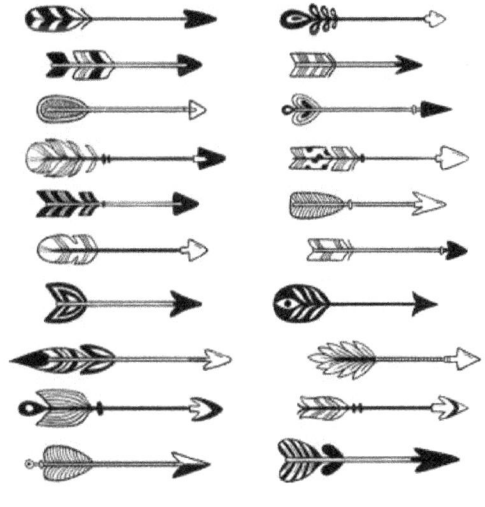

Chapter 4

Liquor, Lies, and Laissez Faire

Chapter 5

Wood, Water and Fire
After the Beaver

Though by 1787 the little village of Detroit had earned a position in the still unsettled Great Lakes region as a permanent and resilient outpost with its own identity, the lands beckoning around and beyond the western shore of Lake Michigan were as yet ill-defined, roiling with the energy and ambition of thousands of land-hungry immigrants who slogged their way to them as best they could by river and rough-hewn road. One thing was certain: the beaver was, for the most part, gone. After a century of predation, of surrendering its soft coat to the sartorial whims of European hat and coat makers, it had been hunted to near extinction, making the ultimate sacrifice for humankind's commerce. Meanwhile, until the final British exit, defiant Indian tribes maintained a stubborn resistance against the onslaught of white migration from the east, their inevitable marginalization and expulsion staved off, for the time being at least, by British arms and support. Only a year before, Daniel Shays and his rag-tag rebels had so shaken the Continental Congress that many close to the seat of power began lobbying for a new constitution, one grounded in a federal authority with the power to put down such rebellious rabble and collect money to compensate those who had invested in the revolution. Before the confederation's demise, however, the otherwise ineffective body realized that the newly acquired land-mass to the west comprising present day Ohio, Indiana, Illinois, Michigan, Wisconsin, and Minnesota should be admitted to statehood in an orderly process, shepherded by provisions codified in what has come to be called the Northwest Ordinance.

In the ensuing scramble to satisfy these pre-conditions for statehood, the boundaries of territorial Michigan and the governmental entity called Wayne County alternately expanded and contracted, their jurisdictions overlapping like a series of Venn diagrams. Between the introduction of the Northwest Ordinance in 1787 and Michigan's admission to statehood some fifty years later in 1837, it had been drawn and re-drawn, shaped by regional competition and internal forces both personal and political. The two charts on the following page compare visually the interaction and varying forms Michigan Territory and Wayne County took between those years.

As one would expect, such conflicting and fluid geographical boundaries made governance likewise uncertain. The region had only just thrown off the last vestige of British influence in 1796, so the perceived seat of authority was as yet also unclear, oscillating between the newly minted but nebulous federal authority and a local cabal comprised of governors, judges, and territorial secretaries whose interests were not always guided by a desire to serve the greater good or a strict adherence to the rule of law. But wasn't that precisely the problem? After all, the rule of law didn't quite exist yet. So, wasn't it the duty of any dedicated local or regional official to proactively craft legislation in the interest of their constituents and create a stable framework for governance to serve everyone's interest? Not so much, as the record shows.

On June 30, 1805, Michigan Territory was officially voted into being. However, laws

Maps adapted from sources in *A History of Michigan* by Silas Farmer[1]

governing the new territory did not issue from selected representative bodies as one would expect given the model offered by the recently crafted federal constitution. Instead, responsibility for the territory was put in the hands of four men, one of whom was William Hull, an ill-fated military man/politician who was appointed governor and Indian agent by President Jefferson in March, 1805,

Chapter 5 *Wood, Water and Fire: After the Beaver*

just months before it became a territory. To help him, four judges were appointed to territorial Michigan's Supreme Court: Augustus Woodward, Frederick Bates, and John Griffin were acquaintances of Thomas Jefferson and were appointed by him personally. James Witherell, on the other hand, was appointed by James Madison, then Secretary of State to Jefferson. While it is impossible to tell if, from the very beginning of their tenure, their motives and integrity were above reproach, the historical record shows that their actions, at least, earned something less than approval from their constituents in the course of their service.

Their first act as a legislative body, drafted on July 9th, 1805, was the creation of a state seal and the adoption of a body of laws already crafted by Judge Woodward known as the "Woodward Code." From this benign and blameless beginning, the group began a descent into increasingly self-serving legislative chicanery, crafting laws not in the interest of their constituents, but for their own aggrandizement. They met for business not, as one might imagine, in august surroundings with marble pillars and wood paneling but, rather, in the more hospitable atmosphere of Richard Smyth's tavern on Woodward Avenue near Woodbridge street.[2] While the group's original mandate had been to

Appointed by Jefferson to administer affairs in the new territory of Michigan, these four men – Hull as governor, the other three as judges – quickly devolved into a cabal dedicated only to self-aggrandizement. Affairs of state were conducted in the august chambers of Smythe's Tavern on Woodward Ave. Tired of the corruption, residents of Michigan begged Jefferson to rid them of the tainted leaders. **(Bates: artist unknown. Public domain; Woodward: Caricature. Woodward Ave. Action Assoc. & Nat'l Scenic Byways Program; Hull: Artist, Rembrandt Peale (1778-1860). Colonial Society of Massachusetts.)**

Chapter 5   *Wood, Water and Fire: After the Beaver*

"'adopt' such of the laws of the original thirteen States as they deemed best suited to the needs of the Territory,"[3] their actions began early on to reflect something quite at odds with the public good. By September, 1808, they had deviated so far from their purported mandate that, in desperation, Michigan inhabitants crafted a letter to President Jefferson, begging him to free them from the whimsical abuses of this group of men. It went unheeded. The extent of their duplicity is summed up in this passage from the inhabitants' letter to the president:

> "They would parade the laws of the original States before them on the table, and cull letters from the laws of Maryland; syllables for the laws of Virginia, words from the laws of New York, sentences from the laws of Pennsylvania, verses from the laws of Kentucky, and chapters from the laws of Connecticut."[4]

Though frustrated in their attempts to gain redress through more formal avenues, their cause was, nevertheless, not lost. Their banner was picked up by a journalist by the name of John Gentle who, in a series of scathing articles appearing in the Philadelphia Aurora and the Pittsburgh Gazette in 1807, chronicled in detail the corruption and abuse of power emanating routinely from Governor Hull and his judicial partners. In his articles, Gentle not only took the group to task for their whimsical and self-serving legislative conjuring, he shined a light on their "…court proceedings and actions as a Land Board, and intimated that they were controlling for their own pecuniary advantage the lots of in the city and the Ten-Thousand-Acre Tract, and that the Detroit Bank was a scheme designed to further the same object."[5] Gentle even insinuated that Hull had secretly been aiding Aaron Burr[6][7][8] whose scheme to conquer and install himself as suzerain of Louisiana and other western lands set him on a course to infamy and charges of treason. But a region already teeming with settlers was an impediment to Hull and the judges who, Gentle asserts, were keen to reap the rewards of ever-increasing land speculation for themselves. Part of Hull's attempt to de-populate the region, Gentle claims, even included false warnings of impending Indian attacks, hoping the settlers would flee in fear.

Detroit did not have a newspaper of its own at the time, so Gentle's inflammatory articles were "hung out during the day from the houses, guarded by arms, and taken in at night."[9] The targets of Mr. Gentle's ire did not, unsurprisingly, suffer these accusations quietly. Not only did Governor Hull, Judge Woodward and his judicial brethren denounce Gentle's exposés as libelous, their indignation took a menacing turn when some of their friends attacked the journalist in his home. Fortunately, Gentle enjoyed the protection of prominent businessman, Joseph Campau. Included among Gentle's chronicle of gubernatorial and judicial malfeasance was the astounding assertion, not by him directly, that the Great Fire of June 11, 1805 – which reduced Detroit to a heap of ashes within a few hours – was perhaps no accident.

The official chronicle of the fire puts the blame on a careless worker in the employ of baker, John Harvey. Some accounts actually attribute the mishap to Harvey himself. On the morning of the fire, one or the other was harnessing a horse in a stable on St. Anne's Street and, after either carelessly knocking the ashes from the pipe, or simply not noticing that an errant glowing ember had settled in the hay, the structure was quickly engulfed in flame. Ironically, Detroit lawmakers had, for some time, been keenly aware of the danger of fire to a town filled with wooden structures and had only recently passed regulations requiring

Chapter 5　　　　　　　　　　*Wood, Water and Fire: After the Beaver*

maintenance of chimneys and the need for buckets in each household. The community even had a pump which, drawing its water slowly from the river, proved unequal to the massive conflagration. Inhabitants formed a bucket brigade in double lines, but to no avail. Residents began piling their belongings into boats and furniture and household items were piled on the river banks.

Except for Fort Lernoult, which was still intact above the city and a stone warehouse by the river, the devastation was total. Thankfully, no lives were lost. Because the fire occurred in the warmth of summer, the weather was at least hospitable to the newly dispossessed. Yet, as in many tragedies of this sort, the finest and the worst of human nature was set in motion. Whereas the country folk rose to the occasion, offering what materials they could to their urban counterparts without demand for repayment until such time as their unfortunate residents were back on their feet, many felt that local purveyors of lumber were viewing the situation through less altruistic eyes.

In a letter to President Madison in September, 1805 (two months after the fire), Governor Hull gave voice to the suspicions of some Detroit citizens who, having recently negotiated some preliminary contracts with the local lumber interests to supply the town's building needs before the fire, were beginning to suspect that pyromania might have been part of the lumbermen's business plans. The motive was certainly there, Hull implies, for after all: "Contracts had been previously made for all the lumber at the mills,

Joseph Campau – from a portrait by Alvah Bradish (1856)

and which could be sawed this season, which was a novel arrangement in this country."(10)

But there was plenty of paranoia to go around regarding the cause of the fire; and, perhaps, the motive. Fingers pointed everywhere, including at Governor Hull himself and the judges who, it was charged, had showed up suspiciously soon after the fire in order to take control of a situation which could have been adequately handled by local officials. Whereas Gentle reports that the Governor and judges came the very next day after the fire, in his letter to Madison, Hull maintains he did not arrive until early September, a full two months after the fire. No matter what the time frame, their arrival becomes more suspect not so much by the time as by their actions immediately upon arrival. For his part, Hull issued a proclamation on September 4th, 1805 "…forbidding all person, on pain of fine and imprisonment, to cut any timber in the St. Clair pinery…."

This led Gentle to question the Governor's motives. Was it, he mused, a sincere attempt to forestall a wholesale exploitation of the desperate citizens or "…was it because he purposed to prevent, as he did prevent, the people from building on their old lots in order to secure the adoption of a new and really better plan?"(11) Though on its face this concern for planning might seem a blameless and even worthy approach, the resulting arrangement of streets and selective platting arising from their plans betrayed uglier ambitions and reinforced the suspicions of Detroit's citizens that Hull and the judges were once again engaged in self-serving business as usual. Ignoring provisions passed in the previous articles of corporation passed in 1802 forbidding such unilateral actions, in September, 1806 the group passed an Act overriding these provisions and, within three months, were actively involved in reconfiguring Detroit's

Chapter 5   *Wood, Water and Fire: After the Beaver*

Artist's rendering of the Great Fire of Detroit, 1805, which completely destroyed the city. Probably as viewed from nearby Fort Lernoult. Blame for the fire has historically gone to baker, John Harvey or a careless employee. However, credible evidence exists linking the blaze to corrupt officials anxious to corner the local lumber market. **(Detroit Historical Society)**

streets and real estate to suit their own schemes. As Gentle recounts:

> "Some time in the month of December following, the Governor and Judges were committing some depredations upon the streets of the new town, entirely blocking up one, laying it out in lots, and disposing of them at an enormous price, to the great damage of the settlers; and removing another street about fifty feet, on purpose to make the bank form the corner of the two streets, and enlarge the avenue to the governor's mansion, to the great damage of the principal range of houses in the new town."[12]

So entrenched was the influence of Hull and the Judges that they remained an implacable force in the life in Detroit until 1812 when, shaken only by the power of another war with Britain, their grip was finally loosened; but only temporarily. For Governor Hull, on the other hand, the war would prove to be his undoing. William Hull's path to the Governorship of the Michigan Territory included honorable service in the Revolutionary conflict, one that earned him the rank of general. Notwithstanding the cloud of suspicion hanging thereafter over his political activity, it was, ultimately, his military role in the surrender of Detroit without a fight on August 6th, 1812 to British General Brock that earned him his infamous reputation.

Though the Treaty of Paris had officially ended hostilities with Britain in 1783, British ships continued to harass and detain American vessels on the pretense of looking for deserters. When the British ship Leopold commandeered an American vessel called the Chesapeake as it lay in harbor off the coast of Virginia, the U.S. government had had enough. President Madison ordered all British vessels away from the U.S. coast. England ignored the order, and Congress declared war on June 18, 1812. On July 12, General Hull crossed the Detroit river to Sandwich (present day Windsor, Ontario) with a force of around two thousand men. This force far outnumbered the British detachment quartered at Fort Malden eighteen miles away, a

Chapter 5   *Wood, Water and Fire: After the Beaver*

detachment headed by Colonel Henry Procter. In an act of hesitation that perplexed many in his ranks and has been the subject of much speculation to this day, Hull remained at a distance from Malden for a month without exploiting his obvious tactical advantage. This was enough time for the Governor of Upper Canada, General Isaac Brock, to rush to Sandwich where he assembled a force of seven-hundred troops and six-hundred Indian allies led by the charismatic chief, Tecumseh. Rather than confronting Brock and his inferior forces, Hull once again puzzled those in his charge by retreating back across the river to Detroit.[13]

Brock, on the other hand, was not indecisive. He wasted no time and, within a week, crossed the river and marched on Detroit. Even with the enemy at his very doorstep, Hull once again did not engage the invading British force. Mysteriously, something other than mere bravery seemed to embolden Brock. "So satisfied, apparently," Farmer recounts, "was Brock that he would not be attacked that he rode several hundred yards ahead of his troops."[14] This was puzzling and a source of great frustration for the troops which included the Fourth Regiment under Colonel Miller, and volunteers from the Ohio and Michigan militia:

> "At this time, Hull had an opportunity to repulse General Brock…The high bluff then existing at that point afforded an excellent and commanding position. Colonel Anderson subsequently told C.C. Trowbridge that he 'had his fuse ready, and by one discharge could have blown Brock's close column to pieces; but instead, he received a preemptory order from Hull not to fire.'"[15]

By noon, the indignity finally came to an end. With nary a shot fired their way, British forces marched into the fort after seven hours of what could hardly be called a battle. The Americans marched out. After striking the colors, the British raised the Union Jack over Detroit. With his victory, Brock hit the jackpot. In the surrender, General Hull turned over about two-thousand men, forty barrels of powder, four-hundred rounds of twenty-four-pound shot, one hundred thousand ball cartridges, twenty-four thousand stands of arms, thirty-five iron and eight brass cannons, and a large supply of provisions.[16] The Michigan and Ohio volunteers were released. Many of the Army regulars were transferred to Montreal, Quebec, and Halifax. Hull, on the other hand, was permitted to return to his home in Massachusetts where, after a trial for treason and cowardice, was found guilty and sentenced to be shot. His sentence, however, was commuted by President Madison whereupon he was forced to endure the more prolonged stigma of disgrace and dishonor.[17]

The motives for Hull's capitulation have, since the event, been a source of historical speculation. Certain testimony from Hull's trial points to collaboration with the British in the surrender of Detroit. While the facts are clear, they do little to illuminate the reasons behind his behavior, leaving the issues of cowardice, complicity, and corruption open to debate.

Whatever the verdict on Hull's shortcomings, his demise opened the door for Lewis Cass who assumed the governorship on October 29th, 1813. Though Cass's own tenure and character has been the source of volumes, he at least displayed a genuine desire to promote Michigan at a time when it was viewed generally as a meritless backwater. Making no initial attempts to reform the corrupt legislative process, he assumed Hull's place at the table with the same cabal of judges, even creating his own version of territorial laws in 1816 called the "Cass Code." This situation was finally rectified when, after more petitions to the federal

Chapter 5   *Wood, Water and Fire: After the Beaver*

government, the Judiciary Committee of Congress ordered a change in Michigan's legislative procedure on January 24, 1823. By order of the committee, the power of the Michigan judiciary (and thereby, the power of the judges) was to be divorced from the legislative process which was to be assumed instead by the governor and a legislative body called "The Council of the Territory," its eighteen members to be elected by the citizenry. This transfer became official on March 3, 1823.[18] This structural fix proved enduring, serving the territory until its admission to statehood in 1836.

With much of the distraction posed by legislative intrigues laid to rest by the changes in Michigan's government to a more representative body, Governor Cass threw himself into the task of refurbishing Michigan's image. In the years before it became a state, Cass pressed his agenda to transform Michigan into a magnet for settlement on a number of fronts. As mentioned above, the survey was an integral part of this vision, laying down a fictive grid-work pattern across the otherwise wild terrain in neat parcels to be sold, donated, or appropriated in the interest of the state.

Then there was the expedition headed by Cass, chronicled by Henry Schoolcraft, and marketed to easterners stuck in cramped cities offering little or no opportunity. Statehood certainly brought a new sense of legitimacy and increased Michigan's appeal, but there was an even more compelling and concrete reason for making tracks to Michigan:

accessibility. Completed in 1825, the Erie Canal realized the dream of a waterway linking the east coast of the U.S. with the Great Lakes. What before had involved a nightmare combination of river travel and portage over land became a mere five-day journey on the 364-mile canal that linked New York and the Hudson River with the Great Lakes.[19]

Cass's writings and performance in his roles as military man, governor, and Indian agent beg, for some, many questions as to his character and motivation. Did his paternalistic treatment of Native Americans mask a deep-seated bigotry and racism? Was his eagerness to develop Michigan a sincere product of his gubernatorial duties, or a manifestation of his own self-interest? While these may forever be the stuff of history, one thing is certain: Cass was a masterful salesman. By the time the Erie Canal was opened for business, Cass had done much to refurbish Michigan's image as a worthless no-man's land. Indeed, he and Schoolcraft had re-invented the soon-to-be state as the "pleasant peninsula," touting its agreeable climate, its soil, and its proximity to the Great Lakes, control of which were vital both to commerce and defense. Now pacified, publicized, and sectioned into a grid-work pattern of townships that would be the template for its orderly settlement (and exploitation) by the end of the century, it was time for the land of Michigan to make another sacrifice to human enterprise. Gorged, now, on the furry denizens of the region who had once called its dense, beautiful forests

Surrender of Detroit –Painting by John C.H. Forster in *Invasion of Canada Before the War of 1812*. **(James Lorimer Ltd., 2011)**

Chapter 5 *Wood, Water and Fire: After the Beaver*

"home," Cass and his successors proffered the trees themselves, offering the ancient pines as the next commodity on the menu for hungry settlers in need of a plot to till, and restless lumbermen anxious for a new harvest, having already stripped the forests of Maine and New York of their finest trees.

To be fair, human settlement could not have occurred without some sort of logging and clearing of forests, and the Great Lakes region was no exception. As proof, copper axe heads and digging tools dating as far back as 3,000 B.C. are among the items excavated at sites along the shores of Lake Michigan in Wisconsin and Minnesota and around Upper Michigan at sites along Lake Superior. This "Old Copper Culture," as it is called, lasted about 2,000 years, cold-forging copper tools and ornaments without the use of smelting or casting.[20] In addition, Iroquois and Huron fortifications and dwellings were made of wood, while many Anishinabeg tribes like the Potawatomi and the Cherokee intentionally set portions of the woods ablaze in order to increase deer habitat.[21] But all these encroachments were limited and based on use. Though natives would clear an area for settlement, it was only one big enough to fulfill their needs. Once they moved on, they surrendered the spot to the forest once again, to be regenerated and overtaken with foliage. Early settlers, like the French and some of their English and European successors, continued this practice, thereby leaving, quite unwittingly, a minimal environmental footprint.

For later arrivals to Michigan, however, development was not nearly so far-sighted. Absent the present sense of urgency bestowed on our own modern consciousness by an awareness of dwindling natural resources and human effect on climate, or the traditional reverence for nature implicit in Native American culture, footprints were simply the physical evidence of where one had been, or where one needed to go. Over the next hill – for the property-less outcasts from the coastal states or refugees from the turmoil and misery of places like Europe and Ireland – was an entire continent waiting to rescue them. Unmolested, like an unsuspecting pig or sheep fattened by millennia of sun and rain, the forests and prairies awaited the first fatal gashes of ax and plow. Far west, on the treeless plains, there were houses and fences to be built. "Prairies that came right up to the Lakes at Chicago held out their treeless arms and cried for succor from the rich green woods of Michigan."[22] Michigan complied.

At the beginning of the nineteenth century, when construction and woodworking tools were powered exclusively by hands and muscle, the rate at which construction lumber could be supplied was naturally constrained by the speed at which humans could work the wood from timber to two-by-four. Given the burgeoning demand for wood to be used in housing and mining at the time, carpenters and craftsmen relegated to hand tools needed a wood that was easily worked, retained its structural integrity and strength, and received a coat of paint or stain without issue. Ask any expert on wood for candidates, and the winner would probably be white pine. Its cooperative behavior in the woodshop is a direct result of its nature. In the wild, if left to compete unhindered with surrounding vegetation for a good length of time, – say, two or three hundred years – the white pine can grow to dominate the dark, primal environment at its base. As de Tocqueville described the pines during his sojourn in the "wilderness" of Saginaw in July, 1831, they:

> "…shot up into the sky. Forced to grow on a very circumscribed plot and almost entirely deprived of the sun's rays, each of these trees rises swiftly in its search for air

Chapter 5 *Wood, Water and Fire: After the Beaver*

and light. As straight as a ship's mast, it soon tops all its surroundings."(23)

Out of this primeval green sprang two-hundred-foot white pines whose trunks often reached up one hundred feet before sprouting any branches and whose diameter could span as much as five feet. This made for sturdy finished lumber with long, consistent grains that was soft enough to be cut, planed and pared easily. Because of the tree's natural girth, it yielded many dry cuts before encountering the inner pith, making it stable wood that would keep its shape. It was ideal for framing and for use in the inner panels of drawers and cabinets.(24)

Not just the white pine, but all the flora, the soil they grow in, the very topography of the region and the Great Lakes themselves are the legacy of glaciers. Over a period of 500,000 years the massive ice sheet alternately advanced and receded. At one time, two miles thick at its center and a quarter of a mile thick at its lead edge, "...it came down on that gentle landscape" as William Ashworth describes it, "like a gigantic battering ram or bulldozer." Existing soft soil and shale was "scooped out like ice cream" and deposited across an enormous area including present day Michigan, Ohio, Indiana, and Wisconsin.(25)

Carried in the glacier's lead edge were the richest soils and minerals, perfect for agriculture. These were deposited farther south in Ohio, Indiana, and southern Michigan. But the glaciers did their ponderous work with very uneven results, leaving Michigan with what are really three kinds

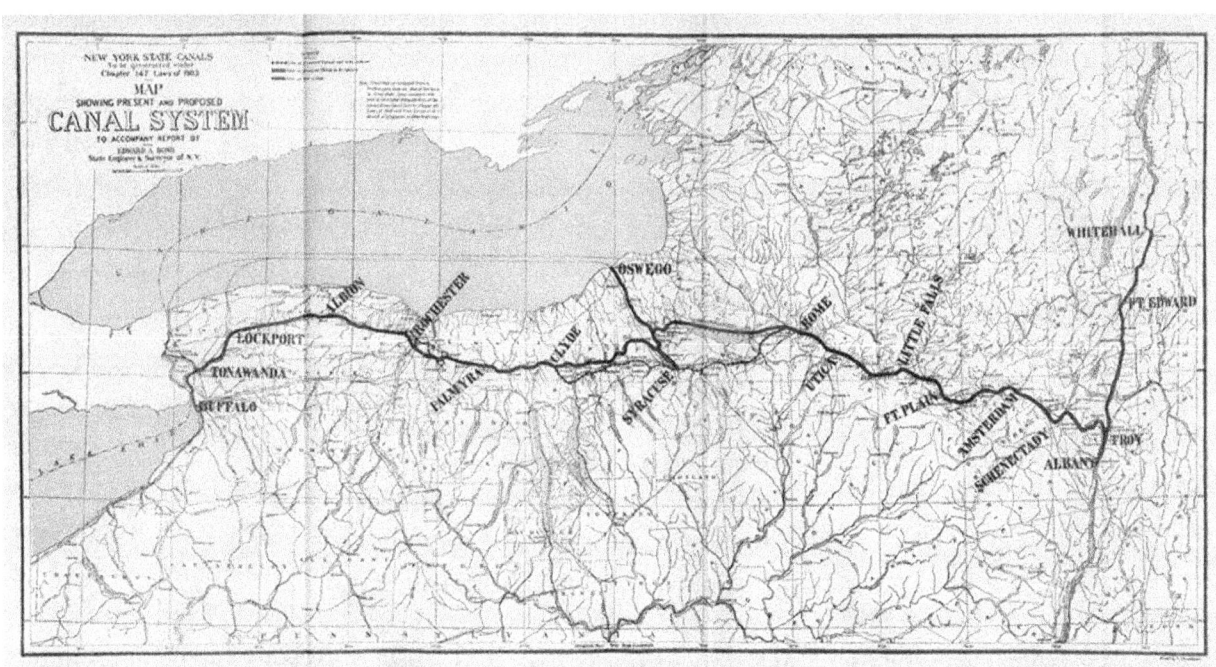

Begun in 1817 and completed in 1825, the Erie Canal made the grueling trip from New York, down the Hudson River to the Great Lakes easier and quicker. Allowing for continuous navigation, it cut the once two-week journey to just five days.

("Map showing Present and Proposed Canal System" -- from: Annual report of the State Engineer and Surveyor of the State of New York, for the fiscal year ending September 30, 1903. (Albany : Oliver A. Quayle, 1904) -- facing p. 60.)

Chapter 5　　　　　　　*Wood, Water and Fire: After the Beaver*

of the state is the "taiga," (also known as the "boreal") forest, a region of rugged trees like the spruce, hemlock, and fir that ring the northern shore of Lake Superior and run down the eastern shore of Lake Huron. The southern part of the region, the area around Lake Erie and the southern tip of Lake Michigan, received the most fertile soil. There, one finds a mixture of oak, ash, maple, and dogwood called the "hardwood forest." What would prove to be Michigan's bumper crop – the coveted white and red pines – grew in the sandy soil of its mid-section called the "transition forest," a vast area also called the "North Woods" that rung Lake Ontario, followed the north shore of Lake Erie, the south shore of Lake Superior, and inhabited much of the state's mid-section from Lake Michigan to Lake Huron.

Settlers who put down roots in the barren loam of Michigan's North Woods were often disappointed by a poor harvest and eventually quit the soil or moved to more productive areas. But eastern lumbermen, who came to be known as "timber beasts" were anxious to wring what dollars they could from any promisingly profitable woodland. They soon realized that in Michigan's North Woods was a veritable mother lode of "green gold." Hard upon the heels of the surveyors and their rattling chains, the timber beasts sent the agents who served as their eyes and ears. Known as "timber cruisers," it was their job to inspect a wooded tract previously purchased by the lumbermen and assess it, both for its potential yield, and the possible impediments to extracting the timber and shepherding it to market. Highly skilled observers, good cruisers were well-paid and sought after, often securing as much as a fourth of the proceeds from an analyzed tract. In addition, once they had identified a likely parcel, it was their job to officially lay claim to it for their boss at the nearest land office – a task in itself. An important part of the timber cruiser's skill set was being able to navigate and, at times, manipulate, the byzantine rules and often corrupt culture of the local government land office.

By the early 1830s, the land survey of much of Michigan had been done twice, once by the pessimistic Tiffin, and again by the indefatigable and optimistic Lewis Cass. At the same time, the federal government had also come into possession of (or, at least, laid claim to) an enormous swathe of as yet unsettled land west of the Mississippi River from the Louisiana Purchase of 1803. But the infant government was more interested in subduing the continent in the interest of manifest destiny than handling the annoying minutiae of managing millions of small parcels. A functioning bureaucracy had already been established in 1812 to do this. Called "The General Land Office," it was tasked with transferring all the federal land it did not want to be bothered with into the loving arms of settlers, speculators and business interests. These scions of the economic order would, or so the government thought, be guided by the zeitgeist à la Adam Smith and Horace Greely. Thus, would the sweet fruit of progress be wrung from these as-yet unproductive lands by the simple magic of *laissez-faire* capitalism. With this sure-fire strategy and such pure and noble intentions, what could possibly go wrong?

> **"Over the next hill – for the property-less outcasts from the coastal states or refugees from the turmoil and misery of places like Europe and Ireland – was an entire continent waiting to rescue them. Unmolested, like an unsuspecting pig or sheep fattened by millennia of sun and rain, the forests and prairies awaited the first fatal gashes of ax and plow."**

Chapter 5   *Wood, Water and Fire: After the Beaver*

Early cruisers evaluated Michigan's North Woods and predicted a bonanza beyond anyone's expectations. Initial estimates of the area's potential yield came in at around 150 billion board feet (a board foot being a standard unit of measure in the lumber industry based on a board one-foot long, one foot wide, and one-inch thick).[26] To put this in context, if this much lumber were sawn and stacked in a pile ten feet high and ten feet wide, it would stretch for 23,670 miles.[27] The only thing standing between a feeding frenzy and the slow and orderly exploitation of the state's coveted pines was the land office where, upon inspection by the cruiser and approval by the potential owner, a prospective parcel had to be registered and approved by the government before any ax or saw could be put to it. That was the theory, at least. This process, as one would expect in an era of slow communication, took a great deal of time: time enough for every sort of scheme and mischief in order to subvert it. One could acquire and harvest a wooded tract by any number of means ranging from legal, to shady, to outright theft. Much of the land was given away. Veterans, for example, were often rewarded for their service with military benefits warrants, a certificate entitling them to eighty acres. Transportation interests – railroad, canal, and road builders – received even greater largesse, often including rights of way encompassing huge tracts of land surrounding potential roads, tracks, and waterways. For those forced to purchase land outright, the government made that less painful as well by setting the price as early as 1820 at $1.25 per acre or less.[28]

Cupidity and ambition were, however, powerful incentives, luring timber hungry interests away from the straight and narrow path. Swindles and schemes to circumvent established procedures were legion. One common ploy was for lumbermen to collude prior to a public sale, only to bid up the price amongst each other once the sale was concluded. Bribery was also a reliable mechanism for facilitating a sale. At this point in time, federal enforcement was so toothless that the palms of elected officials and land agents could be greased with impunity. While the rules dictated that the sale go to the first cruiser to lay claim in the land office, frequently it went instead to those who had made

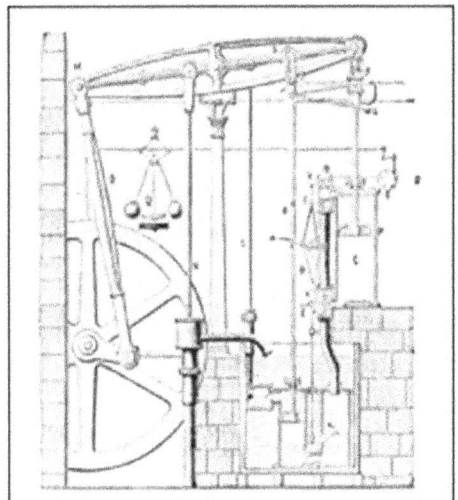

"Though a working steam pump, invented by Thomas Newcomen, had been in existence since 1712, it retained its original design flaw: that is, the need to cool the cylinder after each stroke. This made for frequent stalling and inefficient use of energy. After many trials, James Watt solved this problem by channeling the steam into a separate condenser so that the cylinder could remain constantly hot and, therefore, work more efficiently. After patenting his design in 1769, Watt added to its performance over the years with improvements in gearing and speed control. Immense energy for work, therefore, could be released in a consistent and controlled manner for many different tasks, energy more powerful and tireless than human hands could offer."

Chapter 5   *Wood, Water and Fire: After the Beaver*

"prior arrangements."(29) Timber beasts who managed to acquire parcels with plans to hold it for resale often became victims themselves. Unguarded tracts often fell prey to poachers. Owners had their own schemes to harvest beyond the potential of their legal tracts. One was the "round forty," or "rubber forty" whereby the foreman of a lumber camp was told to not only cut the timber on the property, but all the trees around it as well, then, claim ignorance when called on the "mistake."(30)

For workers relegated to manual tools, logs hundreds of feet long and two or more feet in diameter were unwieldy at best and dangerous at worst. Their great weight meant dragging them impossible in anything but the snow and ice of winter, so most logging in the early days before powered tools and conveyance was done during the winter months. However, even more important to the lumberman than the icy avenues of winter were the waterways where the logs could be stored immediately after being felled, then floated in Spring downriver to the mills for cutting and processing. Part of a cruiser's assessment, then, included an analysis of the water system surrounding the site and the prospective difficulty of shepherding the downed timber into the water for transportation to market.

Of all the Michigan rivers, one became the crown jewel, perfect for lumbering: The Saginaw. Slow moving and only twenty-five miles long, the Saginaw is, on its own, rather unremarkable. As the anchor waterway for the huge network of tributaries that make up the Saginaw watershed, it became a veritable turnpike for North Woods timber that would otherwise have had no way of moving out of camps located in the interior. Four tributaries – the Cass, Flint, Shiawassee and Titabawassee – empty into the Saginaw. In all, the network comprises nine-hundred miles of navigable waters and drains six-thousand square miles of land within the watershed.(31) In 1837, an unemployed timber beast by the name of Harvey Miller sailed up Lake Huron, turned into Saginaw Bay and "…took one look at the tall, straight pines with their thick boles marching off, row upon row, into the muted and misty forest distance and decided that he had found paradise."(32) But Miller employed the new, recently developed weapons in the lumberman's arsenal that would change the nature of logging and, sadly, accelerate the pace of the North Woods' destruction. Among these were the peavey hook (a long pole with a metal point and hook on the end for stabbing and rolling logs), the circular saw, and, most importantly, the steam-powered mill.(33)

Miller adapted a small steamboat engine to the task of sawing lumber and, in his mill on Saginaw Bay, revolutionized the process. But he was only able to produce about 2,000 board feet a day, often taking three days to process a single pine.(34) The speed was less important than the method which was, for the most part, mechanical. Logs were floated into the facility where they were cut, pared, and planed with monotonous precision by soulless metal blades animated by steam, free of the need for nourishment, wages, or a night's sleep. By virtue of its centralized location and its use of tools with little human interaction, Miller's sawmill was a harbinger of industrialization to come. It and other

> **"These scions of the economic order would, or so the government thought, be guided by the zeitgeist à la Adam Smith and Horace Greely. Thus, would the sweet fruit of progress be wrung from these as-yet unproductive lands by the simple magic of laissez-faire capitalism. With this sure-fire strategy and such pure and noble intentions, what could possibly go wrong?"**

Chapter 5   *Wood, Water and Fire: After the Beaver*

facilities like it would forever alter the nature of production and work. It would drive the first wedge into the already splintering relationship between capital and labor. But the success of Miller and other nascent manufacturers was built on engineering and mechanical developments decades in the making. In particular, Miller and his counterparts in the steam-powered flour mill or steamboat business stood on the shoulders of two men: Matthew Boulton and James Watt.

Though a working steam pump, invented by Thomas Newcomen, had been in existence since 1712, it retained its original design flaw: that is, the need to cool the cylinder after each stroke. This made for frequent stalling and inefficient use of energy. After many trials, James Watt solved this problem by channeling the steam into a separate condenser so that the cylinder could remain constantly hot and, therefore, work more efficiently. After patenting his design in 1769, Watt added to its performance over the years with improvements in gearing and speed control. Immense energy for work, therefore, could be released in a consistent and controlled manner for many different tasks, energy more powerful and tireless than human hands could offer.[35] But such a process demanded great precision in design and machining, skills that only highly trained machinists like Watt possessed. After recruiting or training these coveted workers, they were most effective, it was realized, if gathered under one roof and set to work in a production process that was both collaborative and methodical. British Industrialist Matthew Boulton was a proponent of this notion, both championing and subsidizing Watt's work. Thus, the age of the factory and the modern machine was born, a way of producing things that presupposed an army of engineers and mechanics not just to develop it, but to support it and keep it running efficiently.

Steam power had a profound effect on shipping as well, freeing it, in part, from the fickle and arbitrary winds. A full head of steam could propel the ship's pistons under most conditions, thereby assuring more reliable and predictable schedules for commerce and travel on the lakes. Yet, the lakes have always managed to exact their toll, claiming, for instance the mammoth Edmund Fitzgerald which went to the bottom of Lake Superior in November, 1975. Steamships were a mixed blessing, demanding absolute control for their operation. "But man, indeed, is ever the god of the steamer" writes nautical historian James Cooke Mills. "…it depends on him for its every movement; and without his guiding hand is but a helpless hulk upon the waste of waters."

Begun in 1855, the "Soo" Locks (at Sault St. Marie, Michigan) reconciles the previously unnavigable, 21-foot gap between Lake Superior and the Ste. Mary's River. **(Photo: U.S. Army Corp of Engineers)**

Whereas the majestic, multi-masted schooners that had plied the lake waters since La Salle's Griffon were usually undone by the raw, elemental power of a sudden gale, the potentially lethal combination of wood and fire on a steamer introduced a different, deadly and benign human

Chapter 5   *Wood, Water and Fire: After the Beaver*

element to sailing, one which, under unfortunate circumstances, could and often did send a boat to the bottom in a blazing inferno. The Great Lakes were the superhighway of the time upon which was conveyed the grain, the wood, and the ore gleaned from the western frontier. For many escaping far-flung and desperately poor hamlets in places like Ireland or Italy, it was the final watery leg of a long journey to the promised land. Fraught with risk and danger, many gambled on the passage and felt it worth the risk. Too often, fate won the toss:

"The ships, their holds packed stinking-tight with emigrants, traveled over the Lakes like fleas on a gigantic watery wolf, riding low. Some rode too low, going down with all aboard to colonize dark realms from which there was no returning. Some were cast onto reefs in storms; some burned like gigantic Egyptian pyres, sending up fountains of flame and showers of billowing sparks in the dark night to illuminate one last glimpse of water and sky for the screaming, living cordwood packed in their keels."[36]

Still, they came; wave after wave in increasingly greater numbers. Every year during the last half of the nineteenth century roughly three hundred ships were lost, most were carrying human cargo. If the Great Lakes were the superhighways, then the canals were the off-ramps. The great success of the Erie inspired other canals – artificial waterways that accommodated not only barges, but full-blown sailing vessels as well. There was the Welland, begun in 1829, whose eight huge locks lifted ships through a canal that not only connected Lake Erie with Lake Ontario, it rendered obsolete a passage that before required laborious portage around Niagara Falls.[37]

After twelve years and millions of yards of dirt moved by the back-breaking labor of immigrants from other countries, the Illinois-Michigan Canal was opened for business in 1848. Lifted in a single day through its fifteen locks were vessels carrying everything from wheat, to sugar, to lumber, linking Lake Michigan – via the burgeoning port of Chicago – with the Illinois and Mississippi

The first track, between Adrian, Michigan and Toledo, Ohio, was laid down by the Erie-Kalamazoo Railroad in 1833 and was pulled by horses. Four years, later, in 1837, the company deployed its first steam engine, depicted opposite.

As seen in "Railroading Forty-Five Years Ago" (1882) by C.P. Leland. **(Wikimedia Commons.)**

Chapter 5   *Wood, Water and Fire: After the Beaver*

Rivers.[38] By 1855, the network linking the Lakes would be nearly complete with the construction of what was called, initially, the Michigan State Canal, but would come to be known simply as the "Soo" locks after Sault Ste. Marie where it is located.[39] But these were just the water-related parts of the system. Farmers and businesses not located near a river were faced with the impediment of carting their goods to a sometimes far-away port for transport eastward – a problem eventually solved by the railroad.

When the first trunk lines were laid, they were regarded as merely complements to the primary lake and river transportation system. The idea, at first, was for railroads to extend the reach of the waterways by providing greater local access, not to compete with them.[40] And rightly so, as railroad technology was in its infancy. Each step forward came with much stumbling. Inventors grappled not only with the fundamental problems of how to mitigate the inevitable wear involved with iron wheels rolling constantly on iron track, but also with how to keep the cars from derailing in inclement weather. Engineers approached these challenges from a number of angles including tracks rolled at the foundry in myriad different shapes (to cut down on friction and forestall weakening and fracture), differing methods of affixing the rail to the bed, and, finally, reducing the weight of the cars and altering the gripping mechanisms on the wheel itself.[41] Much of this trial and error occurred well before the first steam engine was even introduced in Michigan or anywhere else America.

The first track to be laid in Michigan – put down in 1833 by the Erie and Kalamazoo Railroad – was a line that ran between Toledo and Adrian, pulled by horses. It was not until July, 1837 that the Erie and Kalamazoo put its first steam engine, The Adrian, into service on that line.[42] As long as the volatility of iron tracks, wheels, and cars remained factors, then weight, friction, and fracture would keep railroads from overtaking water routes as the predominant method of moving goods and people, despite the canals' obvious drawback of freezing in winter. Though the railroad offered the promise, theoretically, of metal was needed; something lighter yet resilient enough to stand up to the weight of ever-increasing loads without buckling under the stress or wearing out quickly. That something was steel, and its use in railroading was, it turns out, quite an unintended consequence.

"Michigan had offered up most of its furred creatures and was hard at work stripping the state of its coveted white pine and other trees, an orgy of destruction that would only exhaust itself at the beginning of the next century and come to be known as "The Big Cut," a moniker that does little to express the utter devastation wrought by it."

Before 1844, all the track used in America came from England, and most of it was iron. Up until the late 1840s, much of the research and development in track technology had taken place in England and was tested on English railways. Steel had, of course, existed for centuries. Its use, however, was confined to implements like knives and sabers. Though some imagined it might also be very useful in the form of railroad track, no one had, until 1844, sought to devise a method for forging it in the mass quantities needed for that purpose. In 1844, an American by the name of William Kelley began experimenting in Eddysville, Kentucky with a process involving "...refining and re-carbonizing melted cast iron with the use of an air blast."[43]

In 1854, inspired by a conversation with Napoleon III who expressed frustration at the excessive weight, weakness, and immobility of

Chapter 5   *Wood, Water and Fire: After the Beaver*

existing iron cannons, Henry Bessemer began experimenting with a process that would result in a metal cannon at once lighter, stronger and, therefore, more mobile and effective on the battlefield. Kelly and Bessemer, however, failed in their attempts, always ending up with metal that was simply "melted, de-siliconized and de-carbonized iron." The resulting metal needed to be re-carbonized in order to be turned into steel, and it was another Englishman by the name of Robert F. Mushet who solved the puzzle in 1857, thereby making the first Bessemer steel rail.[44] This was a pivotal moment in the history of railroading, allowing for lighter yet stronger rails, wheels, and engines. Bessemer forged steel made possible heavier loads run on tracks that would stand up to the weight and the wear. Railroads were now poised to claim their share of Great Lakes commerce long dominated by the waterways.

Unlike stubborn and brittle iron, steel would assume the shape of clever humans' ideas, ambitions, and indefatigable schemes for self-enrichment. Steel meant more of everything: steel hulls meant ships could carry more in their holds; steam engines – more and more reliable and powerful – could withstand greater stress and help ships ply the waters more easily, moved by the new steel screw-propellers; steel wheels meant railroad cars could be loaded with more logs and sent off to the mill, even if they weren't felled near a river on which to float them. And finally, steel made for stronger, longer bridges and buildings that reached for the sky. Michigan had offered up most of its furred creatures and was hard at work stripping the state of its coveted white pine and other trees, an orgy of destruction that would only exhaust itself at the beginning of the next century and come to be known as "The Big Cut," a moniker that does little to express the utter devastation wrought by it. Yes, and Michigan had other natural gifts to offer. There was copper, iron ore, and salt, each of which was extracted with the same enthusiasm as the unfortunate, doomed forests. For its part, Detroit – like the growing Gotham of Chicago rising up to the west – was becoming an important link in the commerce between the east and the west. Like Michigan and the new nation, Detroit businesses grew organically in response to commercial and technological developments in the region and beyond. There was ever more grain to mill, ships to build, ore to be smelted and myriad parts needed for the new machinery used to move things, cut things, and make other things. Detroit rose to the task, showing the first signs of the industrial behemoth it would one day become.

Before its heyday as the world center for automobile production, Detroit was known for its stoves. Above is an ad, circa January, 1900, for the Detroit's Garland Stove Co. **(Library of Congress.)**

Chapter 5 *Wood, Water and Fire: After the Beaver*

Chapter 6

The Not So Calm Before the Storm

To say the truth, though there are rich men, the class of rich men does not exist; these rich individuals have no feelings or purposes in common, no mutual traditions or mutual hopes; there are therefore members, but no body.

Alexis de Tocqueville – *Democracy in America*[1]

Coming, as he did, from the turmoil of a post-Napoleonic Europe violently reshaped by revolutionary forces, the young Alexis de Tocqueville was, perhaps, the perfect person to observe life in the infant nation as he found it at the beginning of his journey to the U.S. in 1831. Though his mission was simply to study the American penal system, he and his travelling companion, Gustave de Beaumont, could not resist broadening the scope of their observations from the ins and outs of mere incarceration to the emotional prison that kept much of the American populace enthralled at the time in an irrepressible quest for riches. Absent the impediments to social mobility found across the water and confronted with a rough, unhewn frontier beckoning with possibilities, the promise of riches was simply a part of the new egalitarian order where the only thing between a person and success was hard work and a good idea; or so it seemed. It was, as the epigram above suggests, the beguiling notion of a class-less rich – a country where wealth and success did not confer simultaneously the cudgel of political power. But that was, as de Tocqueville correctly predicted, a delusion.

The America de Tocqueville studied was pre-industrial, the same sort of post-mercantilist world around which Adam Smith had wrapped his own thoughts. Even in the face of emerging manufacturing, both men betray a reverence for the soil as the seat of true wealth and economic stability similar to physiocrats like Quesnay whose own attachment to agriculture, far from being merely sentimental, was based on a clear and clean connection between capital invested in the land, and the very real (and marketable) product of the harvest. "The capital employed in agriculture," says Smith "therefore, not only puts into motion a greater quantity of productive labour than any equal capital employed in manufactures…it adds a much greater value to the

Alexis de Tocqueville – Painting by Théodore Chassériau, 1850. **(In Versailles.)**

"Democracy in America" – Cover, 1st French edition, 1835

annual produce of the land and labour of the country, to the real wealth and revenue of its inhabitants."[2]

Writing a half-century later, de Tocqueville describes an American populace generally intolerant of old-world notions of a landed, privileged gentry as the center of societal power; that is, an aristocracy whose very idleness is a badge of esteem. Conversely, whereas labor in the Old World was anathema to the idle rich and regarded as a sign of inferior status, labor in egalitarian America was instead the great equalizer. "Equality of conditions not only ennobles the notion of labor in men's estimation, but it raises the notion of labor as a source of profit."[3] The American continent – only partially settled at this time – was a *tabula rasa,* just waiting for the hand of the ambitious to write on it, as yet undisturbed by those huge aggregations of wealth that would one day cast a shadow over it. "Labor is honorific in itself," de Tocqueville observes, "when it is undertaken at the sole bidding of ambition or of virtue."[4] Success was, for the time being at least, fluid in its promise. It would prove to be, however, not equally accessible as men like Vanderbilt, Gould, Carnegie, and Rockefeller would one day prove.

A mere month after de Tocqueville's moving visit to the primeval forest surrounding Saginaw, Michigan, Lewis Cass would end his tenure as that territory's governor. In his wake, he would leave a soon to be state whose indigenous people had, for the most part, been evicted and a successful publicity campaign that would open the door to the mass destruction of those very trees by hungry lumber interests and speculators. Likewise, in the same spirit of "development," the Erie and Kalamazoo Railroad would hack a corridor through Michigan's dense landscape and lay the first tracks between Kalamazoo and Erie two years later, in 1833.

> **"Land, therefore, is torn from the center of settled life and thrust, cheapened and debased, into the day to day haggling of the market with the other commodities, as volatile in value as pork bellies, grain, copper, and iron."**

Land in Michigan, as elsewhere throughout the frontier, became something quite different than the revered *terra firma* anchoring the settled culture of the old order. For those impatient for riches "... life is slipping away," muses de Tocqueville, "time is urgent – to what is he to turn? The cultivation of the ground promises an almost certain result to his exertions, but a slow one; men are not enriched by it without patience and toil."[5] For such a person, wheat or corn or any other crop is of little consequence compared to the market value of the land itself. What does he do? "...he brings land into tillage in order to sell it again, and not to farm it: he builds a farmhouse on the speculation that, as the state of the country will soon be changed by the increase of population, a good price will be gotten for it."[6] Land, therefore, is torn from the center of settled life and thrust, cheapened and debased, into the day to day haggling of the market with the other commodities, as volatile in value as pork bellies, grain, copper, and iron.

Severed intellectually from the sclerotic European monarchies and separated physically by an ocean's distance, the new nation imagined it was safe from the social ills and peculations of the old world. It was not so. The promise of endless growth and quick riches once again proved too seductive for the yeoman, the man of business, and the politician. Eager and naïve investors either forgot or simply ignored the fact that the coin of any realm is both universally and eternally fickle and demanding. Whether in the wooded tracts of Michigan, among the poor and peopled warrens of New York and Chicago, or the drawing rooms of Europe's nobility, the scions of the new order would make the painful rediscovery that currency demands a level of security, support, and integrity without which any economy can be thrown into a tailspin. And as is too

Chapter 6 *The Not So Calm Before the Storm*

often the case, those of suspect character who *do* know the dangers of unbridled speculation and inflation are the best situated to exploit it – to fill the bubble until bursting with prospects of an easy, quick wealth without the annoyance of labor or sound and patient capital investment, only to cash in at just the right moment to avoid a ruin shared by the multitude.

Certainly, such financial discord was not a new phenomenon in that time. The lessons of unbridled speculation and the battle between paper and metal money were readily available at the time to anyone curious enough to acknowledge them. One had only to look at the evidence to understand that once the decision to untether money from its metallic anchor is made and to release it from the oversight of some centralized power, any scheme can fill speculation's sails, propelling it ever faster toward the inevitable storm on the horizon. Such schemes are only limited by the imagination, requiring only a small bit of capital as the seed for ever increasing issues of paper notes that eventually exceed any possibility of redemption. Such schemes of times gone by had indeed been diverse, promising boundless riches from gold, silver, and minerals wrung from such varied sources as the South Sea Coast and the Mississippi Basin. Never mind that the former belonged exclusively to Spain's Phillip V – who, in reality, had no intention of sharing – or the latter which, at this time, was under the control of an equally reluctant France.[7] Even simple tulips had at one time blossomed into a speculative mania that ruined thousands.[8] There had been voices of reason, however. Notwithstanding Adam Smith who, though not condemning it outright, had serious reservations about the reliability of speculation as a source of and the power to open branches.,[9] Critics as varied as Jefferson and Horace Walpole lent their voices in condemning the practice. For example, inveighing against the ever growing South Sea bubble, Walpole took to the floor of Parliament and warned that it countenanced "…the dangerous practice of stock-jobbing, and would divert the genius of the nation from trade and industry."[10]

"Whether in the wooded tracts of Michigan, among the poor and peopled warrens of New York and Chicago, or the drawing rooms of Europe's nobility, the scions of the new order would make the painful rediscovery that currency demands a level of security, support, and integrity without which any economy can be thrown into a tailspin."

Democrats like Jackson and Calhoun clearly understood the role metal specie played as a bulwark to any monetary system. What both mistrusted, however, was the idea of a central bank controlling the process and the resources. They regarded it as simply another manifestation of elitist power and privilege. Because they saw it through a distinctly class-based prism, their view was distorted, causing them to ignore a central bank's very real and practical usefulness as a tool for managing the volume of paper currency that too easily fuels speculation and panics. But the perils of loose money had been all too apparent to founders like Hamilton who presented the case for the advantages of a central bank to President Washington. Persuaded, the president appointed Hamilton Secretary of the Treasury in September, 1789; he was the first. Within two years, Hamilton created a federal revenue system, restructured the national debt into Treasury securities paying quarterly interest, and redefined currency in terms of gold and silver coins. Most importantly, he founded the Bank of the U.S. (BUS), a corporation with $10 million capitalization – 20 million shares of which were owned by the government – and the power to open branches.[11]

Before Hamilton's efforts in 1789, there had been only three banks in the new nation.[12] The new BUS provided a secure financial atmosphere for the addition of more banks, something state legislatures did increasingly until, by 1830, there were five to six

Chapter 6   *The Not So Calm Before the Storm*

hundred, all anxious to feed the new hunger for land and, in the time to come, railroads. Between the First Bank's inception in 1791 and the expiration of its charter in 1811, only eight banks had been officially designated as branches of the BUS.[13] After Democrats in Congress revoked the BUS charter in 1811, the number of state banks – no longer restrained by the scrutiny and sound money policies of the BUS – grew to 103 by 1814, their coffers fattened by money rechanneled to them from the vaults of the central bank. As one would expect, free of BUS guidance, the state banks issued paper notes far beyond their supporting reserves. Many state entities printed their own currency, the market becoming flooded with paper notes unpegged to specie and, consequently, of nebulous value. This lack of uniformity was especially apparent on the edges of the country – places like Michigan, Ohio, and Illinois – where reliable banking was virtually an impossibility.

As Farmer recounts,[14] blatant and egregious examples of counterfeiting were openly on display in territorial Michigan in 1819, perpetrated not only by members of the disadvantaged class from whom one might expect such behavior, but also from such august members of the community as Judge Woodward who issued small bill notes referred to as "shinplasters" in meager denominations of one and two cents each.

And there were more legitimate purveyors of self-issued paper money, the revered Father Gabriel Richard being one. Tasked with building Detroit's now iconic St. Anne's Church, the good father paid the workmen in script he issued himself. He was, however, put in a bind when a local printer named Cooper, seeing his opportunity, issued a number of notes with the good father's name forged on them. In keeping with his pristine reputation, Father Richard attempted to redeem as many of these fraudulent notes as he could. For his part, then Governor Cass at least had an inkling of the unsettled atmosphere caused by the watered currency and, in the same year (the year when the economy finally crashed), petitioned the branch of the BUS in Chillicote, Ohio for a draft in specie of $10,000 dollars in order to fulfill the terms of a treaty with the Indians. His request was rebuffed, and went into protest; a sure sign that the halcyon days of loose money had ended.[15]

Alexander Hamilton – Painting by John Trumbull, 1805. **(In White House. Public Domain.)**

Political boundaries began to form around the money issue, following the fault lines between those with expansionist sentiments who favored cheap money and lax regulations to fuel it, and the Hamiltonian wing embracing the restrictive, stabilizing influence of a central bank. In 1819, the two forces collided and the debate was temporarily stymied by a panic and subsequent depression, the first in the new republic's history. The crash was deep and broadly felt. Writing at the time, Baltimore publisher Hezekiel Niles commented on the depth of the contraction, citing the report of a Philadelphia committee which found that 30 industries had declined "…from 9,672 in 1816 to 2,137 in 1819" and that cumulative "weekly wages were down from $58,000 to $12,000."[16]

Reinvigorated by a new charter in 1817, the Second Bank sought to curb the speculative fever through tightened credit, a move that certainly contributed to the contraction. But a more consequential cause came from the collapse of foreign markets after the War of 1812, and the rapid repayment of federal debt, much of it to

Chapter 6 *The Not So Calm Before the Storm*

foreign bond holders.[17] Confidence in the Second Bank waned, provoking the ire of such powerful populist critics as Andrew Jackson who, despite the bank's improvement under the leadership of Nicholas Biddle beginning in 1823, harbored a categorical contempt for it. Unwavering in his efforts to shut down the institution, President Jackson finally effected its demise in July, 1832 when he vetoed the bank's re-charter. After firing two consecutive Treasury Secretaries – Samuel Ingham and Lewis McLane, both of whom expressed confidence in the bank and refused to cooperate in its demise – Jackson found a willing surrogate for his plans and, with a recess appointment, brought Roger B. Taney to the post in 1833.

Like a bumper crop bereft of a silo, the public money had, then, been wrested from the BUS coffers by Jackson and Taney and grew to a gargantuan sum. Absent the autonomous, central, and secure control of the bank, an enormous sum of the peoples' money suddenly needed a new place to reside. It was, in Jackson and Taney's opinion, not only undemocratic to have federal money relegated to the control and the coffers of a single institution, it was inefficient as well – an idea, in fact, inspired by Jefferson himself. The public's money was, in their minds, essentially being hoarded by the BUS,kept from otherwise useful purposes in the economy. Taney expressed this view in a circular: "The deposits of the public money will enable you to afford increased facilities to commerce and to extend your accommodations to individuals..."[18] Jackson echoed this sentiment in an address to Congress: "It is considered against the genius of our free institutions to lock up in vaults the treasure of the nation."[19] Where, then, should the money be stored? For Jackson, Taney,

> "...blatant and egregious examples of counterfeiting were openly on display in territorial Michigan in 1819, perpetrated not only by members of the disadvantaged class from whom one might expect such behavior, but also from such august members of the community as Judge Woodward who issued small bill notes referred to as "shinplasters" in meager denominations of one and two cents each."

and anti-Bank forces it was simple: distribute the money where, they felt, it was actually needed. Instead of a central federal clearinghouse, a certain number of state banks would be designated as official depositories and the funds distributed proportionately according to their representation in Congress. Though the solution seemed simple, the devil was, as always, in the minutiae. In their concern for the health of civil commerce, Jackson and Taney forgot that the public's money must also serve public purposes as well. The plan – and, as it turned out, its Achilles heel – was to make the money subject to stringent terms and then reclaim it back to the government coffers in four installments over a year once it had worked its magic as a stimulus to private commerce. What could go wrong? Much, as history shows.

The surplus was prodigious, much of it amassed from the sale of public lands. Receipts from the sale of public lands between 1823 and 1833 had totaled $1,670,000. Sales for 1835, in turn, were $14,757,600 and rose in 1836 to $24,877,179.[20] Land, however, was not the only river of revenue feeding the surplus. Since 1828, northern manufacturers had enjoyed the profitable protection of a tariff on finished goods and raw materials from abroad. Crafted to increase Jackson's electoral chances in the west and south, this tax overtly discriminated against the southern states with little manufacturing and for whom the cotton industry was their life's blood. Dubbed the "Tariff of Abominations" by southerners, it fueled an already intense sectional rivalry between the north and the south, and laid the political and philosophical foundation for the civil war to come.[21]

In fairness, Taney was aware of the pitfalls of plundering the BUS coffers as early as 1834, and negotiated what he thought might be a model

Chapter 6 *The Not So Calm Before the Storm*

framework for securing the integrity of the system, despite redistribution, with the Girard Bank of Philadelphia. Among the proposed safeguards was a provision that as of March, 1836 "…no bank [was, *sic*] to be a depository which issued notes below five dollars. No notes below five dollars to be received in payment to the United States. No bank which failed to pay specie on demand for its notes was to be a depository."[22] But, as history shows, Taney perhaps had bargained with the wrong agents. The banking practices of an esteemed and established eastern institution like the Girard were not indicative of the no-holes-barred, speculative atmosphere raging in frontier outposts like Michigan. There, and in other far flung settlements at the edge of the young nation, state bankers and speculators were giddy with the infusion of money from Washington. Unrestrained by the tepid legislative preconditions governing its use, they continued to issue low-denomination paper and loaned far above the prescribed capital stock. Looking back on the event some seventy years later, one writer recounted:

> "A time of feverish speculation and over-rush of business activity followed. A large number of new state banks came into existence, and these took part in the inflation. Prices rose rapidly. Business boomed. The treasury overflowed with a surplus. By the end of 1836, credit was strained to its utmost limit, and those familiar with the real situation knew that a crash was imminent."[23]

Taney's tenure as Treasury Secretary came to an abrupt end well before the consequences of his role in the BUS's demise could bear fruit. Jackson had tapped him in a recess appointment to carry out his agenda against the bank, and Congress retaliated by failing to approve his official appointment. Levi Woodbury succeeded Taney, and into his lap was thrown the baggage of an over-heated economy. Not only had free-banking forces in the west blatantly disregarded Taney's suggested restraints, opposition closer to home came from the usual pro-banking lobby like the Whigs who obstructed Jackson's efforts by any and every means possible. Paramount to this campaign were dire warnings of impending economic collapse absent the oversight of the BUS, even though such predictions were, at the time, as yet unwarranted. These jeremiads began to work on the public. After passing the distribution legislation in May, 1836, Congress immediately recessed, leaving Jackson to act unilaterally in an attempt to slow the now runaway train that was the economy. Inspired by a congressional ally, Missouri senator Thomas Hart Benton, Jackson issued an executive order known to history as the now infamous "Specie Circular." The generally unpopular order "…provided that no bank should have the public money on deposit to an amount exceeding three-quarters of its capital stock…"[24] More importantly, it mandated that only specie would be acceptable for payment of public lands. While the Specie Circular and its demand for hard money has historically borne the brunt of blame for the ensuing panic that occurred the next year in 1837, it is more likely that the Distribution Act itself and the speculative contagion triggered by the surplus were the real culprits.[25]

While it is easy, in hindsight, to condemn the custodians of the frontier banks for mismanagement and profligacy, the blame should more correctly be laid at the door of the Twenty-Fourth Congress who passed the distribution legislation. It is hard to imagine any industrious banker on the fringes of the nation who, having just been handed a mammoth infusion of cash and told to stoke the furnace of commerce, would not be tempted to underwrite any speculative undertaking without regard to the metal reserves supporting it.

Taney, Jackson, and the legislators created a situation of cross-purposes. As Farmer so poignantly suggests, "They forgot that the revenue could not be used 'to extend accommodations to individuals' and at

Chapter 6 *The Not So Calm Before the Storm*

the same time be garnered in vaults awaiting the demands of the nation."⁽²⁶⁾ Naturally, once news of the impending distribution was made public, banks in every corner of the country clamored for a piece, and as one would expect, whether one got a portion and how big it might be was based less on economic analysis than the measure of patronage afforded Old Hickory. In many cases, it was "reserves be damned."

Like a perpetual motion machine, the proceeds from land sales circulated and inflated, especially in the wilds of Michigan. "The proceeds of these sales were deposited in the state banks;" says Phillips, "the money deposited was again loaned out to speculators, with which they purchased more land, and so the process was repeated…"⁽²⁷⁾ Many banks held sums of money totally at odds with the capital requirements stipulated by the legislation. The Farmers' and Mechanics' Bank held $1,029,200 of public money in December 1836 and had only $150,000 in capital. Michigan's State Bank, on the other hand, held $1,259,974 against $444,779 in capital stock. Throughout the young nation and especially at its edges, such a situation was the rule rather than the exception. Looking back on the period in a journal article from 1900, one scholar of the time recounted the lesson:

> "To satisfy the needs of this feverish activity, bank paper had been increased from eighty-two -millions in January, 1835, to one hundred and eight-millions in January, 1836, and to one hundred twenty millions the following December. The per capita circulation increased from seven to ten dollars. The specie in the banks rose only two-millions, and that in circulation from eighteen to twenty-eight millions. The currency was largely bank paper."⁽²⁸⁾

"The banking practices of an esteemed and established eastern institution like the Girard were not indicative of the no-holes-barred, speculative atmosphere raging in frontier outposts like Michigan. There, and in other far flung settlements at the edge of the young nation, state bankers and speculators were giddy with the infusion of money from Washington."

The ramifications of such an imbalance only seemed to hit home when it was time to pay it back. Participating banks were suddenly required to pony up $9,000,000 dollars every three months, and furthermore – according to the Specie Circular – only hard currency would be accepted, thank you. Though it might seem obvious to most that withdrawing $9,000,000 from state banks every three months for a year might be a recipe for a disastrous economic contraction, such a prospect seems not to have occurred to the members of the twenty-fourth Congress who let the legislation pass.⁽²⁹⁾ It is worth noting that although Jackson sought the bank's demise, he thought the distribution of the surplus unwise and perhaps even unconstitutional. Clay and Webster were the ones who wanted it and successfully pushed the legislation through congress. By the next year, 1837, the house of cards began to tumble:

> " 'Paper Cities' by the score collapsed, wild lands were returned for unpaid taxes, banks curtailed their loans; circulating notes were returned for coin' and the large sums due the United States for the proceeds of public lands sold or duties collected were required to be transferred East. The State depositories, which were trembling under the pressure, and needed strengthening, were thus left to their own resources. The government account that at first had promised so much, in the end proved one of the most unfortunate and disastrous of accounts. The banks were obliged to pay the Government, but could not collect the loans they had made. Manufacturers suspended, and

Chapter 6 *The Not So Calm Before the Storm*

wholesale and retail merchants toppled like rows of bricks."[30]

The panic of 1837 was devastating and far reaching, an event that certainly must have cast a shadow over Michigan's induction into the union that year as the twenty-sixth state. Through their efforts, former Governor Cass and others had re-crafted the territory's image from a impenetrable sea of trees to a potential ocean of profitable lumber just waiting to be harvested, rich pockets of iron and copper, and vast lakes on all sides ready to ferry westward the anxious easterners arriving in a steady stream via the new Erie Canal. Seduced by the promise of wealth pouring into the soon to be state's coffers, the territorial legislature began mapping out concrete development plans as early as 1835. Were they not merely following the dictates of the state's constitution? Section 3, Article 12 said clearly, after all, that "Internal improvements shall be encouraged by the government of this state; and it shall be the duty of the legislature, as soon as may be, to make provision by law for ascertaining the proper objects of improvement in relation to roads, canals, and navigable waters…"[31] And make provision they did.

Two years later, in the session of 1837, the lawmakers conceived five ambitious projects. No less than three railroads and two canals were envisioned, to be funded with an appropriation of five million (borrowed) dollars. Working under the aegis of the state and to be overseen by a board of commissioners, the new networks would facilitate trade in every part of Michigan, traversing it north and south like life-giving arteries.

But whereas dreams of development are easily and cheaply spun, their realization would only come at a very real price. In their enthusiasm, the lawmakers ignored the reality of Michigan at that time which was still, except for pockets of population like Detroit and Saginaw, essentially wild, sparsely populated, and plagued with an even wilder banking system. Jackson's war on the BUS had been indisputably successful, the unfortunate proof of which was the now chaotic and parochial patchwork of banks whereby each state played by its own rules and selective levels of enforcement. Michigan's banks were some of the wildest, and anyone who appeared to meet the minimum specie threshold (there are tales of specie being hauled in the night from one bank to another in anticipation of a commissioner's visit) could open a bank as easily as an apple stand. Though paper abounded, hard currency and secure capital was in woefully short supply. Writing in a Michigan journal nearly seventy years later, one Michigan historian mused: "…it is difficult to understand how men could be so visionary, so lacking in judgment, that they could organize a system which the needs of the state did not demand and for the carrying out of which they had not a dollar."[32]

Bludgeoned by the downturn, the grand scheme developed cracks quickly. By April, 1837, some lawmakers were already working to shore up the fractures. The original sum allotted to commissioners for projects was reduced dramatically from $40,000 to $5,000. Many contracts were abandoned, in turn, because the commissioners did not have the authority to actually release the funds. By 1839, the number of commissioners was reduced from five to three and their salaries were reduced to $1,400. The ranks of engineers and their assistants was cut as well. Project after project was forsaken as the plan devolved into sectional bickering driven not by the well-being of the community, but by the potential gain for local leaders. As though from a thousand pin-pricks, the grand scheme devolved until, in 1846, the situation had come completely around and legislators were trying desperately to sell the public projects to private developers at the best price possible.[33]

Antebellum Michigan and Detroit were shaped by economic, geographical, and demographic forces they had little resources to resist. The 1837 census put the

Chapter 6 *The Not So Calm Before the Storm*

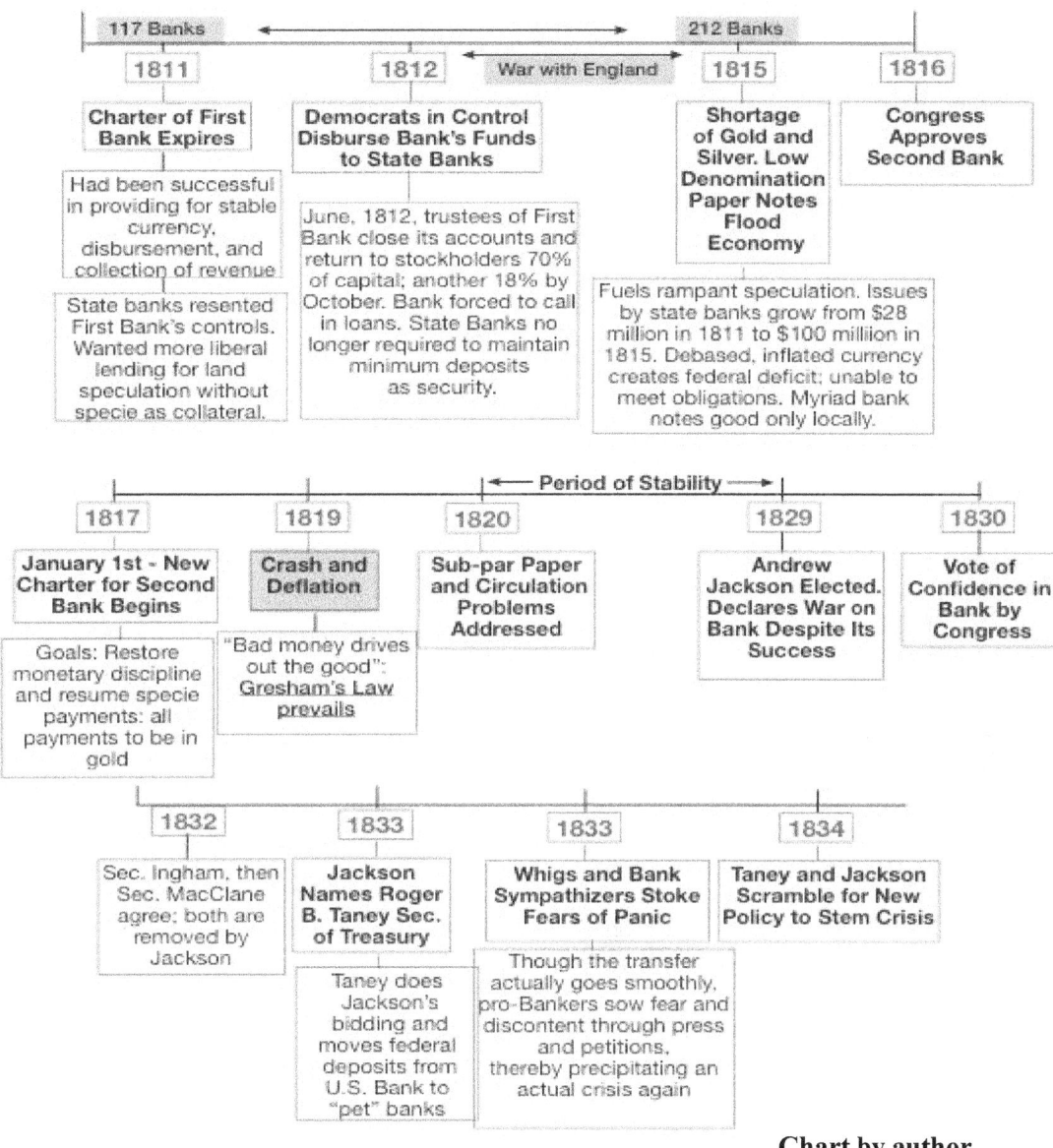

Chart by author

population of the whole state at only 175,000. One of the proposed railroads – the Northern – was to run through a tier of five counties, three of which had around two inhabitants per square mile, the other two counties counting only one per square mile.[34] For its part, Detroit had 9,278 inhabitants, 4,355 of whom were under the age of twenty-one.[35] The city was home to some industry at this time, the most prominent of which was The Detroit Iron Foundry which, for the most part, served the needs of the local community. Detroit's days as an industrial powerhouse were yet to come, but not terribly far off; the conflict to come would change that.

Jackson had sealed the fate of the BUS, and in every corner of the still small nation mountains of paper money fueled speculative undertakings. Budding entrepreneurs hatched schemes to corner the market,

Chapter 6 *The Not So Calm Before the Storm*

unhindered by a government itself totally invested in the same myth of the propriety of unbridled capitalism. And that was okay, because the small scale, local production and the cottage industries which were essentially family owned and catered to parochial needs comported nicely with the Smithian notion of pure, equalizing competition. The misery wrought by the belching factories and Midas-sized fortunes were yet on the horizon. Rooted in this innocent time those who enjoyed those esteemed fortunes foresaw nothing but good in them, and saw no need to use the power of government to restrict them. Against this backdrop, the young Carnegies, Vanderbilts, Goulds and Rockefellers dreamed of wealth, and imagined no practical or moral impediments to it.

(Photo: iStock, "the Vinman" id 145190854)

Many years later in 1889, native son, historian, and mapmaker Silas Farmer would look back with pride on these developments, attributing them to Detroit's advantageous geographical location and Michigan's abundant natural resources:

"No city in America is more favorably situated, and few cities possess so many necessary and desirable conditions for successful manufacturing…the mere recital of facts will amply prove the claim of superior advantages. It is well known that iron, copper, lead, and wood enter largely into the composition of all articles manufactured, and the location of Detroit in the midst of the chief sources of supply of these materials gives it unequalled manufacturing facilities."[36]

As it grew, Detroit's business community reflected both the technological developments and the diverse needs and tastes stimulated by the ever-growing influx of immigrants. As early as 1819, Detroit offered a variety of basic products and services provided by craftsmen skilled in blacksmithing, gunsmithing, carpentry, cabinet making, shoemaking, masonry, etc.. By 1836, the demand for goods was so great that "…every house that could be obtained on Jefferson

"Jackson's war on the BUS had been indisputably successful, the unfortunate proof of which was the now chaotic and parochial patchwork of banks whereby each state played by its own rules and selective levels of enforcement. Michigan's banks were some of the wildest, and anyone who appeared to meet the minimum specie threshold (there are tales of specie being hauled in the night from one bank to another in anticipation of a commissioner's visit) could open a bank as easily as an apple stand."

Avenue from Shelby to Randolph Street had been fitted up for a store and filled with goods."[37]

When the first working steamboat in service on the Great Lakes, the storied "Walk-in-the Water," docked in Detroit on August 26th 1818, it merely signaled the addition of steam-powered vessels to an already vibrant lake-born commerce, carried for decades by wooden sailing ships of all sorts.[38] Steamships, however, demanded more frequent, skilled, mechanical maintenance and it wasn't long before Detroit's waterfront provided this service. The "Argo" was the

Chapter 6   *The Not So Calm Before the Storm*

first steamship built at Detroit in 1827. By 1837, of the thirty-seven steamers plying the Lakes, seventeen were owned at Detroit.(39) Established sometime after John McDermott's arrival in Detroit in 1844, the McDermott Shipyard became the first in the city, followed in 1852 by the Dry Dock Engine Works. Conventional wisdom holds that between 1880 and 1882, a young man by the name of Henry Ford worked in what is now the decrepit remnants of the building that housed this business, acquiring some of his knowledge of combustion and driveshafts. This is, however, only half true. Since the existing building was built ten years later, he more likely worked at a nearby business, long defunct, called the Detroit Shipbuilding Company.(40)(41)

With the advent of steam power and the transition to steel in the middle part of the century, a nucleus of production and support industries gradually appeared in and around Detroit. Businesses like the new shipbuilding and maintenance facilities needed a source of raw materials, and the Eureka Iron Works, founded by Eber B. Ward in 1857 and located in nearby Wyandotte, processed much of the iron ore extracted in Michigan. In 1864, it converted to steel making using the new Bessemer process, the first business in America to do so.(42) Early on, it competed with the Fulton Iron and Engine Works, established in 1851 and located right in Detroit at the corner of Woodbridge and Brush.(43) The new railroads needed engines, and, as early as 1841, The Detroit Locomotive Works began building them.(44) Railroads needed cars: a market the Detroit Car & Manufacturing served, providing twenty-five cars to the Detroit/Pontiac Railway Company began serving in 1853.(44) Michigan was also blessed with an abundance of copper, a fact that did not escape the founders of the Detroit and Lake Superior Copper Company in 1850.(45) And finally, before brothers Jeremiah and James Dwyer formed the J. Dwyer & Company Foundry in 1861 – the Detroit business that would become one of the world's largest producers of iron stoves by 1864 as the Detroit Stove Works in 1864 – most of the iron stoves that warmed Detroiters were imported from Europe.(46) These businesses were seminal, representing only a fraction of the number of industries that would come to call Detroit home after the impending Civil War.

> "The misery wrought by the belching factories and Midas-sized fortunes were yet on the horizon, rooted in this innocent time that esteemed fortune, foresaw nothing but good in it, and saw no need to use the power of government to restrict it."

Nothing arises from a vacuum, as history shows. Detroit and Michigan are no exceptions. Once the region became accessible via new modes of transportation and secured with the expulsion of perceived native and foreign threats, Michigan and Detroit in particular became a magnet for disaffected immigrants fleeing poverty and upheaval in places like Ireland, Germany, and other European countries in the throes of social revolution. Most settled within enclaves in and around Detroit, each bringing their own unique cultural identity to the areas where they settled. Just before 1840, Detroit and the surrounding region was

The storied steamship "Walk in the Water" was one of the first steamships to ply the waters of the Great Lakes. This 1820 sketch by George H. Whistler is an accurate rendering of the ship's distinctive features. (**Library of Congress Prints and Photographs**.)

Chapter 6 *The Not So Calm Before the Storm*

primarily agricultural, with 9,000 people living in Detroit and 103,000 in the entire region. Detroit's population swelled from 9,192 in 1840 to 45,619 on the brink of the Civil War in 1860 – a more than 500 percent increase in twenty years. As the chart above indicates, even though the ethnic component of the population remained relatively steady (not quite half) over the three decades from the beginning of 1850 through the 1870s, the Germans and Irish were consistently the largest immigrant groups in the city during this period.[47]

Certainly, among these groups was a wealth of skill in trades and an important source of manual labor for a service and manufacturing sector still dependent on it. The table above, however, does not reflect the African American component of the workforce, a sub-group marginalized economically and relegated to the shadows by the dark cloud of slavery which, though technically forbidden on the frontier by the Northwest Ordinance of 1787, was still influenced by the slave-owning culture that gripped the southern half of the republic despite the founding documents' *paens* to liberty and freedom. (A political process that also excluded the entire female and Native American population.) Though not as overt as the oppression in the southern slave states, a veil of distrust and suspicion was nevertheless held over the black population in Detroit and Michigan in general, manifesting itself in special codes of behavior, fees for proof of trustworthiness, and segregation in housing and services. Comparatively, so abhorrent was the treatment of blacks in the slave states at this time that anything less than such total subjugation in places like Detroit was regarded as benevolent and tolerant. Much of the white populace was possessed by a sort of smug

> While the white, ethnic makeup of Detroit's population remained consistent at just less than half over the decades between 1850 and 1870, the German and Irish sectors predominated. Subsequently, the Irish presence diminished while the German population steadily increased during this time.

Percentages of Foreign Born Population In Detroit: 1850 - 1870

Census Year	1850	1860	1870
No. Total Population	21,019	45,619	79,603
No. Foreign Born	9,927	21,349	35,381
%. Foreign Born	47.22	46.79	44.44
Ethnic Breakdown Per Decade by Percentage			
Canada (English)	–	–	–
Canada (Unspec.)	–	14.46	21.83
Canada (French)	–	–	–
Great Britain	17.32	16.49	14.03
Ireland	33.13	28.08	19.7
Germany	28.66	33.82	35.75
France	2.84	2.92	2.15

"Table adapted from Zunz, "Detroit's Ethnic Neighborhoods at the End of the Nineteenth Century" Univ. of Michigan, 1977

Chapter 6 *The Not So Calm Before the Storm*

paternalism that included not just the notion that black inferiority was the natural order of things, but also the idea that blacks were complicit with their inferior status.

The image of the African American as a grateful stooge, useful only for white service and amusement held sway, thus laying the groundwork for ugly and persistent stereotypes of African American subservience, laying the groundwork for caricatures like Aunt Jemima, Uncle Ben, and Step 'n' Fetch-It – humiliating caricatures that endured well after the Civil War. Indicative of this "darkies have it good here" are city father Friend Palmer's reminiscences, penned many years later in 1906, of certain black slaves, much beloved for their good-natured compliance with subjugation. "Detroit and vicinity was a heaven to the slave compared to the southern states," Palmer writes. "The master once attached to his 'Sambo,' a great price would have to be paid to buy him."

One iconic Detroit figure, businessman Joseph Campau (who, it will be recalled, helped the imperiled journalist, John Gentle) owned ten slaves. One of them, Palmer recalls, was a man named Crow whom Campau always dressed in scarlet. "This negro, to the amusement of the inhabitants of old town, used to ascend old St. Anne's church steeple and there perform some of his gymnastic tricks. He was supple and elastic as a circus rider." Or consider another of Campau's slaves – Tetro – who, as Palmer suggests "…was a faithful and as honest as the day was long."[48] A diamond in the rough, apparently, among a black population otherwise regarded by the white majority as inherently dubious of character and unworthy of trust.

A few dim yet promising abolitionist sentiments existed here and there in Detroit, Michigan, and in the new territories at this time. They were, however, no match for the heady gusts of old, ugly legislation like Kentucky's 1793 Fugitive Slave Act and the numerous slave codes that ensnared the black populations of states like Virginia and Alabama. Nor could they evade the influence of a southern plantation system that depended for its very existence on slave labor, one that was willing to pay bounty hunters to retrieve their runaway "property" should they be lucky enough to slip their bonds and escape north. Both enabled slavery even at the margins of the new country, ensuring that any faintly glowing embers of racial equality would be quickly snuffed out. For any slaves making the slightest gesture of disobedience, attempting to escape, possessing a weapon, congregating without a white person present, or even showing interest in education, the black slave codes in places like Virginia and Alabama promised swift and certain punishment including everything from beatings, to castration, to execution.[49]

Certainly, compared to the inhumane, barbaric, and oppressive standards set by the southern slave states at the time, Detroit, Michigan, and many of the new territories could be considered bastions of tolerance and respect for human dignity. Beginning at such a low level, though, it is easy to characterize even the slightest movement upward as "raising the bar." True, blacks in Detroit of the 1830s and '40s suffered much less harassment than their unfortunate southern counterparts, but less harassment is not freedom *per se*, and despite the self-congratulatory rhetoric issuing from city fathers like Palmer and Farmer reminiscing fondly on their treatment of resident African Americans in antebellum Detroit, merely misconstruing blacks' stoic acceptance of their fate as complicity is a self-serving delusion. In truth, their condescending and paternalistic treatment of Detroit's black minority was simply a softer version of the same contempt for the black race that countenanced lash and lynching on the plantations. The rot in the national body politic could not be kept at bay by artificial borders, and as long as federal authorities tolerated it on the national level, northern states and localities were forced to deal with it as effectively and justly as possible on their own levels. This engendered a conflicted outlook on the part of white Detroiters, one willing to theoretically accept

Chapter 6   *The Not So Calm Before the Storm*

blacks in the life of the community while at the same time drafting measures calculated to ensure that only those blacks of a certain economic and social mettle were worthy of inclusion.

Blacks were tolerated in Detroit as long as their presence did not invite social disruption. As early as 1827, bounty hunters seeking escaped slaves were regular visitors to the city, their missions tacitly sanctioned by a federal government unwilling to regard escaped slaves as something other than property.[50] Consequently, city authorities were obliged by statute to hand over escaped slaves even as they championed rhetorically the rights of certain black citizens to remain. The unsavory task, then, was to differentiate between the human chattel who had managed to escape, and the blacks with documentation attesting to their status as "free."

The first legal expression of this conflicted civic conscience were Detroit's "Black Codes." For then Assistant Marshal of the Michigan Territory, Benjamin Witherell, the immediate task was to take a census of "free" blacks in the territory. They numbered sixty-six. The next step was to discourage migration of non-free blacks into the region, a goal accomplished by requiring all blacks entering the territory to present a "certificate of freedom." Upon presenting this documentation to the authorities, migrating blacks were then required to post a $500-dollar bond (an enormous sum at the time) as a guarantee for their "good behavior." Once these preconditions were satisfied, any slave catcher attempting to capture and abscond with said "free" blacks were themselves subject to arrest. These stipulations were known as the "Black Codes," and to the credit of those who were citizens at the time, they were, for the most part, ignored. Many lived and worked in and around Detroit without the legally mandated documentation. This unspoken racial détente held sway in the city until June, 1833 when two slave catchers arrived in Detroit. Their mission: to return two fugitive slaves by the name of Thornton and Ruth Blackburn back to their "owner" in Kentucky.

After being delivered to the jail, the Blackburns could not produce the requisite proof of freedom and were incarcerated pending extradition to Kentucky under the 1793 Fugitive Slave Act. After word of the couple's plight circulated among Detroit's blacks, the community threw off the veil of complicity in their second-class status and promised the authorities that the white man's justice would not prevail. Conflicted, perhaps, between the demands of his job and the morality of the situation, Sheriff John M. Wilson locked them away in the jail instead of handing them over to the two bounty hunters. Though he had hoped the situation would resolve in a short time, it only got worse. The next day – Sunday, June 16th – the black population congregated on the commons near the jail. Armed with clubs, they made clear their intention to prevent the couple's extradition by any means possible. During the course of the day, the Blackburns had been allowed visitors, one of whom was a Mrs. George French who, unbeknownst to Sheriff Wilson, had exchanged clothes with Mrs. Blackburn, making it possible for her to walk out of the jail and secure safe passage across the river to Canada. In the evening, the steamboat sailed away without the fugitive cargo, and the crowds dispersed for the night.

Thornton Blackburn was still facing the same fate and, in the morning, a cart was sent to the jail to ferry the man to the steamboat, and then on to bondage once again in Kentucky. Crowds of blacks had again assembled outside the jail. A cart was sent to the door of the jail, intended to spirit Blackburn away to the steamboat, and then once again to bondage in Kentucky. When Wilson appeared at the door with the prisoner, a scuffle ensued whereupon the protestors commandeered the horse and cart, and whisked Thornton Blackburn away to join his wife in freedom on the other side of the river. The unfortunate sheriff paid dearly for executing his duties. After being clubbed

Chapter 6

The Not So Calm Before the Storm

and stoned by the rioters, he was grievously injured, suffering a fractured skull and teeth knocked out. (He would die within the year of the injuries.) Retribution was swift. Though Thornton Blackburn's rescuers were overtaken by a posse a few miles away, he himself had escaped successfully to Canada where he went on to enjoy a prosperous career.[51]

Whatever good will and tolerance that might previously have existed toward the black community became a casualty of the riot. Detroit's white citizens became paranoid and fearful now that African Americans had made clear their true feelings about their relegation to an inferior status and their frustration at the white community's willingness to let them be ensnared by the odious tentacles of slavery reaching for them from the south. In June, 1833, the white population gave formal expression to this fear and distrust by demanding that the 1827 Black Codes be strictly enforced. Fugitive slaves were put on notice by a special (white, of course) citizens' committee who penned this warning: "Composed as the Negroes who resort to this frontier, for the most part are of the most worthless of the slave population; we can have no adequate motive to encourage their emigration hither." In addition, the committee called for a nine o'clock curfew on all blacks and forbade any black person from landing a boat Detroit's shores.[52] Thus, with the Blackburn Riot were the weeds of racial discord rooted in the earliest soil of Detroit's history, a stubborn growth which would come to flower throughout the years and decades to come. There, among the first budding signs of prosperity and industrialism came the first pernicious buds of racial animus as well, a scourge that would one day grow to be a divide separating white from black, city from suburb; a floodgate re-channeling Detroit's wealth from the once great and diverse metropolis to its environs where white inhabitants hunker down behind red lines and not so subtle signs saying: "blacks not welcome."

Runaway slave ad posted by "owner," James Banks who, interestingly, was a northern slave holder living in New York in 1774, nearly twenty years before the passage of the "Fugitive Slave Act." **(Source: African Burial Ground National Monuiment.)**

Chapter 6

The Not So Calm Before the Storm

Chapter 7
A Melting Pot, Boiling

The camel loves the desert; the reindeer seeks the everlasting snows; the wild fowl gather to the waters; and the eagle wings his flight above the mountains. It is equally the order of Providence that slavery should exist among a planting people, beneath a southern sun.

Rep. James Hammond, S.C., 1835[1]

In the mid-1800s, by all outward appearances, antebellum Detroit seemed to be a place at once placid and prosperous. The network of newly built canals like the Erie were now offering a steady stream of material and people in and out of the state, making it no longer a mere entrepot through which goods simply passed to other points of production. Now, Detroit was a rudimentary manufacturing hub in its own right, where iron, copper, and other natural resources were also being crafted into finished goods. Ore from Michigan's mines found its way to Detroit where it was forged into iron rails for the ever-growing railroads and to satisfy the burgeoning demand for iron stoves. Railroad cars and carriages were produced, and parts for the steam engines – the boilers, gears, and shafts – propelling the steam ships that plied the lake waters and the locomotives that chugged along on land. Immigrant influence belied itself in the local, thriving cigar and beer making industry. It seemed to be a good time; so much so that at the turn of the following century, native

A young Ulysses S. Grant as he looked in 1843, sixteen years before being posted in "Old Slow Town", as Detroit was then known. **(Albert Richardson, "A Personal History of Ulysses S. Grant," 1868. Cooper Collection.)**

sons like historians Silas Farmer and Friend Palmer would look back nostalgically on a city which, notwithstanding its reputation as "Old Slow Town," a moniker future Mayor John C. Lodge would remember hearing as a boy, decades later. Actually, Detroit had a diverse commercial sector that supplied its population with all the necessities of daily life, from groceries to dry goods to shoes hats and a good shave. Writing from his new post at the Detroit Barracks in 1859, a young lieutenant named Ulysses S. Grant corroborated the town's laid-back image in a letter to his wife Julia, complaining that Detroit was "dull" and that there was little to do.[2]

At the outset of the 1850s, one could characterize Detroit's economic landscape as proto-industrial. Though it accommodated the needs of a burgeoning steam technology for shipping and railroads in the region, work was still done by small groups of skilled craftsmen either gathered under a single roof, or working independently from their own, in-home shops. Throughout the previous decade production remained relatively true to the old-world craft hierarchy: master workmen worked with hand tools, taking on apprentices and hiring journeymen to help them with the workload. The days of the modern assembly line were far in the future, and businesses employed relatively few workers, rarely totaling more than ten or twenty.[3] More importantly, the wretched working conditions and exploitation that already gripped industrial centers of Europe and the eastern seaboard had not yet found their way to Detroit.

Because much of Michigan was still undeveloped, early immigrants had only to invest the time and energy to clear a patch of land in order to get a new lease on life in places like the German enclave in Frankenmuth. However, increasing demand for cheaper goods produced quicker, and the prospect of easy wealth for merchants willing to circumvent established craft-work culture compelled them to find short cuts in production. Instead of purchasing finished items done entirely by master craftsmen, some Detroit merchants began supplying materials to less-skilled tradespeople who would perform only a portion of the work, then hand the item over to the merchant to complete. These sub-contractors, dubbed "two-thirders" (because they only performed two-thirds of the work) provoked the ire of journeymen who were being by-passed for cheaper labor.[4] Thus was the door to exploitation cracked slightly open, the same door through which one entered, eventually, the poverty and misery already existing in eastern and European industrial centers. For now, the impact was minimal. But the devil had taken a finger and would, someday, return for the whole hand.

Look deep enough, however, and Detroit just before the Civil War reveals a place more complex than the soporific burg Grant and Lodge described. Beneath its quiet exterior, like a dormant geyser threatening and hissing, flowed the boiling cross currents of racial hatred and working-class disaffection that were destined eventually to erupt. These were fed by several streams: by distant European political turmoil and exploitation; by the festering swamp of southern slavery; and by the impoverished refugees from a budding eastern industrial establishment that was bent on recreating the sort of slums and horrendous working conditions already spawned in English cities, places like Manchester whose hellish working and living conditions Engels (his father owned a factory there) would meticulously document in 1844.[5] U.S. coastal cities like Philadelphia and New York had already begun their own descent into misery and exploitation and were rocked by frequent strikes by workers rebelling against miserable conditions. Workers in Philadelphia lived fifty people to a tenement with "…no garbage removal, no toilets, no fresh air or water." In New York "you could see the poor lying in the streets with the garbage." These conditions brought a typhoid epidemic in 1837, typhus in 1842, and cholera in 1832.[6]

Certainly, they – the Irish, the Germans, the Italians – had all come from different places, each escaping their own special torments, each transplanting the seeds of their mother country's traditions, dysfunctions, and hatreds in this place that was supposed to instill hope

> "…Detroit just before the Civil War reveals a place more complex than the soporific burg Grant and Lodge described. Beneath its quiet exterior, like a dormant geyser threatening and hissing, flowed the boiling cross currents of racial hatred and working-class disaffection that were destined eventually to erupt."

Chapter 7 *A Melting Pot, Boiling*

Roberts power loom, 1835. **(Artist: T. Allom, in "History of the cotton manufacture in Great Britain. Sir Edward Baines.)**

for everyone. Yet, many shared a similar fate, a destiny that would profoundly shape the nature of work and the relationship of laborers to work in the centuries to come; not just in Detroit, but the world over. All had had their traditional way of life wrested from them in some way. For many, no longer did their labor serve their own private needs or the needs of their local community. For generations, agricultural workers had followed the same cultural patterns of work characterized by alternating periods of intense labor and idleness dictated solely by the rhythms of the harvest. Increasingly, lone weavers laboring at their single-bobbin spinning wheels could not satisfy the growing demand for textile production dictated by middlemen in faraway markets. "Most work activities emanated from the home," explains Shoshana Zuboff, "and the distractions of the family, the taverns, and the social web of the community limited any undivided commitment to work."[7] Furthermore, writes Engels:

> "They did not need to overwork; they did no more than they chose to do and yet earned what they needed…But intellectually they were dead; lived only for their petty, private interest, for their looms and gardens, and knew nothing of the mighty movement which beyond their horizon was sweeping through mankind."[8]

Their private labors were no longer enough; redundant, in fact. Their meager efforts at the loom in the back of their home or their lone tinkering in their private workshops was insufficient to sustain them or satisfy the insatiable hunger for cheap goods in distant markets. Only machines – ever more complicated and powerful – were fast enough and powerful enough to serve those markets, and only the few and the wealthy owned machinery like the spinning jenny and the new McCormick reaper. And it was the wealthy few who reaped the rewards. There was, after all, money to be made. In England, Scotland and Ireland, the rich gobbled up small farms everywhere, creating huge estates not to raise crops, but to graze cattle: beef intended for export and the aristocratic palate; meat not meant for the poor, indigenous, and starving population. The once independent yeomen were forced to either share the harvest as tenant farmers with wealthy landlords, move to the city where they were faced with the unsavory options of yoking themselves to machines and selling their labor for wages barely enough to keep them alive, or begging in streets filled with the miasma of garbage, excrement of all kinds, and the poisonous vapors from the factories' coal-fired steam engines.

Little wonder, then, that many fled such misery; the Irish, especially, whose all-important potato succumbed to disease on a massive scale in 1846, sending a scourge of famine and disease that ultimately claimed the lives of about two million Irish between 1846 and 1851. Even more fled than died. In the decade between 1845 and 1855, a full two million Irish emigrated from the Emerald Isle to an uncertain future – and in many cases, death – across the ocean.[9] The lucky ones (those who managed to survive the voyage on disease infested ships) were the ones who made it further west to places like Detroit.

Chapter 7   *A Melting Pot, Boiling*

For those with deep roots in Detroit and Michigan, names like Stroh, Oscar-Mayer, von Steuben, Frankenmuth, Pfeiffer and Kiefer have a familiar ring. Compared to the French and English, Germans were relative late-comers to the Great Lakes area, their exodus to Detroit and other places in the state beginning in the mid-1830s. (An exception, of course, were the Moravians who founded a settlement near present day Mount Clemens in 1782.) Certainly, their entry into the region would have been difficult or even impossible before the long and tumultuous issue of possession had been settled between the three great powers: the French, the English, and the nascent republic. It was not until then that much of Michigan was even physically accessible. Had these factors not precluded their involvement in that part of the country, a greater German presence in the area might have occurred much earlier and been coincident with their very early involvement in eastern colonies like Jamestown in 1607.

"Boy and Girl at Cahera," by artist James Mahony shows a famished boy and girl scavenging for potatoes during the Irish famine. **(Illustration appeared in the London News Gazette on Feb. 20, 1847. Wiki Commons.)**

Germans had established themselves in coastal enclaves a full century before the American Revolution. Among the passengers aboard the Mayflower in 1620 were Germans with valuable skills like glass-blowing, carpentry, and brewing.[10] Often passed down through generations, their various trades were a source of pride – a repository of knowledge and ability regulated and protected by a rigorous guild system that governed advancement in each discipline, provided oversight, and thereby guaranteed quality. More importantly, perhaps, the guild system preserved the integrity of the trade, the independence of the tradesmen, as well as their esteem and standing in the community.

The meticulous and long path from apprentice to master was a cultural constant in an otherwise unstable Germany torn by sectarian conflicts like the Thirty Years War (1618 – 1648) and the War of Spanish Succession (fought in 1700 to determine who would succeed Hapsburg Phillip II to the Spanish throne). Whether from wars triggered by religious ideologues or narcissistic aristocrats clawing for power, these battles were invariably fought by common folk whose daily fight for survival was punctuated by periodic conscription in the local noble's army. Pressed into battles over boundaries and titles over which they had no control, they sometimes made the choice to flee the continent rather than stay and bleed for a cause over which they had no say. Even those lucky enough to remain above the fray often became victims of a different sort when foraging armies stole their crops and cattle, leaving them with nothing.

Unlike the Irish who, desperate to escape starvation and the sociopathic indifference of their wealthy overlords, burst forth from their homeland in a huge wave over a rather brief span of history, the German exodus (until the revolutionary upheaval of 1848, as we shall see) was more measured, often religious in motive, and occurring over a much greater length of time. Germany was, after all, the birthplace of the

Chapter 7   *A Melting Pot, Boiling*

Reformation. When Luther drove that first wedge into Catholic Christianity it split into two halves; not fourths, nor eighths, nor any smaller ideological factions of consequence than the two great adversaries – Protestants and Catholics – who squared off against each other in a seemingly endless orgy of violence. For some, the struggle mocked a faith whose founder, as they regarded him, embraced peace and compassion. Locked in a struggle for dominance, the two combatants had no patience for anyone not willing to pick a side, and certainly no stomach for dogmatic hair-splitting over issues like adult baptism or pacifism. Vilified, persecuted, and unwilling to give their lives for what they felt were compromised if not corrupt religious institutions, these disaffected souls – with names like Anabaptists, Amish, Mennonites, and Quakers – took their beliefs, their skills, and their dreams and settled in America in new colonies like Massachusetts, Pennsylvania, and Virginia.[11] This was the first German wave to American shores. Nothing like a tsunami; it was more a long, steady infusion of skilled, hard-working people who just wanted to be left alone.

In July of 1830, Michigan was aspiring to statehood and was peacefully preoccupied with defining its identity and its boundaries, creating an effective and responsive legislature, carving paths through its wilderness, and methodically evicting the native population through lopsided treaties more correctly described as swindles. Meanwhile, an ocean away, French republicans in Paris had had enough of Bourbon Charles X's restrictions on the press, his attempts to disenfranchise most of the population, and his desire to consolidate more and more power in the crown. They had already consigned one monarch's head to a basket, and for those who had steam-rolled across Europe under Napoleon's tricolor banner, Charles' excesses were an unconscionable overreach: an unwelcome reprise of the days of Louis. The rebels threw up barricades and for three days battled the Bourbon authorities in the streets of Paris, demanding a republic. Charles relented and passed the crown to Louis-Phillipe under a new, constitutional monarchy.

The next year, 1831, Alexis de Tocqueville would make his historic journey to America. While de Tocqueville was busy chronicling the young republic and admiring the as yet unmolested wilderness around Saginaw, weavers in faraway Lyon, France – called, "Canuts" (likely derived from the French word "cannette" or, "spool") – rebelled against local merchants who refused to reward them adequately for their work and undercut them with workers from other areas. Several hundred Canuts marched on Lyon where they sacked the armory, confiscated guns, attacked guards, and took over the town.[12]

Violence flared across the channel in England as well. In the East Kent region of England (around Hungerford and Kintbury), agricultural laborers who had been crushed for years in an economic vice of high taxes, compulsory tithes, low wages, and unemployment (made worse by increasing use of mechanical threshing machinery to do what traditionally had been an abundant and reliable source of hand work for them), rebelled. Led, ostensibly, by a fictitious character by the name of "Captain Swing," the so-called "Swing" rioters managed to destroy, over a period of about three weeks, one hundred threshing machines and pen hundreds of threatening letters to farmers, magistrates, and parsons.[13] These clandestine attacks were not new to England. Roughly ten years earlier Luddites had used the same tactic to wreak havoc countrywide, destroying the newly invented wide-frame weaving machines and threatening officials they felt were exploitive and disrespectful of their skills and the value of their labor.[14] Though machines, in each case, bore the brunt of the rioters' anger, it was less the machinery itself than the new merchant class and their use of it for their exclusive enrichment that incurred the wrath of the workers. Many of the rioters were skilled

Chapter 7 *A Melting Pot, Boiling*

operators. But, ironically, the labor-saving devices meant fewer workers were needed to produce more and cheaper goods. The savings, of course, redounded to the benefit of the owners while workers were rewarded with increasing unemployment.

Further east in Austria, Germany, and Prussia, the reigning monarchs monitored these events closely and with dismay, anxious to prevent similar uprisings in their own domains. As they watched their royal counterparts in France and England forcibly put down successive uprisings through the 1830s, the correct response seemed to be: 1) to quash any revolt as quickly and thoroughly as possible; 2) to block the dissemination of republican sentiments internally by controlling the press and arresting those propagating those ideas; and 3) resisting as long as possible in Germany the same sort of exploitive industrialism by clinging to and protecting the old guild and craft system to keep the workers happy. And how could they think otherwise? Consumed by fear of the mobs and haunted by memories of Robespierre and Napoleon, eyes reared in the cloistered environment of the royal court were, it would seem, incapable of seeing or understanding the poverty, misery, and desperation at the root of their subjects' violence; and violence was all they could see. So, these rulers of a still fragmented Germany swatted at the billowing smoke of resistance, unaware that they were actually stoking the fires of revolution.

Inspired by Austria's Klemens von Metternich, fellow ambassadors from Great Britain, Russia and Prussia met in Vienna in September, 1814 to chart the course of post- Napoleonic Europe. The gathering of diplomats from these countries met under a benign name – "The Congress of Vienna."[15] At this meeting they laid the groundwork for another repressive alliance conceived a year later in 1815 between Metternich and Tsar Nicholas I (who was at the height of his popularity after his rout of Napoleon) dubbed "The Holy Alliance."[16] This agreement between Russia, Prussia, and Austria put teeth into the strategies concocted at the Congress of Vienna, its mission: to quash any form of resistance in each realm and preserve monarchy as the

In 1831, in Lyon, France, weavers known as "Canuts" revolted against merchants' increasing use of machinery to undercut weavers' labor and to underpay them. (Aritist unknown: http://traboule.free.fr/images/bataille.jpg)

Led, followers claimed, by a fictitious character by the name of "Captain Swing, disaffected English workers rebelling in the "Swing Riots" against wretched conditions, low wages, and increasing industrialization threatened factory owners with letters like the one below reading: "…the college that though haddest shalt be fired very shortly. Thou shalt here [sic] further from me when it is in flames." (British National Archives)

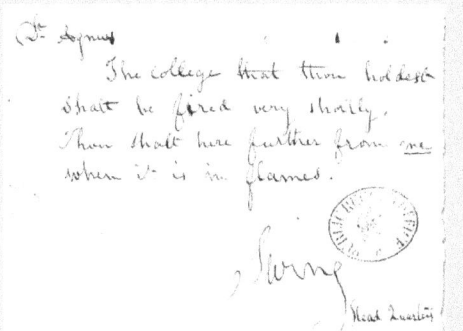

Chapter 7

A Melting Pot, Boiling

preferred form of government. More than the actual revolts, Metternich, Tsar Nicholas and their sympathizers feared the intellectuals who often inspired them, hounding those they regarded as subversive wherever they found them into the next decade.

By 1844, Michigan had been a state for only seven years. Due to its thinly distributed population, still inaccessible interior, chaotic banking system, and the insecurity engendered by the Panic of 1837 (there would be many more to come), its leaders were forced to scale back their ambitious development plans that came with the excitement of statehood. For its part, Detroit was peacefully burnishing its bona fides as an economic hub. Its significance as a Great Lakes shipping center prompted James McDermott to open the McDermott Shipyard in that same year. While Detroit was putting down roots and suffering growing pains as a future industrial behemoth, a monarchy had been forcibly re-installed in France and workers in the northern Prussian province of Silesia tested the peace of Metternich-inspired repression, finally delivering their own worker revolt to the doorstep of Germany. Looking on events in Silesia with great interest was a young editor at the "Deutsche-Französiche Jahrbücher" (the "German-French Yearbook") named Karl Marx.

Writing from his new position at this Paris-based journal (he had moved to France from Germany after Prussian censors closed his previous publication, the "Rheinische Zeitung," located in Berlin), Marx had only recently broken away from the popular thrall of Hegelian idealism.[17] His feet were now planted firmly in the material world where he saw in the struggle of workers to reclaim control of their labor from the new capitalist class a path to a more just and equitable world order. The worker, according to Marx, was being forced into a situation where a task over which he/she formerly had had complete control was now subdivided into myriad small operations and distributed among dozens of other workers for the benefit of the owner of the means of production who did no work at all. Often the task involved little more than monitoring a machine that performed the actual operation. "The worker's labor confronts him as another man's property," Marx says, and "the means of his existence and his activity are increasingly concentrated in the hands of the capitalist."[18] More now than just a mere emotional reaction to a new exploitive environment they could not understand, the workers' growing nemesis, industrial capitalism, was now being defined and marked with a target by the intelligentsia and worker resistance.

For some time, Marx had been monitoring uprisings in France and England, frustrated that Germany had as yet no revolutionary movement of its own (testimony, perhaps, to the success of Metternich et al). When the Silesian revolt finally occurred, Marx was heartened and perceived it, in contrast to the French and English rebellions, as the first real expression of an energized and revolutionized proletariat: a too-long exploited and disaffected class that creates value for someone else even as it itself is rendered increasingly valueless:

> "The Silesian rebellion starts where the French and English workers' finish, namely with an understanding of the nature of the proletariat. This superiority stamps the whole episode. Not only were machines destroyed, those competitors of the workers, but also the account books, the titles of ownership, and whereas all other movements had directed their attacks primarily at the visible enemy, namely the industrialists, the Silesian workers turned also against the hidden enemy, the bankers."[19]

Three years later, in 1847, a bad harvest triggered economic instability which once again enflamed long-simmering revolutionary sentiment.[21] throughout western Europe, beginning with a revolt in Sicily against its Austrian masters. Rebellions by the Czechs

Chapter 7   *A Melting Pot, Boiling*

German revolutionaries at the barricades on Breiten Strasse in Berlin in March, 1848. **(Published in Verlag Winckelman. Artist unknown . https://www.deutsche-digitale-bibliothek.de/item/YSA74GHCTOXUCF2V3JY6ZQ2CC3TKLHP2)**

"The misery wrought by increasing industrial capitalism and entrenched class dominance in Europe gave rise to numerous worker revolts beginning with the Canut rebellion in France in 1831. Even in the face of a united effort among monarchs to repress revolt through the Congress of Vienna, workers revolted everywhere on the continent. Germany was no exception. In 1848, intellectuals and activists in Frankfurt took to the streets, successfully appealing to the reigning monarch – Frederick William IV – to invoke reforms. By 1849, however, due to squabbling and indecision among the rickety worker/intellectual coalition, the aristocracy was able to reassert its power and quash dissent. In response, movement leaders like Karl Marx fled the country to other parts of the world, including the U.S. and places like Michigan. Unlike the first wave of Germans who, religiously motivated and apolitical, came to America in the 1600s in search of anonymity, revolutionaries in 1848 came to the U.S. and actively assimilated into the economic and political life of the country."

and Polish to free themselves from Russia followed. In March, 1848 French Republicans once again took to the barricades as intellectuals and political activists in Germany and Austria also mounted their own insurrection against William Frederick IV in Berlin, thereby testing the reactionary firewall of the Holy Alliance erected by Metternich and his royal sympathizers, Francis the II of Austria, Frederick William IV in Prussia, and Ludwig I of Bavaria (father of the so-called "Mad King"). Whereas the Italians, Czechs and Poles were easily put down, the French succeeded, thereby establishing the Second French Republic which guaranteed universal manhood suffrage in France.

The German revolutionaries fared better as well; or so it seemed. After three days of bloody conflict in the streets of Frankfurt – triggered after shots were fired into a crowd of citizens demanding press freedom and a constitution – King Frederick William finally took action. Whether out of a belated sense of royal responsibility or abject fear and abhorrence at the sight of his citizens killing each other to the tune of two-hundred dead, he mounted his horse, brandished the new flag, and rode amongst the crowd promising reforms and restraints on his power.[20] Germany now seemed to be on a its own path to unity, freedom of the press, and a truly representative government. It was, however, not to be.

As the violence in Frankfurt and other parts of Germany, Austria, and Bavaria unfolded, the American ambassador to Germany, Andrew Jackson Donelson (a nephew of Old Hickory's wife) was an eyewitness. His reports back to then President Polk expressed an admiration for the rebellion, seeing in the rebels a kindred spirit in their desire for the type of representative government that already existed in the U.S.. But Germany – most of Europe, in fact –

Chapter 7

A Melting Pot, Boiling

confronted an ancient reality the new American republic did not. "This system," Donelson reflected, "so difficult in its completion with us, is complicated by a thousand obstructions here, from which we were free. These states have always had a monarchy or a power equivalent to one."[21] However rattled royals like Frederick William might have been, vicegerents like Metternich and Austrian Prince Schwarzenberg held fast to the notion of royal entitlement and merely waited for cracks to develop in the rickety coalition. They didn't have long to wait.

Known now to history as the "Professors' Parliament," the assembly split into three factions including conservatives, liberals, and left-wing democrats. (Peasants and workers were not represented.) Despite the squabbling, the body tried its best to accomplish its goals: a constitution and a centralized government. Though something called an "Imperial Government" was cobbled together, the "Imperial Administrator" chosen to head it was Austrian Archduke Johann whose appointment was regarded as a biased nod to Austrian interests, furthering fracturing the coalition. He inspired no loyalty, especially from royals who were expected to surrender their power to him. With no parliamentary procedures and no unaffiliated civil service to administer it, the "Professors' Parliament" crumbled of its own weight. In the wings, anxiously anticipating its demise, were the monarchists, still deeply rooted in the society with extensive connections not easily disentangled by mere revolutionary sentiment.[22]

By August of 1849, forces sympathetic to the monarchies reasserted their power yet again over the liberal-democratic bourgeoisie and intellectuals in Germany and Austria. However, rather than feel the boot of royal repression on their necks once again, architects of the rebellion fled to Switzerland, France, England, and America. This was the Second German Wave, a group decidedly more engaged politically than their humble and pious predecessors who wanted only a patch of soil and privacy.

The 48ers brought with them uncompromising notions of social justice, human dignity, and human rights. Numbering about 5,000, they settled everywhere including places like Michigan, Wisconsin, Minnesota and Ohio where they inserted themselves unapologetically into the political process and were often at the forefront of social change, the abolitionist movement, and organized labor. Unlike most of their predecessors in the first wave, they were intellectuals – teachers, artists, scientists, publishers, and politicians who immediately expressed their convictions publicly in newspapers, journals, and social activism. Two 48ers of note were Carl Schurz and his wife Margarethe. An ardent abolitionist and advisor to Abraham Lincoln, Schurz also served as a general in the Civil War. Margarethe founded the first kindergarten in America in 1856.[23] Perhaps the most noteworthy of the 48ers was Karl Marx who, after hopefully repatriating back to Germany at the outset of the revolution was forced yet again to flee, settling for good in England where he would work until his death on his most famous work, "Das Kapital."

For all the immigrants who fled their home country to Detroit, Michigan, or any other part of the U.S., America offered a respite from some onerous and unbearable political or economic situation. Once there, however, it did not take long for some to realize (the Irish, especially) that they had merely traded the

Chapter 7 *A Melting Pot, Boiling*

poverty, exploitation, and oppression in one place for much the same dismal life on a distant shore. And for the Irish there was probably an unnerving similarity in that English was the dominant language as well as an equally entrenched Protestant, Anglo/Saxon Yankee society that made it clear whose culture and habits were at the top of the socio-economic pecking order. Yes, it was true: there was no monarchy. But they were soon forced to realize the U.S. had its own aristocracy and that it was rooted not so much in lineage than the more insidious, stratifying, and universal power of money. Whereas in England and Europe the feudal lord's purview had, at least, been restricted to the boundaries of his patrilineal domain, immigrants newly settled in America (especially those on the low end of the social ladder) soon realized that the new elites, no matter where in the world, knew no boundaries and that exploitation based on the new industrial capitalism had grown into a monster with far-reaching, global tentacles. Mere distance and geography no longer offered safe haven. One could not escape it in the next shire, county, or even the next country.

Though generally accepted, the metaphor of America as a "melting pot" is, in reality, quite a shallow one, leaving to the imagination all the socio-political implications of the concept of "melting." While apropos in suggesting diversity, it is insufficient in accounting for the fate of these diverse masses once "melted" into the existing population. For clarity, we take a cue from the physical world: when things are melted, as in the production of steel or butter in cooking, it is a transitory step in a more complex process with a clear, intended end; i.e., a piece of steel, a slice of pie, utility and hunger. So too with newly blended populations. Each group brings to its new environment the memories and fears of past experiences in its native land. Huddling together at first, each in its safe and separate enclaves, it assesses the political landscape in the new country and eventually gravitates toward a party that resonates with its worldview, offers security, and a possible seat at the table in the national dialogue. Viewed through this prism, antebellum Detroit and Michigan were simply microcosms of most of the North and much of the new frontier which, by this time, had extended to mid-western territories like Kansas and Nebraska who were making their own bid for statehood. (Soon to be touchstones, as we shall see, for sectional division and violence.) In future decades, after the Civil War, Italians and Poles would also become an important part of Detroit's ethnic mix. (The French, of course, had had a presence from the beginning, albeit no longer overt.)

> **"Whereas in England and Europe the feudal lord's purview had, at least, been restricted to the boundaries of his patrilineal domain, immigrants newly settled in America (especially those on the low end of the social ladder) soon realized that the new elites, no matter where in the world, knew no boundaries and that exploitation based on the new industrial capitalism had grown into a monster with far-reaching global tentacles."**

After the infusion of the 48ers into Detroit's already substantial German population, they, the Irish, and the Blacks would come to form the principle, three-legged demographic stool of the city, each of whose history, cultural identity, and place in Detroit's social and economic hierarchy would thereafter drive events in the centuries to come. In the political choices each ethnic group made and their response to external events such as recurring economic crises and the Civil War, one can see the roots of the racial tension, segregation, and periodic economic dysfunction that would prove to be Detroit's undoing far in the future.

What, then, were the political options for immigrants and anyone else in the Detroit of the 1850s? Until 1854 and the formation of the Republican Party,

Chapter 7 *A Melting Pot, Boiling*

the political battlelines were chiefly drawn between Whigs and Democrats. One could also sign on to a more clandestine party called the "Know-Nothings," a nativist, racist, and vehemently anti-Catholic party that advocated for free land for white farmers in the new territories; "Free Soilers," they were called. (Upon being questioned about acts of violence against Catholic property obviously perpetrated by them, members would reply that they "know nothing.")

Democrats had dominated Detroit's political scene since the Jackson administration. The Democratic Party in Michigan and elsewhere at this time regarded itself as the unyielding champion of the common folk, embracing a populist Jacksonian agenda that was virulently anti-bank and anti-elite. Egalitarian in its outlook, it represented the economic well-being of the common white man (race and gender emphasized), its views on race and ethnic minorities ranging from indifference to overt hatred. It favored limited government and eschewed the notion that a superior, educated elite was necessary to make political decisions for average working people. The Whigs, on the other hand, were categorically anti-Jacksonian. Formed in 1834 by businessmen and believers in the self-correcting mechanism of capital markets (Smith's "Invisible Hand" was, they would insist, firm but "just,"), tariffs to protect them, and federal involvement in economic projects and development, Whigs were also exclusively Protestant and anathema to anything Catholic. For Whigs, Catholics (read that "Irish") represented the potential co-optation of the American political process by the Vicar of Christ – the Pope. The name "Whigs" was deliberately suggestive of the wigs worn by members of the British Parliament.(23)

For the Irish, the choice was clear. Relegated to the most menial jobs and vilified by the Protestant Whig business community and worker activists who saw the Sons of Erin as irredeemable, drunken, shiftless reprobates, Holy Mother Church was a well of faith and security representing the one constant in their otherwise tragedy-laden passage to American shores.(25) The Church tethered them, at least, to an ancient and venerable organization that accepted and forgave them no matter their transgressions and perceived weaknesses in the eyes of society. The choice was also obvious in a practical sense. Given the Democratic Party's indifference to slavery, its belief in the inherent inferiority of the black race, and its categorical support for black ostracism and disenfranchisement, the Democratic Party of this time represented an institutional imprimatur for the exclusion of the only class of workers who posed a threat to the supply of menial jobs to which the Irish were relegated. And, in these days before objective journalism or journalistic integrity, the Democratic Party's racism and propaganda found a reliable conduit in the Detroit Free Press.

Always a source of populist rage, the Free Press's racial venom was newly invigorated by its editor, Wilbur Storey, who purchased the paper in 1853. Storey introduced the novelties of a Sunday edition and expanded news coverage through use of the telegraph, then a new technology. Storey's hatred for the black race, his support of slavery, and his contempt for abolitionists who helped them was relentless and unequivocal. "No more worthless, vagabond, lazy, good-for-nothing set of mortals can be found," Storey proclaimed on the eve of the bombing of Fort Sumter, "than the negro population of the northern states."(26) Many Germans were Democrats as well and were faithful readers of the Free Press. German political loyalties were more complex, dividing along socio-economic and intellectual lines. Pre-Second Wave Germans were also, like the Irish, not interested in opening the door to an influx of competitive black labor from the south, so fear mongering from racists like Storey often drove less educated Germans into the Democratic camp. The most effective scenario used by

Chapter 7 *A Melting Pot, Boiling*

Democratic Party racists to engender fear among the poor and working class was the specter of black slaves rising up in rebellion, overtaking their masters, then migrating north in a flood to compete with whites for menial jobs.

The alternative political choice at the outset of the decade were the Whigs, but the Whigs' days as a viable political party were numbered when Storey assumed the reigns of the Free Press in 1853. They were primarily a business party, their *raison d'etre* being to champion the cause of liberal capitalism. Whigs reviled the plantation economy in the south not out of moral outrage over the subjugation of the black race, but rather for the fact that it contradicted their own sacrosanct notions of self-determination, the importance of (white) wage labor in the Calvinist equation of success with hard work and virtue, and the acceptance of government involvement in the form of protective tariffs.

But regardless of the moral cloud that hung over it, it could never be said that the southern plantation system was not profitable. Ironically, it was even more profitable for business interests in the allegedly "free" north who were more than happy to turn a blind eye to the institutional injustice it posed as long as much of the profits redounded to their benefit; and indeed they had, from the very beginning of the republic. As historian Howard Zinn reminds us, cotton production grew from a thousand tons in 1790 to a million tons in 1860. More importantly, the 500,000 slaves who worked the cotton in the early south had grown to 4 million in the same period.[27] Naturally, then, in order for such a large group of oppressed, forced labor to exist in a purportedly free society required philosophical, religious, and political justifications of labyrinthine proportions, drawing on everything from biblical passages purportedly affirming black's inferiority, to minimizing their exploitation by relegating them to the level of mere property: human capital of little more worth than machinery. It also required an equally oppressive system of laws and a police state to keep this potentially rebellious population at bay. (Some scholars believe that the South's string of victories in the early years of the Civil War could be attributed to the fact that for decades that had kept a disciplined and experienced militia at the ready to quash any sign of slave rebellion before it could take root.)

Political Parties in Early Michigan and the U.S.

Democrats — Library of Congress

Whigs — Anti-Whig poster, 1848 (Library of Congress)

Know Nothings — Library of Congress

Chapter 7 *A Melting Pot, Boiling*

Apologists for southern slavery like John Calhoun had, as early as 1828, become increasingly incensed at what they regarded as an unfair sectional, economic asymmetry between southern planters and northern business interests, a rift that grew from a small fissure to what ultimately would become a gaping chasm. Contrary to conventional wisdom, the first crack did not occur because of slavery, but, rather, economics. The plantation/cotton economy was very dependent on foreign markets, supplying much of the raw material to British mills who worked it into finished goods that ultimately found their way back to the south. Naturally, then, any sort of tariff was scorned by southern planters who saw it as a governmental intrusion that fell exclusively on the southern economy. As Richard Hofstadter explains, "It was tariffs, not slavery that first made the South militant."(28)

Calhoun hurled his first salvo at the sectional issue in the campaign of 1828 when the so-called "Tariff of Abominations" created an obvious advantage for northern bankers and industrialists. Setting aside for the purpose of inquiry the moral abomination that was slavery (if such a thing is possible), for southern planters there were obvious advantages to a captive, brutalized workforce that never went on strike for higher wages, could never leave the plantation, and who worked from sun-up to sun-down no matter what the weather. With the exception of periodic stress emanating from a volatile Northern banking system, the plantation system was generally stable and profitable, especially throughout the 1850s.

The problem, as Southern planters saw it, was their dependence on foreign markets. This required the use of Northern banks to facilitate that commerce. These banks were, in turn, viewed suspiciously as irresponsible purveyors of "stock jobbing" and speculation, practices southerners (and, frankly, many in the rest of the country with some justification) reviled as the source of the North's periodic problems. Southern businessmen believed that were it not for their dependence on large Northern banking interests – that is, if they could simply deal directly with foreign business interests and governments without routing their business through northern institutions – they could insulate themselves from continuing economic turmoil. They could then, or so they might have imagined, rock on their porches in the summer heat and sip their mint juleps with a smug smile, hearing tales of chaos in northern cities where workers struggled to survive, lived in squalor, and waited with dread for the next downturn.

Through successive panics – 1837, 1857 – without a central bank to regulate it, the northern economy ground through the inevitable cycles of boom, bust, and misery while season after season the dependable cotton crop (and reliable foreign customers to buy it) brought prosperity to southern planters who had no concern for the plight of labor and whose labor costs rarely exceeded the price of whips and chains. Given the relative stability of the southern system in the face of continual, cyclical turmoil in the north, it was not too difficult for Calhoun and fellow southern masters to mistake stability for superiority and – a full hundred years before George Orwell – come to the conclusion that slavery was in fact "a good – a positive good."(29) Though outright secession might secretly have been in the hearts of Southerners, it was not on their lips; not yet, at least. And, frankly, they did not truly want to secede, but rather to insulate themselves and their slave-based culture and economically

> "…without a central bank to regulate it, the northern economy ground through the inevitable cycles of boom, bust, and misery while season after season the dependable cotton crop (and reliable foreign customers to buy it) brought prosperity to southern planters who had no concern for the plight of labor and whose labor costs rarely exceeded the price of whips and chains.

Chapter 7

A Melting Pot, Boiling

dominate the north. Their role and importance in the world economy, or so they believed, was unimpeachable and perpetual. In a hubristic statement, then Senator James Hammond from South Carolina unequivocally answered a fellow senator's insinuation (William Seward from New York – an ardent abolitionist) that the South's days were numbered, whereupon Hammond famously replied:

> "Would any sane nation make war on cotton?...The South is perfectly competent to go on, one, two, or three years without planting a seed of cotton...What would happen if no cotton was furnished for three years?...England would topple headlong and carry the whole civilized world with her save the South. No, you dare not make war on cotton. No power on earth dares to make war upon it. Cotton is King."[30]

Though they inveighed against what they felt were the shortcomings and evils of northern industrialism and wage labor with the fervor of a socialist at the barricades, the difference was that Calhoun and Hammond's alternative stood on the even more rickety and doomed legs of slavery. Cotton had become increasingly lucrative and abundant with the introduction of Eli Whitney's cotton gin in 1794. But Whitney's gin merely solved the technical problem of separating the fiber from the seed – a once long, laborious and therefore unprofitable process. Two insurmountable facts remained. First, cotton, by its nature, is a hungry and inefficient crop, quickly depleting the soil and demanding ever fresher loam to produce its bounty. Secondly, cotton still needed to be picked by human hands; preferably the hands of someone at once physically tolerant of long days in the hot sun and who, in turn, could be forced to do so with little or no resistance and, most importantly, for no pay. Ironically, Whitney's efficiencies made cotton into an irresistible cash crop, one requiring ever more slaves to extract it from the fields. In their constant quest for new land and more slaves, southern planters anxious to cash in looked hungrily at territories like Kansas, Nebraska, and California, eager to sow their fields with cotton and to people them with a black race they deemed inferior and divinely pre-destined for the task. After all, as the same Senator Hammond put it in 1858:

> "In all social systems there must be a class to do the menial duties, to perform the drudgery of life. That is, a class requiring but a low order of intellect and but little skill. Its requisites are vigor, docility, fidelity...Such a class constitutes the very mud-sill of society and of political government; and you might as well attempt to build a house in the air, as to build either the one or the other, except on this mud-sill. Fortunately for the South she found a race adapted to that purpose to her hand...We use them for our purpose and call them slaves."[31]

Though Eli Whitney's cotton gin solved the vexing technical problem of separating the cotton from the seed, it did nothing to mitigate the plant's tendency to suck the life from the soil quickly and totally. Nor did it replace the need for the unique labor – that is, black, slave labor – more tolerant of the brutal, hot climate it requires to grow. Therefore, among the planter class, both the perpetuation of slavery and expansion to fresh growing regions became of paramount importance. Hence, the desire to absorb new western territories into its orbit. **(Photo: Tom Murphy VII. Wikimedia Commons.)**

The southern political establishment knew clearly that without slavery and without the fresh soil in new states where it would be tolerated, the southern economy would crumble. As it weathered each financial storm that blew in from the north, it felt more and more confident of its security and moral rectitude. Seeking to bring this confidence to bear on the course of legislation in the Congress, Calhoun concocted bizarre schemes in which slavery would be justified and/or normalized constitutionally. One was the concept of "nullification," the notion that states who might be harmed by a federal policy have the right to disregard or "nullify" them. Calhoun even floated the idea of electing two presidents, one to represent the North and the South. Each year, the issue of which potential state would allow slavery and which would not increasingly drove the political discourse, enflamed sectional rivalries, and widened the crack in the national identity a little wider.

> "Certain politicians with ordinarily Whig sensibilities realized that their pro-business platform was tepid and ineffectual on the issue of slavery – that a more aggressive stand against the pro-slave agenda was in order; not necessarily on moral grounds, but generally for practical political reasons."

More importantly, decisions over the slavery question reverberated in the economy. For example, Calomiris and Schweikart[32] have argued convincingly that while it is widely accepted that the Panic of 1857 was triggered by the suspension of Ohio Life Bank after the supposed indiscretions of a trader in its New York trader, Edward Ludlow, the actual cause – further removed – was a fall in stocks of railroads serving the Kansas-Nebraska region. Unfortunately, these stocks were a major part of Ohio Life's portfolio. These securities experienced a precipitous fall in their value when aforementioned Free-Soilers stopped migrating to Kansas after Kansans voted (in a rigged election) to allow slavery in the state. This could not, in turn, have happened had Congress not passed, in 1854, the Kansas-Nebraska Act. This legislation not only reversed the no-slavery policy that had existed in the "unorganized territories" west of the Missouri border since the 1820 Missouri Compromise, it granted those two potential states the right to vote on whether they would endorse slavery. A year later, the infamous Dred Scott decision would codify the notion that blacks were simply property. Anti-slavery factions in Kansas cried foul, refused to accept the results of the election for statehood, and militarized. The stand-off devolved into violence and guerilla warfare, each side exacting a murderous toll on the other in a period that is now known to history as "Bleeding Kansas."

As the South's confidence and sense of entitlement increased, so too did their efforts to enshrine it legislatively. Land-hungry Southerners were delighted when, in the Guadalupe Hidalgo Treaty (1848) ending the war with Mexico, that country ceded to the U.S. a vast area encompassing present day Arizona, California, New Mexico, parts of Colorado, Nevada and Utah – virtually the whole of the remaining land mass of the western United States. For Southern planters, these territories loomed like a new calf waiting to be fattened and milked for the cause of King Cotton. As luck would have it, in the election of 1845 they had earlier received a sympathetic and very powerful advocate in the person of James Polk. A protégé of Jackson, Polk was a dark horse candidate who won on a platform of expansionism over the favorite, Martin Van Buren. Embracing expansionism was a wise strategy as the country, regardless of its views on slavery, was intoxicated at this time with the notion of Manifest Destiny, and how could Southerners or anyone else feel otherwise than that the new territories were a gift of divine providence? But whose God: the one who, as Hammond had suggested, justified slavery, or the one who didn't? For the time being, Congress and the federal judiciary seemed to be praying to the God of slavery. There had been, after all, a spate of legislative

Chapter 7

A Melting Pot, Boiling

and judicial actions that seemed to sanction it: the Fugitive Slave Act in 1850, which essentially gave a legal nod to slave-seeking bounty hunters; the Kansas-Nebraska Act, which had reversed previous injunctions against slavery in the Northwest Ordinance of 1787; and the 1855 Dred Scott decision, which unequivocally stated that slaves had no right of legal redress and had no civil status other than as property for Southern planters.

Abolitionists perceived this as evidence that the federal government was being hijacked by southern, pro-slavery interests. Certain politicians with ordinarily Whig sensibilities realized that their pro-business platform was tepid and ineffectual on the issue of slavery – that a more aggressive stand against the pro-slave agenda was in order; not necessarily on moral grounds, but generally for practical political reasons. (Not to insinuate that Whigs were otherwise callous on the slavery issue. Many had heartfelt abolitionist convictions which, though sincere, did not rise to the level of outright activism.) On July 6, 1854 a group of Whigs and anti-slavery Democrats met in an oak grove

Cast over each new western territory as it opened up was the menacing cloud of the slavery question; that is, whether slavery would be part of its economy when it achieved statehood. The issue had been moot since 1820 when the Missouri Compromise dictated that all "unorganized territories" be free of slavery. In need of fresh soil to subjugate and the slave labor to accomplish it, southern planters pressed the issue stubbornly in Congress until, in 1854, President Pierce signed the Kansas Nebraska Act, a legislative sea-change which, instead of enjoining slavery outright, allowed residents of Kansas and Nebraska Territories to decide the issue at the ballot box. When, however, the pro-slavery contingent in Kansas won in an obviously rigged election, violence – a prelude to the carnage that was to come seven years later – erupted in a bloody period known as "Bleeding Kansas." One year later, in 1855, the Supreme Court would rule on the make the infamous "Dred Scott" decision, codifying the notion that blacks could, indeed, be property, thus paving the way to civil war. **(Library of Congress. "McConnell's Historical Maps of the United States." 1919.)**

Chapter 7 *A Melting Pot, Boiling*

in Jackson, Michigan to address the problem. Adopting opposition to slavery as the core of their platform, they formed a new political organization called the Republican Party.(33) For them, the very real prospect of six western territories falling to control of the Southern planter class called for action. Such an outcome had been anticipated nearly ten years earlier by Democrat, David Wilmot who – angered at dark horse, James Polk's election to the presidency over then favorite, Martin Van Buren – introduced an amendment that would preclude slavery in any western territory won in the Mexican War.(34) What was a hypothetical in 1845

(National Constitution Center: https:w/constitutioncenter.org/blog/on-this-day-the-republican-party-names-its-first-candidates)

had, at the time of the meeting under the oaks, become a very real possibility. Members of the new party decided to resurrect Wilmot's earlier proposal and press it legislatively in an attempt to arrest the pro-slavery momentum. Invested with new energy, abolitionists and northern movers and shakers alarmed at the South's increasing influence threw down the Wilmot Proviso as the gauntlet proponents of slavery dare not cross.(36) The Wilmot Proviso proved to be an effective wedge, forcing what was before a crack in the body-politic into a chasm bridged only by the violence of the Civil War. It was a sound strategy and it worked in Michigan where, in 1851, Republican Zachariah Chandler was elected Mayor of Detroit. A successful local businessman and one of the groups that had met in the oak grove in Jackson, Chandler's election opened the door of government to others who were there on that day: future Senator Jacob Howard, and future Governor Austin Blair. All would, as Taylor suggests, "…play important 'Radical Republican" roles in the upcoming Civil War."(35)

Since, it could be argued, the Republican's embrace of abolitionism was in great part a political gambit – more Machiavellian than moral – the fortunes of Detroit's black community did not markedly improve with the rise of the party. There were just 193 blacks in Detroit in 1840. By 1850, that number had grown to 587

> Alarmed at the strength of the southern juggernaut steamrolling pro-slavery legislation, pro-business, anti-slave Whigs and abolitionists saw the need for a new party that could push against slave owner interests. In March, 1854, a group met in an oak grove in Jackson, Michigan and did just that, forming what would become the Republican Party.

– almost a quarter of the 2,583 blacks then residing in Michigan. Most had come in the previous two decades from larger cities in Virginia like Richmond, Fredericksburg, and Petersburg in order to escape that state's increasingly draconian enforcement of its black codes. They came from varied backgrounds, many possessing valuable skills in the trades and business. However, despite their potential value to the community, the door to white society was closed. Relegated to the margins of the dominant white culture, blacks were only allowed to interact with whites in a servile capacity and, more significantly, were confined to a certain area of the city just north of Jefferson Avenue and east of Woodward Avenue, a boundary that would prove to be stubbornly persistent both physically

Chapter 7   *A Melting Pot, Boiling*

and spiritually in the decades to come. Leaders in the black community like George de Baptiste (who went on to become a White House steward in the William Henry Harrison administration) and Henry Bibb (a prominent abolitionist and editor) worked tirelessly, exhausting every legal avenue – both judicial and through political activism – in their efforts to earn for the black community the rudimentary rights enjoyed by the white population.[36]

But by 1850 Detroit's blacks had made only minor inroads into the civil life of the community, winning only the right to vote in school district elections: in black districts, that is. Blacks had to create a rudimentary and separate system of education for themselves even as they also had to pay taxes to support the white system from which they were excluded.[37] At Michigan's constitutional convention in 1850, the prospect of black suffrage was discussed, but not seriously. The event did little to change the dominant view of the white population throughout Michigan and elsewhere in the North that blacks were inferior and unworthy of participation in political life. John Bagg of Detroit was unequivocal on the subject: "I would not let them [Negroes] come into our civil, political, social, conjugal or connubial relations."[38]

In the face of such unmitigated bigotry and racism, Detroit's blacks took refuge in faith, coalescing around a system of churches which served, one could argue, as a surrogate outlet for their thwarted political instincts. Marginalized and frustrated, others directed their energies to more clandestine pursuits, such as helping to shepherd refugee slaves across the Detroit River to freedom on the Underground Railroad. Others turned to emigration as a solution. In 1851, a group of Detroit's black leaders, including William Lambert, Henry Bibb, and Episcopalian leader, William Monroe met at the North American Convention of Colored People in Toronto. Ultimately, Bibb would settle in Canada and Monroe would emigrate to Liberia, becoming a missionary. Lambert remained, his frustration taking a darker turn. Increasingly, he began to sympathize with abolitionist John Brown's scheme for violent insurrection.

On March 12, 1859, prominent black abolitionist Frederick Douglas arrived in Detroit for a speaking engagement. Unbeknownst to Douglas, there to meet him was John Brown who had arrived a few days earlier with fourteen liberated slaves seeking freedom in Canada, and five of Brown's own men. Forced from "Bleeding Kansas," Brown had left behind his own violent and bloody trail. There, he had lost two sons to proslavery mobs and his own men had killed five pro-slavers with broadswords. After Douglas' speech, Brown attended a meeting of Detroit's local black leaders at the home of William Webb. There, he shared his plan to attack an armory in the south, seize the weapons, and turn them over to enslaved blacks. Douglas advised against the action, deeming it too risky. Though Douglas later denied it, Brown ostensibly left the meeting in anger after calling Douglas a coward.[39] Undaunted, Brown remained determined to carry out his plan. He had chosen the object of his attack carefully. The federal arsenal at Harper's Ferry, West Virginia sat at the confluence of the Potomac and Shenandoah rivers. Inside the lightly guarded facility were twenty-thousand rifles, muskets, and pistols – the largest collection of weapons in the south. The plan was simple: he would abscond with the guns before any force of significant size could challenge him and transfer them to the eager hands of slaves who, finally confronted now with the means and a plan for their liberation, would follow Brown in the very rebellion that had so long been a nightmare scenario for slave owners.

Brown seized the arsenal easily enough, the legion of grateful slaves he imagined would join him did not materialize. He managed to arm between only twenty to fifty slaves.[40] King Cotton had done his job well.

Chapter 7 *A Melting Pot, Boiling*

Brown was both a victim of his optimism and his idealism and, like many idealists, could not abide any compromise – no, "misbirths" as DuBois would characterize it – in his moral vision.[41] He failed to realize that the shackles of this dispirited and broken group went deeper than their hands and feet, gripping the slaves' hearts and minds as well in a prison of submission and hopelessness. A people beaten into subservience and docility is often more at home with a hoe than a gun. And yet, there was a soberness and wisdom to their restraint. It was, in fact, a well-advised hesitation born of the grim and brutal reality of the punishment they would suffer should they fail. Yes, there had been tragic precedence for slave resistance in the rebellions of Gabriel, Vesey, and Turner, and even successful uprisings in the Caribbean colonies of the British. But none of the slave rebellions had been successful in the American South. Those that participated paid dearly with the lash and the noose.

As DuBois suggests, though Frederick Douglas and many other slaves admired John Brown for his conviction and his courage, they found his plans suspect. Though laudable, they felt Brown's efforts would be too small to dislodge the entrenched system that had rooted itself so thoroughly throughout the south. The problem was much bigger than a single man and the contents of one arsenal. It would require – as the not too distant future would prove – violence on a massive scale. Given that, scions of the northern economy and government could not, as Zinn explains, leave an upheaval of such magnitude to chance and the fortunes of one zealot at Harper's Ferry:

> "Such a national government would never accept and end to slavery by rebellion. It would end slavery only under condition controlled by whites, and only when required by the political and economic needs of the business elite of the North."[42]

Brown's true significance, like a particle in quantum physics, can be understood only from the perspective of the observer. For slave owners desperate to maintain the brutal status quo, he was a dangerous fanatic and a terrorist who threatened the security of the cotton/slave-based culture. But if Brown was, as southerners insisted, an insane fanatic, then it would have made more sense to keep the incident as quiet as possible, to lock him away and point to the "fact" of his failure and inefficacy. Instead, Southern slavers gave Brown a courtroom and a forum from which to publicly condemn slavery and willingly seal his martyrdom by hanging, which they obliged him on December, 2nd, 1859.

Even before the trial, sick and wounded in the solitude of his jail cell, he had accepted his fate as the one consequential moment in what had been a life filled with tragedy, uncertainty, and a roller coaster of economic success and failure. He had assumed the mantle of a cause that had no payout in cash and power: that of the enslaved and the oppressed. At his trial, he addressed the court:

> "…had I so interfered in behalf of the rich, the powerful, the so-called great, or in behalf of any of their friends, – either father, mother, brother, sister, wife, or children, or any of that class – and suffered and sacrificed what I have in this interference, it would have been all right; and every man in this court would have deemed it an act worthy of reward rather than punishment."[42]

Whereas war requires the resources and power of a nation to prosecute, hope does not. Word of John Brown's failed mission and his fate at the gallows spread quickly among the slave population. No, they could not fight, but they could leave; just leave. And many did, shepherded among "The Black Way" on the Underground Railroad. As DuBois recounts, though the

Chapter 7   *A Melting Pot, Boiling*

black population of Maryland and Virginia increased about four percent between 1850 and 1860,

> "...in the three counties bordering on Harper's Ferry – Loudon and Jefferson in Virginia and Washington in Maryland, the 17,647 slaves of 1850 had shrunk to 15,996 in 1860, a decrease of nearly ten per cent. This means a disappearance of 2,400 slaves and is very significant."[44]

Brown's raid on Harper's Ferry was a tactical failure, but a psychological success. It struck terror in the hearts of plantation owners. The uprising they'd feared so long had finally happened, and had been inspired not by an oppressed black, but by a white Northerner. It underscored for them the need to separate themselves once and for all from the North and its pernicious influence. Lincoln's election in 1860 and anti-slavery Republican electoral victories throughout the North were the proverbial straws for the slave-holding South. On December 20, 1860, South Carolina seceded from the union. Just four months later, in April, 1861, Confederate ships would fire on Fort Sumter and give Lincoln the pretext he needed to wage the war John Brown could not.

"Tragic Prelude" 1938. A mural by John Curry commemorating John Brown in the Kansas State Capitol.
(Source: United Missouri Bank of Kansas City. Wikimedia)

Chapter 7   *A Melting Pot, Boiling*

Chapter 8

A Rich Man's War, A Poor Man's Fight

War is the father and king of all.
                                    Heraclitus

Whereas Heraclitus' war is a philosophical subtlety – an intuition of the constant give and take that pulsates underneath and creates the physical world – its vision is at least positive and constructive. In a much cruder and literal sense, Heraclitus' words could also describe the tendency of actual armed conflict to spawn immense fortunes for a few at the expense of many who are killed and maimed. This, of course, is nothing new. The masters of war have always been the winners in the marriage of martial and mercenary, and the Civil War was no different. For the "young men of '61," as Matthew Josephson calls them[1] – men like Mellon, Carnegie, Rockefeller, and Morgan who each hired a replacement to fight and perhaps die in their stead – the war was an opportunity: a chance to bring wartime profiteering to a new level of sophistication, exploiting the government's need for the tools and resources of mass destruction with corporate efficiency and scale.

Implicit as well in Heraclitus' words is the power of war to drive government policies in new directions, forcing officials to feed war's insatiable hunger for blood and treasure on a new and massive national scale previously deemed ideologically unacceptable. For the country, the conflict was a monumental bloodletting that went only part-way toward redeeming the nation's original sin of slavery. It left intact the deeper sickness of racial hatred that even violence could not undo and still festers. At the beginning of the conflict, the abstraction of national unity trumped the very real horror of slavery. For the "young men of '61," the carnage on the battlefield and the fate of blacks in bondage was only of peripheral importance, simply a more violent manifestation of a world where, for the elite and privileged few, the true business of the world was not war, but business.

Bombardment of Fort Sumter, March, 1861. **(Currier & Ives. Wiki Commons.)**

In the weeks after April 12, 1861, as the dust settled on Fort Sumter and the small garrison of eighty-five Union soldiers led by Major Robert Anderson finally evacuated the island fortress, the newly minted Confederacy could now celebrate complete control of all the federal outposts that had formerly wrung South Carolina's Charleston Harbor. Though the immediate triumph seemed to herald an auspicious beginning for the South's secession from its industrial nemesis in the north, the next four years of carnage it triggered would prove their success at Fort Sumter to be merely short-lived and pyrrhic, the bugles of victory a mere swan song for a doomed plantation system based on the intolerable subjugation of four-million black slaves. Despite the defeat, for newly elected President Lincoln the fall of Fort Sumter was also a strategic victory of sorts. Aware, after the South's formal secession, that war would be the only means of healing the profound cultural rift, Lincoln realized it was imperative the North not be seen as the aggressor: that is, to not strike the first blow. By refusing to surrender Sumter to the rebel government; by sending a ship on a strictly humanitarian mission to resupply the Union garrison with food and supplies, Lincoln provoked a violent response from the Confederate forces who fired on the ship, turning it away. Thereafter, when Southern artillery opened fire on Sumter in the pre-dawn hours of April 12th, Lincoln had won the right to characterize the conflict not as a war to force the North's will on the South, but rather a war to preserve the union against the rebellious states. Lincoln had, it seemed, the moral high ground.

The battle at Sumter was mostly sound and fury, the thirty-four-hour bombardment reducing much of the fort to rubble yet, miraculously, not claiming any lives. Absent the grim reality of the massive death yet to come, the war thus far was relegated to grandiloquent promises for the enemy's destruction and chest thumping on both sides. Both were convinced of their righteousness, and each was sure their own military superiority would bring the other to its knees within three months after one great, decisive battle to come.

After Sumter, the opening salvo of the war – before the endless names of the fallen would march day after day in neat black rows across the pages of local newspapers – volunteers were eager and abundant on both sides of the Mason-Dixon. Aware of the imminent struggle, Lincoln called for each state sympathetic to the Union to contribute its share of 75,000 volunteers to a militia capable, or so he believed, of suppressing the rebellion,[2] a force constrained in number and purpose by the Militia Act of 1795.[3] The standing army, at this time, totaled at most 25,000, most of which was stationed on the western frontier in order to deal with Indian resistance. And, frankly, no one expected much more from the antebellum federal government than to deliver the mail and collect tariff revenue at the border. Most of those with an inkling of the length and breadth of coming destruction kept it to themselves, the majority overcome by patriotic fervor.

> "….the next four years of carnage it triggered would prove their success at Fort Sumter to be merely short-lived and pyrrhic, the bugles of victory a mere swan song for a doomed plantation system based on the intolerable subjugation of four-million black slaves."

Detroit quickly became the epicenter of Michigan's response to the President's call for fighting men, promising to provide the single regiment (roughly 750 to 1000 men) Lincoln had requested. Meeting with local political figures and businessmen on Tuesday, April 16th (just one day after Lincoln's request), the new Republican governor, forty-three-year old Austin Blair, committed the state to the goal. There was, however, one problem: Michigan's treasury was virtually empty. The state's treasurer, John Owen, solved the problem by helping to pass a resolution pledging that the city of Detroit would loan Michigan $50,000. In addition,

Chapter 8 *A Rich Man's War, A Poor Man's Fight*

Owen committed the citizens of Michigan to raise the remaining $50,000 of the total $100,000 it would take to raise and provision such a regiment.(4) Encouraged by these developments, Blair challenged the state further by requesting ten additional volunteer companies, each consisting of a captain, a first lieutenant, a second lieutenant, four sergeants, four corporals, two musicians, and sixty-five privates.(5) Any attention would have been a boon to the existing militia which had been underfunded and neglected for decades, its members ill-equipped both psychologically and logistically for armed combat. The one militia unit with a respectable pedigree, stretching back to 1836, was the Detroit Light Guard whose ranks suddenly became the goal of men from every profession in Michigan. Anxious to become part of the esteemed corps, many even offered up substantial bribes for the privilege of including their names on the unit's roster.(6)

21st Michigan Regiment. "Company of Sherman's Veterans" Photo by Matthew Brady. (Public Domain. **(Wikimedia Commons)**

Under then Governor, Austin Blair, Michigan provided many of the first soldiers to go to the front. (Photo, 1916. **Wikicommons)**

In just a week, by May 2, ten companies from all over the state had come together to form Michigan's First Regiment. By May 11 – in a city awash with displays of red, white, and blue flags and bunting of all sorts – the regiment mustered on the city's Campus Martius to the delight of the immense witness the iconic moment of pomp and pageantry. The day's events included a speech by the venerable and elderly Lewis Cass and, as native son and historian Silas Farmer recounts, "three thousand children sang the "Star Spangled Banner."(7)

Two facilities, the Detroit Barracks and Fort Wayne, would be the focal point of military activity in the city at the outset of the conflict. New recruits were processed and trained at these two forts. Whereas Fort Wayne (named for the hero of the "Battle of Fallen Timbers," General Anthony Wayne) was newly constructed and not quite finished, the Detroit Barracks had been the main mustering point for troops on their way to the Mexican War in 1845. At the beginning of the next decade, it had been overseen by a young officer by the name of Ulysses S. Grant. Over the course of the war, these two forts would be insufficient to handle the increasing amount of men needed to sustain the conflict, creating the need for yet more facilities in the area to house and train the men. On May 13th, The First marched through the streets of Detroit to the docks where it traveled by boat to Cleveland. From there, it went by train to Washington where it finally arrived at its destination in Washington D.C., ready to become the first group to be thrown into the maw of what would come to be a brutal and long war. Upon seeing the regiment, Lincoln is said to have remarked, "Thank God for Michigan."(8)

Chapter 8　　*A Rich Man's War, A Poor Man's Fight*

As for Congress, the political die had been cast nearly five months earlier on January 21st when five southern senators bade their colleagues farewell and officially threw in their lot with secessionist elements in their home states. With eloquence and, for the most part, civility characteristic of the Senate (that most "deliberative body"), five senators from Florida, Alabama, and Mississippi rose and gave the reasons they would be resigning their seats that day. One by one they spoke, enumerating as calmly as possible the issues which, in previous years, had raged like a storm among the august body. First, Florida Senator David Yulee told of an inescapable duty to his constituents who, despite his own reservations, had chosen the course of secession.[9] Fellow Floridian Stephen R. Mallory called for reason over passion and appealed to the well-being of the country rather than the dictates and divisiveness of party politics. After Clemont C. Clay Jr. of Alabama recounted the events that had led to the impasse, Benjamin Fitzpatrick also professed a duty to his constituents. Finally, Jefferson Davis – who shortly thereafter would become the President of the Confederacy – went to the well and gave a restrained yet still emotional accounting of the secessionist viewpoint, beginning with a familiar states' rights argument. He then dismissed Calhoun's notion of nullification as a half-measure whereby southern states would be required to stay in the Union, but pick and choose the laws they felt were justified. Davis felt this was an impossible scenario. Only through secession could the South become a sovereign, self-determining entity. They would, in essence, have the status of a foreign country, unencumbered by federal control:

"Secession belongs to a different class of remedies. It is to be justified upon the basis that the States are sovereign…"[10]

Davis, therefore, implies that only a definitive break can solve the crisis. He then strikes at what he regards (with some justification) as the hypocrisy of a northern adversary who, while publicly and politically rejecting slavery, still embraces founding documents which, though affirming in principle the equality of all people, in practice had from the start denied said equality to blacks, Indians, and women. How then, Davis asks, is the South's use of slavery presently enjoined by that same Declaration and Constitution?:

"She has heard proclaimed the theory that all men are created free and equal, and this made the basis of an attack upon her social institutions; and the sacred Declaration of Independence has been invoked to maintain the position of the equality of the races…When our Constitution was formed, the same idea was rendered more palpable, for there we find provision made for that very class of persons as property; they were not put upon the footing of equality with white men –not even upon that of paupers and convicts; but, so far as representation was concerned, were discriminated against as a lower caste, only to be represented in the numerical proportion of three fifths"[11]

When Davis finished, all five legislators exited the Senate with Davis in the lead.

In other venues less restrained by the Senate's traditional decorum, the matter-of-fact bigotry and racism at the core of the South's secession shone through. On April 23, 1861 Alexander Stephans, soon

Chapter 8 *A Rich Man's War, A Poor Man's Fight*

to be Jefferson's Davis Vice President, stated unequivocally:

> "The great truth, I repeat, upon which our system rests, is the inferiority of the African. The enemies of our institutions ignore this truth. They set out with the assumption that the races are equal; that the negro is equal to the white man."(12)

If the South's economic argument was not persuasive – that is, the immense role "King Cotton" played in both U.S. and world markets – there were also the more visceral reasons. Rooted in ugly and cruel racial stereotypes calculated to strike fear in the hearts of whites, this argument broached the prospect of millions of black slaves suddenly loosed upon the country in a flood. Liberated slaves would then be free to undercut the wages of white workers (a prospect that also unnerved many white workers in the purportedly "free" north), to violently overthrow their plantation over-seers (the memory of John Brown and Harper's Ferry was, after all, still fresh), and worst of all in their estimation, "…to consign their wives and daughters to pollution and violation to gratify the lust of half-civilized Africans."(13) Among the white supremacist gallery of nightmares, miscegenation and the toppling of the barrier between white and black provoked utter terror. And weren't they justified in thinking so? After all, had God not willed it? The venerable S.F. Hale – commissioner to the Alabama Secession Convention – certainly thought so in this letter to then Governor of Kentucky, B. McGoffin:

> "What Southern man, be he slave-holder or non-slave-holder, can without indignation and horror contemplate the triumph of negro equality, and see his own sons and daughters, in the not distant future, associating with free negroes upon terms of political and social equality, and the white man stripped, by the Heaven-daring hand of fanaticism of that title to superiority over the black race which God himself has bestowed."(14)

By April 12, 1861, the South's exit from the Union was complete. The first out the door with Davis had been the deep south states: Alabama, Florida, Georgia, Louisiana, Mississippi, South Carolina, and Texas. After Sumter, the border states – Virginia, Arkansas, Tennessee, and North Carolina – joined the exodus. Though the Confederacy had triggered the conflict with its easy military victory at Charleston Harbor, one could say that the more consequential victory was legislative and belonged to the Union; not a single shot was fired. For decades, the floor of the Senate and House had seen heated battles between sectional interests over economic and social issues like taxation, tariffs, and slavery. Now, with secession, Republicans scored a victory by default, their southern opponents simply walking away and ceding the floor to lawmakers sympathetic to the Union. For the first time in the nation's history, a significant portion of its federal legislative bodies had

"After fate delivered the antebellum government into the lap of the infant Republican party (it had, after all, been born just seven years earlier in that oak grove in Jackson, Michigan), it began its tenure as an entity at once blessed with the gift of no serious opposition, yet still facing the challenge of funding and

Chapter 8 *A Rich Man's War, A Poor Man's Fight*

dropped their proverbial weapons and surrendered their influence to the opposing party.

After fate delivered the antebellum government into the lap of the infant Republican party (it had, after all, been born just seven years earlier in that oak grove in Jackson, Michigan), it began its tenure as an entity at once blessed with the gift of no serious opposition, yet still facing the challenge of funding and prosecuting an impending war. Under these influences it would evolve quickly into a unique and determined political entity, one giving rise to many of the federal institutions of today. At the outset, before the real pressures of war, Republicans began their mission as an ill-formed incarnation of the pro-manufacturing Whigs. While the new party received at first the baton of Smithian *laissez-faire* without much issue, it increasingly cast a weary gaze at British economic hegemony at work across the globe and began to loosen its grip on Smith's "invisible hand."

> "While the new party received at first the baton of Smithian *laissez-faire* without much issue, it increasingly cast a weary gaze at British economic hegemony at work across the globe and began to loosen its grip on Smith's "invisible hand."

Inspired by Hamilton's attempts to shepherd and protect the young U.S. republic with a national banking system, sound currency, tariffs, and support for manufacturing, intellectuals like Friedrich List (a first wave German intellectual who immigrated to the U.S. in 1823) suspected that while "free trade" sounded like a worthy economic principle, it could only work in a world filled with trading partners of equal prowess, and this was certainly not the case in a reality of wars, turmoil, and British manufacturing dominance. "...'Laissez faire, laissez passer,' " List grumbled in 1841, [15]

With its colonial possessions feeding it raw materials and absorbing its finished goods, its vast merchant fleet and extensive manufacturing facilities, England of the day was the acknowledged and formidable giant, not easily challenged. As List observed "...only very few of the inland manufacturers of other nations can, under free

Friedrich List

First wave German immigrant and economist, List saw early on the limits of the Smithian free market philosophy. World markets in the 1840s and '50s were dominated by Britain. In the face of Britain's obvious hegemony, it was foolish to imagine, List believed, that other economies like the infant U.S., could compete on a level playing field. List, therefore, argued for intervention through import tariffs and taxation in order to make domestic markets more competitive. "Laissez faire, laissez passer," he said in 1841, "an expression which sounds no less agreeably to robbers, cheats, and thieves than to the merchant, and is on that account rather doubtful as a maxim." **(Portrait, 1889, by Caroline Hövemeyer, List's daughter. In the Heimat's Museum, Reutlingen, Germany. (En. Wikiquote.org**

Chapter 8   *A Rich Man's War, A Poor Man's Fight*

trade, maintain in their own seaports the same prices as the English manufacturers." Larger capital, a larger home market, and cheaper sea transport "give at the present time to the English manufacturers advantages over manufacturers of other countries, which can only be gradually diverted to the native industry of the latter by means of long and continuous protection of the home market..."[16] The only recourse for budding economies like the U.S. was a strategy of protection utilizing a relatively high (but not prohibitive) tariff on foreign goods, and manufacturing facilities closely located to a strong agricultural center providing food easily without burdensome transportation costs. For List, these two factors – agriculture and manufacturing – were the necessary pillars of any young economy with hopes of trading successfully on the world stage.

When it came to the economic gospel according to Adam Smith, the nascent Republicans who assembled in 1854 in the oak grove at Morgan's Forty were only slightly heretical. While they accepted the soundness of free-trade principles in general, some merely questioned the circumstances under which trade could be "fair" as well as "free." Many Smithian concepts were repeated like a *leitmotif*, one of which was the notion that labor was the seat of all value, an idea that became politically codified as far back as Locke and one that played a significant role in thinkers from Jefferson to Marx. After all, nothing is perhaps more straightforward in a rudimentary craft and agricultural economy than the relationship of human energy to the finished product. With skilled hands, the village carpenter, tanner, silversmith, and potter each produce a thing of utility and/or beauty from raw materials which, but for their efforts, may have remained in a less useful, natural state. Farmers break the soil, sow, and produce a bounty that can be brought to market and exchanged for the *things* others make: products they need or want. It was simple, elegant, and proof that God the Clockmaker who fixed the planets in orbit and governed Newton's gravity also directed the minutiae of economic exchange according to equally precise laws, motivating humans through need and desire. And it was all lubricated with capital – the congealed embodiment of past labors to be used or set aside for future investment.

> "Capital was merely the means – the vehicle – but a beneficent Deity had so designed the machine that the outcome of all exchanges redounded miraculously to the benefit of everyone; especially to the laborer."

Though God the Clockmaker had set the gears of economic exchange in motion and stepped back to let it spin on its own with divine precision, the Holy Ghost was, many thought, still in the machine. Capital was merely the means – the vehicle – but a beneficent Deity had so designed the machine that the outcome of all exchanges redounded miraculously to the benefit of everyone; especially to the laborer. Economics of the time was only generally "scientific" in the modern sense and had not yet untethered itself from its theological underpinnings. This connection was especially strong on the U.S. side of the Atlantic where reality in the infant nation offered nothing to contradict such a roseate outlook. Labor was scarce in many places (therefore, commanding higher wages), and U.S. manufacturing had not yet spawned their own versions of Blake's "satanic mills,"[17] those dens of exploitation already found in English industrial centers like Manchester and London. The pessimistic Europe of Malthus and Ricardo – where a geometrically increasing population was doomed to chase an ever-

Chapter 8   *A Rich Man's War, A Poor Man's Fight*

dwindling food supply, and a tiny cabal of aristocratic landowners commanded higher and higher rent from over-stressed soil – was soundly rejected by the optimistic Republican political economists who insisted that such conditions exist simply when God's preordained laws are not followed; that is, when government compromises the process with wars or unnecessary meddling in the economic process.

Wayland to insist that the capitalist's gain redounds even more to the benefit of the worker. "The accumulation of capital is more for the advantage of the laborer than of the capitalist," Wayland deduced. "The greater the ratio of capital to labor, the greater will be the share of the product that falls to the laborer. Hence, the laboring classes are really more interested in the increase of the capital of a country, than the wealthy

---

Henry Charles Carey

While List's antidote to Britain's market power was to erect a wall of protective tariffs and taxation, Henry Charles Carey (family friend of List and a protege) expressed a more optimistic faith in the power of the new industrialism to produce goods quicker, cheaper, and thus – through the cost savings wrought by mass-produced goods – generate greater (and equitably distributed) income for both capitalist factory owners and their employees While prophetic and correct in his views of industrial productivity, he was naïve in thinking the economic gains from that productivity redounded evenly to both workers and capitalists. It would take someone like Marx to point out, in the very near future, that the economic advantages of increased production flowed into the pockets of industrialists and not workers. Nevertheless, Carey was an integral part of Lincoln's inner circle of advisors.

(Graphic of Henry Carey extracted from Daheim, Jahrgang, 1868, Seite 151. Wikimedia commons)

Never mind that on the eve of the Civil War, Charles Dickens had filled thirteen novels, including "Nicholas Nickleby," "Oliver Twist," and "Great Expectations," with downtrodden and dispossessed characters in whose lives one would be hard pressed to identify any subterfuge regarding God's plan other than being victims of unfettered capitalist greed. Though places like Lowell, Massachusetts were well on their way to imitating England's smoke-laden cities filled with the miasma of exploitation, it was still easy in the U.S. for people like Baptist preacher, dilettante economist, and President of Brown University, Francis

classes."[18] No doubt many a wretched soul languishing in England's poor houses and debtor's prisons would have begged to differ.

While Wayland's faith in free-market forces was uncompromising, a more consequential and nuanced voice in the new Republican economic nationalism was Henry Charles Carey. Carey, a deeply curious and widely read business man, inherited his father's successful publishing house. The elder Carey – Matthew Carey – was himself a noted writer and critic. Henry continued his father's practice of opening the family home to leading intellectuals for routine roundtables on subjects of every kind including economics, politics, and philosophy. A friend of the family, frequent visitor to the Carey salon, and an early influence was none other than Friedrich List who no doubt helped plant the seeds of Carey's sentiments and comprehensive worldview. Though elusive now to any but the most ardent students of history, Henry Charles Carey was, in his day, immensely popular and influential. Translated into five European languages as well as Japanese, he became part of Abraham Lincoln's inner circle and a principle architect of the administration's economic agenda. Like many thinkers of the day, a diverse interest in subjects ranging from sociology, to economics and politics vied for a place in his consciousness. Equally faithful to the notion of a just and loving God, Carey was preoccupied with uncovering the divine thread that wove them all together in a harmonious human quilt. He therefore rejected the notion that high profits and high wages could not co-exist or that God cynically used starvation and death to winnow down excess population. On the contrary. It was not from a lethal, competitive war for the means of survival that humans prospered, but from their interaction and common, productive enterprise. In short, by *association*.

At the core of Carey's thought is Smith's notion of the division of labor. That is, the more hands involved in the production of an article, and the more those hands are assisted by labor saving devices, the greater the number of commodities produced in less time. Since these items are produced with less and less labor, they are more abundant. Given, then, that the amount of labor required to produce a thing bestows on it its value, then articles mass produced with less labor (aided by machines) are cheaper and more plentiful than something laboriously produced from start to finish by a single pair of hands in the back of a cottage. In Carey's words:

> "That as every improvement in the quality of labor tends to diminish the quantity of labour required for the production of any commodity, it follows, that it also diminishes the quantity that can be obtained in exchange for commodities of a similar description already accumulated."[19]

Commodities mass produced by multiple hands aided by machinery have less value and can be exchanged for less of similar items in the marketplace produced previously. Any tool, machine, or money invested to facilitate production or to create a thing is termed "capital." For Carey, the emphasis is on the *quality* of labor; or, how efficiently one works by employing labor saving devices and distribution of tasks. Carey was, therefore, convinced that a laborer's wages were directly dependent on their *productivity* (one of Carey's more enduring theoretical contributions), and not, as was the prevalent notion, that wages were determined by past savings (known as the "wage fund" doctrine.)[20] Furthermore, while it would seem that the diminished value of mass produced items would mean a loss for the owner of capital, in Carey's thought the apparent shortfall is made up by an increase in the *quantity* of items produced: items more abundant and therefore cheaper and more available for sale to the workers who produced them. As Carey himself describes it:

> "…labour is improved in its quality," it becomes more productive, capital is accumulated at less cost of labour, and its owner can demand a smaller proportion of the product in return for granting its aid."[21]

Chapter 8   *A Rich Man's War, A Poor Man's Fight*

It was logical, mutually beneficial, and perfectly in keeping with what one would expect from a loving God. But it made no allowance for the one variable that could send the whole system crashing down; the one element overlooked in a cosmos purportedly overseen by an all-powerful and beneficent Deity: human greed. Though people like Wayland and Carey naively imagined that profits from surplus production would find their way into the pockets of workers with mathematical regularity, they underestimated the ability of the owners of capital to sabotage the scenario. As Kaplan explains:

> "That labor must inevitably obtain a larger share of the product as capital increases, is after all, pure assumption. In the world of realities, from day to day, wages come down as well as go up; unemployment reduces the morale as well as the income of the laborer; captains of industry may increase their gains by reducing output as well as increasing it. The gains of technological advance are not invariably shared with labor."[22]

Smith's invisible hand appeared to be quite arthritic. In short, as Kaplan concludes:

> "The pecuniary side of business, by which economic wealth and power are measured, does not of necessity work hand in hand with the welfare side."[23]

Workers on the east coast in the budding union movement were already struggling against this reality, especially the newly-arrived Irish.

Even before the fall of Fort Sumter made the prospect of war inevitable, Lincoln and his Treasury Secretary, Salmon P. Chase, began looking for money: revenue to fund the very expensive enterprise that is war. Chase was a novice in the world of government finance, but his abilities were good enough to assess the dismal state of the government's financial condition. In addition to a deficit of $65 million, short term bonds that had been issued by the Buchanan administration during the panic of 1857 were coming due. Most of the government's revenue at this time came from customs duties, a source threatened by the secessionist South's professed intention to lower their own tariffs, thereby drawing business to the south. In addition, there were three loans totaling $40 million dollars the government had not yet negotiated, and, finally, government expenses were projected to be about $3 million. The winds of war rattled at the windows of the Union government and whistled through empty coffers.

Faced with raising money for the Union's war effort, Lincoln's Treasury Secretary, Salmon Chase, attempted to sell government bonds to eastern bankers. Regarding his terms as not lucrative enough, even in the face of impending war, bankers rejected the government's offer, causing a financial crisis for Lincoln and his government. **(Photo: Matthew Brady. Library of Congress – Matthew B. Brady National Photographic Art Gallery.)**

Chapter 8 *A Rich Man's War, A Poor Man's Fight*

Money – much money – would be needed; and fast. As his predecessors at Treasury had done in the past in times of war, Chase decided to approach the big eastern banks in New York and Boston with a bond issue which they could, in turn, sell for a profit to smaller investors. Probably out of an unconsidered urge to woo the bankers with irresistible terms, Chase opened up bidding of $30 million on $8 million in bonds of 94 percent at par. Eastern financiers were ecstatic until Chase reneged on the initial proposed bid by reducing it to a mere $3 million with terms still 94 percent at par. Bankers slammed the door on Chase, laying waste to the Secretary's illusion that the money-men, out of patriotism, would support their government in time of war under any terms.[24] They would not. Thus, Chase was presented with the first evidence that the interplay of economic forces was not, in fact, so naturally harmonious. God had indeed stepped away from the machine and the machine was broken.

The situation was dire. Projections were that the deficit would reach nearly $11 million by August. In addition, expenditures on the war had already reached $2 million in June.[25] Desperate, Chase went before the recently convened Thirty-seventh Congress and broached a combination of both foreign and personal loans. While a foreign loan was simply a means of soliciting foreign capital in addition to native sources, the prospect of a personal loan was, on the other hand, quite novel in terms of government financing. It was simple: the government would raise funds directly from the citizenry by offering them low-denomination bonds, redeemable in three years at generous interest.[26]

> **"Thus, Chase was presented with the first evidence that the interplay of economic forces was not, in fact, so naturally harmonious. God had indeed stepped away from the machine and the machine was broken."**

The idea of raising money directly from the electorate seemed, to Chase, a good way of giving them a personal interest in the outcome of the war, a tangible way of expressing their patriotism and, frankly, a way to bypass the banking establishment which, in the eyes of many, was regarded as untrustworthy, opportunistic, even parasitic and the cause of the nation's periodic economic crises. But the need was immediate and the logistics of preparing such a large subscription for personal loans were formidable. Chase was compelled, for the time being, to pursue more traditional avenues and revise his offer to bankers in New York and Boston. He offered $5 million in short-term Treasury Notes, but refused to entertain low bids, a move that so irritated bankers, they turned their back on Union securities completely, thus proving that patriotism and the war effort were not significant factors in the bankers' agenda.[27]

Chase's faith in the bankers was further shaken in May when he invited bids for another bond issue of $14 million dollars which, by law, had to be sold at par, a fact the bankers would not accept and caused them yet again to shun the bidding. In response, Chase relented and made a second issue for $9 million, this time with no par restrictions. Bankers bought only $7 million in bonds and $1.5 million in Treasury Notes; still not enough.

Enter Jay Cooke *et al.* Cooke and his family already had a foot in the administration's door. Jay Cooke's father had shared a podium with Chase, who had been governor of Ohio before being sent to the Senate, then tapped by Lincoln for Secretary of Treasury. In addition, Jay's brother Henry – a prominent newspaperman and politico – was friends with John Sherman who inherited Chase's Senate seat and, in addition to being a member of the powerful Finance Committee, was also the older brother of General William Tecumseh Sherman. The Cookes hailed from Pennsylvania, a state that ranked somewhere below New York and Boston in the eastern bank pecking order. Seeing their opportunity to make an honest profit while also helping the war effort, the Cookes marshalled their assets and bought a $200,000 chunk of the May loan, a gesture that caught Chase's attention and opened the door to more cordial relations with the family.[28]

After soliciting yet again the banking community for funds through August, 1861 with limited success, Chase decided to move forward with the personal loan plan. Among the 148 agents appointed to sell the subscription to the public was Jay Cooke, a task he would embrace with enthusiasm. After the first week, the other 147 agents had together sold $25 million worth of the issue. Cooke was selling over $100,000 worth of bonds and personally sold $5 million dollars, a talent for fund raising he would repeat again and again throughout the war.[29] Cooke proved so adept at selling the bonds to the public that by October, 1862, Chase named him "special agent" with exclusive responsibility for selling subscriptions of the 5-20s. Using his own network of 2,500 agents and utilizing the media for mass ad campaign extolling the virtues of patriotism and personal involvement through bond sales, Cooke revolutionized the practice of government fund raising and gave the general public a feeling of personal responsibility and inclusion in the war effort.[30] Government funding was no longer the exclusive province of bankers, foreign and domestic.

Money was only part of the demands of war; the bill would also come in blood. Sumter's lack of casualties was, perhaps, a noisy but inconsequential prelude to the real carnage to come. Sons and husbands had yet to fall when Chase and Cooke were first scrambling to raise money, so patriotic fervor was stoked in the press on both sides and cries for a definitive, epic battle rang over a landscape as yet un-littered with corpses. Blood lust is easy when there is no blood. That changed on July 21st, 1861 at a little creek near Centreville, Virginia called Bull Run. Under pressure from the press and the public, and concerned that the 90-day enlistments of the volunteer army would expire before being utilized, Lincoln goaded Irvin McDowell – the general in charge of the recently raised army – to move

Jay Cooke – "…Cooke revolutionized the practice of government fund raising and gave the general public a feeling of personal responsibility and inclusion in the war effort." **(Photo: "The Century" monthly magazine, Jan. 1, 1865. Wikimedia Commons.)**

his 28,400 men and confront the 21,900-man Confederate army massed in Virginia's Shenandoah Valley. McDowell protested, insisting his troops were green and not yet ready for battle. Lincoln countered, arguing that the other side was green as well.

Chapter 8   *A Rich Man's War, A Poor Man's Fight*

McDowell dutifully moved his army 25 miles into neighboring Virginia where, after some initial skirmishes, a full-blown battle erupted on the banks of Bull Run Creek. By afternoon, a throng of spectators who made the seven-hour carriage ride from Washington had amassed on a ridge about five miles away, anxious to see the clashing army like fans at a football game. They could see little from their perch and few realized that by day's end, after an initial back and forth, the Union forces would be routed and sent into a panicked, terror-filled, humiliating retreat back to Washington D.C.. The cost in blood had now come due: out of 2,896 Union casualties (wounded, missing), 460 were killed. Of the 1,982 casualties on the Confederate side, 387 were killed. This was merely a prelude to the death and destruction to come. Thus, for the first time the real face of war reared its ugly head and Lincoln, Chase, and the Republican dominated Thirty-seventh Congress struggled to confront it.

Out of necessity, the Thirty-seventh Congress of 1862 was productive. Its flurry of legislation was born of both the constant challenges presented by the war and a dedication, despite the conflict, to realize the Republicans' Wayland/Carey inspired goals of protectionism, westward expansion, and technological development, especially railroad building. Two elements remained constant, however: the demand for men and money. To satisfy that demand, the legislature was pushed in policy directions it probably would not, under normal circumstances, have considered. On the economic side, the body had already, in August of the previous year (1861), passed the Revenue Act which established the first tax on income – a flat tax of three percent on incomes above $800. The following February, 1862, the Thirty-seventh addressed the lack of a viable currency in the Union caused, in part, by the suspension of specie payments by large eastern banks. The amount of currency in circulation was of questionable value and not enough for an expanding economy to which the government was adding an additional $1 billion a year. "To leave that economy dependent on a motley array of irredeemable, often counterfeited, frequently worthless bank paper was not only to invite, but to insure, disaster."[31] The legislators solved the problem of conversion to scarce gold and silver by simply ignoring it, thereafter declaring paper currency called "greenbacks" legal tender for all government debts and flooding the economy with $150 million worth of them.[32]

By July, 1862 – with the costs rising and casualties escalating into the tens of thousands,[33] – the bulk of the war was being funded by bond issues and revenue from tariffs which, though substantial, were still not enough to cover the growing conflagration. The income

The first major battle of the Civil War occurred at a little creek called Bull Run near Centreville, Virginia on July 21, 1861. Ignoring the potential danger, spectators brought picnic lunches to observe the battle from a distance. The battle quickly turned fierce and violent, forcing not only the revelers to flee for their lives, but the Union forces as well. **(Engraving: "The Soldier in Our Civil War" by Frank Leslie. Manassas National Battlefied**

Chapter 8   *A Rich Man's War, A Poor Man's Fight*

tax created the previous year had yielded nothing, in great part due to the fact that it didn't come into effect until June, 1862. Even if it had been implemented sooner, there was, frankly, no entity designated to collect it. After flirting briefly with the idea of a land tax, Congress opted to scrap the earlier tax plan and replace it with something more comprehensive – one that would both cast a wider net for revenue and create a permanent infrastructure to sustain it. While the original tax had fallen short because it exempted incomes under $800 a year, the new legislation would be progressive, retaining a three percent impost on incomes over $600 and five percent on $10,000 and above. The act also included a three percent *ad valorem* on manufactured goods, a stamp and liquor tax, and a surcharge on the total receipts of railroads, banks, insurance companies and other large entities.[34] But the greatest change was institutional in that it created an enduring new government sub-agency within the Treasury Department and a person to head it. The Office of the Commissioner of Internal Revenue was established to oversee tax collection within 185 designated districts.[35] Thus, revenue formerly tethered to the changing fortunes of commerce was now firmly anchored in income whose collection was entrusted to a non-elected, bureaucratic entity.

Less than two months after the Legal Tender Act, the war insinuated itself on the Congress' business like an unwanted guest demanding attention. On April 6, 1862, Confederate forces launched an attack on an unsuspecting Ulysses S. Grant at a little town on the Tennessee River called Shiloh. With reinforced ranks, Grant counter-attacked the next day. In two days of fighting, the battle left over 13,000 Union soldiers killed or wounded, with over 10,000 Confederate fallen: more than all the casualties in all the previous wars.[36] Tragically, it would become the new normal. In the body count was the implicit message that Lincoln had finally found, in Grant, a general willing to prosecute the war despite the human cost, a tally that would grow even larger on both sides as the conflict ground on. Despite the loss, the Thirty-seventh stayed focused on its larger political agenda of settling the western expanse with what it imagined would be independent, apolitical, taxpaying farmers committed only to the soil and bound, from coast to coast, by a network of railroads.[37] Both could be realized, or so Republicans imagined, by appropriate legislation with dedicated funding for farming and land grants to railroads for construction. This agenda had been part of the Republican platform since the 1850s but had been thwarted continually in Congress by pro-slave, southern states fearful of free-soil, free-labor interests and eastern industrialists concerned that the act would drain their factories of cheap labor. Now, with those states absent through secession, the Thirty-seventh Congress was free of this political obstacle and, between May 15th and May 20th, 1862, passed both the Homestead Act and an act creating the Department of Agriculture to oversee the settlement process and nurture the farmers' skills.

As with previous government-sponsored land grants going back to the Northwest Ordinance of 1787 (*see* Chapter Five), the legislation was full of generous giveaways which ultimately, just as it had in the past,

> "The Office of the Commissioner of Internal Revenue was established to oversee tax collection within 185 designated districts. Thus, revenue formerly tethered to the changing fortunes of commerce was now firmly anchored in income whose collection was entrusted to a non-elected, bureaucratic

Chapter 8 *A Rich Man's War, A Poor Man's Fight*

wound up in the hands of unscrupulous business interests and speculators and not, as time would prove, those sturdy, honest yeomen for whom it was intended. The war banged again on Congress' door just a month later with even deadlier effect. Between June 25th and July 1st, Union General George McClellan and his 100,000-strong army fought six different battles against a rebel army of 93,000 led by General Robert E. Lee.[38] After the final day, 15,500 Union Soldiers had been killed or wounded with the battered but victorious Confederacy suffering 20,000 casualties. Though McClellan's ultimate retreat put a tactical victory in the Confederate column, it came at high cost for the South. It burnished the image of Robert E. Lee but was yet another dispiriting defeat for the Union and a clear signal of both the length of the war to come and the cost in lives. For Lincoln and legislators in Washington it was a disturbing reminder that in the struggle for money and manpower, coffins were being filled as quickly as coffers.

Nevertheless, despite yet another battlefield setback for the Union, Republicans continued to press their domestic agenda into July of 1862, passing the aforementioned Revenue Act, the Railroad Act, and the Morrill Land Grant College Act. Like the land legislation, the Railroad bill provided a purse full of government money with very loose strings. Unfortunately, with its attention necessarily focused on the war, the Republicans had neither the time, the resources nor, perhaps, the inclination for effective management, so its largesse came with very little oversight. Laying track quickly from the Atlantic to the

Real time photo, 1863, of Capitol Building under construction. Two years into the Civil War, and the 37th Congress – without the opposition of the entire, secessionist southern contingent – became one of the most productive in the nation's history. Along with funding and prosecuting the war, the 37th laid the foundation for our modern government, passing such legislation as The Revenue Act, The Railroad Act, and the Morrill Land Grant College Act. ("Capitol, Washington, north-east view." Andrew J. Russell, photographer. Library of Congress.)

Pacific was the priority, so land-grants were thrown at railroad tycoons who opportunistically brokered parcels on either side of the route, sometimes selling them to the highest bidder, sometimes holding onto them, bidding up the price beyond the reach of the homesteaders for whom they were intended.[39] Priced out of the land near the tracks from where it would be easier to bring their goods to market, farmers were forced further out on the plains where soil was much less hospitable and Native Americans – tired of being swindled out of their patrimony – often violently challenged their right to be there.

And the vultures circled, not just around the western lands and railroad tracks, but above the battlefields as well. It was the usual suspects; predators for whom the horrors of the conflict were just mute references in the daily papers and mere opportunities to be exploited.

There was, for instance, shipping magnate, Cornelius Vanderbilt. As designated shipping agent for the War Department, Vanderbilt worked through his

Chapter 8   *A Rich Man's War, A Poor Man's Fight*

agent (a man named Southard) and "exacted a purchasing commission of 5 to 10 per cent, while paying what were afterward thought high rentals of $800 to $900 a day for obsolete river or lake steamers."[40] There was Pierpont Morgan who, after underwriting a purchase of $17,486 for 500 defective rifles, sold the same carbines to a Union government desperate for weapons for a cool $109,912. The weapons had the potential to blow the thumbs off the soldiers unfortunate enough to use them.[41] These were just two, as Josephson recounts, "of the great mass of citizens…engrossed in the multifarious industrial activities evoked by the immense destroying and consuming of a modern war."[42]

The accounting sheets of the rich swelled, fed by war's ceaseless appetite for food, munitions, and clothing. At the same time the lists of those killed and wounded that hung on posts and windows in myriad towns throughout the north and south got longer and longer, telling the truth of the ugly enterprise: it was a rich man's war and a poor man's fight. After Sumter, when the marching bands and flag-waving crowds sent the first troops off to war in '61, the thought of war was much easier than the reality of it. Early on, when it became obvious that the rich on both sides – the businessmen, the industrialists, the plantation owners – were the benefactors of the common soldiers' sacrifice, abstractions like the "Union" and "states' rights" bowed, for the average man, to the urge to survive. With crops to take in and families to support, the martial music and the red, white, and blue bunting faded to a memory.

After McClellan's Peninsular campaign failed in July, 1862, Lincoln asked for volunteers to replenish the Union ranks, sending out a call to the northern states for 300,000 more troops. Michigan's share of this total would be six new regiments, or, 6,000 men. On July 15 – just ten days after the bloody Seven Days' Battle – Detroit's mayor and wealthy brewer, William C. Duncan, organized a rally to encourage recruitment. The event, held in Detroit's Campus Martius, began at 7:30 pm. To date, it was the largest public gathering in Detroit's history and though it began auspiciously enough, it became clear that many in the audience were less than enthusiastic about the prospect of serving and perhaps losing their lives in yet another Union defeat. Speaker after speaker who went to the dais to extol the virtues of patriotism and recruitment were greeted with cat calls and derision. "Bull Run," one voice intoned, reminding the city fathers of that humiliating defeat.

The mob got more and more brazen and provocative until finally, as Detroit's largest employer and owner of Eureka Iron Works, Eber B. Ward arose to speak, the crowd lunged at him and might have injured or killed him were it not for the intercession of Sheriff Mark Flannigan and his deputies who spirited Eber to safety at a nearby hotel. As the wealthiest person in town, the class overtones at the root of the attack on Eber were unmistakable.[43] It was a harbinger of things to come. Even the venerable, now quite old, Lewis Cass barely escaped the melee. For the city fathers, the horrible optics of this event could not stand. To counter it, they organized another event the next day which was a success. As inducements, the event's finance committee offered bounties of $50 to any single man and $100 to any married man who would enlist. Well-off Detroiters also pledged varying amounts to the cause, and Detroit's Common Council offered $40,000 to help raise the regiment.[44] It was only through these efforts that further cannon fodder was recruited. Thereafter, the Union would have to resort to the more compulsory and less savory mechanism of a draft,

Chapter 8 *A Rich Man's War, A Poor Man's Fight*

something it would do a little over a year from the time of the Campus Martius riot.

In its need for bodies, the Union began to consider a once forbidden resource: free blacks. On July 17, 1862, Congress passed the Militia Act, a bill allowing men and boys "of African descent" to aid in "constructing intrenchments, or performing camp service or any other labor, or any military or naval service for which they may be found competent…"(45) In other words, blacks would be relegated to menial tasks, thus freeing more white soldiers for duty in the meat grinder on the front lines. For some in the north, especially those of Democratic ilk who were okay with the war effort as long it strictly involved the abstract goal of preserving the union, black service (and especially emancipation, which would legally put blacks on an equal and competitive footing with poor whites) was a bridge too far, and stoked the simmering fires of racial tension. But those anxious to bar blacks from the field at the time of the bill's passing would be, perhaps, less particular in a matter of months.

On September 22, 1862, Union General George McClellan clashed with Confederate General Robert E. Lee at Antietam Creek in Sharpsburg, Maryland. After twelve brutal hours of fighting, the war claimed another 12,469 Union casualties with 10,316 Confederate soldiers killed or wounded. Frustrated, the President could not understand why Union armies, with their obviously superior numbers and resources, could not score a clear-cut victory.(46) Assuming McClellan's habitual hesitation was the reason for the North's continual poor performance, Lincoln replaced him with General Ambrose Burnside. The President urged Burnside to attack General Lee who was dug in on the hills above Fredericksburg, Virginia. Burnside did just that on December 13th, 1862, sending wave after futile wave up the hill into Confederate rifle-fire until, after just two hours, 6,000 Union soldiers were mowed down. It would be the worst defeat yet for the Union which suffered 12,653 casualties – more than twice as many as Lee whose total casualties, in comparison, were 5,377.(47)

"But the string of Union defeats, and Lincoln's calculated evasiveness and pragmatism on the issue of slavery became a liability in terms of international politics. By leaving the door to the South ajar, Lincoln was, in the beginning, inviting the Confederacy to forsake their rebellion and re-join the fold with slavery still in place."

While the Militia Act could be regarded as the first legislative nod toward black freedom, it was hardly a sea-change and may never have come about were it not for the rapidly escalating body count of white soldiers and the dire need for manpower. Even though the gesture was codified in the congressional record, it was more practical than moral in spirit. For his part, Lincoln – ever the politician – did not initially embrace abolition publicly as a definitive goal of the war effort, lest he alienate those border states still wobbly on the Union and abolition. His goal at the outset of the conflict was, as Hofstadter suggests, "to bring back the South *with slavery intact."*[sic.](48) But the string of Union defeats, and Lincoln's calculated evasiveness and pragmatism on the issue of slavery became a liability in terms of international politics. By leaving the door to the South ajar, Lincoln was, in the beginning, inviting the Confederacy to forsake their rebellion and re-join the fold with slavery still in place. By doing so, Lincoln muddied the political waters in England and France where, with the Union blockade of imports to the Confederacy and the protectionist cocoon thrown up

Chapter 8   *A Rich Man's War, A Poor Man's Fight*

around Northern industry by the punishing Morrill Tariff of 1862, the conflict was perceived by Europeans (deprived of Southern cotton and barred from U.S. markets) as a war over the Morrill Tariff, and not the moral issue of slavery. Business interests sympathetic to the South deliberately fed the mis-perception that the conflict was purely a war over the tariff rather than a struggle over slavery.[49]

Quite frankly, Lincoln did little to dispel this view until, with consecutive Southern victories on the battlefield, England (starved for the South's cotton) began to consider recognizing the Confederacy as a viable and sustainable political entity. In order to forestall this, Lincoln had to switch the center of gravity of the conflict from an economic to a moral one. Since slavery had been reviled and opprobrious throughout Europe for some time, Lincoln and his allies in Congress decided to make the war clearly about slavery rather than trade. On January 1st, 1863 the President did precisely that. By issuing the Emancipation Proclamation, Lincoln successfully shamed Europeans into keeping their distance from the pro- slave South.[50]

No matter how Lincoln's personal views on slavery might have evolved at the time, the Emancipation Proclamation of January, 1863 was an act of pragmatism, more political than moral in spirit. While conventional wisdom has, in hindsight, graced it with a loftier purpose, it is not too cynical to regard it as a gambit to keep Europeans, particularly the British, from allying with the Confederacy; a gamble that worked. One has only to study the language of the Proclamation to appreciate its very limited scope. The Proclamation does not free slaves in every state, but rather, only those seceding states enumerated in the document; those, at the time, at war with the Union. As the Proclamation reads:

> "I do order and declare that all persons held as slaves within said designated States, and parts of States, are, and henceforward shall be free; and that the Executive government of the United States, including the military and naval authorities thereof, will recognize and maintain the freedom of said persons."[51]

"The Proclamation, no matter how disingenuous, changed that. With the stroke of a pen it officially invited blacks to the table of citizenship; not just citizenship in the legal sense, but, more frighteningly for poor whites, in the economic sense as well."

The Emancipation Proclamation, therefore, "had all the moral grandeur of a bill of lading," says Hofstadter, and was, in terms of the war effort, quite ineffectual except for its value as propaganda.[52] Symbolically, however, the Proclamation was a menacing development for the poor, white, northern wage earner (the Irish, in particular) who saw it as an invitation to newly freed blacks to come and compete for (and perhaps take from them) a limited number of menial jobs by working for an even lower wage.

If only Southern planters, early on, could have been lured back into the Union with their subjugated black workforce still in place. If only a deal could have been struck whereby half a country filled with wage earners could coexist with another half built on slave labor, then perhaps the horrific, North-South conflagration would not have devolved into such bloodletting. But such a peaceful scenario was never possible. In his heart, Lincoln the Senatorial candidate knew morally in 1858

Chapter 8 *A Rich Man's War, A Poor Man's Fight*

what Lincoln the President made a reality with the Proclamation of 1863: only violence (violence on a scale that could not be entrusted to an individual like John Brown, no matter how righteous; state-sponsored violence initiated and fed by all the resources of an organized government unwilling to entrust such an important agenda to anyone but itself) could mend the rift. "In my opinion, it will not cease," said Senatorial candidate Lincoln in a speech to Republican colleagues five years earlier, "until a crisis shall have been reached, and passed. A house divided against itself cannot stand. I believe this government cannot endure, permanently half slave and half free."[53] As long as four-million blacks remained an abstraction, safe and contained, on the southern periphery of the nation, then poor whites needn't be concerned.

Yes, blacks already lived and worked among them in the north, but they existed in an unspoken capsule of inferiority, away from the white population. The Proclamation, no matter how disingenuous, changed that. With the stroke of a pen it officially invited blacks to the table of citizenship; not just citizenship in the legal sense, but, more frighteningly for poor whites, in the economic sense as well. For working class white workers driving the wagons, working the docks, and tending the monotonous wheezing machines in the factories, it was the realization of all the nightmares painted by the pro-Slave Democratic press for decades, one that warned of black hordes loosed on the North.[50] Through the Proclamation, by government imprimatur, blacks were elevated from the nothingness of slavery to the status, albeit the lowest, of the working class. It was momentous. It was life changing. And for the white workers struggling to exist in the over-heated, inflated economy of the north where prices rose and wages not so much, it was intolerable and, more importantly, it was a recipe for civil disorder.[54]

Even with the Emancipation Proclamation, blacks were not allowed to perform one crucial service: they could not fight – not yet, anyway. Though black leaders like Frederick Douglas and abolitionist Wendell Phillips saw in blacks a reliable and capable source of manpower, racial prejudice and bigotry dismissed the prospect of blacks serving, doubting both their courage and willingness to stand in the face of enemy fire. More and more white soldiers were fed into the pipeline of battle, each deadlier than the last. So, the government asked for more. More and more, however, began to resist what they regarded as certain death. On March 3rd, 1863, Congress added an element of compulsion and passed the Enrollment Act, a sanitized moniker for what amounted to the first government draft.[55]

The bill generally designated those males between twenty and forty-five for at least a two-year stint. Among the exempt were: only sons of dependent widows, only sons of dependent elders, those with minor siblings dependent on their care, fathers of motherless minors dependent on the father's care, and those among multiple family members already serving. Also, convicted felons, those intellectually incompetent, and those physically disabled need not apply [Sec. 2 & 3]. Most controversial, however, (and as it turned out a recipe for violent resistance) was the bill's Commutation Clause [Sec. 13], a provision whereby those who could afford it could either pay a substitute to take their place, or, pay a fee of $300. This, of course, was a sum well out of reach of the average person at this time and as one might expect, an invitation for young men of means – men like J.P. Morgan, John D. Rockefeller, Andrew Carnegie and others – to avoid service and avail themselves of the

Chapter 8 *A Rich Man's War, A Poor Man's Fight*

mountain of money being pumped into the war economy instead.

Anticipating resistance, Congress divided the congressional districts into specified areas, each overseen by an official dubbed "Provost-Marshall" who would be charged with ensuring enrollment and bringing recalcitrants and deserters who refused to enroll either to justice or to the front line [Sec. 5-12]. For many young white men on the farms and in the cities, the Emancipation Proclamation freeing certain blacks (blacks who could not fight) and the draft (a conscription the rich could buy their way out of) were unconscionable. The Union's recent lopsided defeat at Fredericksburg did not exactly inspire patriotism or courage. Nor did the casualties thereafter at Chancellorsville (14,000), Vicksburg (4,800), and, above all, the "victory" at Gettysburg with 23,000 plus killed or wounded.[56] Unmoved by the prospect of a glorious demise by bullet or lance on the battlefield, some even maimed themselves, choosing to cut off fingers or other appendages in the hope that their self-inflicted deformity might deliver them from the carnage. Some fled to Canada. More, however, expressed their rage through rebellion. There were anti-draft riots in cities as diverse as Newark, Troy, Toledo, and Evansville, but none would match the mayhem and death that reigned in New York.[57]

On Saturday, July 11th, 1863 draft officials in New York held the first successful lottery without incident. The following Monday, however, was quite a different story when, upon opening their doors for the next round of selections, they were greeted by an angry mob, made up mostly of Irish firemen called the "Black Joke Engine Company" who felt the volunteer fire-fighting services they provided exempted them from military service and, in particular, the draft lottery.[58] By July, 1863, the issue of white conscription was merely the latest tinder thrown on a smoldering pyre of working class unrest that had existed among the ranks of white labor in the north since the massive influx of Irish migrants in the mid 1800s. Prior to this influx, ironically, the menial jobs the Irish so jealously guarded had actually been done by blacks who were slowly edged out by the Sons of Erin.[59] Of the manual labor jobs in New York and elsewhere in major eastern ports, dock workers and longshoremen positions were perhaps the most insecure and volatile, paying at most, $1.50 per day and often less. To make matters worse, dockworkers were lucky to get three days of work a week and, in lean times, were often let go with no income. There were, in other words, too many people for too few jobs.[59] This meant that it was an employers' market, with the owners and managers setting the terms of employment with impunity. With no secure employment and no steady job to lose, militancy came easy.[60]

Longshoremen had struck for higher wages in 1855 and 1862. But after the war had begun, the government could not sit by waiting during a strike for much needed supplies while labor and capital fought over their differences. Under the wartime regime, capital, therefore, had its way. Under the watchful eye and rifles of federal troops, employers used blacks and foreign workers as strike breakers, further enraging Irish workers, injecting an element of racism into what was already an entrenched economic struggle. A pattern of violent resistance and racial animus was already established when conscription became law in 1863. The original mob of 500 that attacked the lottery office on July, 13th grew in size and fury, rampaging, looting, and murdering blacks for five days. Zinn characterizes the

Chapter 8 *A Rich Man's War, A Poor Man's Fight*

By July, 1862, the conflict was becoming one of attrition, with both sides feeding the war machine not only prodigious amounts of weaponry and materiel, but bodies as well. Lincoln asked for 300,000 more volunteers. On July 15th, a rally held by Detroit city fathers to encourage recruitment turned into a riot. Subsequently, another year of carnage passed and increasingly, the call to duty – eagerly heard in the early days of the war – fell on deaf ears. Still, the war's appetite for bodies remained. To fill the need, the government in Washington made service compulsory in 1863 and implemented a draft. The move was not well received and resulted in riots across the country, the worst occurring in New York City, depicted above. (**Engraving in the** *Illustrated London News*, **1863. Wiki commons.**)

motives of rioting workers, factors much more complex than simple racism:

\ "White workers of the North were not enthusiastic about a war which seemed to be fought for the black slave, or for the capitalist, for anyone but them. They worked in semislave conditions themselves. They thought the war was profiting the new class of millionaires. They saw defective guns sold to the army by contractors, sand sold as sugar, rye sold as coffee, shop sweepings made into clothing and blankets, paper-soled shoes produced for soldiers at the front, navy ships made of rotting timbers, soldiers' uniforms that fell apart in the rain."[61]

The first day of the riot, the mob focused its ire on symbols of the government and pro-abolitionist establishments. After looting and burning the draft facility, they moved on to attack the offices of Horace Greely's pro-war, pro-abolitionist *New York Tribune* where they were beaten back by armed *Tribune* employees. As the crowd grew larger and bolder, they fell upon the Colored Orphan Asylum (230 children escaped), destroyed and burned it. A night of heavy rain brought a respite, but the mob resumed its fury the next day with even more violence to property and people. They forcibly entered the homes of blacks and businesses where blacks were employed, dragged them to the street, beat them, then ransacked and burned their houses. Bodies were abused – one dragged through the street – and eleven black men were lynched. After three days, the mob had grown so huge and out of control that the police could not contain them. The rioters erected barricades and fought pitch battles with police and anyone trying to restore order. Only the arrival of 4,000 federal troops, already exhausted from battle at Gettysburg just ten days earlier, was enough to quell the insurrection. After the smoke settled, about 115 people had lost their lives (no one knows, actually, how many black bodies were thrown into the river), 100 buildings were damaged, many burnt to the ground. Though the riot was put down, their goal – to destroy or minimize the black presence in New York – was successful. Many blacks fled permanently, leaving the city with only

Chapter 8 *A Rich Man's War, A Poor Man's Fight*

10,000 blacks, a population hearkening back to the 1820s. Thereafter, white business owners were also hesitant to employ blacks.[62]

Detroit had experienced its own violent racial discord six months earlier in March when, two nine-year-old girls – Mary Brown, who was white, and Ellen Hoover, black – accused the bi-racial, forty-year-old owner of an eatery named William Faulkner of rape. The girls' testimony was convincing enough to convict Faulkner who was thereby incarcerated. The Emancipation Proclamation, just three months old at the time, had engendered hatred toward blacks in the Irish and German communities. Many in these ethnic enclaves clamored for something more dramatic for Faulkner than standard jurisprudence; something more akin to a rope and a sturdy tree limb. As always, the Democratic leaning *Free Press* could not resist fanning the flames of racial division and whipped the Germans and the Irish into a vindictive frenzy. Guarded by a group of federal soldiers, Faulkner was being led from the courthouse back to his cell when a mob gathered around the soldiers protecting him, demanding he be turned over to them for their own brand of instant justice. Tensions were high, and one of the soldiers fired, killing one Charles Langer.[63] Enraged and frustrated, the vigilantes proceeded to the black neighborhood around Beaubien where they burned black homes and businesses and violently set upon any black person they came across. Order was only restored after soldiers from Fort Wayne and the Twenty-seventh Infantry were deployed to quell the riot. Two blacks were killed, more than ten injured. Thirty to thirty-five homes of blacks had been destroyed. Faulkner languished in jail for six-and-a-half years when, in 1869, now sixteen-year-old Ellen Hoover admitted that she and Mary Brown had falsely accused Faulkner in order to escape trouble at home. Faulkner was pardoned on December 30, 1869 and provided with a subsidy to open a produce business as an attempt at restitution.[64]

Detroit, then, was not immune to the violence nor to the bitterness and resentment of forced conscription and the trauma of battlefield death on such a massive scale. But, unlike many northern communities far from national borders, potential draftees from Detroit were geographically fortunate in that Windsor, Canada– and what seemed like an easy escape – was just a short boat trip across the Detroit River.

Within days of the Enrollment Act's implementation, little Windsor's population swelled with "skedaddlers," the popular term for young men fleeing the draft. The *Free Press* made reference to this exodus, remarking: "the influx of skedaddlers fills the hotels and boarding houses."[65] After two-and-a-half years of blood soaked battlefields and what many communities regarded as increasing and very selective government intrusion by the Republican congress in its desperation for victory, the moral opprobrium that no doubt would have fallen on draft evaders with the first bugles in 1861 was now, in many cases, lifted once more of those bugles were playing over the graves of the fallen. Outraged that their sons and fathers were just $300 dollars short of exemption (and safety), cities and counties began to collaborate legally in the avoidance, establishing funds from various taxes and collections to pay the fee of their native sons called up for duty.[66]

> "…the moral opprobrium that no doubt would have fallen on draft evaders with the first bugles in 1861 was now, in many cases, lifted once more of those bugles were playing over the graves of the fallen."

Chapter 8   *A Rich Man's War, A Poor Man's Fight*

Some businesses pooled their resources with small contributions from employees to create an insurance fund of sorts to cover the fees of inducted employees. Others formed "draft insurance societies" and "draft protection clubs," charging fees of from $50 to $100 dollars, still a prohibitive sum for workers, especially the Irish.[67]

As early in the war as Sumter and Shiloh, abolitionist Republicans in the administration like Thaddeus Stevens (Ways and Means) and Owen Lovejoy (Agriculture Committee) urged the recruitment of blacks into the Union fighting force. Ever the pragmatist, Lincoln, however, was afraid such black empowerment would drive slave owners in the border states into an alliance with the Confederacy, thereby increasing its ranks. Unencumbered by such political considerations, certain generals in the field began early on to recruit blacks into their regiments without official government sanction. On August 30th, 1861 the commander of Union forces in St. Louis, Major General John C. Fremont, proclaimed all blacks in Missouri to be free. A furious Lincoln fired and replaced him.[68] Less than a year later, in May, 1862, General David Hunter declared all slaves owned by Confederates in his jurisdiction (Georgia, Florida, South Carolina) to be free. Hunter had even created a black regiment – the "First South Carolina (African descent) – which Lincoln ordered disbanded.[69] Two years in, and once it was clear that it would be a war of attrition with the North having the advantage with regard to men and resources, what had long seemed practical to command on the ground finally became policy for the administration. On Monday, February 3rd, 1863, a front page headline in the *New York Times* announced "The Passage of the Negro Soldier Bill."[70] Though a step forward, the language of the bill still bore a taint of racial distrust, specifying that any black contingent was to be "officered by white men."

Anxious to make black participation a reality was (white) Detroit newspaper editor and long-time supporter of the Underground Railroad, Henry Barnes who, in the editorial section of his newspaper, the *Detroit Advertiser and Tribune*, advocated for the plan. Barnes, an Englishman by birth, proposed the plan to Michigan Governor Austin Blair who, although receptive, was afraid of arming blacks so soon after the Emancipation Proclamation. Undaunted, Barnes personally lobbied Secretary of War Edwin Stanton who – obviously, by virtue of his position, was very aware of the need for soldiers – was receptive and, on July 24th, 1863 (nearly a month after the immense loss of life at Gettysburg) gave Blair permission to raise a black regiment. Barnes demonstrated his conviction by trading his desk for a commission as colonel at the head of the black regiment. Despite venomous attacks from anti-black Democratic publications like the *Free Press*, Barnes enlisted a sizable number of black volunteers and finally, by Fall's end, had gathered what was to be named the "First Michigan Colored Infantry."[71] After more recruiting and enduring a brutal winter in the wretched, freezing conditions at shoddy Camp Ward, the regiment was absorbed into the U.S. Army as the "102nd U.S. Colored Infantry." Without any of the fanfare accorded previous columns of white soldiers, Barnes marched his 102nd down Jefferson Avenue to the depot on Brush Street where they would board the train to Annapolis, Maryland and, thereafter, to valorous service on battlefields in South Carolina and Florida.[72] In all, the black Michigan contingent would become part of a total population of 180,000 black soldiers in the Union Army who would participate in thirty-nine full blown battles and 400 smaller engagements. They

Chapter 8   *A Rich Man's War, A Poor Man's Fight*

comprised 139 regiments and ten artillery batteries, suffering total casualties of 68,178.[73]

The epic battle at Gettysburg and the hard-won Union victory was the beginning of the end for the Confederacy who, throughout the next year-and-a-half, would mount a dogged resistance, their resources and manpower dwindling in inverse ratio to a Union force that increased in size, strength, and territory. Many more on both sides would fall at places with names like Chickamauga, Spotsylvania, and Cold Harbor, but the end was inevitable once Grant had cut the Confederacy in half by controlling the Mississippi and Sherman cut a swathe of destruction through the South on his march to the sea.

When Robert E. Lee surrendered at Appomattox on April 9th, 1865, it was only the end of formal hostilities and just the beginning of nation still wracked with racial hatred and class conflict. Even though Abraham Lincoln, the man who had shepherded the conflict to its momentous conclusion, would meet his end with a bullet to the head at Ford's theater just five days later on April, 14th, what he and the Thirty-seventh Congress

1st Michigan Colored Regiment – Formed and led by abolitionist newspaper editor, William Henry Barnes in 1863. **(Library of Congress.Wikicommons)**

had set in motion – an expanded federal bureaucracy, an industrial sector newly infused with federal subsidies and protective tariffs, and a black population freed, at least, in theory – was firmly planted, unfazed by one mere assassin's bullet. Detroit was ready. The factories that had churned out the guns, uniforms and the parts for steamships and wagons could now beat their swords into ploughshares and set Detroit on its course for the industrial behemoth it would one day become.

Chapter 8 *A Rich Man's War, A Poor Man's Fight*

Chapter 9
In God We Make Trusts

What do I care about the law? H'aint I got the power?

Cornelius Vanderbilt [1]

On April 9th, 1865, Robert E. Lee succumbed to the relentless onslaught of Union forces and resources. At McClean's Courthouse in Appomattox, Virginia, General Ulysses Grant sat next to Lee in an unpretentious, dirt-splattered uniform. Their attire spoke much. Lee, in contrast, was regaled in his finest dress uniform as though to give sartorial expression to the notion that even defeat could not rob him of his pride and dignity. The two generals exchanged awkward pleasantries (they had known each other from the Mexican-American War, seventeen years earlier). For his part, Grant – anxious for peace and not the South's humiliation – immediately stopped a union band from playing a celebratory tune, saying simply, "the war is over; and the best sign of rejoicing after the victory will be to abstain from all demonstrations in the field. The Rebels are our countrymen again."[2] It was, as history would show, more a wish than reality. Nevertheless, as the highest-ranking officers of both armies and as battle-hardened warriors who had sent thousands of men to their deaths, they were as anxious to implement as swift and as just a peace as only men who have experienced the horror of war were capable. After receiving a pledge from Lee that Confederate forces would lay down their arms and cease resistance, Grant allowed Confederate soldiers who owned their horses to keep them, aware they would need them for the more productive purpose of spring planting.

Slowly, the men from every state who, in the crucible of war, had come together and forged a common bond in order to execute the methodical

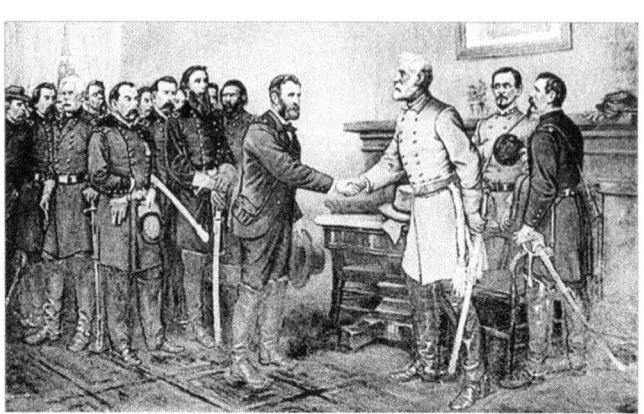

With a handshake between the reigning generals, the Civil War ends on April 9th, 1865 at McClean's Courthouse in Appomattox, Virginia. (**"Peace in Union." Reproduction of painting by Thomas Nast. Granger Historical Picture Archive. Wikimedia Commons.**)

mechanism of mass slaughter that is warfare trickled back to the towns to pursue independent lives in the cities that had sent them off to glory four years earlier. Now, instead of the wooden stocks of their rifles pressed against their cheeks and the gleam of bayonets in the sun, their hands would once again grip the handles of hammers and guide their scythes through the tall grain; or would they? With a telling hint of dread, the June, 1865 edition of *Fincher's Trades Review* assessed the situation: "As was to be expected, the returned soldiers are flooding the streets already, unable to find employment."[3] Those returning to the big cities of the east had little to look forward to:

"The cities to which the soldiers returned were death traps of typhus, tuberculosis, hunger, and fire. In New York, 100,000 people lived in the cellars of slums; 12,000 women worked in houses of prostitution to keep from starving; the garbage, lying 2 feet deep in the streets, was alive with rats. In Philadelphia, while the rich got freshwater from the Schuylkill River, everyone else drank from the Delaware, into which 13 million gallons of sewage was dumped every day."[4]

Even the chaos of war and a profound tear in the body politic strong enough to focus the nation's attention on that singular, bloody struggle for years was not enough to keep the northern industrial behemoth

B.F. Spinney & Co. shoe factory, Lynn Mass. 1872. (**NY Public Library. Wikimedia Commons.**)

from its slow, inevitable march toward reproducing working and living conditions as wretched or worse than any to be found anywhere in English and European cities. The wartime government's insatiable need for uniforms, guns, wagons, and all the sundry artifacts of war had fattened and emboldened that appetite. Driven by an unregulated banking system and an owner/business class that justified its exploitation and predations with a sordid combination of Smithian laissez-faire and a Calvinist meritocracy equating poverty with divine disfavor, workers – including women and children (most laboring twelve, fourteen hours a day for a pittance in factories that were hot as ovens in the summer and cold as meat lockers in the winter) – began early on to push back against their new industrial overseers.

Women led the way. As early as 1825, female members of the United Tailoresses of New York, struck for "a just price for our labor." In 1834, female workers imprisoned in the "dormitories" at Lowell Massachusetts struck, protesting a wage cut and dismal working conditions. One year later, in 1835, female mill workers in Exeter New Hampshire walked off the job, demanding the overseer stop setting back the time clock. That same year workers in twenty mills went on strike, demanding a reduction in the work day from thirteen and a half hours to eleven hours, and to be paid in cash instead of company scrip. Worker protests and strikes occurred with greater frequency and size. After the Panic of 1857 devastated the manufacturing sector, owners attempted to recoup their losses on the backs of

Shoemaker riot, Lynn Mass. March 17th, 1860. (**NY Public Library. In: Civil War Research Engine, Dickenson College. Wikimedia Commons.**)

workers by firing them and reducing their wages. By 1860, shoemakers in Lynn, Massachusetts had had enough and sparked a strike that spread to neighboring communities like Salem and Marblehead. At one point, ten-thousand workers paraded through the streets of Lynn.[5] These were only the first skirmishes in the ongoing battle between labor and capital, one that would only get bloodier and more desperate.

For a variety of reasons, however, veterans returning to Detroit and other Michigan cities in the years immediately following the war confronted conditions not nearly as dire. Michigan's soldiers had served loyally and sacrificed much. From April 1861 to April 1865, the state had furnished 90,747 men. In the course of the war, Michigan men had engaged the enemy on more than 800 occasions. Of 177 officers killed, 85 died of wounds, 96 of disease. 2,643 enlisted men were killed. 1,302 died of wounds, 10,040 of disease.[6] Unlike the heavily mechanized mills and factories in the east, veterans returning to factories and workshops in Detroit found, in the first two decades following the peace at Appomattox, a work

Chapter 9 *In God We Make Trusts*

environment still grounded in skill-centered, family owned and managed enterprises where a limited number of craftsmen adhered to an hierarchical master, journeyman, apprentice model. Whether a shoe, a coat, or a railroad wheel, the produced article was still in great part the province of the workman's expertise, guided from beginning to end by subtle movements perfected over years of practice, and stored in the consciousness of the man or woman wielding the needle, scissors, saw, or lathe. In this environment there was not, as yet, the extreme division of labor that likewise created a "division of head and hands."[7] That, and Henry Ford's production line, were as yet a half-century away.

Not so for workers in places like Lowell, Lynn, New York, Philadelphia, and Chicago. In those places, through the use of ever more sophisticated machines, what was once the gratifying and creative process of production was wrenched from the workers' hands, surrendered to the machine, and ground into hundreds of mindless, mechanized motions the workman no longer controlled. Increasingly, the laborer was becoming a skill-less custodian and observer of the machine's work rather than the master of his own. The result: "The manufacturing worker, unable to perform or even understand the process of production as a whole, loses the intellectual command over production that the handcraft worker possessed."[8] As such, the skill-less worker became more manageable and, most important for the capitalist, easily replaceable.

Robbed of the independence and power once conferred by his or her work, the worker was forced to recoup some semblance of social power in other ways. One obvious course of action was to band together in organizations – that is, in unions – with others suffering a similar plight. If it were true, as socialists in England and Europe were writing, that only labor can create value, then, withholding mass labor through a boycott or a strike should restore the worker's bargaining power in the marketplace. Though theoretically sound, the logic took no account of the capitalist's own logic and determination which surmised (at the time backed by the power of those who governed) that what was good for business was good for everyone – period. Therefore, when workers took to the streets to protest poor wages or conditions, the halt in production would be tolerated only for a short time if at all, the full force of an unsympathetic government forcing them back to the machines and looms, the truncheons and guns of militia and police often employed as persuasion.

To conclude, however, that Detroit and Michigan were islands of complete labor peace would be an error. Though spared for the time being from the violence and outright warfare roiling much of the rest of the national economic landscape (see labor timeline following), winnowing down to a few rich and politically powerful magnates, and a laboring class stratified by skill and ethnicity simmered like a pot just near the boiling point. Geography, as well, still offered a sort of buffer. With the nation stretching now beyond the Mississippi to the Great Plains, only in the most general sense could Michigan now be regarded as the "frontier." Certainly, the state's northerly latitude and its embrace by what were essentially three inland seas still gave it a semblance of geographic autonomy. But geography was not enough to insulate it from the technological developments changing the nature and conditions of work and the workplace everywhere. "Apprentice, journeyman, Master, and merchant; it was supposedly,"

> "Unlike the heavily mechanized mills and factories in the east, veterans returning to factories and workshops in Detroit found, in the first two decades following the peace at Appomattox, a work environment still grounded in skill-centered, family owned and managed enterprises where a limited number of craftsmen adhered to an hierarchical master, journeyman, apprentice model."

according to Detroit historian Steve Babson, "one big family, free from the class conflict that characterized Europe and the eastern United States."[10] Detroit's Potemkin façade of labor peace belied the forces squaring off behind the scenes, waiting for that inevitable economic downturn or depravation to set it ablaze. The crucial variable, however, were the thousands of immigrants pouring into the city. Still steeped in their native languages and cultures, they became Detroit's "lumpen proletariat," as Marx called them, willing to work for any wage under any conditions and, more consequentially, to cross a picket line to do it.

Strikes were not uncommon in the city. The first strike in Detroit occurred in the wake of the 1837 Panic. Thereafter, workers would react similarly and with increasing fervor to future panics in 1857, 1873, and 1893. However, the strike on April 4th, 1837 was, on the whole, a quiet and civil affair with a properly dressed group of journeyman carpenters marching solemnly down the street with signs reading: "Ten hours a day/Two dollars for pay."[11] As early as 1818, Detroit was home to the Detroit Mechanics' Society which, sixteen years later in 1834, constructed a library with technical information available to workers and employers alike.[12] Detroit Typographers and their employers were joined in a similar co-operative society until 1853 when, after employers' increasing use of lower-wage apprentices and contracting out of work, journeymen typographers expelled the employers from the society and joined forces with the National Typographers Union (NTU).[13]

In Detroit – before the mass infusion of foreign labor into the city after 1880 – less people meant less competition for jobs, a shortage of skilled workers, and comparatively higher wages. In addition, land was still abundant in Michigan, making agriculture an option for those unable to find employment in the state's cities. The population, therefore, expanded outward rather than concentrating in high-rise hovels filled with sickness and poverty like those in the east. Over the course of the war, many of the men at the front had left behind jobs to which they would not return. In their absence – and compelled by survival – women filled many of the vacancies, performing in positions previously reserved for men. Traditionally relegated to lower paying needlework or teaching, many women moved into the better paying manufacturing jobs vacated by men. Even retail jobs, an exclusive province of men before the war, became an option. Women could bring home an enviable nine dollars a week. Women even took spots in Michigan's manufacturing sector. According to the 1860 census, 1,046 women worked in 3,448 manufacturing concerns throughout the state.[9]

Yet, despite the increased female presence in the war-time workplace, many more were forced into more traditional, less lucrative occupations. For these women, there were three options: traditional needlepoint work, domestic service, and prostitution. Since "proper" women shunned domestic service as lowly toil reserved for poor Irish and blacks, and most would rather die than sell their bodies, all that was left for women was needlework. It was a craft that required a measure of skill and, therefore, brought a measure of dignity as well. But its paltry level of remuneration had much less to do with the skill it required than with the gender of those practicing it. Though necessity was certainly strong enough to crack the glass ceiling in manufacturing and retail, patriarchal attitudes regarding the inferiority of women were entrenched and unyielding when it came to women's pay for sewing.

> "Though necessity was certainly strong enough to crack the glass ceiling in manufacturing and retail, patriarchal attitudes regarding the inferiority of women were entrenched and unyielding when it came to women's pay for sewing."

Chapter 9　　　　　　　　　　　　　　　　　　*In God We Make Trusts*

Wages were barely enough for survival, and the Democratic leaning Detroit Free Press – always the champion of the white laborer, male or female – took up their cause in its pages and demanded better pay for them. Labor leader Richard Trevellick had a better idea.

Born in Britain's Scilly Isles in 1830, Richard Trevellick's[14] path to Detroit was colorful and circuitous. Beginning in Calcutta, the ship's carpenter and caulker prospected for gold in Australia and New Zealand, then did a stint in the Peruvian navy after being shipwrecked off that country's coast. Thereafter, he worked in Panama, then moved to New Orleans where he became active in the trade union movement and became a crewman on a riverboat. After secession, the Confederacy offered him a captain's position. He not only refused, but, with the help of the British Consul, fled north to New York, all the while burnishing his organizing credentials and elocution skills. Finally, he found his way to Detroit where, by 1865, he had not only become the head of the Ship's Carpenter's Union, but president of the Detroit Trades Assembly as well. Using his influence with the DTA, Trevellick took under his wing the newly organized Detroit Sewing Women's Protective Association. After purchasing eight sewing machines, Trevellick rented a hall for the women where anyone needing tailoring could by-pass the recalcitrant middle-men and bring their tailoring directly to the women. To aid the women further, Trevellick promised to monitor the women's situation, send a committee to investigate any offending employer, and call for a boycott of that business should they deem it necessary.[15]

To appreciate the nature and diversity of Detroit's economic development from the mid-1800s to the turn of the last century, a reliable, real-time visual account can be compiled from Silas Farmer's voluminous "History of Detroit and Michigan." (See diagram above.) In Chapter seventy-nine of this work, published in 1889, Farmer offers a detailed list of Detroit's

RICHARD F. TREVELLICK.

Labor leader and orator, Richard Trevelick, founder of Detroit's Women's Protective Association and champion of the city's female laborers. **(Toledo Lucas County Public Library.)**

principle businesses at the time along with their start-up dates and company information. (Included, for those interested enough to seek out a copy of Farmer's history, are beautiful pen and ink renderings of each establishment.) While no means accounting for every Detroit business during the period (native Detroiters may notice that iconic Detroit brands such as Vernor's Ginger Ale and Stroh's beer are not included), when placed visually on a timeline, Farmer's list serves as a sort of snapshot of Detroit's business growth. To make the exercise even more instructive and to illustrate the contrast between Detroit's comparatively benign work environment compared with the struggle of working people in much of the rest of the country, when this chart is placed opposite another timeline chronicling the increasingly violent struggle of organized labor elsewhere, one can truly appreciate the difference. The following chart attempts to do just that.

Chapter 9   *In God We Make Trusts*

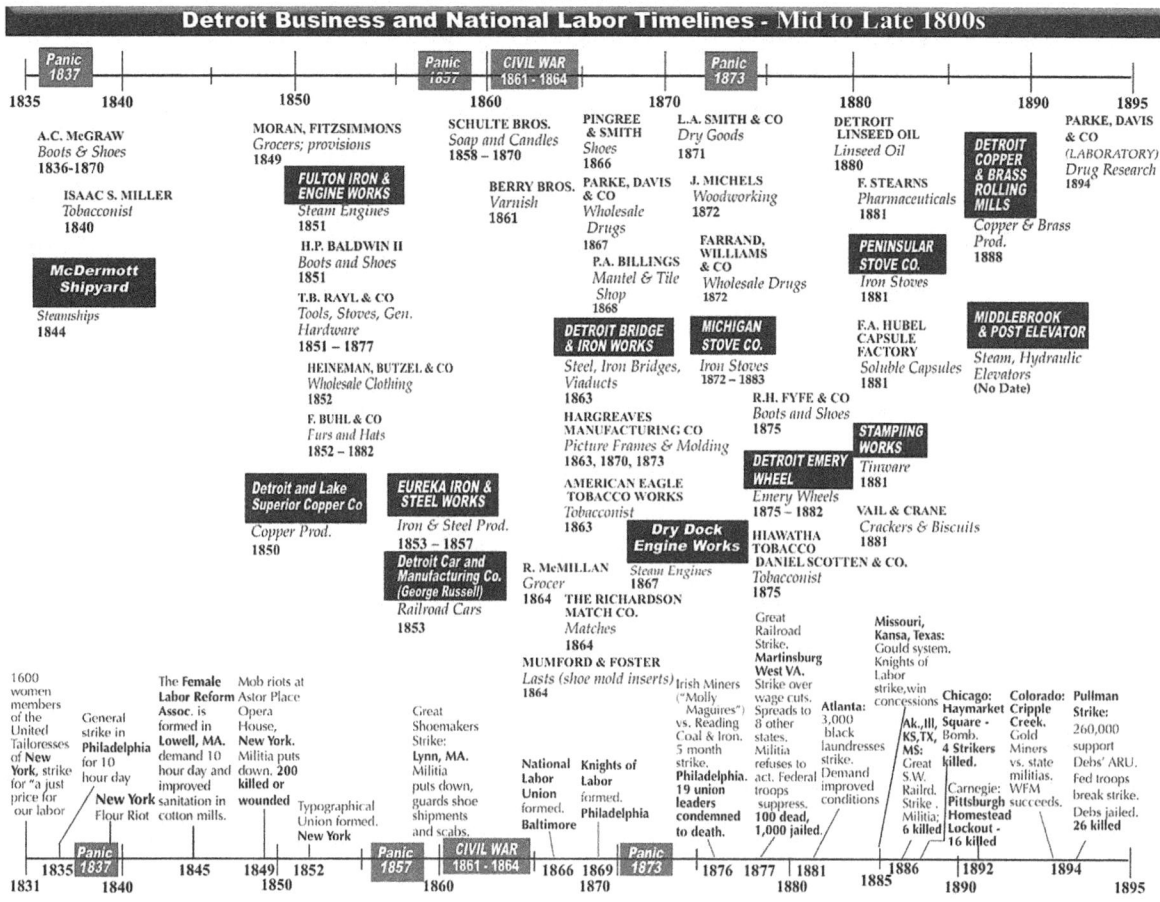

Chart above compares development of Detroit businesses, 1831 – 1895, (top half) with successive labor actions nationally. **(Chart by author. Based on Silas Farmer's "The History of Detroit and Michigan, 1889."")**

At work beneath these developments are socio-economic forces on several levels. First of all, of the Detroit businesses listed across sixty years from 1835 to 1895, roughly 67 percent are general merchandise and retail outlets dealing in products like shoes, groceries, dry goods, and matches. The remaining 33 percent (those with company names in black boxes) could be considered heavy and or capital goods industries. On its face, the mix between commercial and industrial enterprises might not appear much different than the rest of the country. What, then, explains, the stark contrast between Detroit's rather benign work environment and the violent upheavals rocking labor-business relations elsewhere in the U.S.? Two factors, it could be argued, account for the radically divergent environments: 1) a more personal, family-based business structure with owners still closely involved with day-to-day management, even in the industrial sector; and 2) controlling interest – thus, influence – in the company locally focused and undiluted by extended ownership through stocks, bonds, securities, and less personal methods of subsidy that put the decision-making process further and further away from the business, thus routing its destiny through the volatile exchanges on Wall Street and surrendering the fate of the enterprise to those with only a monetary interest in the survival of the company. It is no accident that many of the major, violent strikes listed on the bottom timeline occurred in railroad, mining, and industrial interests which were merely money-making schemes for acquisitive speculators like Drew, Vanderbilt, Gould, Fisk, and Carnegie, men with little or no concept

Chapter 9 *In God We Make Trusts*

nor concern for the needs of workers and their survival; predators undeterred by corrupt governments that were often complacent in their schemes.

Contrast this with someone like Detroit business man and owner of Eureka Iron Works, Eber Ward who, in the midst of the 1857 panic, tried his best to keep his employees at work, even though it meant operating at a loss.[16] Throughout the period, this was the rule rather than the exception for labor-management relations in Detroit with small and large concerns alike. This would, as we shall see, come to an end only when Detroit business owners began to adopt, after the introduction of Ford's assembly line early in the next century, the impersonal, extended corporate model ascendant in the rest of the country. In the interim, however, it is interesting to note that though one might expect the family-owned model to be found only in smaller, retail businesses, the opposite is, in fact true as evidenced by employment figures of the time. As late as 1900, recounts Detroit historian, Thomas Klug, "…the mass of small employers claimed only 39% of the city's factory workers, while 61% were employed by just 113 middle or large-size firms. Indeed, a mere twenty large companies (employing 500 or more workers) engaged nearly one-third of the city's manufacturing workforce."[17] One may justifiably conclude that had Detroit's industrial enterprises conformed to the more predatory model at work in the rest of the national economy, then Detroit may have been rocked by the same degree of labor-business violence.

The family enterprise was, therefore, a stabilizing and pacifying force in the economic life of Detroit up to 1880. According to U.C. Berkeley sociologist, Melanie Archer, Detroit's self-employed of the time could be divided into three occupational levels: 1) industrialists and elite merchants (large merchants, manufacturers, and wholesalers); 2) general merchants and proprietors (general retail and artisan merchants); 3) petty merchants and proprietors (peddlers, hucksters, petty retailers).[18] Zooming in closer, census figures for the year 1880 show that "of 353 self-employed household heads, 75 or 21.2% were elite merchants and industrialists; 192 or 54.4% were general proprietors; and 86 or 24.4% were petty proprietors.[19] Each category, in turn, were joined in varying degrees of association ranging from formal legal partnerships, to shared management, use of family labor, transfer of ownership, and apprenticeships. Which type was used depended on how many family members were involved, whether the business was extended and required, for instance, shared management, or, whether the family business required the pooling of capital by relatives.[20] No matter which strategy was used, ownership and management of Detroit businesses at the time were grounded in kinship and, perhaps more important for stability, were intergenerational. "Between 40.0% to 60.0% of all businesses, regardless of family strategy, involved intergenerational kinship relationships, mostly fathers and sons."[21] This would seem to indicate, as one would expect at the time, a strong and persistent male gender bias despite the inroads made by women in the workforce after the Civil War.

In the ten years before the Civil War, Detroit's population more than doubled, swelling from 21,019 in 1850, to 45,619 in 1860. By 1880, it had climbed to

> "No matter which strategy was used, ownership and management of Detroit businesses at the time were grounded in kinship and, perhaps more important for stability, were intergenerational. "Between 40.0% to 60.0% of all businesses, regardless of family strategy, involved intergenerational kinship relationships, mostly fathers and sons."

Chapter 9 *In God We Make Trusts*

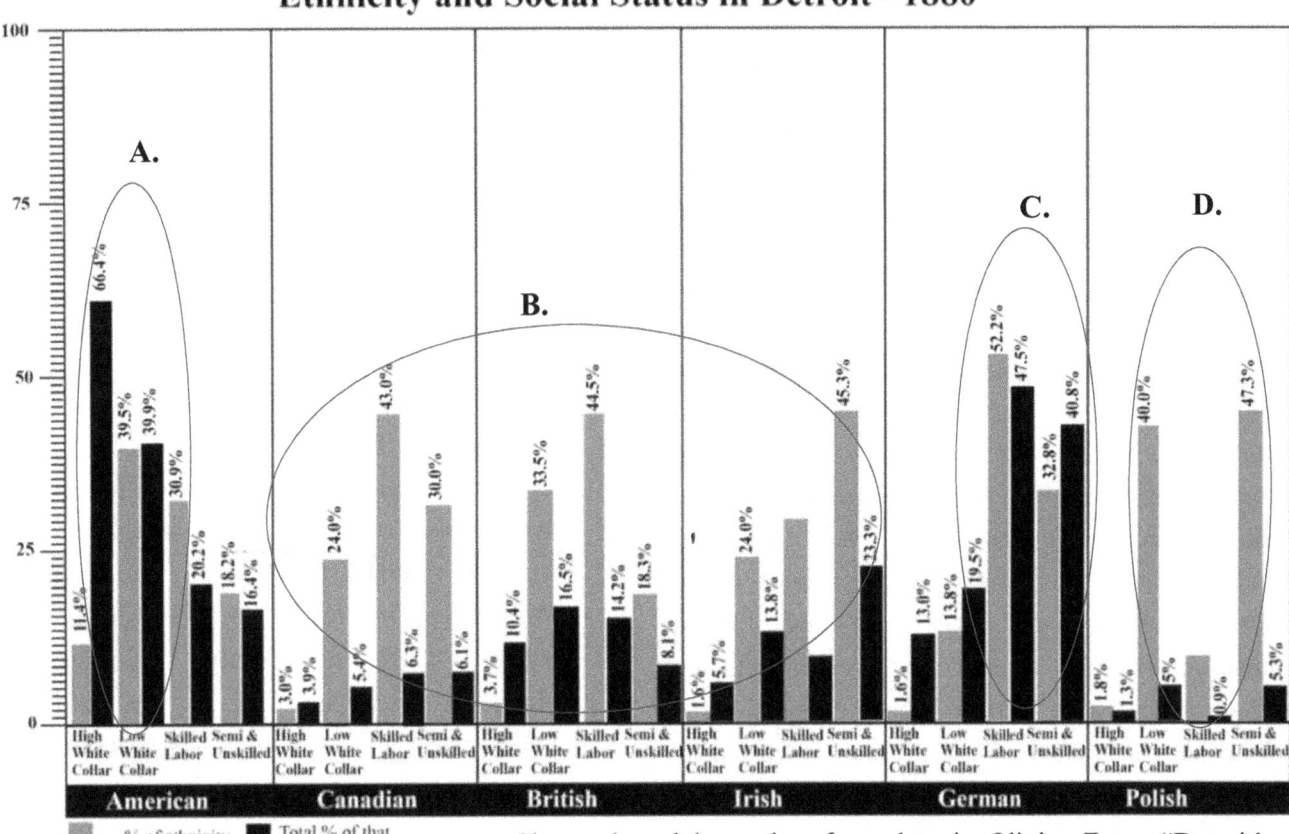

Chart adapted by author from data in Olivier Zunz, "Detroit's Ethnic Neighborhoods at the end of the Nineteenth Century," 1977.

116,340, 44.4% (51,709) of which were foreign born. Twenty years later, in 1900, Detroit had 285,704 residents. Of these, 96,166 (33.7%) were foreign born.[22] Under these circumstances, language was a mitigating factor in the lives of Detroiters who spoke little or no English. Obviously, for Canadians, British, and Irish the language barrier was inconsequential. But for Germans, Poles, and Italians who did not speak English, much of their lives were spent in the relative isolation of their ethnic enclaves. Though Poles, for example, represented 35.54% of the city's population, 27.18% of men, and 44.80% of Polish women did not speak English. Italians, on the other hand, were 28.52% of Detroit's population. 26.43% of Italian men did not speak English; 32.09% of Italian women. Germans fared a little better. Though they made up 14.81% of the city's population, 9.87% of German men and 19.77% of German women had no command of English.[23] Language and ethnicity, therefore, not only shaped the nature of work in Detroit and who did it, it established a social hierarchy of work, with Americans and native speakers dominating the jobs involving more prestige and less toil.

The chart above illustrates the social stratification of work in Detroit of 1880. Under each ethnicity are four categories: 1) high white collar; 2) low white collar; 3) skilled labor; and 4) semi-skilled labor. When applied like a template to each ethnic category, the data establishes an unmistakable relationship between ethnicity and the type of work being done. This is not to imply anything conspiratorial or that the framework was preconceived or deliberately constructed. Rather, the stratification developed naturally, based on

Chapter 9 *In God We Make Trusts*

language, social clannishness, isolation, and cultural work habits. Moving from left to right, the data in oval **A.** illustrates a privileged native-born minority in control of a full 66.4% of high white-collar work, and 30.8% of low white-collar production. No other ethnic group competes in this category. Of the foreign-born English speakers – Canadian, British, and Irish – skilled and semi-skilled labor pre-dominates. Oval **B.** illustrates this, but it also displays an interesting anomaly: though all the bars in these categories are in the 40th percentile, it is crucial to notice that all the bars are *gray*. This is significant, for it is only an accounting of the number of people in that ethnic group doing that work, and not an indication of their production. Their actual output is shown by the black bars, none of which reach the 20th percentile. Only the Germans show relative equality in both ethnic presence and output. Oval **C.** indicates the German workers maintained a lock on the skilled and semi-skilled labor category with little or no presence in either white collar sector. Finally, like the English-speaking foreigners, the Polish community (oval **D.**) shows a strong presence in both low white collar and semi-skilled labor, but very little output compared to Americans and Germans.

By the gravitational pull of family ownership, the economic life of Detroit was held for a time within the limited orbit of the city and its environs, the national gospel of success and the unquestioned virtue and reverence ascribed at the time to the successful, self-made man fed the cultural life of Detroit as surely as Vanderbilt, Astor, and Gould had fixed themselves as worthy and envied luminaries in the larger cosmos of the national economy. The image of armed socialist partisans behind the barricades of the Paris Commune still was enough to strike fear in the hearts of Detroiters – laborer and businessman alike. The city's work environment, though admittedly less oppressive, was anything but egalitarian. While the skilled laborers of the city demanded a modicum of dignity and fair remuneration, they did not begrudge their employers the outward trappings of their success – their fine houses, carriages and servants. So naturally, just as in places like New York, Philadelphia, and Boston, Detroit's neighborhoods followed a logical platting based on wealth and/or the lack of it, and the desire of people to live in their respective ethnic communities. Had it been possible to ascend above Detroit of 1880 in a helicopter, one could have gleaned the social stratification of Detroit according to its neighborhoods and housing:

> "Not only did Detroit's neighborhoods look different in their architecture and in their physical arrangement, but they were inhabited by people with different family structures, different jobs and sometime different languages. There was a large Yankee and Anglo-Saxon portion of the city with a low fertility rare and with households headed by white collar workers inhabiting large brick or wooden houses; the families were often extended, and often employed servants. On the other side there was a working class Celtic, German and Slavic city divided into several neighborhoods. There, large households consisting of nuclear families lived in small wooden house and occupied the few multiple dwellings of Detroit."[24]

Rapid post-war industrialization fueled the fortunes of certain Detroit businessmen, lending credence to the notion of the "self-made man" gospel that was the bellwether of the times (and, as we shall see, also gave philosophical cover to the schemes of economic predators with less constructive motives). There was Frederick Stearns who, working with one assistant, made prescription drugs in the back of his drugstore opened in 1856. Twenty-five years later, Stearns oversaw a major drug manufacturing operation with 400 employees. There was Hazen Pingree. Once a simple shoe leather cutter in a factory in Massachusetts,

Chapter 9 *In God We Make Trusts*

Canadian born James McMillan became a business and political powerhouse across the border in Detroit. Born to wealthy Scottish immigrants, McMillan rubbed elbows, in his youth, with the common folk. However, once economic adversity struck in the panic of 1857, he reached for the silver spoon and quickly rose through the ranks of his father's railroad business. While McMillan lived nearly fourteen miles away in what today is affluent Grosse Pointe, he was unencumbered by the muddy and undeveloped roads of the time by taking to the water and sailing daily to Detroit on his now famous yacht named "the Truant." In contrast to the growing number of parvenus at the time who sunk their wealth into the nebulous casino of Wall Street, McMillan, to his credit, invested his fortune in tangible businesses that "made" things." Thereafter, he moved into politics, becoming first governor of the state, then, a powerful and influential U.S. senator.

Sen. James McMillan

McMillan Home - Grosse Pointe, MI

Pingree came to Detroit and, after a modest investment of hard-earned savings, began a shoe making business of his own. From his original eight employees, Pingree grew the company to a major shoe manufacturer in 1886 with 700 employees using semi-skilled machine production instead of the original and slower hand-cutting techniques. In 1856, the same year Frederick Stearns opened his humble pharmacy, Daniel Schotten began processing tobacco (one of the principle niche businesses captured by German immigrants). By 1875, he presided over a huge three-story factory on West Fort Street, handling two-million pounds of tobacco a year.

After a day's work overseeing their facilities, these men would return to fine homes in exclusive new areas opening up along Woodward and Cass Avenues and West Fort Street.[25] And there were those parvenus who rejected entirely the confines of Detroit. Taking our helicopter a short eight miles to the east, we hover over Grosse Pointe (one of the future homes of the Ford family). There, we look down on the mansions of two other wealthy Detroiters: James McMillan and John Newberry. In order to avoid what would have been a grueling six-hour buggy ride over barely passable roads, Newberry and McMillan took to the water in Newberry's yacht, the "Truant," commuting to the city in a manner the less-fortunate denizens of Detroit could only dream of.

In the economic pantheon of post-Civil War Detroit, industrialist James McMillan was most esteemed and influential. Lost now to only the most assiduous students of Detroit's history, he is the city's most important businessman few have heard of. McMillan was, in fact, Canadian. Born to Scottish immigrants, William and Grace McMillan, in 1838, it could hardly be said that James was of humble origins since his father was the founder of the Great Western Railway. Nevertheless, at fourteen, James put the silver spoon aside for a time, quit school, and took up a job at a hardware store in Hamilton where he distinguished himself as a diligent and resourceful worker. Building on this foundation, he moved across the border in 1855 to Detroit where he took another more lucrative position at one of the city's major hardware businesses, Buhl and Ducharme. He distinguished himself there as well, but his feet were not planted firmly enough to tether him in the financial storm to come: the Panic of 1857.

Chapter 9   *In God We Make Trusts*

Though forced by the downturn out of the position at Buhl and Ducharme, McMillan did not join the swelling ranks of the unemployed and destitute. He reached instead for that silver spoon he had laid aside as a boy, accepting a position his father arranged for him as a purchasing agent on the Detroit-Milwaukee Railroad. Now, in his father's railroad milieu, he advanced yet again, becoming thereafter the credit manager for a financially strapped freight-car business by the name of Dean and Eaton in 1864. To this partnership he brought his life-long friend and business associate, John Newberry. The move was timely and profitable. Satisfying the Union's need for railroad cars to transport men and equipment, the Michigan Car Company became one of the many businesses to become fat on the carrion of war. In 1865, when the slaughter had ended, McMillan *et al* founded the Detroit Car and Wheel Company. Thereafter, McMillan and Newberry began collecting businesses in Detroit like tokens on a Monopoly board, adding to their list many of the industrial concerns rendered in black on the right side of the forgoing business timeline. Among others, these included solid Detroit enterprises like Detroit Iron Furnace Company, the Baugh Steam Forge Company, and the Detroit Pipe and Foundry Company, all of which McMillan was the president.[26]

Unlike tycoons such as Vanderbilt, Drew, and Fisk for whom the tangible assets of their business – the cars, track, and stations – were but a material pretense for

When the engines from the Union Pacific and Central Pacific railroads met on May 10, 1869 at Promontory Ridge, Utah after spanning half the continent from different directions, it not only signaled a race to crisscross the nation with tracks, it triggered a sea change in business culture. The massive capital demands of railroad building and its need to increasingly acquire land to facilitate construction meant an increasing role for government and short, a new corporate model. However, despite the fluid and massive demand for money and resources, the country was still under the thrall of Smithian capitalism, a view that held market forces as the disinterested and objective arbiter of resources and capital. Therefore, in homage to Smith, money from the government came with strings – strict rules regarding par levels for bonds and the stipulation that money would only be released in accordance with business' own efforts to raise capital. Faced with these restrictions, railroaders found ways around government restrictions in their quest for money. **(Photo: Wikimedia Commons)**

what they regarded as the real but volatile value of their enterprise rendered in stocks and bonds (paper sums whose value shifted daily like sand on the exchanges) McMillan was, to his credit, concerned with making things. He founded business after business to provide *real* goods and services. Unlike his "stock-jobbing" eastern counterparts obsessed with Wall Street, McMillan and Newberry were laser focused on Main Street, funneling their assets locally until they were the very center of Detroit's economic life. And, as one would expect, along with the crown of economic power came the scepter of political might as well. After winning a seat on the Detroit Board of Estimates in 1877. For McMillan, merely another ladder, one he climbed through various positions in Michigan's Republican establishment until, in 1879, he had risen to the position of State Party Chairman upon the death of

Chapter 9 *In God We Make Trusts*

the iconic Zachariah Chandler.[27] It was, however, not a good time to assume control of the Republican party, its fortunes and its reputation having been set into a tailspin six years earlier by none other than the venerable and trusted "financier of the Civil War," Jay Cooke, whose ambition to span the northern edge of the country with a railroad from the Great Lakes to the Pacific failed, triggering the Panic of 1873.

It was not an unreasonable idea. The scheme was, in fact, a logical sequel to the success of the trans-continental railroad that came together on that momentous day a few years earlier in 1869 at Promontory Ridge, Utah when an engine from the Union Pacific met one from the Central Pacific, finally closing that nationwide gap between oceans. Inspired by unequal parts patriotism, ambition, and jingoism, and cheered on by the likes of "go west young man" Horace Greeley," Cooke's plan was to build another transcontinental railroad line hundreds of miles north, one straddling the rugged and nebulous border with Canada. It would stretch from Duluth on Lake Superior (at the time, a sparsely settled burg of 3,000 plus souls) all the way to Puget Sound on the Pacific. Because the land across the length of the proposed project was still pristine and untrammeled, it was easy for the imagination to fill in the blanks where hard, topographic knowledge was lacking. General Sherman, however, had had actual first-hand experience with the area and was quite forthright in his efforts to disabuse potential investors. The entire region was, Sherman warned, "as bad as God ever made or as body can scare up this side of Africa."[28]

Nevertheless, undeterred by anything as inconvenient as facts, proponents of the enterprise swung into action, producing fanciful pamphlets depicting Duluth and all parts west of it as a magical, lush paradise filled with exotic flora and fauna, just waiting for hardscrabble settlers to come and partake of the unexploited bounty that was the Northwest. Rumors even told of "monkeys and orange groves" on the route which ran through Idaho, Montana, and the Bad Lands of Dakota.[29] As with any project of this magnitude, land was needed. The U.S. Government accommodated Cooke in 1869 with the North Pacific Charter. It granted him rights to 47,000,000 acres.[30] Now, all he needed were investors and settlers, a task that should have been the easiest part of the enterprise for the banker who helped subsidize the Union in the Civil War. Instead, it proved to be Cooke's undoing and the start of a national economic disaster.

> "Federal subsidies, therefore – coming as they did *after* the fact of construction and based on the amount of track laid – were like a carrot dangled constantly in front of a rabbit."

One can only speculate about the reasons for Cooke's departure from the security of the banking world to the morally challenged realm of railroading. Certainly, as with his efforts in the war, there was a genuine element of patriotism and a desire to see the nation expand and prosper. Or, perhaps he needed a distraction after the untimely death of his beloved wife, Dorothea Elizabeth Allen, in 1871. Then again, and more cynically, maybe his decision involved a desire to nurture the substantial financial investments he had made in Duluth. Whatever his motivation, it was a worthy idea that had come at a very bad time. Why? In one sense, the country's taste for railways was souring. That is, not so much railways themselves (they were, after all, necessary) as their intravenous attachment to government funding. Railroads had been a glorious addiction, one whose ugly alliance of legislation and largesse had long been obscured, hidden first under the veil of manifest destiny, then wrapped up in the uniform of military necessity during the war. But after the veil was lifted and the bugles fell silent, the extent of the government shake-down and the unholy roll-call of lawmakers as larders and cronies of the business elite became increasingly clear.

Chapter 9

In God We Make Trusts

It was nothing new. Since the beginning of the republic, the government's schemes for harnessing the land mass of the nation from coast to coast and its well-intentioned goal of securing meager patches of land for eager settlers, or the building of a canal had been routinely hijacked by speculators and business interests. As early as 1834, a government report was providing evidence that "...in Ohio and elsewhere, combinations of capitalist speculators, at the sale of public lands, had united for the purpose of driving other purchasers out of the market and in deterring poor men from bidding."[31]

But the railroad put a new, insidious twist on the old swindle. By their very nature, railroads defied the traditional brick and mortar business model. Their inherently dynamic function as an ever-evolving vehicle for transporting goods and people made them something quite different than factories or other businesses competing within a limited region. In the old milieu, factory owners would square off in genuine competition, restrained in their ambitions by another local factory owner who could put him out of business for good. More importantly, as Gustavus Myers emphasizes, their physical restrictions were also a brake on their fortunes. "Fortunate was that factory owner regarded," remarked Meyers, "who could claim $250,000 clear. All those modern complex factors offering such unbounded opportunities for gathering in spoils mounting into the hundreds of millions of dollars, were either unknown or in an inchoate or rudimentary state."[32] Those "modern complex factors" referring, of course, to the stocks, bonds, securities, and other financial instruments that were mere paper approximations of the real, material capital involved in the business. Once again, Adam Smith's admonitions about the dangers of "stock-jobbing" went unheeded. But for speculators, they were irresistible. Such intangible expressions of value as a stock or bond were magically prone to multiply exponentially, one only needed to pursue the right course, as outlined by Myers, to make them propagate:

"With a grandiloquent front and a superb bluff they would organize a company to build a railroad from this to that point; an undertaking costing millions, while perhaps they could not pay their board bill. An arrangement with a printer to turn out stock issues on credit was easy; with the promise of batches of this stock, they would then get a sufficient number of legislators to vote a charter, money and land."[33]

In all fairness, railroads did require massive amounts of capital. Because of their complexity and extensive reach – their routes passing through numerous municipalities and local jurisdictions on their way – only the federal government, it was agreed, had both the resources and the legal purview to override regional claims using eminent domain, thus clearing the way for construction in the "national" interest. As such, railroads were the first large scale corporate entities in the modern sense, forming conglomerates that would become the rule rather the exception. It was, as a report by the American Economic Association would conclude in 1887, a "system of transportation, under which the construction and ownership of the road-bed, the fixing of tolls and the actual carrying business of transportation should all be vested in one and the same body, was surely destined to bring about entirely new combination in business which could not fail to call for a new system of regulation of commerce."[34] Because railroads needed resources and capitalization on a much larger scale, why not, then, nationalize them, making them purely creatures of the government. Their construction and operation would be controlled directly, from concept through completion, by federal authorities: a truly socialist enterprise. This would have been impossible at the time; a heretical assault on the established, free market philosophy of Friedrich List, Henry Carey, and Francis Wayland that had become the economic cornerstone of the Republican Party since its founding.

The economic Zeitgeist, therefore, demanded that private enterprise execute the designs of any public project, with government subsidies the incentive and the prize for business' successful efforts. Competition, or so the theory went, would ensure the greatest and speediest effort at the cheapest price. Still steeped in their naïve faith in the inherent certainty and distributive justice of market capitalism, the Republican Civil War congress crafted legislation based on this alliance. Thus, the Pacific Railway Act of 1862 provided the grist for the capitalist mill. No government money was provided for construction up-front. Instead, funds would be released according to the amount of actual track laid. Construction companies were granted "a right of way through the public lands four hundred feet wide, the rights to take material for construction from adjacent public land, and twenty sections of public land for each mile railway constructed…"[35] Funding, therefore, would be raised by the construction companies themselves whereupon they would be reimbursed based on their progress. Depending on the terrain where the track was laid, the government released thirty-year bonds at six-percent in amounts ranging from $16,000 per mile east of the Rockies, to as much as $48,000 per mile in certain areas of the Rockies and Sierra Nevadas.[36] Federal subsidies, therefore – coming as they did *after* the fact of construction and based on the amount of track laid – were like a carrot dangled constantly in front of a rabbit. Forced to raise money as they proceeded, the land itself – real estate – became a big money-making component of the enterprise. Railroads held towns and municipalities hostage, threatening to by-pass them if they did not purchase parcels at dictated rates. Many towns were forced to make bond issues they often could

Political cartoon depicting Uncle Sam directing the corrupt politicians in the Crédit Mobilier scandal to commit hari kari. (From: Frank Leslie's Illustrated Newspaper, March 8, 1873. Public Domain. Wikimedia Commons.)

Crédit Mobilier Scandal

Anxious to promote the proliferation of railroads in the country, the U.S. 37th Congress passed the Pacific Railroad Act in 1862, legislation not only making huge land grants for right of way to railroads, but government backed bonds as well. The government stipulated, however, that the bonds were not to be sold below par, a pre-condition that made them unattractive to eastern investors. To circumvent the government's restrictions and to increase their chance of greater profits, Union Pacific Vice-President Thomas C. Durant created a bogus company, named after a defunct French bank, called Crédit Mobilier. Unlike the parent company – Union Pacific – the proxy, Mobilier, could sell bonds well below par, which it did. Construction was assigned to the phony company which, per plan, billed the government-backed Union Pacific to the tune of $94 million, a sum more than $44 million more than the cost originally proposed by engineers. Along with lining the pockets of Union Pacific shareholders, some of the $44 million profit went to politicians in Washington to purchase favorable legislation.

ill afford lest the track be routed elsewhere, thus forcing them to travel miles to the nearest station in order to bring their goods to market.

As for the government securities, the legislation opened the door to mischief by demanding the bonds not be sold under par. Investors, in turn, were disinclined to purchase them at face value. Oakes Ames, a congressman from Massachusetts, and Vice-President of the Union Pacific, Thomas Durant, came up with a solution. The Union Pacific Board of Directors would set up a separate agency called Crédit Mobilier (after a bankrupt French company with the same name), one not subject to the constraints of the legislation and, technically, free to sell the bonds below par. This the agency did, thus creating a shortfall. To make up for the deficit, Crédit Mobilier inflated the cost of construction, over-capitalizing the endeavor from the originally projected $50 million to $111 million. "For this work," Josephson recounts, "the directors of the Union Pacific had ingeniously contracted with themselves at prices which rose from $80,000 to $90,000 and $96,000 mile, twice the maximum estimates of engineers; so that the total cost eventually was $94 million." This was a full $50 million above the original $44 million cost projected by engineers, a sum never accounted for.[36]

The Crédit Mobilier scandal pulled back the curtain on the American economy, revealing the true, evolving nature of business after the Civil War from a constellation of small enterprises fighting for dominance, to ever larger corporate entities with far flung interests, interlocking directorates, and complex management spread across state borders. They were, as they saw it, giants serving a national, even international market. They were not eager to subject their stability to the "purifying" crucible of competition, preferring instead the safe haven of collaboration. It was only logical. After all, were workers not combining in greater and greater numbers to defend their own interests *en masse*.

First recorded trust in the U.S.: the Saginaw and Bay Salt Company, 1868. Among its members, a young John D. Rockefeller who applied the concept to the petroleum market with astounding success.

John D. Rockefeller **(Scientific Amer. 1907. Wikimedia Commons)**

Caseville Salt and Coal Mine, Caseville, MI. **(Caseville Hist. Society and Thumbwind Publications)**

As fate would have it, the first such organization inspired by this idea was begun in Saginaw, Michigan and centered around the salt business. Salt was a lucrative market for the state, one that, at the time, produced a full 40 percent of the salt in the United States.[37] Such white gold, it was thought, had to be protected from the verities of the marketplace and a group of salt producers moved to do just that on April 16th, 1868 by forming the Saginaw and Bay Salt company, a trust that would be the official clearing house for most of the salt manufacturers of the region. In the first year, the trust handled four-fifths of the salt produced in Michigan.[38]

For manufacturers, membership in the organization brought a number of advantages, including: 1) a fixed price for their product; 2) monthly updates on personal accounts as well as sales and expense figures, freight and storage charges; 3) inspection of salt by qualified agents to ensure quality.[39] Two members of the trust were the prominent whiskey distiller and salt producer, S.V. Harkness, and his son-in-law, Henry Flagler. Both are significant not so much for their membership in the trust as with their mutual friend, a young oil refiner in Cleveland who struggled to survive the cut-throat competition that characterized the infant oil business:

Chapter 9 *In God We Make Trusts*

John D. Rockefeller. It was they, perhaps, who planted the seed in the young man's mind for what would become a behemoth in the oil business, Standard Oil Company, and the infamous network of corporations tied to it in the monopoly known as the South Improvement Company.[40] Though Rockefeller and his South Improvement Company is a story unto itself, Rockefeller's mindset and vision is best summarized by Josephson:

> "All the political institutions the whole spirit of American law still favored the amiable, wasteful individualism of business, which in Rockefeller's mind had already become obsolete and must be supplanted by a centralized, one might say almost *collectivist* – certainly cooperative rather than competitive – form of operation."[41]

After the war, the country was eager for the extension of the railways, so eager that they were willing to wink and nod at the financial indiscretions that would devolve into full-blown corruption, impossible to ignore. Too much was at stake, and too many were profiting, at first, to listen to those arguing for caution, dismissing them simply as "Cassandrian prophets, scarcely worth consideration.[42] It was only after trusts like the South Improvement Company had proliferated, controlling great swathes of the economy from coal to steel and other commodities, that the people began to finally press government for relief from their all-encompassing grip. Political cartoonists like Thomas Nast (himself a victim of Crèdit Moblier), academics like Gustavus Meyers, and journalists like Ida Tarbell began to peel back the veneer of legitimacy surrounding the trusts, exposing the stranglehold corporations such as Rockefeller's Standard Oil had on the on the economic life of the nation.

It was a day fraught with consequences when, on September 19, 1873, the iconic banker J. Cooke closed and locked for good the doors of his New York office on Third Street. And there was irony as well, for news of the bank's failure was sent immediately over the telegraph, its demise announced instantly in papers as far away as California. The lead on the front page of the Sacramento Daily Union that day was simple and to the point: "the Great Banking House of J. Cooke and Co. has failed."[43] The speed of the announcement was both fitting and ironic, since it was Cooke who had pioneered the use of the telegraph to speedily trade the securities that both helped make his fortune and quickly told of his undoing. As Cooke's biographer, Ellis Oberholtzer, described the event: "...he turned his face away from the men who surrounded him, the tears streamed from his eyes."[44] Others would weep as Wall Street collapsed, bank after bank failed, and bankruptcies mounted in an ugly and devastating chain reaction. Of course, as in all previous downturns, workers became the biggest losers in the constant struggle between owners' surplus and labor's sustenance. Legions of workers were either let go or forced to work longer hours with wages cut as much as 40 percent. Laborers' lives were put at risk as they were overworked and put in dangerous

"With each downturn – 1837, 1857, and 1873 – the misery and depravation suffered by workers offered empirical evidence that not only was the notion of a classless society in the U.S. a lie, but that the very opposite was true."

Closing of Wall St. Exchange in Panic of 1873, triggered by bankruptcy of Jay Cooke & Co. **(Frank Leslie's Illustrated Newspaper. Library of Congress.)**

Chapter 9   *In God We Make Trusts*

situations. By 1877, 40 percent of the workforce was idle for seven months of the year and unemployment reached 20 percent nationwide.(45)

With each downturn – 1837, 1857, and 1873 – the misery and depravation suffered by workers offered empirical evidence that not only was the notion of a classless society in the U.S. a lie, but that the very opposite was true. In their misplaced reverence for wealth by any means, their indifference to the predatory practices of unscrupulous tycoons, and their tolerance for legislation sold as though at auction, the American citizenry had helped create a ruling class as empowered and immovable as the aristocracies of Europe. But whereas Europe's was founded on blood, America's was built on money. For plutocrats like Cornelius Vanderbilt (at the time worth $100 million), William Astor ($100 million), and Jay Gould ($50 million), the poverty, unemployment, and desperation were of no consequence, their fortunes as secure as medieval barons perched in castles on the Rhine or the Danube.

For unemployed and dispossessed workers, whose very lives became the ballast to right the sinking profits of the rich, the choice was simple: despair or resistance. To surrender meekly to penury or to protest; to withhold the one component of capitalist production as yet not subsumed by a machine: one's labor. This they did in increasing numbers, the strike being the only recourse in the face of such overwhelming economic power. After the 1873 crash, workers struck in textile mills in Fall River Massachusetts and Irish miners– the ill-fated "Molly Maguires (46) In a time when railroads by their sheer size and complex nature were changing the very meaning of "corporation," the thousands of employees it needed to function in prosperous times could, during a strike, become like logs caught in the wheels of its engines when the economy crashed, paralyzing extended systems across multiple states.

In 1877, in response to a 10 percent wage cut, railroad workers struck the Baltimore and Ohio Railroad in Martinsburg, West Virginia. A massive crowd, too big for local police, gathered in support. B&O officials petitioned the governor for protection whereupon the state militia was called and violently set upon the crowd. Six-hundred freight cars jammed the yard in Martinsburg. Sympathizers in Baltimore mounted their own strike, surrounding the National Guard armory. As the militiamen emerged, the crowd pelted them with rocks. A pitch battle ensued with ten dead and many injured. Federal troops were called. The strike then spread to Pittsburgh, Harrisburg, and Lebanon, Pennsylvania. Workers at the Carnegie steel plant walked out in sympathy. Federal troops brutally suppressed the action. The strike then spread to St. Louis where bakers, coopers, cabinetmaker, cigar makers, and brewers supported the railroaders. All were violently put down at the behest of government officials sympathetic to business interests. "When the great railroad strikes of 1877 were over," Zinn recounts, "a hundred people were dead, a thousand people had gone to jail, 100,000 workers had gone on strike, and the strikes had roused into action countless unemployed in the cities." (47)

Workers of the Michigan Central Railroad dutifully joined the action and struck. Alarmed by the wide-ranging violence, Detroit's business elites girded themselves, calling out three-hundred reserve policemen and recruiting volunteers for their own "Protective Association."(48) For custodians of Michigan's economic order like McMillan, the barbarians were at the gates, threatening their control and the illusion of labor peace. "There was no bloodshed – just intimidation," recalls Babson. "By year's end, the combined impact of this employer repression and the continuing economic depression had destroyed all but a handful of Detroit's unions,"(49) Employers were, however, aided in their repression by a much more complex, subtle, and insidious factor than the simple threat of violence, one exploiting the increasingly growing and diverse immigrant population of the city.

Chapter 9 *In God We Make Trusts*

For strikers to be effective, a united movement – solidarity – was of the utmost importance. Unlike business owners who, in their ever-growing combinations, were united in the common pursuit of profit despite their diverse interests, worker solidarity was fragmented and compromised by ethnic rivalries and a paranoid, protective attitude toward remaining craft skills not yet taken over by machinery. Consequently, in contrast to the fervid support coming from workers of all stripes in the great strike of 1877, members of the railroad "brotherhoods," i.e., brotherhoods of Locomotive Firemen and Engineers, distanced themselves from the conflict, fearing the violence was too "communistic." Though Marx, from his perch in London, viewed the chaos optimistically as the first signs of a working-class rebellion, the class consciousness so necessary to movement cohesion was actually lacking. Solidarity was fragmented, broken into a destructive hierarchy based on ethnicity and false conflict between skilled and unskilled labor, one exploited by owners of struck businesses who simply used immigrant labor as strikebreakers. Thus, the class consciousness so necessary to the cohesion of the nascent union movement was undermined internally. In Detroit and elsewhere, one faction was pitted against another not merely on the basis of abilities, but on ethnicity and race as well. This, unfortunately, became the template for labor and race relations far into Detroit's future.

For members of Detroit's black community, who at the time of the railroad strike of 1877 accounted for only three percent of the city's population,[50] the storm clouds of class conflict were far off and, frankly, completely white. Systematically excluded from white craft unions, blacks could not hope to acquire the skills necessary to enter the middle-class, nor to add their voices to the groundswell of labor discontent that swirled around them. "In 1890 there were no blacks in the brass and ship industries," Katzman recounts, "and only twenty-one blacks were found among the 5,839 male employees in the tobacco, stove, and iron and shoe industries.[51] The skill-less drudgery of factory work was primarily done by foreign-born (white) immigrants, many of whom did not speak English. In exchange for those menial, servile jobs, immigrants provided the employers with a subservient and submissive workforce, unlikely to join nor even understand the agenda of organized labor. In their fear and isolation, they were a dependable go-to source of replacement workers when skilled workers took to the streets. Whether out of *naivté* or a simple will to survive in a foreign environment, immigrants became a wedge for employers to fracture working class solidarity. So marginalized were black workers, they were even regarded as unfit to be "scabs" (the traditional moniker for replacement workers). The chart, *Figure 2* below (reproduced from Katzman's *Before the Ghetto*), illustrates the extent of black ostracism from the economic life of Detroit at the end of the 1800s:

Clearly, black employment is skewed over four decades to the right of each graph. The black bars captured by the ovals indicate that throughout this period, about half the "service" jobs – i.e., live-in domestic servants, waiters, and barbers –were being done by blacks, even though blacks were only three percent of Detroit's population. Blacks still filled half the domestic service jobs in 1900, a time when their percentage of the population fell by more than half to 1.4 percent. Dangerous jobs were also dominated by blacks, especially dock work. Employment was erratic and seasonal, with lost and crushed limbs always a possibility. Prospective dock-hands gathered at the docks each day, hoping to be picked by a boss or stevedore.[52] As for live-in domestics, isolation was their lot. With few days off and on-call most of the day, they had little or no time to themselves, their own lives subordinated to that of their employer's. Certainly, there were black professionals of some stature in Detroit – men like Robert Pelham (a politician who invented a tabulating machine for figuring the census),

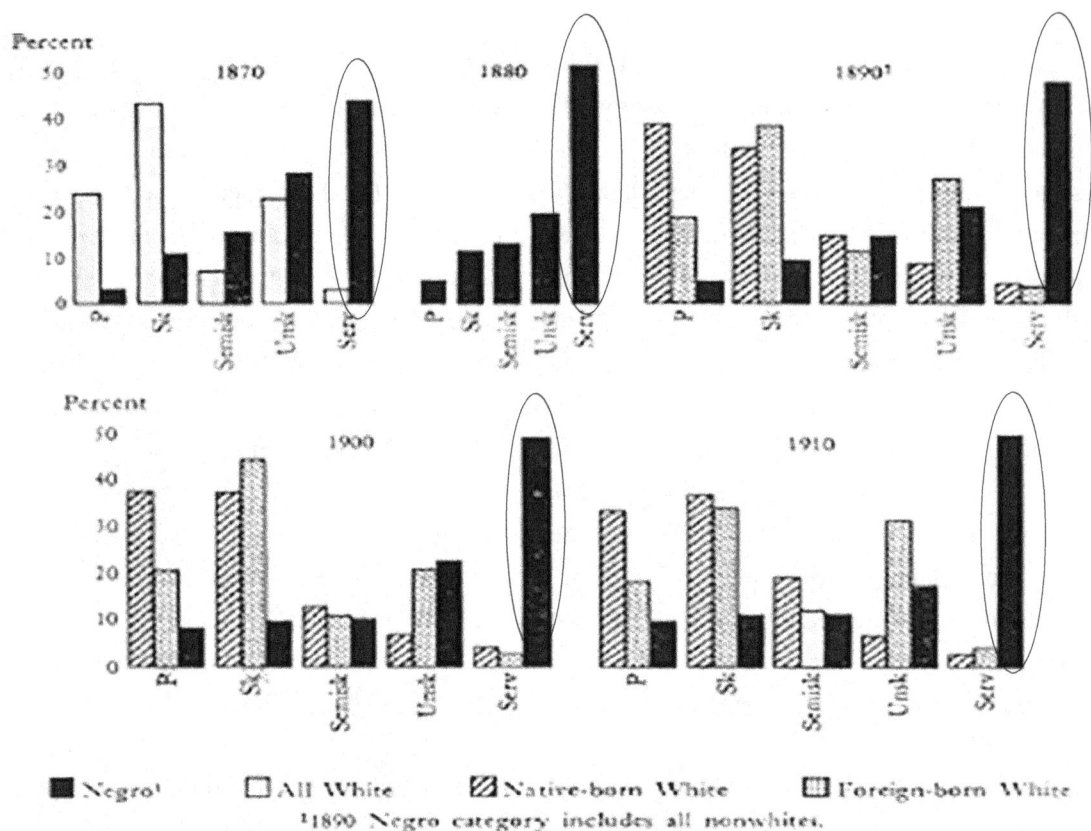

FIGURE 2 *Occupational Distribution, by Percent, of White and Black Males, Detroit, 1870–1910.* From: Katzman, "Before the Ghetto"

and D. Augustus Stryker (a lawyer, born in Barbados, who was Dean of Law at Allen University before moving to Detroit in 1887). But their skills and energies were confined to the city's proportionally small black community.[53]

That the door to the union hall was closed to blacks throughout the 1800s was, at the time, merely the latest form of discrimination. Since the city's founding, blacks had been relegated to a small section of the city. Though the evolving electric street-car system expanded the range of working people in Detroit in the 1880s, making it possible to live further out on the periphery of the city and commute to work, for most of Detroit's blacks, this development was moot. Whereas blacks as a percentage of the population peaked in 1870 at 2.4 percent (2,235), it fell thereafter incrementally to 1.2 percent in 1910. Yet, even though their actual numbers had more than doubled in that year to 5,741,[54] what remained consistent in size was the area to which they were confined. As Katzman indicates, before re-districting in 1881, most blacks lived in a small slice of what were then wards 3, 4, and 7 (see map below) bounded by Gratiot on the north, Atwater (by the river) to the south, Randolph Street to the west, and De Quindre to the east.

With a growing black demographic squeezed decade after decade into the same small area, the law of supply and demand for housing took a devastating toll

Chapter 9   *In God We Make Trusts*

both in terms of price and quality. Detroit at this time was known as a city of predominantly single-family homes; not so for its black population. Within this area were a warren of service alleys. They were, however, not used for this purpose. Originally intended as secondary, utility paths to expedite the removal of trash and ashes, there arose there instead poorly constructed tenements. Most of the city's blacks and many newly arrived immigrants were housed here. The tenements were, as Katzman describes them, "...former sheds and stables converted into one-, two-, and three family dwellings."[55] Because the city did not provide services of any kind to the area, it became not just a health hazard, buy a magnet for Detroit's unsavory elements.

Dirty and decrepit, however, did not mean cheap. Because blacks had no living options anywhere else, they were helpless victims of predatory landlords who charged more for these run-down domiciles than white workers paid to rent single family homes in Detroit's other areas restricted to blacks. Though not physically or officially designated by the city with signs or any other indications, the racial boundaries of Detroit were well-established and intractable. Woodward Avenue became the hard boundary between white and black Detroit, a line blacks crossed at their own peril.

Immediately to the west of Woodward was the Irish district, Corktown. Though not officially chronicled, the area's history includes tales of a black family who attempted to settle there. After a short time, their house mysteriously caught fire. Responding to the fire, the volunteer fire department proceeded to put out the fire in the house next door, after the fire chief pronounced what could be a watchword for race relations in the city a hundred years hence: "Lave the nager's house be," he ordered.[56]

"Lave the nagger's house be...."

Workers (mostly black) eating dinner on the docks, Jacksonville Florida. Detroit Publishing Co. USA. (**Alamy, image: M1T312**)

Chapter 9 *In God We Make Trusts*

Endnotes

Chapter One:
Before the French

1. Ryan, Vince. "Ignatius Loyola and the Ideas of Catholic Reform." *Ignatius Insight*, IgnatiusInsight.com. (orig. in *Catholic Dossier*, Sept. 2001) Web. http://ignatiusinsight.com/features2007/vryan_jesuitsreform_jan07.asp

2. "About Beavers." . Beavers: Wetlands and Wildlife, n.d. Web. . http://www.beaversww.org/beavers-and-wetlands/about-beavers.

3. "Native Americans in the Great Lakes Region" n.d. Web. http://web2.geo.msu.edu/geogmich/paleo-indian.html.

4. *Ibid.*

5. "Native American Tribes of Michigan" n.d. Web. http://www.native-languages.org/michigan.htm.

6. Strayer, Joseph R., Hans W. Gatzke, and E. Harris Harbison. "The Mainstream of Civilization to 1715." 2nd. New York/Chicago/San Francisco/Atlanta: Harcourt, Brace, Jovanovich, 1974. Pg. 412. Print.

7. Ebenstein, William. "Bodin (Six Books On The State)." *Great Political Thinkers*. 5th ed. Princeton: Rhinehart, 1958. 328. Print.

8. Johnson, Ida. "The French Regime – 1634 to 1760." *The Michigan Fur Trade*. Lansing: Michigan Historical Society, 1919. 4 - 5. Print.

9. A group of wealthy French merchants began the first monopoly in 1603. It lasted until 1610 when Richelieu – ever one to insist on control – reconstituted the monopoly as the "Company of Hundred Associates with a range Florida to the Arctic Circle, and revenue stream more tightly controlled by the Crown (meaning himself). Johnson, *loc cit.* pg. 4.

10. Juen, Rachel B., and Michael S. Nasseney. "The Fur Trade." *Fort St. Joseph Archaeological Project* Booklet Series, No. 2 (2012): 6. Print.

11. Johnson, *op cit.* pg. 5.

12. Johnson, *op cit.* pg. 10.

13. Gallway Patricia (Editor),, and Conrad, Glenn R. (Author). "Reluctant Imperialist: France in North America (Part II). *La Salle and His Legacy: Frenchmen and Indians in the Lower Mississippi Valley*. Mississippi Historical Society, 1982. Pg. 93. Print.

14. "The one feature by which they might, to some close observer, have given an inkling of the future was that they hung about the universities and impressed youths with their learning; or that, while they served the poor, they were pleased to direct the consciences of noble and wealthy women." McCabe, Joseph. *A Candid History of the Jesuits*. London: Eveleigh Nash, 1913. pg.19. Print.

15. "The one feature by which they might, to some close observer, have given an inkling of the future was that they hung about the universities and impressed youths with their learning; or that, while they served the poor, they were pleased to direct the consciences of noble and wealthy women." McCabe, Joseph. *A Candid History of the Jesuits*. London: Eveleigh Nash, 1913. pg.19. Print.

16. McCabe, *Ibid*. Pgs. 7-8.

17. Parkman, Francis. *England and France in North America/* Vol. II: *The Jesuits in North America in the Seventeenth Century*. Boston: Little/Brown and Company, 1879. Pgs. 111-112. Print.

18. Notwithstanding possible questions surrounding Loyola's motivations in aiding the poor, one can argue, as Alves has done, that Ignatius' efforts (along with his contemporaries, Calvin and Vives) were some of the first concrete efforts to collaborate with local authorities on secular aid to the downtrodden: "…he turned to the material needs of the communal body by persuading the magistrates to draw up a list of ordinances to provide for the regular relief of the poor. Typically, a list of penalties was also drawn up to punish sturdy professional beggars. Openly crediting Ignatius for the reforms, the magistrates appointed the *major domos* of the poor to make regular collections on Sundays and festivals, and to then distribute money to those paupers officially registered for the reception of aid." Alves, Abel Athouguia. "The Christian Social Organism and Social Welfare: The Case of Vives, Calvin and Loyola." *Sixteenth Century Journal*, University of Massachusetts, XX, No.1. Spring (1989): Pgs. 14-16. Print.

19. McCabe, *op cit*. pg. 9.

20. Stayer, Gatzke, Harbison, *ibid*. Pg. 388.

21. Juen and Nasseney, *ibid*. Pg. 29.

22. *Loc.cit.*

Chapter Two:
Rule Britannia

1. " ...the failure of the Long Parliament to make peace after the Civil War was the same error that had ruined Charles and was to vitiate the Restoration settlement, the inability of any party to admit the need for religious tolerance." Trevelyan, G.M. "The Stuart Era/Parliamentary Liberty and Overseas Expansion." *History of England*. 3rd ed. London: Longmans, Green, 1937. 417. Print.

2. Osgood, Herbert L. "The Corporation as a Form of Colonial Government." *Political Science Quarterly* 11.4 (1896): 695-96. Print.

3. *Op cit*, Osgood. 694.

4. Fiske, John. "Chapter IV: The West India Company." *The Dutch and Quaker Colonies in America*. Vol. 1. Boston: Riverside, Cambridge, 1899. 112. Print.

5. *Op cit*, Fiske. 133.

6. "Dutch Colonies." *nps.gov/Kingston:Discover 300 Years of New York History*. National Park Service/U.S. Dept. of the Interior. Web. 1 Nov. 2014 http://www.nps.gov/nr/travel/kingston/colonization.htm

7. Nelson, William E. "The Utopian Legal Order of the Massachusetts Bay Colony, 1630-1686." *The American Journal of Legal History* 47.2 (2005): 183. Print.

8. "The Charter of Massachusetts Bay." *The Avalon Project/Documents in Law, History, and Diplomacy*. Yale Law School Lillian Goldman Law Library (in Memory of Sol Goodman), 1 Nov. 1629. Web. 1 Nov. 2014 http://avalon.law.yale.edu/17th_century/mass03.asp.

9. "Jamestown Settlement and the Starving Time." *Britain in the New World*. Independence Hall Foundation in Philadelphia, 1 Jan. 2008. Web. 1 Nov. 2014 http://www.ushistory.org/us/2c.asp.

10. Tawney, R.H. *Religion and the Rise of Capitalism*. 3rd. New York: Mentor, 1951. 153. Print.

11. Schama, Simon. *A History of Britain/The Wars of the British 1603-1776*. 1st. 2. New York: Hyperion, 2001. 217. Print.

12. Hobbes, Thomas. "From Diffidence Warre." *Leviathan*. (ISBN 13: 9781484033814 (978-1-4840-3381-4)) San Bernadino, CA, 2013. 19. Print.

13. Hobbes makes a distinction between the covenants at the center of civil law – what he calls, "humane politiques" (entered into in order to compel positive social behavior), and the original covenant between Moses and the Deity, regarded as the original seat of all morality in general (what he calls, conversely, "Divine Politiques): "For these seeds have received culture from two sorts of men. One sort have been they, that have nourished, and ordered them, according to their own invention. The other, have done it, by Gods commandement, and direction: but both sorts have done it, with a purpose to make those men that relyed on them, the more apt to Obedience, Lawes, Peace, Charity, and civill Society. So that the Religion of the former sort, is part of humane Politiques; and teacheth part of the duty which

Earthly Kings require of their Subjects. And the Religion of the later sort is Divine Politiques; and containeth Precepts to those that have yielded themselves subjects in the Kingdome of God. Of the former sort, were all the Founder of Common-wealths, and the Lawgivers of the Gentiles: Of the later sort, were Abraham, Moses, and our Blessed Saviour; by whom have been derived unto us the Lawes of the Kingdome of God."
Ibid, Hobbes. 69.

14. *Ibid*, Hobbes. 85.

15. Ebenstein, William. "Hobbes." *Great Political Thinkers*. 5th ed. Princeton: Rhinehart, 1958. 336. Print.

16. "The final Cause, End, or Designe of men…is the foresight of their own preservation, and of a more contented life thereby; that is to say, of getting themselves out from that miserable condition Warre, which is consequent…when there is no visible Power to keep them in awe, and tye them by feare of punishment ot the performance of their Covenants…" *Ibid*, Hobbes. 97.

17. *Ibid*, Hobbes. 75.

18. *Ibid*, Hobbes. 107.

19. *Op cit*, Hobbes. 108.

20. *Op cit*, Hobbes. 109.

21. *Op cit*, Trevelyan. 444.

22. *Op cit*, Trevelyan. 443.

23. *Loc cit*, Trevelyan.

24. Juen, Rachel B., and Michael S. Nasseney. "The Fur Trade." *Fort St. Joseph Archaeological Project* Booklet Series, No. 2 (2012): 7. Print.

25. Johnson, Ida. "The French Regime – 1634 to 1760." *The Michigan Fur Trade*. Lansing: Michigan Historical Society, 1919. 31-32. Print.

26. "Beaver Wars (1642-1698)." *The Patriot Files (Dedicated to the Preservation of Military History)*. 14 Oct. 2014. Web. http://www.patriotfiles.com/index.php?name=Sections&req=viewarticle&artid=8531&page=1'

27. *Ibid*, "Beaver Wars."

28. When Charles II of Spain died in 1700, Louis XIV tried to install his grandson, Phillip of Anjou on the throne and proceeded to declare France and Spain to be unified. France was a *force majeur* at the time, and Italy, Germany, and Holland did not want to see Louis' power increase to such an extent. War ensued on such a wide scale that the conflict came to be known as the First of the World Wars. Louis lost a number of battles over the issue and settled for peace with all the countries involved in a settlement called the Treaties of Utrecht. Newfoundland and Nova Scotia – both part of France's holdings in New France prior to the conflict – were given to England, thus vastly expanding its influence in North America. "War of the Spanish Succession." hyperhistory.com
http://www.hyperhistory.com/online_n2/civil_n2/histscript6_n2/span_succ.html.

29. Fiske, *Ibid*, "Chapter XI: Dutch and English." 326. Print.

30. Fiske, *Op cit.* 243. Print.

31. Schama, *Ibid,* "Chapter 6: "The Wrong Empire." 404. Print.

32. Emerson, F.V. "Geographic Influences on American Slavery. Part I." *American Geographical Society* 43.1 (1911): 15. Print.

33. B.J.R., "Features of American Slavery." *The Sewanee Review* 1.4 (1893): 477. Print.

34. Harper, Douglas. "French Slavery." *The SCIOLIST*. 1 Jan. 2005. Web
    http://etymonline.com/columns/frenchslavery.htm

35. Simons, Stefan. "Memorial to the Slave Trade: French City Confronts Its Brutal Past." *Spiegel Online 2012*. SPIEGELnet GmbH, 1 Jan. 2012. Webs
    http://www.spiegel.de/international/euope/nantes-opens-memorial-to-slave-trade-a-829447.html.

36. Emerson, *loc cit*.

37. "Cadillac's Village or "Detroit Under Cadillac," with List of Property Owners and a History of the Settlement 1701 to 1710.e." C.M Burton/Detroit, 1 Jan. 1896. Web
    file://localhost/Bill Martin, Thunder Bay, Ontario, Canada. email bmartin@tbaytel.net
    http/::www.tbaytel.net:bmartin:.

38. *Ibid*, Johnson. 35-36.

39. *Op cit*, Johnson. 37.

40. *Ibid*, "Cadillac's Village."

41. *Op cit*, Johnson. 41.

42. *Ibid*, Johnson. 49.

43. *Loc cit*.

44. Wraxall, Peter, and C.H. McIlwain (Editor). "The Early Fur Trade." *An Abridgement of the Indian Affairs*. Vol. XXII. New York: Harvard U/Department of History, 1915. 9. Print.

45. "Pickawillany." *Ohio History Central*. Ohio History Connection. Web
    http://www.ohiohistorycentral.org/w/Pickawillany?rec=792

46. *Ibid*, Wraxall. xix.

47. "British Detroit 1760-1796." *Historyofdetroit.com*. City Beautiful Design. Web
    http://historydetroit.com/index.php

48. *Ibid*, Schama. 440 - 441.

49. *Op cit*, Schama. 441.

50. "Battle of Quebec." *United States History*. Web. 31 Jan. 2015
    http://www.u-s-history.com/pages/h787.html.

Chapter Three:

51. Smith, Adam, *The Wealth of Nations*, Book I Chapter VIII,. "Of Restraints Upon the Importation from Foreign Countries of such Goods as Can Be Produced at Home." *The Wealth of Nations*. New York: Barnes and Noble, 2004. (Orig.: 1776) 300. Print.

52. Robinson, Dennis. *Robert Rogers*. Web. http://www.u-s-history.com/pages/h1186.html

53. Hough, Franklin Benjamin,. *Journals of Major Robert Rogers*, 1765. Harvard College Library (from the Francis Parkman Memorial Fund for Canadian History Joel Munsell's sons. 1883. pg. 196. Print.
https://books.google.com/books?id=KXqlHwLIaP8C&pg=PA196&lpg=PA196&dq=Robert+Rogers+I+acknowledge+the+receipt+of+your+two+letters,&source=bl&ots=6XPaJYRQ17&sig=ACfU3U1YhgowTZ72pxOsVL2nY_LLSh7HgQ&hl=en&sa=X&ved=2ahUKEwjr48Tak8n3AhUzLn0KHUMuBCoQ6AF6BAgREAM#v.

54. Granzo, Tina. "Detroit Places: Fort Detroit – British Rule – 1760-1796." *Detroit History*. Tina Granzo, 1 Jan. 2015. Web. 1 Feb. 2015
http://historydetroit.com/eras/british_rule_1760_1796.

55. Burton, Clarence. "*Detroit Under British Rule.*" *Early Detroit*. Ann Arbor: University of Michigan, 1909 (Reprint). 15. Print Op cit, Burton. pg. 16. Print.*Ibid*, Granzo

56. Op cit, Burton. pg. 23.

57. Op cit, Burton. pg. 21.

58. *Ibid*, Granzo

59. *Ibid*, Granzo.

60. *Ibid*, Granzo

61. "If anything, Loudoun's [General Loudoun: British general who succeeded Braddock] contempt for the colonials and their savage allies was even more patrician than Braddock's. Convinced that the whole bloody shower needed smartening up, he courted the hatred of American officers by insisting on the War Office policy of ranking Americans far below their counterparts in the regular British regiments and alienated the men by demanding that the British whip-happy discipline (500 lashes for insubordination, 1,000 for stealing a shirt) be imposed on the colonial troops who had never seen it, much less endured it."
Schama, Simon. *A History of Britain/The Wars of the British 1603-1776*. 1st. 2. New York: Hyperion, 2001. 443-444. Print.

62. Trevelyan, G.M. "Book V/From Utrecht to Waterloo." *History of England*. 3rd ed. London: Longmans, Green, 1937. 512. Print.

63. Op cit, Trevelyan. pg. 514.

64. "It follows that 'the most perfectly virtuous' actions are 'such as appear to have the most universal unlimited tendency to the greatest and most extensive happiness of all the rational agents, to whom our influence can reach.' " Quoted from Hutcheson's Inquiry by:
Seth, James. "Scottish Moral Philosophy." *The Philosophical Review* VII.6 (1898): 563. Print.

65. "If usefulness, therefore, be a source of moral sentiment, and if this usefulness be not always considered with a reference to self; it follows, that everything, which contributes to the happiness of society recommends itself directly to our approbation and good-will."
Hume, David. "Section V/Part II." *Enquiries Concerning Human Understanding and the Concerning the Principles of Morals*. 3rd ed. Oxford: Clarendon, 1975. 219. Print.

66. Smith, Adam. "Of the Propriety of Actions" *The Theory of Moral Sentiments*. 1st ed. Mineola: Dover, 2006. I.I.3. pp 3-4. Print.

67. *Ibid*, Smith. "Of the Foundation of Our Judgments Concerning Our Own Sentiments and Conduct, and of the Sense of Duty." III.I.3. 111-112.

68. *Ibid*, Smith. "Of the beauty with which the appearance of Utility bestows upon the characters and actions of men." IV.1.2. 186.

69. 'The love and admiration which we naturally conceive for those whose character and conduct we approve of, necessarily dispose us to desire to become ourselves the objects of the like agreeable sentiments, and to be as amiable and as admirable as those whom we love and admire the most." Op cit, Smith. III.2.3. 114.

70. "The more I sympathize with the parties, the less are my own values involved."
Leroch, Martin. "Adam Smith's Intuition Pump: The Impartial Spectator." Homo Oeconomicus 25.1 University of Hamburg (2008): 6. Print.

71. *Ibid*, Smith. VI.I.9. 216.

72. *Ibid*, Smith. III.II.8. 116.

73. *Op cit*, Smith. III.I.5. 116.

74. *Ibid*, Smith. II.III.2. 86.

75. *Ibid*, Smith. III.VI. VI.11. 170.

76. *Loc cit,* Smith.

77. Hume, David. *Introduction." Dialogues Concerning Natural Religion*. 2nd ed. Indianapolis/Cambridge: Hackett, 1990 (Orig. pub., 1776). viii. Print.

78. *Ibid*, Smith. III.IV.7. 153.

79. Sidgwick, Henry. *Outlines of the History of Ethics*. McMillan/St.Martin's Press. New York, 1967. pg. 217.

80. Loc cit., Sidgwick.

81. Stevens, Wayne E. "The Organization of the British Fur Trade, 1760-1800." Mississippi Valley Historical Review 3.2 (1916): 180-81. Print.

82. Op cit, Stevens. 179.

83. Wraxall, Peter, and C.H. McIlwain (Editor). *The Early Fur Trade. "An Abridgement of the Indian Affairs. Vol. XXII*. New York: Harvard U/Department of History, 1915. xli. Print.

84. *Ibid*, Burton. pp. 24-25.

85. "Trade and policy were inseparable, but trade was the ultimate end of all policy; it was practically the sole means in all Indian relations."
    Op cit, Wraxall. xl.

86. Webster, J. Clarence. "Introduction." *The Journal of Jeffery Amherst / Recording the Military Career of General Amherst in America from 1758 to 1763*. Vol. 1st. Toronto: Ryerson, 1931. pp. 18-19. Print.

87. In a journal entry dated July, 7th, 1763, Amherst reflects: "There is absolutely nothing but fear of us that can hinder them from committing all the cruelties in their power."
    Ibid, Webster. Pg. 310.

88. Clark, James T. "Sir William Johnson and Pontiac." Proceedings of the New York State Historical Association 13 (1914): 100. Print.

89. *Op cit*, Clark. Pg. 98.

90. "The Confederacy, a representative alliance of six tribes including the Oneidas, Onondagas, Cayugas, Senecas, and Tuscaroras, acted together as one nation for defense and mutual welfare. Matters were discussed at periodic councils at Onandanga among representatives chosen by tribal matriarchs. Acting through the council, and proactively exploiting his many connections to the diverse native population, Johnson shielded Amherst for as long as possible from the disastrous consequences of his own bigoted, racist attitudes and policy. *History of the Iroquois*. Sunbury: A History. Bucknell Environmental Center (Bucknell University). Web. 11 Mar. 2015 http://www.departments.bucknell.edu/environmental_center/sunbury/website/HistoryofIroquoisIndians.shtml.

91. "The great role of the Iroquois was that of middle-men between the 'Far Indian' and the English, a role which enabled them no only to obtain material benefits, but to retain that position of superiority over the Indians of the eastern half…" *Ibid*, Wraxall. xlii.

92. Adams Jr., Charles E. "Interregnum: The Zagonaash, 1760 - 1783." *Assault on a Culture: The Anishinaabeg of the Great Lakes and the Dynamics of Change*. 1st ed. Xlibris, 2013. 81. Print.

93. *Loc cit*, Adams.

94. Op cit, Adams. 83.

95. *Ibid*, Webster. 308.

96. Op cit, Adams. 85.

97. Op cit, Adams. 84-87.

98. It is noteworthy, as Burton recalls, that French and Canadian farmers around the perimeter of Detroit remained generally unmolested by the Indians, suggesting a very selective ire reserved exclusively for the British who were captive in the fort.
    Ibid, Burton. 22.

99. Op cit, Adams. 92.

100. How and Where Did Pontiac Die?" St. Louis Sage Magazine. August 1st, 2019. Web. https://www.stlmag.com/history/st-louis-sage/how-and-where-did-chief-pontiac-die/.

101. Trevelyan's contempt for the American revolutionaries is even more evident in a footnote to this passage when he writes: "The temper and programme of the party which overcame the American 'Tories' and effected the separation from Britain is best described as 'Radical' to English readers, whatever meaning that term may now bear in America. The Revolutionists were not 'Whigs' in the English sense of the word, for they savoured neither of aristocracy nor of moderation. They were not 'Liberals," for they did not wish to allow liberty of speech or opinion to their opponents, whom they eventually expelled from the country. They were not 'Socialists,' for they had no designs of redistributing property, and were individualists in economic theory. They were democrats, with less than no reverence for any authority not derived directly from the people: they sought to enforce the will of the majority on the minority and to make the poor man count as much as the rich man in politics." Ibid, Trevelyan. 553.

102. Burton, Clarence M. "The City of Detroit Michigan, 1701-1922." Michigan County Histories. Web.
https://quod.lib.umich.edu/m/micounty/BAD1447.0002.001?rgn=main;view=fulltext

103. Smith, Adam. "Of Restraints Upon the Importation from Foreign Countries of such Goods as Can Be Produced at Home." The Wealth of Nations. New York: Barnes and Noble, 2004. (Orig.: 1776) 300. Print.

104. Though enclosure – the practice of encompassing and "enclosing" numerous parcels of land hitherto traditionally held in common – had existed in limited form since the fifteenth century, it accelerated apace in the in the mid to late 1700s, driven by an increasingly profit-induced motive. "Under the medieval, open-field system of agriculture, arable land was divided into strips that were cultivated by individual farmers…After harvest, the open-fields became 'common' and anyone in possession of common rights could graze animals on the land. Enclosure put an end to this." Thompson, S.J.. "Paliamentary Enclosure, Property, Population, and the Decline of Classical Republicanism in Eighteenth-Century Britain." The Historical Journal 51.3 (2008): 623. Print.

105. Ibid, Smith. I.II.1. 11.

106. "A monopoly granted either to an individual or to a trading company, has the same effect as a secret in trade or manufactures. The monopolists, by keeping the market constantly understocked by never fully supplying the effectual demand, sell their commodities much above the natural price, and raise their emoluments, whether they consist in wages or profit, greatly above their natural rate." I.VII.24. 51.

107. Ibid, Smith. I.I.10. 8.

108. Hitchcock, Tim. "Begging on the Streets of Eighteenth-Century London." Journal of British Studies. 44.3 (2005): 478-498. Web. 5 Jun. 2015.
http://www.jstor.org/stable/10.1086/429704 .

109. "By 1776…there were 13,605 workhouse inmates north of the river in London and Middlesex, and a further 3,288 in the urban parishes of Southwark and Surrey south of the river, giving a total of nearly 17,000, or around 2 per cent of a population of about 800,000." Payne, Diane Elizabeth. "Children of the Poor in London 1700-1780." A thesis submitted in partial fulfilment [sic] of the requirements of the University of Hertfordshire for the degree of Doctor of Philosophy." (2008): 41. University of Hertfordshire.UK. Web. 5 Jun 2015.

110. Ibid, Schama. pp. 369-370.

111. Ibid, Smith, Wealth of Nations. I.V.2. 26.

112. "But the value of every commodity is determined by the labour-time requisite to turn it out so as to be of normal quality." Marx, Karl. Capital (A Critique of Political Economy). 4th. New York: Modern Library, 1906. 192. Print.

113. Ibid, Smith, Wealth of Nations. I.V.1. 26.

114. Ibid, Smith, Wealth of Nations. I.IV.2. 20

115. Ibid, Marx. pg. 646.

116. "If the prodigality of some was not compensated by the frugality of others, the conduct of every prodigal, by feeding the idle with the bread of the industrious, tends not only to beggar himself, but to impoverish his country." Ibid, Smith, Wealth of Nations. II.III.21. 234.

117. Zinn, Howard. A People's History of the United States. 1st. New York: Harper and Row, 1980. 49. Print.

118. Loc cit.

119. Ibid, Smith, Wealth of Nations. IV.VII.prt.II.para.56.

120. Ibid, Smith, Wealth of Nations. I.XI.prt.I.para.29.

121. Zinn, Howard. A People's History of the United States. 1st. New York: Harper and Row, 1980. 49. Print.

122. Phillips, Kevin. Wealth and Democracy. 1st. New York: Broadway, 2002. 11. Print.

123. United States. National Park Service/U.S. Dept. of the Interior. Yorktown Battlefield. Washington D.C.: U.S. Government, Web. http://www.nps.gov/yonb/learn/historyculture/history-of-the-siege.htm.

124. Gavrilovitch, Peter, and Bill McGraw. The Detroit Almanac/300 years of life in the Motor City. 1st ed. Detroit, Michigan: Detroit Free Press, 2001. 35. Print.

125. Loc cit

Chapter Four:
Liquor, Lies, & Laissez Faire

1. Seelinger, Matthew. "The Battle of Fallen Timbers, 20 August 1794." *National Museum/United States Army*. U.S. Army, 2015. Web. 18 July 2015. https://armyhistory.org/the-battle-of-fallen-timbers-20-august-1794/

2. *Ibid*, Seelinger.

3. The 1795 Treaty of Greenville was only the first of a string of land cessations that would, through successive treaties over the coming decades, appropriate most of the Indian land in

and around Michigan, Ohio, and Indiana. Beginning in the northeast with a large segment of Lake Erie's southern shoreline, the victorious new republic claimed for itself an area bounded on the north by a line following roughly the mouths of the Wabash, Maumee, and Ohio Rivers, the Ohio River on the south, and the southwestern point where the Ohio River first meets and intersects Ohio's border with Indiana. See map:
https://www.pinterest.com/pin/295267319291054805/ and
https://www.cmich.edu/library/clarke/ResearchResources/Native_American_Material/Treaty_Rights/Text_of_Michigan_Related_Treaties/Pages/Fort-Greenville,-Ohio,-1795.aspx

4. Zinn, Howard. *A People's History of the United States*. 1st. New York: Harper and Row, 1980. 39-42. Print.

5. *Op cit,* Zinn. 58.

6. *Ibid*, Zinn. 92-94.

7. See map of treaty area: Library of Congress. Item number:71005487
http://memory.loc.gov/cgi-bin/query/h?ammem/gmd:@field%28NUMBER+@band%28g3700+ar075200%29%29

8. Hatter, Lawrence B. "The Transformation of the Detroit Land Market and the Formation of the Anglo-American Border, 17983-1796." *Michigan Historical Review/Central Michigan University*. 34.1 (Emerging Borderlands) (2008): 83. Print.

9. *Ibid*, Hatter. 84.

10. *Loc cit.*

11. *Op cit.* 87

12. *Op cit.* 87-88.

13. *Loc cit.*

14. It was, however, too late for members of the group who had been given permission to return to the original Gnadenhutten on the Sandusky to harvest crops. In locating a settlement in the Tuscawaras Valley, Zeisberger, it seems, had made a fatal blunder. The valley was home to a hunting and raiding trail used by both hostile Shawnees to attack settlements in Kentucky and Pennsylvania, and white militia alike. After repetitive, deadly attacks by hostile tribes, the Pennsylvania militia mounted a campaign of retribution. Convinced that the peaceful Gnadenhutten Indians were aiding their warring brethren, members of the white militia captured ninety-six of them without incident, imprisoned them, then bludgeoned them to death while they were praying.
Cummings, Jim. "The Story of The Moravian Massacre "A Day of Shame"." *Pioneer Times USA*. Web News Service/An Online Journal of Living History, Feb. 2005. Web. 11 Aug. 2015. http://www.graphicenterprises.net/html/times_2011_4_.html

15. Burton, Clarence. "Sec.IV:Letters and Papers:1786." *Burton Historical Collection. Vol.1: The John Askin Papers*. Detroit: Detroit Library Commission, 1928. 223. Print.
https://www.google.com/search?q=archive.lib.msu.edu%2FMMM%2FJA%2Fa%2FJA09a001p006&ie=utf-8&oe=utf-8

16. "In the first stage, the Congress was responsible for selecting the territory's leaders. There would be a governor, a secretary, and three judges. The governor and judges would jointly select laws from already existing states to create their territory's legal code. The Congress reserved the right to accept or reject all selected laws. The governor would have power over the militia and Native Americans matters. He also could select law enforcement officials and judges for the lower courts. All five members of the territorial government were to have large holdings of land and be residents of the territory."
"Northwest Ordinance." *Ohio History Central*. Ohio History Connection. Web. 1 Aug. 2015 file://localhost/.
http/::www.ohiohistorycentral.org:w:Northwest_Ordinance%3Frec=1747

17. Hofstader, R. (1989). Thomas Jefferson: The Aristocrat as Democrat. In *The American Political Tradition and the Men Who Made It* (4th ed., p. 40). New York, New York: Random House.

18. *Loc cit*.

19. "History of Cuyahoga County." *One Cuyahoga: Official Government Website of Cuyahoga County, Ohio*. County of Cuyahoga, Ohio. Web. 26 Aug. 2015.
http://www.cuyahogacounty.us/en-US/history.aspx

20. Johnson, Ida. Chapter 6: "American Regime – 1796 to 1840. U.S. Policy and Extension of its Trade" *The Michigan Fur Trade*. Lansing: Michigan Historical Society, 1919. 102. Print.

21. *Ibid*, Johnson. Chapter 5: "Fur Trade in Revolutionary Times." 85-86.

22. *Op cit.*, Johnson, Chapter 6. 103.

23. *Op cit.*, Johnson, Chapter 6. 104.

24. Myers, Gustavus. *History of the Great American Fortunes*. 3rd ed. Vol. 1; Part 1: Conditions in Settlement and Colonial Times. Chicago: Charles H. Kerr, 1910. 109. Print.

25. *Loc cit*.

26. With regards to the size and the way Astor's fortune was procured, Youngman observes: "However great the ability displayed in effecting such transactions, it is felt to have no connection to the size of the return, and the cry of "unearned" is immediately raised. Then an explanation of his unusual gains is sought for in the wickedness of his acts, rather than in the institutions and the situations which condition his activity." Youngman, A. (1908). "The Fortune of John Jacob Astor: III" *University of Chicago Press, 16*(8), 523
http://www.jstor.org/stable/1820382

27. Gray, Charles Gilmer. "Lewis and Clark at the Mouth of Wood River: An Historic Spot." *Journal of the Illinois Press* (1920): 182.
http://www.jstor.org/stable/40194492

28. Holman, F. (1911). Some Important Results from the Expeditions of John Jacob Astor, to and from the Oregon Country, 12(3), 208-208. Print.
http://www.jstor.org/stable/20609876

29. *Ibid*, Haeger. 188

30. "In 1800, Astor, and at least four partners, shipped a cargo of furs, specie, ginseng, and cochineal on board the *Severn*. The return cargo of silks and teas was so profitable that the Severn was again bound for China in March 1802 carrying 2,454 beaver skins and 600 otter skins, plus $43,000 in specie. The voyages became so frequent that in 1803 Astor built the *Beaver*, the first of several vessels designed especially for the China trade."
Haeger, John D. "Business Strategy and Practice in the Early Republic: John Jacob Astor and the American Fur Trade." *The Western Historical Quarterly/Utah State University* 19.2 (1988): 188-89. Print.
http://www.jstor.org/stable/968394

31. *Op cit.*, Holman. 208-209.

32. *Ibid*, Haeger. 191.

33. *Ibid*, Haeger. 193-194.

34. *Ibid*, Haeger. 195.

35. *Op cit.*, Myers. 114.

36. *Op cit.*, Myers. 116.

37. *Op cit.*, Myers. 120.

38. *Op cit.*, Myers. 122.

39. *Op cit.*, Myers. 123.

40. *Ibid*, Youngman. 516.

41. *Op cit.*, Youngman. 519.

42. Burton's account of General Hull's surrender of Detroit, though underscoring what he imagines to be Hull's weakness as a commander, at least mentions his descendants' attempts to vindicate his memory by introducing mitigating circumstances they felt justified his surrender of the post to the British. *See*:
Burton, Clarence. "Detroit Under British Rule." *Early Detroit*. Ann Arbor: University of Michigan, 1909 (Reprint). 35-36. Print.

43. "Battle of the Thames." *Ohio History Central*. Ohio History Connection. Web. 28 Oct. 2015. http://www.ohiohistorycentral.org/w/Battle_of_the_Thames?rec=481.

44. Fuller, George N. "Settlement of Michigan Territory." *Mississippi Valley Historical Review* 2.1 (1915): 26. Print. http://www.jstor.org/stable/1889104.

45. Goodwin, Cardinal. "A Larger View of the Yellowstone Expedition, 1819-1820." *The Mississippi Valley Historical Review* 4.3 (1917): 310. Print. http://www.jstor.org/stable/1888594.

46. Fearing the threat of burgeoning northern industrialism in the early decades of the nineteenth century, southern planters led by John C. Calhoun rebelled against protective tariffs they believed worked disproportionately to the advantage of northern businesses, locking them out of foreign markets. Grasping for a constitutional basis to reject the tariffs, Calhoun and South Carolina legislators conceived a state law based on the concept of "nullification." Calhoun *et al* argued that because the tariffs were unilaterally imposed by the federal government without first consulting the electorate, such taxes could be legitimately rejected or "nullified"

by states like South Carolina because they represented, or so they claimed, taxation without representation.
Nullification Proclamation." *Web Guides/Primary Documents in American History*. Library of Congress. Web. Nov. 2015

47. *Loc cit.*, Goodwin.

48. Narrative Journal of Travels from Detroit Northwest through the Great Chain of American Lakes to the Sources of the Mississippi River in the Year 1820." *American Memory/Pioneering the Upper Midwest: Books from Michigan, Minnesota, and Wisconsin, Ca. 1820-1910*. Library of Congress. Web. 77. Nov. 2015. http://memory.loc.gov/cgi-bin/query/r?ammem/lhbum:@field%28DOCID+@lit%28lhbum01453div10%29%29

49. *Op cit.*, Narrative Journal 74.

50. *Ibid*, Narrative Journal 91-92.

51. *Ibid*, Fuller. 29.

52. *Ibid*, Goodwin. 300.

53. In his sweeping chronicle of American fortunes, Gustavus Myers describes an entry from one of the early ledgers of Astor's American Fur Company that came to light in 1909 when they were put on auction in New York City shows a payment of $35,000 from Astor to Cass for "services not stated." It would not be hard to surmise, however, the nature of the services rendered since Cass was the governor of the Michigan Territory and, as Myers explains, "…he [Cass] became the identical Secretary of War to whom so many complaints of the crimes of Astor's American Fur Company were made." *Ibid*, Myers. 125.

54. Berrnard C. "Hypocrisy on the Great Lakes Frontier: The Use of Whiskey by the Michigan Department of Indian Affairs." *Michigan Historical Review* (Fall, 1992): 4. Print. http://www.jstor.org/stable/20173343.

55. *Op cit.*, Peters. 5.

56. Lewis, Francis Paul and Donald F., Cass, Prucha and Carmony. "A Memorandum of Lewis Cass: Concerning a System for the Regulation of Indian Affairs." *The Wisconsin Magazine of History* 52.1 (Fall, 1968). 36. Print.

57. Cass, Lewis. "Removal of the Indians." *North American Review* (1830): 1. Print. https://archive.org/details/removalindiansa00frangoog

58. *Ibid*, Cass, "Removal…" Para. 130, 5. Print.

59. Pearce, Margaret Wickens. "The Holes in the Grid: Reservation Surveys in Lower Michigan." *Michigan Historical Review* (Fall, 2004): 137. Print. http://www.jstor.org/stable/20174084.

60. *Loc cit.*, Pearce.

61. *Ibid*, Pearce. 143-144.

62. *Ibid*, Pearce. 136.

63. *Ibid*, Zinn. 137.

64. *Op cit.*, Zinn. 136.

65. *Op cit.*, Zinn. 137.

66. "What Happened on the Trail of Tears?/Federal Indian Removal Policy." *Trail of Tears/National Historic Trail*. National Park Service. Web. 1 Nov. 2015. http://www.nps.gov/trte/learn/historyculture/stories.htm

67. *Ibid*, "What Happened on the Trail of Tears?"

68. *Ibid*, "…Trail of Tears?"

69. *Ibid*, "…Trail of Tears?"

70. *Op cit.*, Zinn. 124.

Chapter Five:
Wood, Water & Fire: After the Beaver

1. Farmer, Silas. *The History of Detroit and Michigan/The Metropolis Illustrated*. Vol. 1. Detroit: Silas Farmer, 1889. Print.

2. *Ibid*, Farmer. Chapter XVII, 95.

3. *Op cit,* Farmer. 97.

4. *Loc cit.*

5. *Op cit,* Farmer. 96.

6. *Op cit,* Farmer. 97.

7. Known to history as the man who killed Alexander Hamilton in a duel, Burr's role in this dramatic and infamous event was, in fact, merely a tragic footnote to a larger political crisis inherent in the conflict between entrenched Federalist and Republican contingents vying, at the time, for control over the post-revolution government. Federalist John Adams was at the end of his term, and the political forces arrayed against each other in the U.S. election mimicked the colossal, military struggle for Europe that was ensuing between the purported republicanism of Napoleonic France, and caste laden constitutional monarchies like England. Adams – who, to his credit, sought a peaceful rapprochement with the revolutionary French government regarding its suppression of U.S. trade – was seeking re-election and recruited staunch Federalist Alexander Hamilton as his ally. On the other side was Thomas Jefferson who saw the Adams/Hamilton agenda (and their sympathies with the British government in the European conflict) as an attempt to re-introduce British influence into U.S. affairs, and an effort to undo what Jefferson regarded as the hard-won, democratic principles forged in the revolution. Ferling, John. "Thomas Jefferson, Aaron Burr, and the Election of 1800." *Smithsonian.com*. Smithsonian Institution, 1 Nov. 2004. Web. http://www.smithsonianmag.com/history/thomas-jefferson-aaron-burr-and-the-election-of-1800-131082359/?no-ist

8. Burr's descent from a space at the top of the Democratic Republican ticket in the election of 1800 to a cell in the stockade at Fort Stoddard Louisiana just seven years later is indicative both of a personality desperate to retain the reigns of power, and a monumental

miscalculation of how to do so. Had he enjoyed the august reputation of his partner on the ticket, Thomas Jefferson (with whom he was virtually tied for electoral votes) he might well have secured the highest office for himself. But a President Burr was not meant to be, and the iconic Jefferson seized the brass ring. Whether deserved or not, Burr's reputation as a corrupt opportunist dogged him, the most persistent and visceral criticism coming from Alexander Hamilton who never missed an opportunity to disparage Burr in the press and halls of power with the most brutal ad hominem attacks. Hamilton's attacks took their toll, and were probably instrumental in causing Burr to lose his own independent run for the presidency in 1804. Frustrated and humiliated, Burr sought to vindicate his honor by challenging Hamilton to a duel, a deadly exchange that took place on July 11, 1804. Hamilton was slain, adding a charge of murder to Burr's already tarnished reputation of which he was ultimately acquitted. But Burr's bitterness still festered, causing him to concoct a scheme to establish himself as leader of Louisiana and lands beyond. Still under Spanish control, its place in the union was as yet unsettled. After clandestine attempts to raise an army to forcibly accomplish his designs – which even included overt solicitations to the British government for assistance – Burr's plans ultimately became public, bringing on himself charges of treason. Again he was lucky in court and was acquitted of these charges as well in September, 1807. Burr was, however, forever discredited and died in 1836 in New York after spending the rest of his days as an obscure, run of the mill lawyer.
"1804 Burr Slays Hamilton in Duel." *History.com/This Day in History*. A E Networks, 2009. Web http://www.history.com/this-day-in-history/burr-slays-hamilton- in-duel

9. *Op cit,* Farmer. 96.

10. *Ibid,* Farmer. 491.

11. *Loc cit.*

12. *Ibid,* Farmer *r.* 134.

13. Burton, Clarence. "Detroit Under British Rule." *Early Detroit*. Ann Arbor: University of Michigan, 1909 (Reprint). 35-36. Print.

14. *Op cit,* Farmer *r.* 277.

15. *Loc cit.*

16. *Loc cit.*

17. *Op cit,* Burton. 36-37.

18. Ibid, Farmer. 98.

19. "Erie Canalway." *Happy Birthday National Park Service*. National Park Service. Web. https://www.nps.gov/erie/learn/historyculture/index.htm

20. Fregni, Giovanna. "A Study of the Manufacture of Copper Spearheads in the Old Copper Complex." *The Minnesota Archeologist* 68 (2010): 122.Web. http://www.academia.edu/227583/A_Study_of_the_Manufacture_of_Copper_Spearheads_in_the_Old_Copper_Complex

21. Ashworth, William. *The Late Great Lakes*. 2nd ed. Detroit: Wayne State UP, 1987. 69. Print.

22. *Op cit,* Ashworth. 71.

23. De Tocqueville, Alexis. *Aristocracy on the Saginaw Trail: Tocqueville in Michigan.* Clark Historical Library. Central Michigan University. Web.
https://www.cmich.edu/research/clarke-historical-library/explore-collection/explore-online/michigan-material/tocqueville-michigan#a11

24. Casper, Tom. "The Magic of White Pine." *Popular Woodworking Magazine.* American Woodworker Magazine, Apr.-May 2001. Web.
http://www.popularwoodworking.com/projects/the-magic-of-white-pine

25. *Op cit,* Ashworth. 74-75.

26. Wengert, Professor Gene. "What Is a Board Foot? /Explanation and Glossary of Lumber Terms by Professor Eugene Wengert." Woodweb. Woodweb, 2 May 2001. Web.
http://www.woodweb.com/knowledge_base/What_is_a_Board_Foot.html

27. Dickman, Donald L., and Larry A. Leefers. *The Forests of Michigan.* Vol. 1. Ann Arbor: U of Michigan, 2003. Print. 120.

28. *Op cit,* Dickman/Leefers. 121.

29. *Loc cit.*

30. *Op cit,* Dickman/Leefers. 121-123.

31.

32. Kilar, Jeremy. *Michigan's Lumbertowns: Lumbermen and Laborers in Saginaw, Bay City, and Muskgegon, 1870–1905.* Vol. 1. Detroit: Wayne State UP, 1990. Print. 22.

33. *Op cit,* Ashworth. 70.

34. *Op cit,* Ashworth. 71.

35. *Loc cit.*

36. Carl, Lira T. "Watt's Famous Experiment with the Separate Condenser." *Introductory Chemical Engineering and Thermodynamics.* Michigan State University. Web. 2001.
http://www.egr.msu.edu/~lira/supp/steam/wattexp.htm

37. *Ibid,* Ashworth. 53-54.

38. Welland Canal Section of the St. Lawrence Seaway." St. Lawrence Seaway Management Corporation. Web.
https://greatlakes-seaway.com

39. Putnam, J. W. "An Economic History of the Illinois and Michigan Canal: III." *Journal of Political Economy* 17.4 (1909): 419. Print.

40. "Soo Locks." Randal Schaetzl /Michigan State University. Web.
http://geo.msu.edu/extra/geogmich/SooLock.html

41. Tunell, George G. "The Diversion of the Flour and Grain Traffic from the Great Lakes to the Railroad." *Journal of Political Economy* 5.3 (1897): 340-45.3 (1897): 340-41. Print.
http://www.jstor.org/stable/1817751

42. An excellent and thorough examination of the technical development of metal rails. This treatise, penned by G.P. Radabaugh in 1915, is, it could be argued, without peer.

Radabaugh, G. P. *Origin and Development of the Railway Rail/English and American Wood, Iron and Steel*. Pennsylvania Steel/Maryland Steel. 64 pages. Print.

43. *Michigan's Railroad History/1825-2014*. Michigan Department of Transportation, 2014. Web. http//www.michiganrailroads.com › railroad-history.

44. *Ibid*, Radabaugh. 31-32.

45. *Loc cit.*

Chapter Six:
The Not so Calm Before the Storm

1. de Tocqueville, Alexis. *Democracy in America*. Vol. 1 & 2. University Park: Pennsylvania State U, 2002. Translation by Henry Reeve. Web. 628. http://www.hn.psu.edu/faculty/jmanls/Tocqueville.htm

2. Smith, Adam. "The Different Employment of Capitals." Book two; Chapter 4. *The Wealth of Nations*. New York: Barnes and Noble, 2004. (Orig.: 1776) 256. Print.

3. *Op cit,* de Tocqueville. 620.

4. *Loc cit.*

5. *Op cit,* de Tocqueville. 621.

6. *Op cit,* de Tocqueville. 625.

7. Mackay, Charles, *Memoirs of Extraordinary Popular Delusions and the Madness of Crowds*. 1852. Chapter 2: "The South-Sea Bubble." Library of Economics and Liberty. 17 July 2016. Web.
http://www.econlib.org/library/Mackay/macEx.html

8. According to Mackay, the tulip was introduced to Europe by one Conrad Gesner who first saw it in 1559 among the collection of "... the learned Counsilor Hewart," an influential resident of Augsburg. Considered a rare specimen in Europe at the time, as with most rarities, it became a coveted part of any horticulturist's collection, its value increasing more and more with the demand for it until it became the center of a full-blown speculative mania. "The rage for possessing them soon caught the middle classes of society," Mackay observes, "and merchants and shopkeepers, even of moderate means, began to vie with each other in the rarity of these flowers and the preposterous prices they paid for them."
Op cit, Mackay. Chap. 3: "Tulipmania"; 3.2.

9. *Ibid*, Smith. *Wealth of Nations*. I.X. pg. 98.

10. *Ibid*, Mackay. Chap. 2, 2.8.

11. Sylla, Richard. "The U.S. Banking System: Origin, Development, and Regulation." *The Gilder Lehrman Institute of American History*. Gilder Lehrman Institute of American History, n.d. Web.
https://ap.gilderlehrman.org/history-by-era/economics/essays/us-banking-system-origin-development-and-regulation

12. These were: The Bank of North America at Philadelphia, The Bank of New York at New York, and the Bank of Massachusetts at Boston.
    Phillips, John Burton, Ph.D. "Methods of Keeping the Public Money of the United States." *Publication of the Michigan Political Science Association* 4.3 (1900): 64. Web.
    https://play.google.com/books/reader?printsec=frontcover&output=reader&id=GfggAQAAMAAJ&pg=GBS.PA2

13. These banks were: Bank of Maine, Bank of Saco, Bank of Newport, Bank of Alexandria, Roger Williams Bank, Bank of Marietta, Bank of Kentucky, and Bank of Pennsylvania at Pittsburg. As the locality of each suggests, all were in the eastern part of the country with as yet unsettled and dangerous areas on the western frontier (i.e., Illinois, Michigan) still without branches.
    Op cit, Mackay. 68-69.

14. Farmer, Silas. *The History of Detroit and Michigan/The Metropolis Illustrated*. Vol. 1. Detroit: Silas Farmer, 1889. 847. Print.

15. *Op cit,* Phillips. 36.

16. Haulman, Clyde A. "The Panic of 1819 - America's First Depression." *Magazine of American Finance* (2010): 20. Web.
    http://www.moaf.org/search_out?query=Panic+of+1819&search.x=12&search.y=9.

17. *Op cit,* Haulman. 21.

18. *Ibid*, Farmer. 848.

19. *Loc cit*

20. *Op cit,* Phillips. 73

21. For an excellent and thorough examination of Van Buren's role in the tariff and the political intrigue surrounding it, see: Rimini, Robert V. "Martin Van Buren and the Tariff of Abominations." *The American Historical Review*, vol. 63, no. 4, 1958, pp. 903–917. http://www.jstor.org/stable/1848947.

22. .From Taney's report to Ways and Means Committee, 1834. *Op cit,* Phillips. 59.

23. *Op cit,* Phillips. 67.

24. *Op cit,* Phillips. 75.

25. *See:* Timberlake, Richard H., Jr. *The Specie Circular and Distribution of the Surplus*. No. 2 ed. Vol. 68. Chicago: U of Chicago, 1960. 110. Print
    http://www.jstor.org/stable/1829706

26. *Op cit,* Farmer. 848.

27. *Op cit,* Phillips. 73.

28. *Op cit,* Phillips. 74.

29. *Op cit,* Phillips. 77.

30. *Op cit,* Farmer. 849.

31. Hannah, Keith Emily, M.L. "An Historical Sketch of Internal Improvements in Michigan 1836-1846." *Publication of the Michigan Political Science Association* 4.1 (1900): 2. Web.
    https://play.google.com/books/reader?printsec=frontcover&output=reader&id=GfggAQAAMAAJ&pg=GBS.PA2

32. *Op cit,* Hannah. xxiii.

33. *Op cit,* Hannah. 20-25.

34. *Ibid,* Hannah. 9.

35. *Loc cit.*

36. *Ibid,* Farmer. 802.

37. *Ibid,* Farmer. 769-770.

38. Mills, James Cooke. *Our Inland Seas/Shipping and Commerce for Three Centuries.* 1st ed. Chicago: A.C. McClurg, 1910. 110. Print.

39. *Ibid,* Farmer. 909.

40. "Hon. John McDermott (from: "History of Saginaw and Bay Counties, Mich., 1892")". *Bay Journal.* Aug. 2008. Web.
    http://www.bay-journal.com/bay/1he/writings/mcdermott-john.html

41. "Dry Dock Engine Works, Detroit MI." *The Midwest.* Substreet/History Underground. Web.
    http://substreet.org/dry-dock-engine-works/

42. Donovan, Andrew. "Ward, Eber Brock." *Encyclopedia of Detroit.* Detroit Historical Society. Web.
    http://detroithistorical.org/learn/encyclopedia-of-detroit/ward-eber-brock

43. *Ibid,* Farmer. 807.

44. *Ibid,* Railway Car Builders of North America.
    http://www.midcontinent.org/rollingstock/list/bldr_list_D.htm

45. *Op cit,* Farmer. 817

46. Brennecke, Caitlin. "Dwyer, Jeremiah and James." *Detroit Historical Society.* 2016. Web.
    http://detroithistorical.org/learn/encyclopedia-of-detroit/dwyer-jeremiah-and-james

47. Zunz, Oliver. "Detroit's Ethnic Neighborhoods at the End of the Nineteenth Century." *Working Paper #161: Center for Research on Social Organization/Univ. of Michigan* (1977). 8. Web.
    http://scholar.google.com/scholar?oe=...ie=UTF 8&lr&cites=1521314618193317653

48. Palmer, Friend. *Early Days in Detroit.* 1st ed. Detroit: Hunt & June, 1906. 105. Print.https://books.google.com/books?hl=en&lr=&id=Gkt5AAAAMAAJ&oi=fnd&pg=PA17&dq=Detroit+early+OR+industry+"commerce"&ots=cJw3E28bZr&sig=4iSc4a1JRtsymJwwFk6Kjbu_tC4 - v=onepage&q=negores&f=false

49. Bunn, Curtis. "10 Slave Codes That Were Designed To Oppress And Humiliate Black People." *Atlanta Blackstar.* 23 May 2016. Web.
    http://atlantablackstar.com/2014/12/22/10-slave-codes-that-were-designed-to-oppress-and-humiliate-black-people/

50. "The Articles of Capitulation, providing the for the surrender of Montreal to General Amherst; the Treaty of Paris of 1783, ending the American Revolution; and Jay's Treaty of 1794, ceding the Northwest posts, including Detroit, to the United States, all protected slavery." Katzman, David M. *Before the Ghetto/Black Detroit in the Nineteenth Century*. 2nd ed. Urbana: U of Illinois, 1975. 5. Print.

51. *Op cit,* Katzman. 9-10.

52. *Op cit,* Katzman. 11.

Chapter Seven:
A Melting Pot, Boiling, Boiling

1. Clerk's office of the District Court of the United States for the Southern District of New York. "Selections from the Letter and Speeches of the Hon. James H. Hammond of South Carolina." *Congressional Record* (1866): Pgs. 33-34. Print.

2. Taylor, Paul. *"Old Slow Town" Detroit During the Civil War*. 1st ed. Vol. 1. Detroit: Wayne State University Press, 2013. Print. 25.

3. Babson, Steve, et al. *Working Detroit*. 1st ed., Adama Books, 1984. p.4. Print

4. Loc cit

5. Engels Friedrich. *Condition of the Working Class in England*. 1st ed. Leipzig: n.p., 1844. 46. Web: *https://www.marxists.org/archive/marx/works/.../condition-working-class-england.pdf*

6. Zinn, Howard. *A People's History of the United States*. 1st. New York: Harper and Row, 1980. 213. Print.

7. Zuboff, Shoshona. *In the Age of the Smart Machine/The Future of Work and Power*. 2nd ed. New York: Basic Books, 1988. Print. 31.

8. Op cit, Engels. 47.

9. Beginning around 1846, wealthy landowners – many, absentee Englishmen – were aided in their quest for increased landholdings by a country-wide failure of the potato crop. After much of the rural population migrated to the cities for work in the factories, fewer farmers were left to feed a rapidly increasing population. Because it was grown quickly and easily in the Irish soil, the "lumper" potato became the prevalent crop and, in many instances, the primary food source for the poorer classes. The "lumper," however, was a clone lacking genetic diversity and was, consequently, weak and susceptible to disease. Therefore, when the crop was finally struck with a rot called *Phytophthora infestans,* the potatoes upon which most of the population subsisted were reduced to an inedible slime. With failing crops, farmers could not pay their landlords who, in turn, could not foreclose fast enough in order to acquire their land.
http://evolution.berkeley.edu/evolibrary/article/agriculture_02

10. "Timeline of Emigration – Uncover the history of your ancestors." *German Information Center U.S.A.* German National Tourist Board, 2015. Web
    http://www.germany.travel/en/ms/german-originality/heritage/timeline/timeline.html

11. *Ibid.* "Timeline….."

12. "The Canuts Revolt." *Histoire de Lyon.* Gadagne Musée, n.d. Web.
    http://www.gadagne.musee.lyon.fr/

13. Philens, Hugh. "1830 Agricultural "Swing" Riots." *Hungerford Virtual Museum.* Hungerford Historical Association, n.d. Web.
    http://www.hungerfordvirtualmuseum.co.uk/

14. More well-known historically, the Luddites also took their name from a fictitious leader – General Ned Ludd – who, it was told, lived a Robin Hoodish existence in Sherwood Forest, coming out only to lead his men in attacks.
    "Luddites" *Power, Politics & Protest/The Growth of Political Rights in Britain in the 19th Century.* A/The National Archives, n.d. Web
    http://www.nationalarchives.gov.uk/education/politics/g3/

15. Several Congresses were held: Aix-la-Chapelle, 1818; Karlsbad (a conference of ministers), 1819; Vienna, 1820; Troppau, 1820; Laibach, 1821; and Verona, 1822. "Metternich Biography & The Congress of Vienna." *Age-of-the-sage.org/Transmitting the Wisdom of the Ages*. N.p., n.d. Web.
    http://www.age-of-the-sage.org/historical/biography/metternich.html

16. Wetzel, David. "Holy Alliance." *Encyclopedia.com/Encyclodpeia of Russian History.* The Gale Group, 2004. Web.
    http://www.encyclopedia.com/history/modern-europe/treaties-and-alliances/holy-alliance

17. For Hegel, the world is made up of individual minds who, though conscious, are unaware of their true selves as part of the universal mind from which they are estranged, or "alienated." Their task is to transcend their role as limited manifestations of this larger mind and to find their way to the whole. They confront each other, each, at one point, dominating and enslaving the other (dubbed "synthesis-antithesis" by Hegel) until they realize the futility of the struggle and accept their common existence in the larger, universal mind. Marx, via the work of Feuerbach, flipped Hegel's thought on its head, asserting that the real conflict takes place in the material world and is a struggle of the worker to preserve the product and dignity of his labor from the capitalist who would makes labor a commodity to be cheapened and exploited. For an excellent and concise summary of Marx's thought *cum* Hegel, see: Singer, Peter. *Marx/A Very Short Introduction.* 2nd ed. Oxford: Oxford U Press, 1996. Print

18. Marx, Karl. "Economic and Philosophic Manuscripts of 1844." *Marx/Engels Gesamtausgabe* Abt. 1.Bd. 3 (1932): 4. Print.

19. Marx, Karl. "Critical Notes on the Article: "The King of Prussia by a Prussian"." *Vorwarts!* No. 63 (1844): n. pag. Web.
    https://www.marxists.org/archive/marx/works/1844/08/07.html.

20. An eye witness to these events was President Polk's then ambassador to Germany, Andrew Jackson Donelson (nephew by marriage to the Andrew Jackson) who chronicled the event in real time and provided this eyewitness commentary:

> "The King now goes into the crowd waving the new flag of freedom promising unconditional acceptance of the constitutional limitations which the representatives of the people may demand, putting himself ahead of the new movement, and imploring his subjects to put faith in his royal word."

21. Donelson, Andrew Jackson. The American Historical Review Jan 23.2 (1918): Pg. 362. Web http://www.jstor.org/stable/1836572

22. *Op cit*, Donelson. 369.

23. "The German Revolution of 1848/49." *German American History & Heritage*. The German Corner, n.d. Web. http://www.germanheritage.com/Essays/1848/unity_and_justice_and_freedom.html

24. Frost, Helen. *German Immigrants 1820 - 1920*. Mankato (MN): Blue Earth /Capstone Press, 2002. Pgs. 8-9 Print.

25. *Ibid*, Taylor. Pgs. 25-26.

26. Even as staunch an advocate of the dignity and rights of workers as Engels harbored a profound contempt for the Irish proletariat, seeing them as bereft of self-respect and dignity and negligent of their duty to lift themselves up as workers and fight for something better:

> "The uncivilized Irishman, not by his strength, but by the opposite of strength, drives the Saxon native out [of the English workplace], takes possession in his room. There abides he, in his squalor and unreason, in his falsity and drunken violence, as the ready-made nucleus of degradation and disorder."

Op cit, Engels. Pg 103.

27. *Op cit*, Taylor. Pg. 36.

28. *Ibid*, Zinn. Pg. 167.

29. Hofstader, R. (1989). John C. Calhoun: The Marx of the Master Class. In *The American Political Tradition and the Men Who Made It* (4th ed., p. 101). New York, New York: Random House.

30. *Op cit*, Hofstadter. Pg. 103.

31. "Full text of "James Henry Hammond, 1807-." *Johns Hopkins University Studies in Historical and Political Science*. Departments of History, Political Economy, and Political Science, n.d. Web. https://archive.org/stream/jameshenryhammon01merr/jameshenryhammon01merr_djvu.txt

32. *Op cit*, Hammond.

33. Calomairis, Charles W., and Larry Schwiekart. "Panic of 1857: Origins, Transmission, and Containment." *The Journal of Economic History* 51.4 (1991): pg. 813. Print.

34. *Op cit*, Taylor. Pg. 30-31.

35. Robertson, Andrew, Micheal Morrison, William G. Shade, Robert Johnston, Robert Zieger, Thomas Langston,, and Richard Valelly. *Encyclopedia of U.S. Political History*. Vol. 7. Washington D.C.: CQ Press, 2010. Pgs. 384-386. Print. 1976-Present.

36. *Op cit*, Taylor. Pg. 32.

37. Katzman, David M. *Before the Ghetto/Black Detroit in the Nineteenth Century*. 2nd ed. Urbana: U of Illinois, 1975.13. Print.

38. *Op cit* Katzman. 40

39. *Loc cit*

40. *Op cit*, Taylor. 37 -38.

41. As DuBois recounts in his biography of Brown: "He could fight the devil and his angels, and he did, but he could not cope with the million mis-births that hover between heaven and hell."DuBois, W.E. Burghardt. *American Crisis Biographies/John Brown*. Ed. Ellis Paxon Oberholtzer. Philadelphia: George W. Jacobs, 1909. 69. Print.

42. *Ibid*, DuBois. 314.

43. *Op cit*, Zinn. 182.

44. *Ibid*, DuBois. 361.

45. *Op cit*, Dubois. 354.

Chapter Eight:

A Rich Man's War and a Poor Man's Fight

1. Josephson, Matthew. *The Robber Barons*. 2nd. San Diego/New York/London: Harvest/Harcourt, 1948. 32 - 34. Print.

2. Taylor, Paul. *"Old Slow Town" Detroit During the Civil War*. 1st ed. Vol. 1. Detroit: Wayne State University Press, 2013. 41. Print.

3. "Militia Act of 1792, Second Congress, Session I. Chapter XXVIII Passed May 2, 1792, providing for the authority of the President to call out the Militia." *Constitution Society*. http://www.constitution.org/mil/mil_act_1792.htm

4. *Op cit*, Taylor. 42.

5. *Op cit*, Taylor. 44.

6. *Op cit*, Taylor. 45.

7. Farmer, Silas. *The History of Detroit and Michigan/The Metropolis Illustrated*. Vol. 1. Detroit: Silas Farmer, 1889. 305. Print.

8. *Op cit*, Taylor. 50.

9. Long, E. B., and Barbara Long. *The Civil War Day by Day/AN ALMANAC 1861-1865*. Garden City, New York, Doubleday, 1971. Speech given: January 21, 1861. Web https://books.google.de/books?id=LGoYsAkAknwC&pg=PT67&lpg=PT67&dq=farewell+speech+David+Yulee&source=bl&ots=rwbdjnfnfS&sig=xZ0DhuYzki-W5zvkWl44o1GiNpw&hl=en&sa=X&ved=0ahUKEwikpeuH6eXVAhUQZVAKHZ6dCg4Q6AEIKjAB#v=onepage&q=farewell%20speech%20David%20Yulee&f=false

10. From *The Papers of Jefferson Davis*, Volume 7, pp. 18-23. Transcribed from the *Congressional Globe*, 36th Congress, 2d Session, p. 487. Web. https://jeffersondavis.rice.edu/archives/documents/jefferson-davis-farewell-address

11. *Op cit*, Davis.

12. Stephans, Alexander H. Speech before the Virginia Secession Convention, April 23, 1861. From *Alexander H. Stephans in Public and Private* by Henry Cleveland, National Publishing Company, 1966. 741- 743. Also, see: *Proceeding of the Virginia State Convention of 1861*, Vol. 4, reprinted by the Virginia State Library. 385-388. http://www.confederatepastpresent.org/

13. Hale, S.F., Alabama Secessionist Commissioner's letter to then Governor of Kentucky, B. McGoffin urging that state's secession from the Union. From: *The History and Debates of the People of Alabama, begun and held in the city of Montgomery, on the seventh day of January, 1861*. Reprinted: 1975, Spartanburg, South Carolina. Or, see: *Confederate Truths: Documents of the Confederate & Neo-Confederate Tradition from 1787 to the Present*. Web http://www.confederatepastpresent.org/

14. *Op cit*, Hale.

15. List, Friedrich, and Loyd S. Sampson (Translation). *The National System of Political Economy*. 2nd ed., New York, Bombay, Calcutta, Longmans, Green, and Co., 1909. 208. Print.

16. *Ibid,* List. 150-151.

17. "And did the Countenance Divine,
    Shine forth upon our clouded hills?
    And was Jerusalem builded here,
    Among these dark Satanic Mills?"
        from *Jerusalem* by William Blake – 1808
    https://literature.stackexchange.com/questions/935/what-are-the-dark-satanic-mills-in-blakes-jerusalem.

18. Vance, Laurence M. "Francis Wayland/Preacher-Economist." The Independent Review, X, no. 3, 2005, p. 405.

19. Carey, Henry Charles. *Principles of Political Economy of the Production and Distribution of Wealth*. Philadelphia, PA, Carey, Lea & Blanchard , 1837. 338. Web https://books.google.de/books?id=CfEtAAAAIAAJ&pg=PA7&source=gbs_toc_r&cad=4 - v=onepage&q&f=false

20. Kaplan, A. D.H. "Henry Charles Carey/A study in American Thought." *John Hopkins University Studies in Historical and Political Science*, 1931. 38-39.

21. *Loc cit*, Carey.

22. *Op cit.,* Kaplan. 38.

23. *Op cit.,* Kaplan. 39.

24. Cox Richardson, Heather. *The Greatest Nation of the Earth*. Vol. 1, Harvard University Press, 1997. 31-32. Print.

25. *Op cit.,* Cox Richardson. 40.

26. *Op cit.,* Cox Richardson. 41.

27. *Op cit.,* Cox Richardson. 38.

28. *Op cit.,* Cox Richardson. 39.

29. *Op cit.,* Cox Richardson. 44.

30. "The 5-20s were authorized February 1862 in an amount of $500 million and were 6% interest bearing bonds with a maturity of 20 years that could also be redeemed by the government in gold after 5 years…" Cooke went on to even greater success selling "7-30s" to the populace. These were just two of the bond issues overseen by Cooke and, by the end of the war, he had sold bonds covering a full 51.8% of the total U.S. debt of $2,587,347,000. Newman, Patrick. *The Origins of the National Banking System: The Chase-Cooke Connection and the New York City Banks*. Florida Gulf Coast University, Nov. 2016. 7-8. Web
https://papers.ssrn.com/sol3/papers.cfm?abstract_id=2865721

31. Leonard, P. *Blueprint for Modern America/Non-Military Legislation of the Frist Civil War Congress*. Vol. 1, Vanderbilt University Press, 1968. p. 197.

32. "Be it enacted by the Senate and House of Representatives of the United States of America in Congress assembled that the Secretary of the Treasury is hereby authorized to issue, on the credit of the United States, one hundred and fifty millions of dollars of United States notes, not bearing interest, payable to bearer, at the Treasury of the United States, and of Denominations, such denominations as he may deem expedient…" Legal Tender Act of 1862.
THIRTY-SEVENTH CONGRESS. Sess. II. Ch 32, 33. 1862. pg 345
https://fraser.stlouisfed.org/scribd/?title_id=1107&filepath=/files/docs/historical/congressional/legal-tender-act-1862.pdf

33. 2nd Shiloh and 7 days casualties

34. Pollack, Sheldon D. "The First National Income Tax, 1861-1872." *The Tax Lawyer*, vol. 67, no. 2, 2014, p.11.
https://udel.edu/.../The First National Income Tax 12-18-2013.pdf

35. *Op cit,* Pollack. p.12.

36. History.com Staff. "Battle of Shiloh." *History.com*.
http://www.history.com/topics/american-civil-war/battle-of-shiloh

37. "Agriculture also seemed be the root of American political security, for only a person who was self-supporting could remain politically independent and thus help preserve a pure republican government." *Ibid*, Cox Richardson. p.152.

38. No author. "Seven Days in History" *Civil War Trust*.
https://www.civilwar.org/learn/articles/seven-days-history

39. "…extensive areas of good land were withdrawn from entry in order to allow the corporations to make their selections. The process of selection was slow; even as late as 1880, only 34,000,000 out of approximately 180,000,000 acres granted, had been definitely

located. Moreover, many of the land-grant selections were exempt from taxation, hence the railroads would generally hold their lands off the market until they brought a high price." Robbins, Roy M. "The Public Domain in the Era of Exploitation." *Agricultural History*, vol. 13, no. 2, Apr. 1939. p. 96.
http://www.jstor.org/stable/3739712

40. *Ibid,* Josephson. p.67.

41. *Op cit,* Josephson. p.61.

42. *Op cit,* Josephson. p.51.

43. *Ibid,* Taylor. p.80.

44. *Op cit,* Taylor. p.82.

45. The Militia Act of 1862, U.S., *Statutes at Large, Treaties, and Proclamations of the United States of America*, vol. 12 (Boston, 1863), pp. 597-600. *In* Freedmen and Southern Society Project.
http://www.freedmen.umd.edu/milact.htm

46. No author. "Antietam/Sharpsburg" *Civil War Trust*
https://www.civilwar.org/learn/civil-war/battles/antietam

47. History.com Staff. "Battle of Fredericksburg." *History.com*.
http://www.history.com/topics/american-civil-war/battle-of-fredericksburg

48. Hofstadter, Richard. (1989). Abraham Lincoln and the Self-Made Myth. In *The American Political Tradition and the Men Who Made It* (4th ed.) New York, New York: Random House. p.163.

49. NYT opinionator Emancipation

50. *Transcript of the Proclamation,* National Archives,
http://www.archives.gov/exhibits/featured-documents/emancipation-proclamation/transcript

51. *Ibid, Proclamation,* National Archives,

52. *Op cit,* Hofstadter. p.169.

53. Basler, Roy P. *et al*, editor(s). "House Divided Speech." *Abraham Lincoln Online/Speeches & Writings*.
http://www.abrahamlincolnonline.org/lincoln/speeches/house.htm

54. "The money created by this large-scale borrowing helped produce the near doubling of prices by war's end." Phillips, Kevin. *Wealth and Democracy*. 1st. New York: Broadway, 2002. p.35.

55. No author. "THE CONSCRIPTION ACT.; The Bill for Enrolling and Calling Out the National Forces, and for Other Purposes." (reprint) *New York Times*, 19 Feb., 1863.
http://www.nytimes.com/1863/02/19/news/conscription-act-bill-for-enrolling-calling-national-forces-for-other-purposes.html?pagewanted=all

56. Civil War Battles/Major Battles from the American Civil War." *Historynet*, HistoryNet.com
http://www.historynet.com/civil-war-battles

57. Bushey, Anastasia. "The Draft Riots: Its Roots and Occurance." *History of New York City/A TLC Blog*, Seton Hall University, 21 Dec. 2016.

58. *Op cit,* Bushey.

59. Man Jr., Albon P. "Labor Competition and the New York Draft Riots of 1863." *Journal of Negro History*, vol. 36, no. 4, (University of Chicago Press on behalf of the Association for the Study of African American Life and History) Oct. 1951. p.392.
http://www.jstor.org/stable/2715371

60. *Loc cit,* Man, Jr.

61. Zinn, Howard. *A People's History of the United States*. 1st. New York: Harper and Row, 1980. 230. Print.

62. Maranzani, Barbara. "The Most Violent Insurrection in American History." *History Stories*, History.com, 5 July 2013.
http://www.history.com/news/four-days-of-fire-the-new-york-city-draft-riots

63. Poem, "The Riot," by B. Clark, *Narrative of the Detroit Riot.* Quoted in Katzman, David M. *Before the Ghetto/Black Detroit in the Nineteenth Century*. 2nd ed. Urbana: U of Illinois, 1975. p.46 Print

64. *Ibid,* Taylor. p.103.

65. *Op cit*, Katzman. p. 47.

66. *Ibid,* Taylor. p.89.

67. *Op cit*, Taylor. 90.

68. "Colored Troops...The Debate." *Historic la Mott*, Chambres & Associates/WordHerd.
https://historic-lamott-pa.com/colored-troops-the-debate/

69. *Op cit*, Historic la Mott
https://historic-lamott-pa.com/colored-troops-the-debate/

70. Negro Soldier Bill in the House." *New York Times (Archives)*, Feb. 3rd, 1863
http://www.nytimes.com/1863/02/03/archives/important-from-washington-passage-of-the-negro-soldier-bill-in-the.html

71. *Ibid,* Taylor. pp.73-74.

72. *Op cit*, Taylor. 77.

73. Townsend, William R. "William R. Townsend Civil War Diary: Negro Regiments/Excerpts from the Civil War diary of William R. Townsend, 42nd Ill. Infantry." *Southern Illinoiis University Edwardsville*, Southern Illinois University. Web.
http://libguides.siue.edu/c.php?g=332975&p=2239134

Chapter Nine

In God We Make Trusts

1. Josephson, Matthew. *The Robber Barons*. 2nd. San Diego/New York/London: Harvest/Harcourt, 1948. 72. Print.
2. Rubenstein, Harry. "The Gentlemen's Agreement That Ended the Civil War." *Smithsonian.com*, Smithsonian Institution, 5 Apr. 2015. Web. https://www.smithsonianmag.com/smithsonian-institution/gentlemans-agreement-ended-civil-war-180954810/
3. Zinn, Howard. *A People's History of the United States*. 1st. New York: Harper and Row, 1980. p. 235. Print
4. *Loc cit.*, Zinn
5. *Op cit.* Zinn. pg. 226-227.
6. "The Civil War/Michigan Answers the Call to Arms." *Michigan Department of Military and Veterans Affairs*, State of Michigan, 2018. http://www.michigan.gov/dmva/0,4569,7-126-2360_3003_3009-16995--,00.html
7. Mackenzie, Donald. "Marx and the Machine." *Technology and Culture*, vol. 25, no. 3, July 1984, p. 485. http://links.jstor.org/sici?sici=0040-165X%28198407%2925%3A3<473%3AMATM>2.0.CO%3B2-6
8. *Loc cit.*
9. Taylor, Paul. *"Old Slow Town" Detroit During the Civil War*. 1st ed. Vol. 1. Detroit: Wayne State University Press, 2013. p 133. Print.
10. Babson, Steve, et al. *Working Detroit*. 1st ed., Adama Books, 1984. p. 4. Print.
11. *Loc cit.*
12. *Loc cit*
13. *Op cit.,* Babson. p. 5.
14. Montgomery, David. *Beyond Equality/Labor and the Radical Republicans 1862-1872*. Vol. 2, University of Illinois Press, 1981. p. 223. Print.
15. *Op cit,* Taylor. p. 128.
16. *Ibid,* Taylor. p. 80.
17. Klug, Thomas. "RAILWAY CARS, BRICKS, AND SALT: THE INDUSTRIAL HISTORY OF SOUTHWEST DETROIT BEFORE AUTO." Presentation, 5 Nov. 1999, Detroit, Marygrove College. Web. http://www.academia.edu/3625080/Railway_Cars_Bricks_and_Salt_The_Industrial_History_of_Southwest_Detroit_before_Auto.
18. Archer, Melanie. "Family Enterprise in an Industrial City: Strategies for the Family Organization of Business in Detroity, 1880." *Social Science History*, vol. 15, no. 1, 1991. p. 72. Web. http://www.jstor.org/stable/10.2307/1171483http://www.jstor.org/stable/10.2307/1290351.
19. *Ibid*, Archer. p. 73.

20. *Ibid*, Archer. p. 75.

21. *Ibid*, Archer. p. 81.

22. Gavrilovitch, Peter, and Bill McGraw. *The Detroit Almanac/300 years of life in the Motor City*. 1st ed. Detroit, Michigan: Detroit Free Press, 2001. 289. Print.

23. Zunz, Oliver. "Detroit's Ethnic Neighborhoods at the End of the Nineteenth Century." *Working Paper #161: Center for Research on Social Organization/Univ. of Michigan* (1977). 64. Web.
http://scholar.google.com/scholar?oe=…ie=UTF 8&lr&cites=1521314618193317653

24. *Ibid*, Zunz. p. 72.

25. *Op cit*, Babson. pp. 5-6.

26. Drutchas, Geoffrey G. "Gray Eminence in a Gilded Age: The Forgotten Career of Senator Jmes McMillan of Michigan." *Michigan Historical Review*, vol. 28, no. 2, 2002. pp 79-82.
http://www.jstor.org/stable/20173984

27. *Ibid*, Drutchas. p.87.

28. *Ibid*, Josephson. p.94.

29. Loc cit.

30. *Op cit*, Josephson. p.93.

31. Meyers, Gustavus. *History of the Great American Fortunes*. II: Great Fortunes from Railroads, Charles H. Kerr & Co. , 1910. p.21. Print.
http://www.archive.org/details/historyofgreatam)@myeroft

32. *Op cit*, Myers. p.12.

33. *Op cit*, Myers. pp.28-29.

34. James, Edmund J. "'The Agitation for Federal Regulation of Railways.'" *American Economic Association*, vol. 2, no. 3, July 1887. p 22. Print.
http://www.jstor.org/stable/2696699

35. Davis, John P. "The Union Pacific Railway." *The Annals of the American Academy of Political and Social Science*, vol. 8, Sept. 1896. p. 52. Print.
http://www.jstor.org/stable/1009233

36. *Op cit*, Josephson. p.92.

37. Jenks, J. W. "The Michigan Salt Asssociation." *Political Science Quarterly*, vol. 3, no. 1, Mar. 1888. p. 79. Print.
http://www.jstor.org/stable/2138986

38. *Ibid*, Jenks. p.81.

39. *Ibid*, Jenks. p.87.

40. *Ibid*, Josephson. p.113.

41. *Op cit*, Josephson. p.118.

42. *Ibid*, James. p.24.

43. "Failure of Jay Cooke and Company" - Sacramento Daily Union, Volume 45, Number 7008, 19 September 1873. pg 2. *California Digital Newspaper Collection*: https://cdnc.ucr.edu/?a=d&d=SDU18730919.2.9&e=-------en--20--1--txt-txIN--------1

44. Oberhotzer, Ellis Paxon. *Jay Cooke – Financier of the Civil War,* Volume Two. George W. Jacobs and Co., 1907. pg. 422. Print

45. *Op cit,*, Babson. p.10.

46. *Ibid*, Zinn pg. 239.

47. *Ibid*, Zinn pp 245-246.

48. *Loc cit.,* Babson.

49. *Op cit,*, Zinn. p.244.

50. Katzman, David M. *Before the Ghetto/Black Detroit in the Nineteenth Century*. Vol. 1, University of Illinois Press, 1973. p.83. Print.

51. *Ibid*, Katzman. p.105.

52. *Op cit,*, Katzman. p.118.

53. *Ibid*, Katzman. center illustrations. Reproduced from Simmons, *Men of Mark*, 1887.

54. *Ibid*, Katzman. p.62.

55. *Op cit,*, Katzman. p.74.

56. *Op cit,*, Katzman. p.79.

Bibliography

Books

Adams Jr., Charles E. *Interregnum: The Zagonaash, 1760 - 1783. Assault on a Culture: The Anishinaabeg of the Great Lakes and the Dynamics of Change*. 1st ed. Xlibris, 2013. Print.

Babson, Steve, et al. Working Detroit. 1st ed., Adama Books, 1984. Print

Burghardt, W.E. *American Crisis Biographies/John Brown*. Ed. Ellis Paxon Oberholtzer. Philadelphia: George W. Jacobs, 1909. Print.

Burton, Clarence. *Early Detroit*. Ann Arbor: University of Michigan, 1909 (Reprint).

Carey, Henry Charles. *Principles of Political Economy of the Production and Distribution of Wealth*. Philadelphia, PA, Carey, Lea & Blanchard, 1837. 338. Web
https://books.google.de/books?id=CfEtAAAAIAAJ&pg=PA7&source=gbs_toc_r&cad=4 -v=onepage&q&f=false

Cox Richardson, Heather. *The Greatest Nation of the Earth*. Vol. 1, Harvard University Press, 1997.

de Tocqueville, Alexis. *Democracy in America*. Vol. 1 & 2. University Park: Pennsylvania State U, 2002. Translation by Henry Reeve. Web.
http://www.hn.psu.edu/faculty/jmanls/Tocqueville.htm

Dickman, Donald L., and Larry A. Leefers. *The Forests of Michigan*. Vol. 1. Ann Arbor: U of Michigan, 2003. Print.

Drutchas, Geoffrey G. *Gray Eminence in a Gilded Age: The Forgotten Career of Senator James McMillan of Michigan*. Michigan Historical Review, vol. 28, no. 2, 2002.
http://www.jstor.org/stable/20173984

Ebenstein, William. *Great Political Thinkers*. 5th ed. Princeton: Rhinehart, 1958.

Farmer, Silas. *The History of Detroit and Michigan/The Metropolis Illustrated*. Vol. 1. Detroit: Silas Farmer, 1889.

Fiske, John. *The Dutch and Quaker Colonies in America. Vol. 1*. Boston: Riverside, Cambridge, 1899. Print.

Frost, Helen. *German Immigrants 1820 - 1920*. Mankato (MN): Blue Earth /Capstone Press, 2002.

Gavrilovitch, Peter, and Bill McGraw. *The Detroit Almanac/300 years of life in the Motor City*. 1st ed. Detroit, Michigan: Detroit Free Press, 2001.

Hobbes, Thomas. *Leviathan*. San Bernadino, CA, 2013.

Hofstader, R. (1989). *The American Political Tradition and the Men Who Made It* 4th ed. New York, New York: Random House.

Hough, Franklin Benjamin, *Journals of Major Robert Rogers, 1765*. Harvard College Library (from the Francis Parkman Memorial Fund for Canadian History Joel Munsell's sons. 1883. pg. 196. Print.

Hume, David. *Enquiries Concerning Human Understanding and the Concerning the Principles of Morals*. 3rd ed. Oxford: Clarendon, 1975.

Johnson, Ida. The Michigan Fur Trade. Lansing: Michigan Historical Society, 1919.

Josephson, Matthew. *The Robber Barons*. 2nd. San Diego/New York/London: Harvest/Harcourt, 1948.

Juen, Rachel B., and Michael S. Nasseney. *The Fur Trade*. Fort St. Joseph Archaeological Project Booklet Series, No. 2 (2012): Print.

Katzman, David M. *Before the Ghetto/Black Detroit in the Nineteenth Century*. 2nd ed. Urbana: U of Illinois, 1975.

Leonard, P. Blueprint for Modern America/Non-Military Legislation of the Frist Civil War Congress. Vol. 1, Vanderbilt University Press, 1968.

List, Friedrich, and Loyd S. Sampson (Translation). *The National System of Political Economy*. 2nd ed., New York, Bombay, Calcutta, Longmans, Green, and Co., 1909. Print.

Mackay, Charles, Memoirs of Extraordinary Popular Delusions and the Madness of Crowds. 1852. Chapter 2: "The South-Sea Bubble." Library of Economics and Liberty. 17 July 2016. Web. http://www.econlib.org/library/Mackay/macEx.html.

Marx, Karl. *Capital (A Critique of Political Economy)*. 4th. New York: Modern Library, 1906. Print.

McCabe, Joseph. *A Candid History of the Jesuits*. London: Eveleigh Nash, 1913. Print.

Mills, James Cooke. *Our Inland Seas/Shipping and Commerce for Three Centuries*. 1st ed. Chicago: A.C. McClurg, 1910. 110. Print.

Myers, Gustavus. *History of the Great American Fortunes*. 3rd ed. Vol. 1; Part 1: Conditions in Settlement and Colonial Times. Chicago: Charles H. Kerr, 1910.

Oberhotzer, Ellis Paxon. *Jay Cooke – Financier of the Civil War, Volume Two*. George W. Jacobs and Co., 1907. pg. 422. Print

Palmer, Friend. *Early Days in Detroit*. 1st ed. Detroit: Hunt & June, 1906. Print.
https://books.google.com/books?hl=en&lr=&id=Gkt5AAAAMAAJ&oi=fnd&pg=PA17&dq=Detroit+early+OR+industry+"commerce"&ots=cJw3E28bZr&sig=4iSc4a1JRtsymJwwFk6Kjbu_tC4_-v=onepage&q=negores&f=false

Parkman, Francis *The Jesuits in North America in the Seventeenth Century: Vol. II*. Boston: Little/Brown and Company, 1879.

Parkman, Francis. *The Old Regime in Canada*. Vol. Two. Cambridge: John Wilson and Son, 1902. Print.

Phillips, Kevin. *Wealth and Democracy*. 1st. New York: Broadway, 2002. 11. Print.

Schama, Simon. *A History of Britain/The Wars of the British 1603-1776*. 1st. 2. New York: Hyperion, 2001.

Sidgwick, Henry. *Outlines of the History of Ethics*. McMillan/St.Martin's Press. New York, 1967.

Singer, Peter. *Marx/A Very Short Introduction*. 2nd ed. Oxford: Oxford U Press, 1996. Print

Smith, Adam, *The Wealth of Nations*. New York: Barnes and Noble, 2004. (Orig.: 1776) Print.

Smith, Adam. *The Theory of Moral Sentiments*. 1st ed. Mineola: Dover, 2006. I.I.3. pp 3-4. Print.

Strayer, Joseph R., Hans W. Gatzke, and E. Harris Harbison. *The Mainstream of Civilization to 1715*. 2nd. New York/Chicago/San Francisco/Atlanta: Harcourt, Brace, Jovanovich, 1974. Print.

Tawney, R.H. *Religion and the Rise of Capitalism*. 3rd. New York: Mentor, 1951. Print.

Taylor, Paul. *Old Slow Town/ Detroit During the Civil War*. 1st ed. Vol. 1. Detroit: Wayne State University Press, 2013. Print.

Trevelyan, G.M. *History of England*. 3rd ed. London: Longmans, Green, 1937. Print.

Wilson, Margaret (Editor). *The Essential Descartes*. 1st ed. New York: Mentor, 1969. Print.

Wraxall, Peter, and C.H. McIlwain (Editor). *The Early Fur Trade. An Abridgement of the Indian Worth*. The Late Great Lakes. 2nd ed. Detroit: Wayne State UP, 1987. Print.

Youngman, A. (1908). *The Fortune of John Jacob Astor:* University of Chicago Press
http://www.jstor.org/stable/1820382

Zinn, Howard. *A People's History of the United States*. 1st. New York: Harper and Row, 1980. Print.

Zuboff, Shoshona. *In the Age of the Smart Machine/The Future of Work and Power*. 2nd ed. New York: Basic Books, 1988. Print.

Journals

Alves, Abel Athouguia. "The Christian Social Organism and Social Welfare: The Case of Vives, Calvin and Loyola." Sixteenth Century Journal, University of Massachusetts, XX, No.1. Spring (1989). Print.

American Memory/*Pioneering the Upper Midwest: Books from Michigan, Minnesota, and Wisconsin*, Ca. 1820-1910. Library of Congress. Web. 77. Nov. 2015. http://memory.loc.gov/cgi-bin/query/r?ammem/lhbum:@field%28DOCID+@lit%28lhbum01453div10%29%29

Archer, Melanie. *Family Enterprise in an Industrial City: Strategies for the Family Organization of Business in Detroit, 1880."* Social Science History, vol. 15, no. 1, 1991. Web. http://www.jstor.org/stable/10.2307/1171483http://www.jstor.org/stable/10.2307/1290351.

Beauvais, Fred, Ph.D. *American Indians and Alcohol*. Alcohol Health and Research World/Spotlight on Special Populations Vol. 22, No. 4 (1998): 253. Print.

Berrnard C. *Hypocrisy on the Great Lakes Frontier: The Use of Whiskey by the Michigan Department of Indian Affairs*. Michigan Historical Review (Fall, 1992): 4. Print. http://www.jstor.org/stable/20173343.

B.J.R. *Features of American Slavery*. The Sewanee Review 1.4 (1893): 477. Print.

Calomairis, Charles W., and Larry Schwiekart. "Panic of 1857: Origins, Transmission, and Containment." The Journal of Economic History 51.4 (1991): pg. 813. Print.

Carey, Henry Charles. *Principles of Political Economy of the Production and Distribution of Wealth*. Philadelphia, PA, Carey, Lea & Blanchard , 1837. Web https://books.google.de/books?id=CfEtAAAAIAAJ&pg=PA7&source=gbs_toc_r&cad=4 - v=onepage&q&f=false

Cass, Lewis. *Removal of the Indians*. North American Review (1830): Print. https://archive.org/details/removalindiansa00frangoog

Clark, James T. *Sir William Johnson and Pontiac*. Proceedings of the New York State Historical Association 13 (1914): 100. Print.

Davis, John P. *The Union Pacific Railway*. The Annals of the American Academy of Political and Social Science, vol. 8, Sept. 1896. Print. http://www.jstor.org/stable/1009233

De Tocqueville, Alexis. *Aristocracy on the Saginaw Trail: Tocqueville in Michigan*. Clark Historical Library. Central Michigan University. Web. https://www.cmich.edu/research/clarke-historical-library/explore-collection/explore-online/michigan-material/tocqueville-michigan#a11

Emerson, F.V. *Geographic Influences on American Slavery. Part I*. American Geographical Society 43.1 (1911). Print.

Frank, MD, John W., Roland S. Moore, PhD, and Genevieve Ames, PhD. *Historical and Cultural Roots of Drinking Problems Among Native Americans*. American Journal of Public Health/Public Health Then and Now Vol. 90. No. 3 (2000). Print.

Fregni, Giovanna. *A Study of the Manufacture of Copper Spearheads in the Old Copper Complex*. The Minnesota Archeologist 68 (2010): Web. http://www.academia.edu/227583/A_Study_of_the_Manufacture_of_Copper_Spearheads_in_the_Old_Copper_Complex

Fuller, George N. *Settlement of Michigan Territory*. Mississippi Valley Historical Review 2.1 (1915): 26. Print. http://www.jstor.org/stable/1889104. http://www.jstor.org/stable/1888594.

Full text of James Henry Hammond, 1807-1864. Johns Hopkins University Studies in Historical and Political Science. Departments of History, Political Economy, and Political Science, n.d. Web. https://archive.org/stream/jameshenryhammon01merr/jameshenryhammon01merr_djvu.txt

Gallway Patricia (Editor),, and Conrad, Glenn R. (Author). *Reluctant Imperialist: France in North America (Part II). La Salle and His Legacy: Frenchmen and Indians in the Lower Mississippi Valley*. Mississippi Historical Society, 1982. Print.

Goodwin, Cardinal. *A Larger View of the Yellowstone Expedition, 1819-1820*. The Mississippi Valley Historical Review 4.3 (1917): 310. Print.Gray, Charles Gilmer. *Lewis and Clark at the Mouth of Wood River: An Historic Spot*. Journal of the Illinois Press (1920). http://www.jstor.org/stable/40194492

Harper, Douglas. *French Slavery*. The SCIOLIST. 1 Jan. 2005. Web http://etymonline.com/columns/frenchslavery.htm

Hatter, Lawrence B. *The Transformation of the Detroit Land Market and the Formation of the Anglo-American Border, 17983-1796*. Michigan Historical Review/Central Michigan University. 34.1 (Emerging Borderlands) (2008): Print.

Haeger, John D. *Business Strategy and Practice in the Early Republic: John Jacob Astor and the American Fur Trade*. The Western Historical Quarterly/Utah State University 19.2 (1988): 188-89. Print. http://www.jstor.org/stable/968394

Hannah, Keith Emily, M.L. *An Historical Sketch of Internal Improvements in Michigan 1836-1846*. Publication of the Michigan Political Science Association 4.1 (1900): 2. Web. https://play.google.com/books/reader?printsec=frontcover&output=reader&id=GfggAQAAMAAJ&pg=GBS.PA2

History of the Iroquois. Sunbury: A History. Bucknell Environmental Center (Bucknell University). Web. 11 Mar. 2015 http://www.departments.bucknell.edu/environmental_center/sunbury/website/HistoryofIroquoisIndians.shtml

Hitchcock, Tim. *Begging on the Streets of Eighteenth-Century London*. Journal of British Studies. 44.3 (2005): 478-498. Web. 5 Jun. 2015. http://www.jstor.org/stable/10.1086/429704 .

Holman, F. (1911). *Some Important Results from the Expeditions of John Jacob Astor, to and from the Oregon Country*. Print. http://www.jstor.org/stable/20609876

Hon. John McDermott (from: *History of Saginaw and Bay Counties, Mich., 1892*). Bay Journal. Aug. 2008. Web.
http://www.bay-journal.com/bay/1he/writings/mcdermott-john.html

James, Edmund J. *The Agitation for Federal Regulation of Railways*. American Economic Association, vol. 2, no. 3, July 1887. p 22. Print.
http://www.jstor.org/stable/2696699

James Seth,. Scottish Moral Philosophy. The Philosophical Review VII.6 (1898). Print.

Kilar, Jeremy. *Michigan's Lumbertowns: Lumbermen and Laborers in Saginaw, Bay City, and Muskgegon*, 1870–1905. Vol. 1. Detroit: Wayne State UP, 1990.

Klug, Thomas. *RAILWAY CARS, BRICKS, AND SALT: THE INDUSTRIAL HISTORY OF SOUTHWEST DETROIT BEFORE AUTO*. Presentation, 5 Nov. 1999, Detroit, Marygrove College. Web.
http://www.academia.edu/3625080/Railway_Cars_Bricks_and_Salt_The_Industrial_History_of_Southwest_Detroit_before_Auto.

Jenks, J. W. *The Michigan Salt Asssociation*. Political Science Quarterly, vol. 3, no. 1, Mar. 1888. Print.
http://www.jstor.org/stable/2138986

Lewis, Francis Paul and Donald F., Cass, Prucha and Carmony. *A Memorandum of Lewis Cass: Concerning a System for the Regulation of Indian Affairs*. The Wisconsin Magazine of History 52.1 (Fall, 1968). Print.

Leroch, Martin. *Adam Smith's Intuition Pump: The Impartial Spectator*. Homo Oeconomicus 25.1 University of Hamburg (2008). Print.

Mackenzie, Donald. *Marx and the Machine."* Technology and Culture, vol. 25, no. 3, July 1984.
http://links.jstor.org/sici?sici=0040-165X%28198407%2925%3A3<473%3AMATM>2.0.CO%3B2-6

Man Jr., Albon P. *Labor Competition and the New York Draft Riots of 1863*. Journal of Negro History, vol. 36, no. 4, (University of Chicago Press on behalf of the Association for the Study of African American Life and History) Oct. 1951. http://www.jstor.org/stable/2715371

Marx, Karl. *Economic and Philosophic Manuscripts of 1844*. Marx/Engels Gesamtausgabe Abt. 1.Bd. 3 (1932). Print.

Montgomery, David. *Beyond Equality/Labor and the Radical Republicans 1862-1872*. Vol. 2, University of Illinois Press, 1981. Print.

Nelson, William E. "The Utopian Legal Order of the Massachusetts Bay Colony, 1630-1686." The American Journal of Legal History 47.2 (2005). Print.

Newman, Patrick. *The Origins of the National Banking System: The Chase-Cooke Connection and the New York City Banks*. Florida Gulf Coast University, Nov. 2016. 7-8. Web https://papers.ssrn.com/sol3/papers.cfm?abstract_id=2865721

Osgood, Herbert L. *The Corporation as a Form of Colonial Government*. Political Science Quarterly 11.4 (1896): 695-96. Print.

Payne, Diane Elizabeth. *Children of the Poor in London 1700-1780*. A thesis submitted in partial fulfilment [sic] of the requirements of the University of Hertfordshire for the degree of Doctor of Philosophy." (2008): 41. University of Hertfordshire.UK. Web. 5 Jun 2015.

Pearce, Margaret Wickens. *The Holes in the Grid: Reservation Surveys in Lower Michigan*. Michigan Historical Review (Fall, 2004): Print.

Phillips, John Burton, Ph.D. *Methods of Keeping the Public Money of the United States*. Publication of the Michigan Political Science Association 4.3 (1900): Web. https://play.google.com/books/reader?printsec=frontcover&output=reader&id=GfggAQAAMAAJ&pg=GBS.PA2

Pollack, Sheldon D. The First National Income Tax, 1861-1872. The Tax Lawyer, vol. 67, no. 2, 2014. https://udel.edu/.../The First National Income Tax 12-18-2013.pdf

Putnam, J. W. *An Economic History of the Illinois and Michigan Canal: III*. Journal of Political Economy 17.4 (1909). Print.

Quoted from Hutcheson's Inquiry by:
Seth, James. *Scottish Moral Philosophy*. The Philosophical Review VII.6 (1898): 563. Print.

G.P. Radabaugh in 1915, is, it could be argued, without peer.
Radabaugh, G. P. *Origin and Development of the Railway Rail/English and American Wood, Iron and Steel*. Pennsylvania Steel/Maryland Steel. 64 pages. Print.Rimini, Robert V. *Martin Van Buren and the Tariff of Abominations*. The American Historical Review, vol. 63, no. 4, 1958. http://www.jstor.org/stable/1848947.

Robbins, Roy M. *The Public Domain in the Era of Exploitation*. Agricultural History, vol. 13, no. 2, Apr. 1939. http://www.jstor.org/stable/3739712

Schaetzl, Randal *Soo Locks*. /Michigan State University. Web. http://geo.msu.edu/extra/geogmich/SooLock.html

Stevens, Wayne E. *The Organization of the British Fur Trade, 1760-1800*. Mississippi Valley Historical Review 3.2 (1916): 180-81. Print.

"The Charter of Massachusetts Bay." The Avalon Project/Documents in Law, History, and Diplomacy. Yale Law School Lillian Goldman Law Library (in Memory of Sol Goodman), 1 Nov. 1629. Web. 1 Nov. 2014
http://avalon.law.yale.edu/17th_century/mass03.asp.

Thompson, S.J.. *Paliamentary Enclosure, Property, Population, and the Decline of Classical Republicanism in Eighteenth-Century Britain*. The Historical Journal 51.3 (2008): Print.

Townsend, William R. William R. Townsend *Civil War Diary: Negro Regiments/Excerpts from the Civil War diary of William R. Townsend, 42nd Ill. Infantry*. Southern Illinois University Edwardsville, Southern Illinois University. Web. http://libguides.siue.edu/c.php?g=332975&p=2239134.

Tunell, George G. *The Diversion of the Flour and Grain Traffic from the Great Lakes to the Railroad*. Journal of Political Economy 5.3. Print. http://www.jstor.org/stable/1817751

Wetzel, David. *Holy Alliance*. Encyclopedia.com/Encyclodpeia of Russian History. The Gale Group, 2004. Web. http://www.encyclopedia.com/history/modern-europe/treaties-and-alliances/holy-alliance

Vance, Laurence M. *Francis Wayland/Preacher-Economist*. The Independent Review, X, no. 3, 2005, p. 405.

Zunz, Oliver. *Detroit's Ethnic Neighborhoods at the End of the Nineteenth Century*. Working Paper #161: Center for Research on Social Organization/Univ. of Michigan (1977). Web http://scholar.google.com/scholar?oe=…ie=UTF 8&lr&cites=15213146181933176 53

Web

1804 Burr Slays Hamilton in Duel. History.com/This Day in History. A E Networks, 2009. Web http://www.history.com/this-day-in-history/burr-slays-hamilton- in-duel.

About Beavers. Beavers: Wetlands and Wildlife, n.d. Web. . http://www.beaversww.org/beavers-and-wetlands/about-beavers.

Basler, Roy P. et al, editor(s). *House Divided Speech*. Abraham Lincoln Online/Speeches & Writings. http://www.abrahamlincolnonline.org/lincoln/speeches/house.htm.

Battle of Fredericksburg. Battle of Quebec. United States History. Web. 31 Jan. 2015. http://www.u-s-history.com/pages/h787.html.

Battle of Shiloh. History.com Staff. History.com. http://www.history.com/topics/american-civil-war/battle-of-shiloh.

Battle of the Thames. Ohio History Central. Ohio History Connection. Web. 28 Oct. 2015. http://www.ohiohistorycentral.org/w/Battle_of_the_Thames?rec=481.

Beaver Wars (1642-1698). The Patriot Files (Dedicated to the Preservation of Military History). 14 Oct. 2014. Web. http://www.patriotfiles.com/index.php?name=Sections&req=viewarticle&artid=8531&page=1'

Brennecke, Caitlin. *Dwyer, Jeremiah and James*. Detroit Historical Society. 2016. Web. http://detroithistorical.org/learn/encyclopedia-of-detroit/dwyer-jeremiah-and-james

British Detroit 1760-1796. Historyofdetroit.com. City Beautiful Design. Web
http://historydetroit.com/index.php

Bunn, Curtis. *10 Slave Codes That Were Designed To Oppress And Humiliate Black People*. Atlanta Blackstar. 23 May 2016. Web.

Bushey, Anastasia. *The Draft Riots: Its Roots and Occurance*. History of New York City/A TLC Blog, Seton Hall University, 21 Dec. 2016.

Cadillac's Village or Detroit Under Cadillac with List of Property Owners and a History of the Settlement 1701 to 1710.e." C.M Burton/Detroit, 1 Jan. 1896. Web
file://localhost/Bill Martin, Thunder Bay, Ontario, Canada. email bmartin@tbaytel.net http/::www.tbaytel.net:bmartin:.

Civil War Battles/Major Battles from the American Civil War. Historynet, HistoryNet.com http://www.historynet.com/civil-war-battles.

Cummings, Jim. *The Story of The Moravian Massacre. A Day of Shame*. News Service/An Online Journal of Living History, Feb. 2005. Web. 11 Aug. 2015.
http://www.graphicenterprises.net/html/times_2011_4_.html

Donovan, Andrew. *Ward, Eber Brock*. Encyclopedia of Detroit. Detroit Historical Society. Web. http://detroithistorical.org/learn/encyclopedia-of-detroit/ward-eber-brock

Dry Dock Engine Works, Detroit MI. The Midwest. Substreet/History Underground. Web. http://substreet.org/dry-dock-engine-works/.

Dutch Colonies. nps.gov/Kingston:Discover 300 Years of New York History. National Park Service/U.S. Dept. of the Interior. Web. 1 Nov. 2014
http://www.nps.gov/nr/travel/kingston/colonization.htm

Emerson, F.V. *Geographic Influences on American Slavery. Part I*. American Geographical Society 43.1 (1911). Print

Encyclopedia of U.S. Political History. Vol. 7. Washington D.C.: CQ Press, 2010. Print. 1976-Present.

Erie Canalway. Happy Birthday National Park Service. National Park Service. Web. https://www.nps.gov/erie/learn/historyculture/index.htm.

Ferling, John. *Thomas Jefferson, Aaron Burr, and the Election of 1800*. Smithsonian.com. Smithsonian Institution, 1 Nov. 2004. Web.
http://www.smithsonianmag.com/history/thomas-jefferson-aaron-burr-and-the-election-of-1800-131082359/?no-ist

From the Papers of Jefferson Davis, Volume 7, pp. 18-23. Transcribed from the Congressional Globe, 36th Congress, 2d Session, p. 487. Web.
https://jeffersondavis.rice.edu/archives/documents/jefferson-davis-farewell-address.

History of Cuyahoga County. One Cuyahoga: Official Government Website of Cuyahoga County, Ohio. County of Cuyahoga, Ohio. Web. 26 Aug. 2015.
http://www.cuyahogacounty.us/en-US/history.aspx

Haulman, Clyde A. *The Panic of 1819 - America's First Depression.* Magazine of American Finance (2010): 20. Web.
http://www.moaf.org/search_out?query=Panic+of+1819&search.x=12&search.y=9.

Jamestown Settlement and the Starving Time. Britain in the New World. Independence Hall Foundation in Philadelphia, 1 Jan. 2008. Web. 1 Nov. 2014
http://www.ushistory.org/us/2c.asp.

Jerusalem by William Blake – 1808
https://literature.stackexchange.com/questions/935/what-are-the-dark-satanic-mills-in-blakes-jerusalem.

Lira, Carl T. *Watt's Famous Experiment with the Separate Condenser*. Introductory Chemical Engineering and Thermodynamics. Michigan State University. Web. 2001.
http://www.egr.msu.edu/~lira/supp/steam/wattexp.htm

Long, E. B., and Barbara Long. *The Civil War Day by Day/AN ALMANAC 1861-1865*. Garden City, New York, Doubleday, 1971. Speech given: January 21, 1861. Web
https://books.google.de/books?id=LGoYsAkAknwC&pg=PT67&lpg=PT67&dq=farewell+speech+David+Yulee&source=bl&ots=rwbdjnfnfS&sig=xZ0DhuYzki-W5zvkWl44o1GiNpw&hl=en&sa=X&ved=0ahUKEwikpeuH6eXVAhUQZVAKHZ6dCg4Q6AEIKjAB#v=onepage&q=farewell%20speech%20David%20Yulee&f=false.

Luddites -Power, Politics & Protest/The Growth of Political Rights in Britain in the 19th Century. A/The National Archives, n.d. Web
http://www.nationalarchives.gov.uk/education/politics/g3/

Maranzani, Barbara. *The Most Violent Insurrection in American History*. History Stories, History.com, 5 July 2013.
http://www.history.com/news/four-days-of-fire-the-new-york-city-draft-riots

Metternich Biography & The Congress of Vienna. Age-of-the-sage.org/Transmitting the Wisdom of the Ages. N.p., n.d. Web.
http://www.age-of-the-sage.org/historical/biography/metternich.html.

Michigan's Railroad History/1825-2014. Michigan Department of Transportation, 2014. Web.
http//www.michiganrailroads.com › railroad-history.

Militia Act of 1792, Second Congress, Session I. Chapter XXVIII Passed May 2, 1792, providing for the authority of the President to call out the Militia." Constitution Society. http://www.constitution.org/mil/mil_act_1792.htm.

Native Americans in the Great Lakes Region n.d. Web. http://web2.geo.msu.edu/geogmich/paleo-indian.html.

Native American Tribes of Michigan n.d. Web.
http://www.native-languages.org/michigan.htm.

Northwest Ordinance. Ohio History Central. Ohio History Connection. Web. 1 Aug. 2015 file://localhost/. http/::www.ohiohistorycentral.org:w:Northwest_Ordinance%3Frec=1747

Nullification Proclamation. Web Guides/Primary Documents in American History. Library of Congress. Web. Nov. 2015. https://guides.loc.gov/nullification-proclamation.

Paris treaty: map https://www.pinterest.com/pin/295267319291054805/ and https://www.cmich.edu/library/clarke/ResearchResources/Native_American_Material/Treaty_Rights/Text_of_Michigan_Related_Treaties/Pages/Fort-Greenville,-Ohio,-1795.aspx.

Pickawillany. Ohio History Central. Ohio History Connection. Web
http://www.ohiohistorycentral.org/w/Pickawillany?rec=792

Pioneer Times USA. Web Casper, Tom. *The Magic of White Pine*. Popular Woodworking Magazine. American Woodworker Magazine, Apr.-May 2001. Web. http://www.popularwoodworking.com/projects/the-magic-of-white-pine

Simons, Stefan. *Memorial to the Slave Trade: French City Confronts Its Brutal Past*. Spiegel Online 2012. SPIEGELnet GmbH, 1 Jan. 2012. Webs
http://www.spiegel.de/international/euope/nantes-opens-memorial-to-slave-trade-a-829447.html.

Robinson, Dennis. *Robert Rogers*. Web. http://www.u-s-history.com/pages/h1186.html.

Seelinger, Matthew. *The Battle of Fallen Timbers, 20 August 1794*. National Museum/United States Army. U.S. Army, 2015. Web. 18 July 2015.
https://armyhistory.org/the-battle-of-fallen-timbers-20-august-1794/

Seven Days in History Civil War Trust. https://www.civilwar.org/learn/articles/seven-days-history.

Stephans, Alexander H. *Speech before the Virginia Secession Convention*, April 23, 1861. From Alexander H. Stephans in Public and Private by Henry Cleveland, National Publishing Company, 1966. 741- 743. Also, see: Proceeding of the Virginia State Convention of 1861, Vol. 4, reprinted by the Virginia State Library. 385-388.
http://www.confederatepastpresent.org/.

United States. National Park Service/U.S. Dept. of the Interior. *Yorktown Battlefield*. Washington D.C.: U.S. Government, Web.
http://www.nps.gov/yonb/learn/historyculture/history-of-the-siege.htm.

The Militia Act of 1862, U.S., Statutes at Large, Treaties, and Proclamations of the United States of America, vol. 12 (Boston, 1863), pp. 597-600. In Freedmen and Southern Society Project. http://www.freedmen.umd.edu/milact.htm.

The German Revolution of 1848/49. German American History & Heritage. The German Corner, n.d. Web.
http://www.germanheritage.com/Essays/1848/unity_and_justice_and_freedom.html.

THIRTY-SEVENTH CONGRESS. Sess. II. Ch 32, 33. 1862. pg 345
https://fraser.stlouisfed.org/scribd/?title_id=1107&filepath=/files/docs/historical/congressional/legal-tender-act-1862.pdf.

Timeline of Emigration – Uncover the history of your ancestors. German Information Center U.S.A. German National Tourist Board, 2015. Web
http://www.germany.travel/en/ms/german-originality/heritage/timeline/timeline.html

Treaty of Greenville: map https://www.pinterest.com/pin/295267319291054805/ and https://www.cmich.edu/library/clarke/ResearchResources/Native_American_Material/Treaty_Rights/Text_of_Michigan_Related_Treaties/Pages/Fort-Greenville,-Ohio,-1795.aspx

War of the Spanish Succession. hyperhistory.com
http://www.hyperhistory.com/online_n2/civil_n2/histscript6_n2/span_succ.html.

Welland Canal Section of the St. Lawrence Seaway. St. Lawrence Seaway Management Corporation. Web http://www.greatlakes-seaway.com/en/pdf/welland.pdf.

Wengert, Professor Gene. *What Is a Board Foot? /Explanation and Glossary of Lumber Terms by Professor Eugene Wengert*. Woodweb. Woodweb, 2 May 2001. Web.
http://www.woodweb.com/knowledge_base/What_is_a_Board_Foot.html

Wetzel, David. Holy Alliance. Encyclopedia.com/Encyclodpeia of Russian History. The Gale Group, 2004. Web.
http://www.encyclopedia.com/history/modern-europe/treaties-and-alliances/holy-alliance.

What Happened on the Trail of Tears?/Federal Indian Removal Policy. Trail of Tears/National Historic Trail. National Park Service. Web. 1 Nov. 2015.
http://www.nps.gov/trte/learn/historyculture/stories.htm.

Newspapers

Failure of Jay Cooke and Company - Sacramento Daily Union, Volume 45, Number 7008, 19 September 1873. pg 2. California Digital Newspaper Collection:
https://cdnc.ucr.edu/?a=d&d=SDU18730919.2.9&e=-------en--20--1--txt-txIN--------1

THE CONSCRIPTION ACT.; The Bill for Enrolling and Calling Out the National Forces, and for Other Purposes. (reprint) New York Times, 19 Feb., 1863.

http://www.nytimes.com/1863/02/19/news/conscription-act-bill-for-enrolling-calling-national-forces-for-other-purposes.html?pagewanted=all

INDEX

A

Abolitionist 109, 120 (and 48ers), 125 (and William Seward), 127, 129 (and Whigs), 149 (and Wendell Phillips), 154 (and Republicans). 155 (and Colored Regiment).

Abominations 101 (Tariff of), 124, 1.

absolutism 4 (French).,

Adams, John 57.

Adrian 94, 95.

African 25, 26, 108 (American), 109, 135 (and Alexander Stephans), 148 (and Militia Act).

Algonquin 22 (and French), 23, 41, 42 (linguistic group).

Allen, Dorothea Elizabeth 167.

Amherst, Jeffrey 30 (and French surrender), 31 (surrounds Montreal), 33, 39-40 (hatred of Indians), 41 (and gifts), 41, 42 (and Pontiac).

Anabaptists 116.

Ancrum, William 59-60 (partners with John Askin), 61 (Moravian purchase), 63.

Anderson, Colonel (at Detroit surrender) 86, 132 (Major Robert at Fort Sumter).

Anishnaabeg 42-43.

Antebellum 104 (Detroit), 109, 112, 133 (federal government), 136.

antidraft 149.

Antietam 147 (battle of)

Antoinette, Marie 54.

Appomattox 155-156.

Aquinas 9.

Ashworth, William 89.

Askin, John 59- 61, 63.

Astor, John Jacob 64-71, 73, 164.

Astor, George Peter 66.

Astor, William 172.

Augustine, Saint 9.

B

Baggataway 42.

Barnes, Henry 154-155.

Bartholomew's, Day Massacre 3.

Baugh, Steam Forge Co. 166.

Beaubien 153.

Beaumont, Gustave de 97.

Belestre, Picoté de 31-32.

Benton, Thomas Hart 69-70, 102.

Berkeley, Governor William 57, 160.

Bessemer, Henry 96, 107.

Biddle, Nicholas 101.

Blackburn, Thornton and Ruth 110- 111.

Blair, Governor Austin 128, 133-134, 154.

Bodin, Jean 3- 4.

Bonaparte, Napolean 54, 67.

Boulton, Matthew 93.

Bourbon (Charles X) 116.

Braddock, General Edward 29-32 (and Battle of Monongahela Valley).

Brulé, Etienne 1, 10.

Buchanan, James 140.

Burnside, General Ambrose 147.

BUS (Bank of United States) 99-102, 104- 106.

Butler, Elizur 79.

C

cabal 80, 82, 86, 138.

Cadillac, Antoine la Mothe 11, 23 (and Detroit founding), 27 (invites Indians), 28 (income).

Cahokia 44.

Calhoun, John C. 72 (and states' rights and nullification); (exploration), 73 (letter from Lewis Cass), 75, 99 (and specie), 124, (apologist for slavery) , 125, 126.

Calvin, John 18-19, 24.

Calvinist 3, 16, 18-19, 20, 57, 75, 123, 155.

Campau, Joseph 83-84 (and John Gentle), 109.

Campbell, Captain Donald 31- 33.

Canut 119 (rebellion).

Canuts 116-117.

capital(ist,ism) 47 (efficient use of), 48-50 (in industry and agriculture), 63, 93, 99, 102-104, 118-119, 121-123, 139-143, 152, 157, 161-162, 166, 168-169.

Carheil, Father Etienne 12.

Carnegie, Andrew 98, 132, 151 (and Civil War replacement), 161, 172 (and steel plant walkout).

Cass, Lewis 54, 69, 71-72, 73 (and Astor) 74 (and treaties) 75, 76, (and surveyors), 77, 86-88, 90, 92, 98, 100, 104, 134, 147, 165 (Avenue).

Cavagnal, Veudreuil de 30.

Céleron de Blainville, Pierre Joseph 28.

Centreville, Virginia; Battle of Bull Run 143-144.

Champlain, Samuel de 11, 41.

Chancellorsville (Battle of) 151.

Chandler, Zachariah 128, 166.

Cherokee 77-79, 88.

Chesapeake 85 (American vessel).

Chicago 88, 94 (Port of), 96, 98-99, 158.

Chickamauga (Battle of) 155.

Chickasaws 78.

Chillicote (Ohio; BUS branch) 100.

Chippewa 41- 42.

Chippewas 73.

Choctaws 78.

Christian 13, 17-18 (and Magna Carta), 19 (and

Christianity 13, 38 (and Adam Smith), 116.

Christianized 60 (and Moravians), 74 (and Indians).

Cromwell, Oliver 15, 23-24 (agreement on colonies), 31, 47, 75- 76.

Clark, Lieutenant William 68.

Cleaveland 3.

Clay, Clemont C. 134.

Clinton, DeWitt 68.

Clockmaker (God the) 46, 138-139.

coastal 16 (and English colonies), 25-26 (and plantations), 56, 58, 68 (and Astoria), 88, 113, 115 (and Germans).

coureur de bois 1, 5, 12-13, 17, 28.

Colbert, Jean Baptiste 6.

colonies (French), 15-17, 20, 22-24 (English and Dutch), 30, 34-35, 38, 40 (and Jeffery Amherst), 45- 46, 50-54 (and Adam Smith), 61, 115-116, 130.

Columbia 67- 68 (River Basin).

commonwealth 16, 19, 19, 20- 21, 24.

Confederacy 28, 40, 41 (and Iroquois), 132, 135 (and Jefferson Davis), 136, 146-147, 149 (and Emancipation Proclamation), 154-155, 160.

Confederation 57.

conscription 115, 151-152 (and Civil War).

Cooke, Jay 142-143, 167, 171.

Coram,Thomas 49.

covenant 20-21, 25.

Creek 77, 142-147

Cromwell, Oliver 15- 16, 19.

Crow 109.

cruiser 91.

Cuyahoga 59.

D

Dakota 167.

de Baptiste, George 129.

de-carbonized 96.

DePeyster, Colonel Arent Schuyler 53.

Descartes, Rene 13.

de-siliconized 96.

Detroit-Milwaukee (Railroad) 164.

Dickens, Charles 48, 138.

Donelson, Andrew Jackson 119, 120.

Doty, James 72.

Douglas, Frederick 129-130, 150.

Dred 126, 127, 127

DTA (Detroit Trades Assembly) 160.

DuBois, W.E.B. 130.

Ducharme, Buhl and 165.

Duluth 5 (Daniel Greyselon "Du Luht"), 167 (and Cooke's railroad).

Dutch 12, 14-17, 19, 22-24, 41, 54.

Dwyer, Jeremiah and James 107.

E

eastern 16, 45-46 (and Dutch traders), 50, 56, 61, 63, 66, 73, 76, 90 (and forests), 102-103, 113, 115, 140-143 (and banking), 143-144, 145 (and industrialists), 151 (and ports), 159, 166 (and "stock jobbing), 169 (and Crédit Mobilier).

Eaton, Dean and 166.

Echota, Treaty of New 78-79.

Eddysville, Kentucky (and Bessemer process) 95.

emancipation 149-151, 153 (Proclamation).

Engels, Friedrich 113-114.

Erie 23 (Canal), 63, 87, 87, 89, 90 (Lake), 94, 95 (and Kalamazoo Railroad), 98, 104, 112.

Etherington, Major George 42-43.

ethnic 22, 75 (cleansing), 79 (cleansing, Cherokee), 108 (and Detroit), 121- 122, 153, 162-164, 173.

Evansville 151.

expeditions 53, 68.

F

Fitzgerald, Edmund 93.

Fitzpatrick, Benjamin 135.

Flannigan, Sheriff Mark 147.

Flèche, La 13.

Foundling (Hospital) 49.

G

Gallatin, Albert 68.

Gentle, John 83.

George (King, the III), 40, 43 (III, birthday), 44 (king and Indians), 45-46 (the III), 66, 107, 110, 124, 129.

Georgia 55 (and Henry Knox), 77-78 and Indian treaties), 79 (and Treaty of New Echota), 136, 154 (and Anthony Wayne).

German(y) 30 (and George III), 50&52 (immigrants), 55 (and von Steuben), 60 (Moravian Church), 108 (and Detroit population), 113 (and Frankenmuth), 115-116 (and immigration), 117-118 (and Monarchs), 119-120 (and 1848 revolution), 121-122 (in Detroit), 161-163 (and Detroit population).

Gettysburg 151, 152, 155 (Battle of; casualties).

Ghent 69 (Treaty of).

Gladwin, Major Henry 42- 43.

Gloucester (cheese) 29.

Gnadenhutten, (New) 60.

Gotham 53 (Court), 96.

Gothenburg 68.

Gould, Jay 98, 161-162, 172 (net worth).

Greeley, Horace 90, 92, 167.

greenbacks 144.

Greenville (Treaty of) 56.

Griffin, John 82.

Griffon (vessel) 93.

Guadalupe Hidalgo (Treaty of) 126.

H

Haldimand, General Frederick 46, 59.

Halifax 86.

Hamburg 68.

Hamilton, Alexander 57, 99-100, 136.

Hammond, Rep. James 112, 125-126 (and South; cotton)

Hancock, John 45.

Harmer, General Josiah 54.

Harper's 56, 129-131 (Ferry), 136.

Harrisburg 172.

Harrison, General William Henry 129.

Harvey, John (and Detroit fire) 83, 85, 92.

Hay, Jehu 59.

Heckewelder, John 60.

Hickory, "Old" 103.

Hidalgo, Guadalupe 126.

Hudson River 16-17, 22 Bay, 87, 89.

Huguenots 3, 15.

Hull, General William 71, 81- 86

Hume, David 34-35, 38, 51.

Huron 27 (Indians), 58 (Lake), 60 (River), 88 (fortifications), 90 (Lake), 92 (Lake).

Hutcheson, Francis 34-35.

I

Illinois-Michigan (Railroad) 94.

industrialists 118 (and Selisian Revolt), 124 (and tariff), 139 (and Carey), 145, 147, 162.

industrialization 92 (and Miller's sawmill), 117 (and Swing riots), 164 (post-Civil War).

Italians 113, 119, 121, 163.

J

Jackson, Andrew 71, 74-79, 99, 101-103, 105, 119, 122, 126, 128.

Jackson, Michigan 137.

Jacobites 29.

Jamaica 29.

Jamestown 17-18, 24-25, 56-57, 115.

Jefferson, Thomas 57, 62-63 (and Physiocrats), 66-68 (and Louisiana Purchase), 81-83, 99, 101 (and "stock jobbing"), 106 (and BUS), 138.

Jemima, Aunt 109.

jingoism 167.

jobbing, stock 124.

Johnson, Ida 5, 12-13, 63-64.

Johnson, Sir William ("Waraghiyagey") 40-41.

Josephson, Matthew 132, 145, 170, 171.

Juniata (Valley) 29.

K

Kalamazoo (Erie and Kalamazoo Railroad) 94-95, 98.

Kansas-Nebraska (Act) 126.

Kapital, Das 120.

Kickapoo 2.

Knox, Henry 55.

L

laissez-faire 35, 48, 51, 54, 55-79 137.

Lambert, William 129.

Langer, Charles 153.

Lawrence, St. (waterway) 22-23.

Lincoln, Abraham 120, 131, 133 (and Fort Sumter), 134 (and Michigan Regiment), 141 (and Salmon Chase), 142 (and Jay Cooke), 145 (and Grant), 145, 146-147 (and General McClellan) 148 (and "House Divided" speech), 150, 154 (and Black regiment).

liquor 5, 12-13, 40 (and William Johnson), 145.

Locke, John 138.

Locks, "Soo" 93-95.

locomotive 107, 173.

London 1, 16 (and colonies), 25, 34 (and Whigs), 39, 47, 48 (and beggars), 59, 66, 68, 115, 138, 173.

Louis-Phillipe 116.

Louisbourg 29, 30.

Louisiana 10 (and French influence), 28 (and Cadillac), 30, 62, 66-67 (Purchase), 83 (and Aaron Burr), 90, 136.

Loyola 7-9.

Luddites 116.

Ludlow 126.

lumber 64 (...man), 84-85 (and Detroit fire), 88 (and Lewis Cass), 89 (best for construction), 91- 92 (measure and swindle), 94, 98, 104.

M

Machiavelli, Niccólo 4.

Madagascar 53.

Madeira 29.

Madison, James 57, 82 (and Judges), 84-86 (and Gentle).

Malden 85-86 (Fort).

Mallory, Stephan R. 135.

Malthus, Thomas 138.

Manassas 144.

Manchester 47, 113, 138.

mandate 82, 83 (and Detroit judges).

Manichean 26.

manifest 72 (and Cass expedition), 75;79; 90; 126; 167 (destiny).

manufacturing 11(textiles; Indians), 97 (de Tocqueville; Adam Smith), 101 (and Tariff of Abom.), 106-108, 112, 137-138 (Hamilton and List), 157 (and 1857 Panic), 158-159 (and workers; strikes), 160, 164 (and Frederick Stearns).

Marquette, Father Jacques 10.

Marshall, Justice John 78.

Martin, Matthew 48.

Martinsburg 172.

Marx 49 (and Adam Smith), 118-120, 138, 139 (and Karl Marx), 159 (and "lumpen proletariat"), 173.

Mason-Dixon 133 (line).

Mayflower 16, 115.

McCabe, Joseph 7.

McClellan, General George 146 (retreat), 147 (and Peninsular Campaign), 148 (hesitation).

McCloskey, James 76.

McCormick, Cyrus ("reaper") 114.

McDermott, James (shipyard) 107, 118.

McDowell, General Irvin 143-144.

McGoffin, Governor Beriah 136.

McLane, Lewis 101.

McMillan, James 165-66, 172.

Mellon, Andrew 132.

mercantilism 48.

mercantilist 27, 35, 51

Metternich, Klemens von 117-120.

Mexican 128, 134 (war).

Mexican-American 156.

Miamis 27, 28, 44, 54-55.

Michigan 1- 2, 10 (and archaeology), 13 (and liquor ban), 16, 17, 22, 54, 57-58 (and Treaty of Paris), 59 (and real estate), 61 (and Moravian deal), 63 (and Western reserve), 67 (and Astor), 69, 71-73 (and Lewis Cass), 75-76 (Native evictions), 79, 80-81 (and Wayne County), 82-83 (and judge cabal), 85,-86 (and Hull surrender), 87 (judiciary and judges), 88 (history and geography), 89,-90 (geological formation), 92 (and Saginaw River), 93, 94 (and Illinois-Michigan Canal), 95 (Michgan State Canal), 96 (and de-forestation), 98-99 (and land speculation), 100-104 (banking), 107 (and Eureka Iron

Works: Eber Ward), 108 (population chart), 109, 110 (and "Black Codes"), 113 (and immigrants), 115 (and Germans), 116, 118, 119, 120 (and 48ers), 121, 122 (and Democratic Party), 123, 128, 128, 128 (and Republican Party), 129 (Black ostracism), 133 (and Fort Sumter), 134 (and troop recruitment), 137 (Jackson), 154 (and First Michigan Colored Infantry), 157 (and veterans), 158 (and labor), 159 (and land), 160, 161, 166 (and Michigan Car Company), 170 (and Saginaw and Bay Salt Co.; monopoly), 173 (and railroad strike).

Michilimackinac 5, 23, 39, 41- 43, 67.

Mobilier, Crédit 169-170.

Molly (Maguires) 172.

Monangahela (Valley) 29, 54.

monopoly 5, 5, 27, 47, 56, 66, - 67, 166, 171.

Monroe, James 67 (and Louisiana Purchase), 71-72, 129.

Montana 167.

Montreal 5, 23, 30, 31, 59, 59, 61, 86.

Moravian 59-61, 63.

Morrill (Land Grant College Act) 146, 149.

Muskingum 60.

N

Nantes, Edict of 15, 26.

Napoleon (Bonaparte) 53, 54, 67, 67, 95, 117, 117.

Nebraska 121, 125, 127.

neo-liberal 53.

Neolin 42.

Neshnabe 76.

Netherlands 3, 17.

Newberry, John 163-164.

Newcomen (steam engine) 91, 93.

Newton, Sir Isaac 46.

Nickleby, Nicholas 139.

Nicolet, Jean 2.

Niles, Hezekiel 100.

Notary 59.

NTU (National Typographers' Union) 159.

nullification 72, 126, 154.

O

Oakes, Ames 170.

Ojibwe 2, 42.

Ontario 1, 85, 90, 94.

Orontio 43.

Oswego 44.

Ottawa 31, 42.

Outfitters 5.

outpost 6, 12, 26-28, 42, 46, 50, 55, 57, 68, 80.

Owen, John 133, 154.

P

Pacific 63; 65 (Northwest), 67- 68 (and Astor), 146, 166 (Union and Central railroads), 167 (North Pacific Charter), 169 (and Crédit Mobilier) 169 (and Pacific Railway Act).

Pampelona 9.

Panama 160.

Panic 70 (of 1837), 99-100, 102, 104 (of 1837), 118 (and Michigan), 124, 141, 157 (of 1857), 159 (successive), 162 (and Eber Ward), 165 (and McMillan), 167 (of 1873), 171.

pantheism 13.

papists 16, 25.

Pottawatomi 27.

Pax (Britannia) 20, 25, 35.

Peninsular 147.

Pennsylvania 54, 63, 83 (and judge cabal), 116, 143 (and Jay Cooke), 172.

Petersburg 128.

Peyster, Colonel Arent Schuyler 46, 60.

Pfeiffer 115.

Philadelphia 45, 57, 83 (Aurora and Pittsburgh Gazette), 100 (financial committee), 102

(Girard Bank of), 113 (and tenements), 157-158 (and workers), 164.

physiocrat(s) 51, 97.

physiocratic 62, 66.

Pickawillany 27-28.

Pini 44.

Plymouth 24.

Ponchartrain 14, 27, 31, 32.

Pontiac (Chief) 41- 44, 107.

potato 114.

Potawatomi 2, 88.

Potomac 129.

pragmatism 148-149.

protectionism 144.

Protestant(ism) 8 (and Bartholomew massacre), 8-9 (and Jesuit opposition), 15-16 (and France), 24 (and Navigation Act), 116, 121, 122.

Puritan 17-19.

Puritanism 22.

Q

Quakers 116.
Quebec 30, 59, 59, 59, 86.
Quesnay, Françoi 51, 97.

R

railroad(s) 91, 94 (Erie-Kalamazoo), 95- 96 (and Bessemer steel), 98, 100, 104-105, 107, 112-113, 126 (and Panic of 1857), 129-130 (Underground), 144, 146 (Railroad Act), 152, 158, 161, 165 (and James McMillan), 166 (and Promontory, Utah), 167-168 (and Jay Cooke), 168-169, 172.

rails 51, 96, 112.

Raisin, River 76.

re-carbonized 96.

Realpolitik 4.

rebellion 33, 43-44 (Pontiac's), 45, 46 (and colonists), 51, 53, 54 (and Anthony Wayne), 56-57 (Nathaniel Bacon; Daniel Shay), 118, (Canut), 119, 120 (Germany), 123 (slave) 129, 130 (and John Brown), 133, 148, 151 (and draft riots), 173 (and working class).

Reformation 18, 116.

Republican(s) 16 (and Cromwell), 20 (and Hobbes), 116 (French), 119 (French), 136-137 (U.S. party), 144-146 (and 37th Congress), 150, 153.

revolution 19, 46 (American and Detroit), 50, 52-53 (American), 54 (French) 57 (and Treaty of Paris), 60, 63, 80, 92 (and Saginaw sawmill), 107, 115, 117-118, 120.

Rheinische (Zeitung) 118.

Ricardo, David 138.

Richelieu, Cardinal 1, 4, 5, 15.

Richmond 128

riot(s) 111, 111, 117, 148, 152-153.

River 10 (St Joseph), 16-17 (Hudson), 22, 23 (Detroit), 29 (Niagara; Ohio), 32, 33, 39, 55 (and Fallen Timbers), 56, 58 (Mississippi) 59 (Cuyahoga), 60 (Muskingum), 66, 67-68 (Mississippi; Columbia), 72, 76 (Raisin), 77, 80, 84, 84, 84, 85 (Detroit), 86, 86, 87, (Hudson) , 89 (and Erie Canal), 90, 93 (Ste. Mary's), 95, 95, 96, 101, 110, 129 (Detroit), 145 (Tennessee), 145, 153 (Detroit), 157 (Schuylkill), 172 (Fall.

Robespierre, Maximilien 117.

Rockefeller, John D. 98, 132, 151, 170-171.

Rogers, Robert 31- 32.

S

Saginaw 73 (and Chippewas), 88 (and de Tocqueville), 92 (river network), 92 (Bay), 92-93, 98, 104, 116, 170.

Salem 157.

Sandusky 63.

Sandwich 85-86.

Sauk 2, 42.

Sault, St. Marie 1, 2, 5, 23, 93, 95.

Schoolcraft, Henry 72, 87.

Schwarzenberg, Prince 120.

Scilly (Scilly Isles) 160.

Scotch-Irish 52.

secession 124, 133, 135-136, 146, 160.

seigneur 27.

Seminoles 78.

Sequoya 77.

Seward, Senator William 125.

Shenandoah 129 (River), 143 (Valley).

Sherman, General William Tecumseh 134, 143, 155, 167.

Shiawassee (River) 92.

Shiloh, Battle of 145, 154.

Shinplasters 100-101.

Shipbuilding 107.

shoemakers 157.

Silesia 118.

single bobbin 114.

slavery 25, 40, 45 (in southern plantations), 52 (in the north), 57, 108-109 (and Detroit workforce), 111, 112 (and James Hammond), 113, 122 (Democratic indifference), 122 (and Wilbur Storey), 124 (and John Calhoun), 124, 124 (and southern economy), 124, 125, 126, (and Kansas-Nebraska Act), 127 (and Dred Scott), 127 (and Whigs), 128 (and Wilmot proposal), 129-130 (and John Brown), 131-132, 135 (and Jefferson Davis), 136, 148 (and Lincoln), 149.

Smythe's Tavern 82.

Snelling, Josiah 69- 70.

south 24, 25, 58, 76, 77 (and Andrew Jackson), 78 (and Indian Removal bill), 89, 90, 99, 99, 101 (and surplus), 104, 111, 122 (and black labor), 123, 123 (and Whigs), 124 (and British mills), 125 (and Hammond), 126 (and nullification), 129 (john Brown in Detroit), 130 (and rebellions), 131, 132 (and Charleston Harbor), 133, 135 (and secession), 136, 141, 145, 146 (…ern), 149 (and Lincoln), 154 (and Major Gen. Hunter and General Fremont), 154 (Carolina), 171-172. (Improvement Company).

Southard 147.

sovereign(ity) 4, 5, 16, 20, 21, 24, 58, 59, 64, 135.

Spain 8, 67.

Spinney, B.F. 157.

Spotsylvania, Battle of 155.

Stove 96, 107, 112.

strike(s) (157-159), 161, 172-173.

strikebreakers 174.

Stroh 115.

Stryker, D. Augustus 174.

Sumter, Fort 122, 132-134, 136, 141, 143, 147, 154.

Surrender 5, 21, 30, 31, 38, (and Adam Smith), 51, 53 (Yorktown), 55 (Fort Miamis), 63, 71 (Detroit), 85-87 (Detroit), 120, 133 (Fort Sumter), 172 (and labor).

Swing, riots 116- 117.

T

taiga 89.

Tailoresses 157.

Tarbell, Ida 171.

Ten-Thousand-Acre 83.

territories 13 (Michigan), 58 (Mich. and Ohio), 61, 73, 109, 121 (Kansas), 122 (new), 125, 126 127 ("unorganized"), 128.

territory 2, 22 (French), 23 (Iroquois), 38, 56 (Ohio; Treaty of Greenville), 57 (Michigan), 61 (unsettled), 62 (Northwest), 67 (Louisiana), 69, 71- 72 (Michigan), 75-76 (and Native Americans; surveying), 78 (and Cherokees), 80 (Michigan), 81-83 (Michigan), 85 (Michigan and Detroit fire),

87 (Council of), 110 (and Black Codes), 127, 128, 155.

Ticonderoga, Fort 30.

Tiffin, Surveyor Gen. Edward 71, 90.

timber 55-57 (Battle of Fallen Timbers), 84, 88, 90-92 ("beasts").

Titabawassee (River) 92.

tobacco 18, 24-25, 165, 173.

Tocqueville, Alexis de 88 (ands Saginaw pines), 97-98 (and American wealth), 116.

tomahawk 42, 44.

tributaries 72, 92.

Turgot, Anne Robert Jacques 51.

Turner, Nat 130;

Twist, Oliver 138.

two-thirders 113.

U

unemployment 62, 116-117, 141, 172.

uprisings 117- 118, 130.

V

Vanderbilt, Horace 98, 146, 156, 164, 166, 172.

Vaudreuil-Cavagnial, Pierre de Rigaud 31.

Vicksburg 151.

villein 27.

W

Walpole, Horace 99.

Warraghiyagey 40, 41, 44.

Washington, George 29 (as lieutenant-colonel), 35, 53 (and General Cornwallis), 55 (as President), 99.

Washington, D.C. 69, 102, 131 (county in Maryland), 134, 144.

Waterways 23, 58-59, 91-92, 94, 90- 96.

Wayland, Francis 139-141, 144, 168.

Wayne, Anthony 54, 55-56 (and Battle of Fallen Timbers), 71.

Wayne, County 80.

Wayne, Fort 134, 153.

weapons 12, 33, 42, 43, 92, 129, 137, 147.

Weavers 114, 116-117 (Canut).

Webb, William 129.

Webster, Rep. Daniel 103.

Whig(s) 34, 102, 122-123, 127-128, 130.

whiskey 70, 74, 170.

white(s) 2, 10, 11 (merchants), 12-13 (and liquor), 17, 22 (and wilderness), 23, 26, 29, 40, 42 (and Minnevana), 43, 44, 46 (settlers), 52 (indentured servants), 53 (flag, Yorktown), 53 settlers), 54, 56 (immigrants), 57 (and Bacon rebellion) 59 (settlement), 61 (man's concept of property), 75- 80 (settlement, process of), 88-90 (pine), 96, 108 (Detroit, ethnic makeup), 109, 109, 110 (and Blackburns), 111, 122 (farmers, free land), 123, 128 (door to white society), 129 House, and George de Baptiste), 130 (whites and slavery), 131 (and John Brown), 135-136, 148-149 (soldiers), 150 (workers), 153 (business owners), 154 (and Henry Barnes), 160 (labor; Richard Trevelick), 163-164 (collar), 170 (gold;salt), 173, 175.

Wilmot, David 128.

Windsor 85, 153.

Wisconsin 80, 88, 89, 120.

Witherell, James 82, 110.

Wolfe, James 30.

Woodbury, Levi 102.

Woodward, Augustus 82-83, 100.

Woodward (Avenue) 128, 165, 175.

workhouse(s) 48, 70.

Wyandottes 44.

Z

Zeisberger, David 60.

www.ingramcontent.com/pod-product-compliance
Lightning Source LLC
Chambersburg PA
CBHW080434110426
42743CB00016B/3166